The Midrashic Imagination

The Midrashic Imagination
Jewish Exegesis, Thought, and History

edited by Michael Fishbane

State University of New York Press

Published by
State University of New York Press, Albany

© 1993 State University of New York

All rights reserved

Printed in the United States of America

For information, address State University of New York Press,
State University Plaza, Albany, N.Y., 12246

Production by Marilyn P. Semerad
Marketing by Dana E. Yanulavich

Library of Congress Cataloging-in-Publication Data

The Midrashic imagination : exegesis, thought, and history/edited by
    Michael Fishbane.
        p.   cm.
    Includes bibliographical references and index.
    ISBN 0-7914-1521-X. — ISBN 0-7914-1522-8 (pbk.)
        1. Midrash—History and criticism.   2. Bible.   O.T.—Criticism,
    interpretation, etc.,   Jewish—History.   I. Fishbane, Michael A.
    BM514.M44 1993
    296.1'406—dc20   92-27070
                                                            CIP

10   9   8   7   6   5   4   3   2   1

Contents

Introduction

Michael Fishbane

O ne of the most compelling and characteristic features of Jewish creativity is its "midrashic imagination." Growing out of the earliest interpretations of the Bible, the genres of Midrash, as they developed in classical Judaism, extend genres found in the Bible itself. Thus just as the Bible is marked by legal, theological, legendary, historiographical, and rhetorical materials—which are variously, though not systematically, subject to clarifications and expansions *within* the biblical corpus—so are the earliest collections of Midrash (*outside* the Bible) marked by sustained hermeneutical attention to just these literary texts. The result is a rich harvest of interpretations that virutally transform the Bible into a rabbinic work, so profoundly and vigorously do the sages project their own theological and legal agenda into Scripture. What is more, rabbinic Midrash expands and develops the native biblical genres themselves. The result of this development is sustained legal and theological discussions, homilies of various sorts and types, and legendary accretions to the historical narrative of the Bible.

All this is Midrash—forged out of a subtle, serious and even playful imagination, as it comes to grips with life and Scripture. As interpretations succeeded or complemented one another, a massive texture of texts and techniques formed the warp and woof of rabbinic culture, setting its patterns and forms for the ages. Each new period saw successive developments along these lines, even as radically new expressions emerged. In some areas like law, midrashic correlations of biblical texts soon gave way to correlations among the rabbinic solutions, in increasing subtlety. In theology, the impress of philosophy or theosophy led to different uses of the scriptural inheritance, and therewith different conceptions of the nature of the biblical text. And finally, even in the area of medieval historiography, where scholars have often pondered the balance of fact and fiction, one may discover a midrashic template at the core. Therefore across the breadth of Judaism, it is not only the insistent recourse to the Bible that marks its creativity, but the very midrashic mode of correlating Scriptures among themselves and with new values, virtues or events. From this perspective, "Midrash" is not only a (multifaceted) literary genre but itself a generic structure of Jewish tradition.

The chapters in this book provide a select but significant sampling of the dimensions of the topic. As hermeneutics roughly subdivides into the three broad areas of theory of textual meaning, strategies of interpretative technique, and modes of actualizing received authors or authorities, a threefold structure underlies this collection. There is not only a repeated concern of the authors to address the presuppositions or conditions of a certain body of texts, through specific examples, but an attempt to clarify the exegetical techniques used and the way these contribute to the texts at hand. In this way one can see how interpretation retrieves its sources and shapes them for the ongoing culture. Even historiography could not escape the grip of exegesis.

The opening part of this collection therefore begins with a discussion (by I. Gruenwald) of Midrash as a fundamental constituent of the Jewish imagination. The conditions of textual creativity are reflected on, as are the innovative results. Indeed, the role of historical conditions in providing many of the preconditions of exegetical revision are considered. The result is a wide-ranging reflection on exegetical creativity and tradition. To begin to mark the move from the text in itself and in its primary contextual sense (the *Peshat*) to these midrashic transformations (*Derash*), is the burden of the second essay (by D. Weiss Halivni). Here we immediately begin to see how the shift from the one (*Peshat*) to the other (*Derash*) inevitably involves a different sense of the text and its authority. By the same token, the authority of the test to sponsor or legitimate radically new readings, and to consider them as "always already" present to the textuality of Scripture, inevitably involves matters bearing on the authority of the interpreter. A whole spate of theological matters follow—all the more challenging as the *Derash* seems to diverge from the *Peshat*. Rabbinical sages are deeply concerned to validate their readings through reference to the original divine revelation at Sinai. Just as deeply must they ponder the perplexing problem of how their interpretations reveal the real sense of Scripture when it often seems to break with the latter, both lexically and ideologically. Bold constructs emerge to save appearances, including both the notion of an apparently "faulty text" and an apparently unbiblical exegetical tradition.

The final chapter of the part (by M. Idel) comes at the matter of *Derash* from a more phenomenological and typological perspective, and also provides a fitting transfer to latter discussions of rabbinic and kabbalistic Midrash. Once again—but now in bold conceptual terms— the effect of exegesis on the notion of the biblical text is articulated, as also the differing theologies that may result. Differences and continuities between ancient rabbinic Midrash and midrashic ventures in the medieval period are sharply formulated. The full bounty of *Derash* is thus heralded. The subsequent studies provide details.

Part II of the book turns to rabbinic Midrash itself and explores aspects of its hermeneutical creativity through two fundamental modes: mythmaking (by M. Fishbane) and parables (by D. Stern). The role of each mode as a shaping power of the exegetical imagination is explored. In different ways, both essays also treat matters of history and theology. The complex interrelationships that result indicate just how much Midrash is not just a reservoir of ancient exegetical activity and creativity, but also a source for penetrating the mental realities of the sages. The ancient rabbis thought textually, and to following their mind one must learn to follow Midrash.

Part III of the book turns to the Middle Ages and unfurls a broad canvass of Jewish interpretation. Both because of its inherent importance and to set more midrashic dimensions of medieval exegesis in perspective, we begin with an exacting study (by S. Japhet) on the revival of the *Peshat* in Franco-Germany; from here we turn to a study (by J. Stern) on the role of *Remez* or philosophical allegory in Spain and another (by E. Wolfson) on the more midrashic dimension of the esoteric sense, or *Sod,* in the Kabbalah (the *Zohar,* in particular). A study of aspects of renaissance exegesis (by A. Lesley), in its exquisite balance of types, follows. Moving among this spectacular array of themes and examples, the reader will see further how different authors hold multiple exegetical modes in creative tension, place them in different hierarchies, or actually subvert the apparent tensions or hierarchies. It will not follow, therefore, that *Peshat* is simply the "lower" form of interpretation. For this would hardly conform to the task and agenda that the practitioners of this craft set for themselves (or, indeed, of the caustic way they regarded other types of interpretation); nor would it conform to the unexpected way that masters of the *Sod* claimed (in one way or another) that this truth is the truth of the *Peshat* and that only a proper understanding of the *Peshat* (or even the *Derash*) will reveal the *Sod.* Thus we come to see the paradoxical relations among the methods and are forced to recognize that for many exegetes the *Peshat* is the "deepest" of all levels of interpretations—concealing the *Sod.* The philosophical allegorists have a completely different perspective on this issue and quite different appreciations of the functions of *Derash* and *Remez.* In short, the famous rabbinic dictum, that "Scripture never loses its *Peshat* sense," is parsed in altogether different and paradoxical ways in the history of Jewish interpretation.

The final part of the book takes us into an unexpected realm: historiography. Here we see in no uncertain terms just how much the "midrashic imagination" prevailed on the masters and formulators of Jewish memory, in both medieval Italy and Germany. The implications of the essays (by R. Bonfil, S. Bowman, and I. Marcus) are far ranging and far reaching, and they return us to the opening point that "Midrash" is a fundamental habit of mind, imagination, and creativity for rabbinic culture. Indeed, the very notions of fact and fiction must be qualified here. For once we talk of midrashic fact and midrashic fiction there is a certain collapse of old polarities. The enmeshment of medieval Jewish culture in textuality thus had its inevitable result in historical texts of equally complex textuality—of a type that the authors convincingly describe as midrashic.

I am particularly grateful to the kind offices of Mr. William Eastman, director of the SUNY Press, for his interest in this volume. The chapters by M. Fishbane and I. Marcus appeared earlier in *The Journal of Jewish Thought and Philosophy* 1 and *Prooftexts* 10, respectively. They are reprinted here thanks to the editors and publishers of these journals.

PART I

Midrashic Hermeneutics:
Some Conceptual and Comparative
Considerations

1

Midrash and the "Midrashic Condition": Preliminary Considerations

Ithamar Gruenwald

I

The study of Midrash has recently gained in academic attention, for it has dawned on the scholarly world that Midrash is not restricted to idiosyncratic, isolated, and even esoteric forms of rabbinic exegesis of Scripture. Indeed, scholars and literary critics have gradually realized that Midrash as a literary genre and form of interpretative expression is present in almost all form of literary creation, and that the study of Midrash raises hermeneutical questions that have interesting consequences for the study of literature and philosophy.[1]

Yet, despite this new awareness of the vitality of Midrash as a form of thinking and expression, it still awaits a full-scale epistemological assessment. The present study aims at making a few steps in that direction. To begin with, we consider Midrash to be an important factor in the development of the religious tradition of the Jews and not merely a literary form and exegetical technique used in the interpretation of Scripture.[2] Even beyond that, Midrash is a form of cognition that supplies terms of reference and channels of perception for people who organize their lives in accordance with a scriptural world of ideas.[3] Midrash thus helps maintain Scripture as the normative constant of Judaism. In the face of historical and ideological change, it not only regulates the development of Jewish traditionality but supplies its essential substance as well. Finally, Midrash also embodies the principles of interpretative elasticity that are the basic invigorating forces of that traditionality.

In the light of these remarks, I would like to develop a few ideas that may be helpful in realizing the full impact of Midrash on Jewish culture. My approach will mainly be of an epistemological nature; therefore, over against

6

the philosophical or theological aspects of Midrash and its concern with the second ideational content. I shall focus on *the philosophy of Midrash*; that is, its unique forms of thinking expression and interpretation. In this regard, I should now like to introduce the rubric *The midrashic condition(s)*. This phrase refers to a number of factors in Midrash:

1. The centrality of Midrash in Jewish culture and traditionality.
2. The various conceptual, literary and exegetical presuppositions that sustain the midrashic activity.
3. The cognitive potentials of Midrash. Midrash in a vital instrument in creating patterns of perception, conceptualization, and realization in which scriptural terms of reference are applied for existential purposes.
4. The ability of Midrash to create meanings that engender attitudes of relevance and relatedness to the world of Scripture. By *relevance* and *relatedness* I mean the desire of people to continue the modes and norms established by Scripture.
5. Midrashic-like modes of relating to a scriptural or canonical text can be extended to any type of mental relationship that entails the concern for establishing relevance or relatedness to any given fact or piece of information.

In brief, the term *midrashic condition* points to a mental attitude or disposition in which the interpretative attention expressed entails more than a concern for lexicological or plain-sense meaning of a text or piece of information. What really matters, therefore, is not the mere act of understanding texts, but the creation of the meaning that is attached to them. In this regard, a third part aims at appropriating texts by creating a spiritual environment that makes that act of appropriation possible. The act of creating meaning is a vital part of that process of appropriation.[4]

II

In discussing the history of a Scripture, or of a religious tradition in general, two complementary stages may be distinguished: revelation and interpretation.[5] Scripture, as distinct from interpretation, would figure in the eyes of many people as a collection of writings who chief asset is the fact that it claims divine inspiration for itself. It follows, then, that interpretation is a human-made product. However, three crucial problems somewhat spoil the intellectual appeal of such a distinction. To begin with, not every book included in Scripture is divinely inspired in the full sense of the term. Among these are most of the books included in the *Ketuvim* ("The Hagiographa": Psalms, Proverbs, and Chronicles). Then, too, it is important to note that the process of interpretation has already begin in Scripture itself. This fact has recently become part of the standard understanding of Scripture, and it certainly results in blurring the clarity of the previously mentioned distinction. And finally, it must be observed that some interpretations of Scripture (e.g., the *persharim* of the Qumran Community) also claim for themselves the status of diving inspiration.

Since Midrash belongs to the sphere of interpretation, everything that is said about the one is almost automatically valid with respect to the other. Thus if interpretation is part of revelation, then certain aspects of midrashic activity can be expected to exist in Scripture. However, the subject of the presence of Midrash in Scripture has to be introduced with caution. The Hebrew word *midrash* is only twice mentioned in Scripture (2 Chron.13:22;24:27) and apparently in a noninterpretative connection.[6] The verb *darash* is more often used in Scripture, mostly in connection with people who seek the presence of God. However, in a few cases the verb *darash* is used apparently in the sense of finding out something (notable, the decrees of God: Ps. 119:45, 94; or judicial justice: Isa. 1:17). Only once in Scripture is the verb *darash* used in connection with Torah: Ezra 7:10 ("For Ezra had set his heart to study the law of God [Hebrew: *li-drosh 'et torat . . .*], and to do it, and to teach His statutes and ordinances in Israel"; RSV). Similarly, we find the expression *li-drosh* in connection with wisdom (Eccles. 1:13: "And I applied my mind to seek [Hebrew: *li-drosh*] and search out by wisdom all that is done under heaven"; RSV). None of these cases actually reflects an interpretative activity. The first case in which the word *midrash* can be viewed as reflecting such an activity in relation to the Torah is the term *midrash ha-torah* in the Qumranic "Damascus Covenant" (fol. XX, 1.6). Parallel to this term we find in the same text the expression *perush ha-torah* (fol. VI, 1.14; fol. XIII, 1.6) and *serekh ha-torah* (fol. VII, 1. 8; *serekh* = rule). The term *doresh ha-torah* ("the explicator of the Torah") also occurs in the same text (fol. VI, 1.7; fol. VII, 1.18). In other words, and interpretative activity, mainly in relation to the Torah, which undergoes a clear terminological classification is to be found only in later, extrascriptural literature.[7] However, the interpretative work on Scripture began already in scriptural times and can in fact be found in Scripture itself. In addition, it should once again be noted that some collections of extrascriptural interpretation claim some kind of divine relevation as their ultimate source. The Qumran *pesharim* ("Commentaries") are a notable case in point.[8]

The purpose of the foregoing observations was to make it clear that in the mind of the users of Scripture a complementary activity to that of the mere acceptance of revelation took place. That activity generally goes by the name of Midrash, whether it was included in the literary corpus of revelation (= Scripture) itself or added to it at a later stage. In any event, the chief characteristic of that midrashic activity is its almost exclusive concern with matters relating to meaning, and less so with regard to the literal or lexicological interpretation of the scriptural text. Epistemologically speaking, this fact has far-reaching consequences in our assessment of Midrash as an intellectual attitude in general. We shall see that it implies a unique theory of scriptural language, as well.

The dimension of subjective creativity so typical of Midrash has already been highlighted in the important work of I. Heinemann.[9] In relating to the fictional, even fictitious, type of philological and historical information incorporated in the midrashic expositions of Scripture, Heinemann argues that the philology and historiography of Midrash should be qualified as "creative." Heinemann thus speaks both of the "creative philology" and the "creative historiography" of the Aggadah produced by the midrashists. But in so doing, I believe he betrays a somewhat apologetic approach. This is to say, Heinemann wants to emphasize that readers of the Aggadah should not have scientific, or critical, expectations with regard to the interpretative information contained in the aggadic midrash; viz., Midrash does not contain verifiable information. By contrast, when I speak of the creative elements of midrashic interpretation I wish to stress that *Midrash is chiefly concerned with the creation of meaning*—not with exegesis. Previously, even when viewed with respect to its creative thrust, Midrash was usually assessed according to its exegetical functions. However, when people engage in the quest of meaning in general, they go beyond exegesis. Very commonly, meaning is not discovered *in* the text, but attributed *to it*. In other words, Midrash not only creates exegetical information, as Heinemann asserts, but also the spheres of meaning in which new halakhic and theological norms are established and realized.[10]

By way of example; when many medieval commentators interpret the word *bara* ("created") in Gen. 1:1 as meaning "created ex nihilo," they read a philosophical meaning into the scriptural text. Their reasons for so doing need not be discussed here; but it has to be pointed out that, on a purely philological level, the word *bara* actually means "separated." That is to say, God did not so much *create* heaven and earth, as make a separation between them. This notion of separation is stressed in Ibn Ezra's commentary to the verse, and it actually implies a completely different notion; namely, that the act creation entailed the separation between two already existing entities. Similarly, Nahmanides interpreted the words *tohu wa-bohu* in Gen. 1:2, as indicating the hylic, formless quality of primal matter that was, at the beginning, still separated from primal form. In so doing, Nahmanides in all likelihood incorporated into his commentary a notion that was first suggested by the eleventh century Jewish philosopher, R. Abraham bar Hiyya, in his *Hegyon Ha-Nefesh.* There too we find that a philosophical meaning has been read into a scriptural expression conceived in a mythopoetic, not philosophical, setting. Accordingly, it would be more in line with the scriptural passage to say that *tohu wa-bohu* indicates "chaos" in its mythic or mythopoetic sense. For the medieval scholars, those notions were probably the ultimate "scientific" truth; whereas for a modern reader, these are two specimens of what may be called *philosophical midrash.* A midrashic saying does not change its character when qualified as philosophical; it remains a midrash with no change of status. Although its starting point is felt some difficulty in the scriptural text, the solution, both on the level of the lexicological sense and the contextual meaning, reflects the knowledge, predilections, and intellectual needs of the interpreter. In this sense, despite all pretensions to be explicatory in nature (i.e., to serve only the text), such readings reflect the urge of a third party to relate to that text by injecting new meanings *into* it.

Let us now turn to another example of how new conditions create radically new midrashic expositions. The case in point is the famous decree that every person who maims another person should be punished "an eye for an eye." This ruling is repeated three times in the Pentateuch (Exod. 21:24; Lev. 24:20; Deut. 19:21) and presumable thereby indicates that the lawgiver is serious about the kind of physical punishment that has to be inflicted on the person causing the damage. However, as is well-known, the rabbis thought differently about that kind of punishment. For them an "eye for an eye" meant "paying the worth of an eye for the damaged eye" (*Mekhilta de-Rabbi Yishmael* to Exodus; *b. Baba Qama* 83b–84a). Although one of the sages, Rabbi Eliezer, thought that a literal understanding of the injunction was in order, the majority of the sages thought differently. They simple read "a monetary recompense" for the first *eye.* Practically speaking, they rewrote Scripture for judicial purposes. The reasons for so doing are well-established in rabbinic jurisprudence and leave no doubt that this 'change' is the correct halakhic application or enactment of the scriptural text. Everybody knows what an eye is; what the rabbis were concerned with was the meaning of the phrase *an eye for an eye* when the case came before the judges of their times. In face of a literal, and most probably also a correct, understanding of the text, they stressed the question of the text's meaning. And that meaning was formulated by them *almost in spite of* the text itself.

A different "midrashic condition" affects Jesus' reuse of the foregoing injunction. This is what he has to say: "You have heard that it is said, 'An eye for an eye and a tooth for a tooth.' But I say to you, Do not resist one who is evil. But if any one strikes you on the right cheek turn to him the other also;

etc." (Matt. 5:38–39). Whereas the rabbis were principally perturbed by the judicial problem posed by the scriptural verse, such that no moral or other considerations were directly brought into their interpretation, Jesus was mostly concerned with a moral issue. It is thus not only a matter of how the phrase *an eye for an eye* was understood in each case that attracts attention, but also the different direction each takes. In both cases meaning is established in relation to a scriptural ruling; but that meaning is not implied by the scriptural wording itself and was, as remarked, even imposed upon the text by new readers.

The power of interpretative discretion cannot be underestimated—here or elsewhere. An interpreter can do with the scriptural word (even the Word of God), almost anything he considers fitting and proper. To be sure, there are certain fixed rules which the halakhist has to obey (the so-called *Middot*, or "rules," by which the Torah is explicated),[11] but the limits of permitted interpretation are not given. In other words, if it comes to establishing meaning, the word of Scripture can be stretched in almost every direction and to almost any length. On the lexicological level, philological and etymological rules cannot be bypassed. Yet when it comes to establishing meaning, the rules of the game change. Therefore, for instance, we find it said: "See! The Lord has given you the sabbath, therefore on the sixth day he gives you bread for two days; remain every man of you in his place, *'let no man go out of his place on the seventh day'* (Exod. 16:29; RSV). The context here is the story of the manna. As stated, it was forbidden to gather the manna on the sabbath day. But matters (or "midrashic conditions" did not stop here. The italicized words eventually became an interpretative cornerstone on which rabbinic *halakhah* regulated human movement on the sabbath in general. On the strict, literal level of the text, no person is allowed to leave his place—whatever that may mean. Indeed, the Karaites followed such verses to their strict limit. By contrast, the rabbinic sages defined *his place,* and thus gave that verse an interesting twist: " 'Let no man go out of his place'—those are the two thousand ells (of permitted travel)" (see *Mekhilta de-Rabbi Yishmael, ad locum*). A similar ruling is found in the sabbath-rule of the Qumran Damascus Covenant (fol. X, 1. 21: 1,000 ells; fol. IX, 1. 5: 2,000 ells, when one takes one's beast to pasture). In other words, the halakhic interpretation of the injunction mentioned in Exodus reads *one's place* as "one's place + an *x-number* of ells." Needless to say, this is a lenient way of interpreting the scriptural—law whose aim is to render the Law practicable.

The preceeding example may also give us an idea of the power that interpretation enjoys over the interpreted text. The text is realized in being interpreted. For all practical purposes, the text lives in the interpretative mode: nothing can hold it back from succumbing to the inevitable process of interpretations and reinterpretation. In a wider sense, this is precisely the essence of Jewish religiousness; viz., the culture of Midrash as enacted in traditionalism.[12] Yet for all the elasticity that the scriptural text undergoes via midrashic hermeneutics, it is not so "deconstructed" as to make every interpretation possible. Midrash is certainly creator of a tradition; but it obeys certain basic presuppositions that safeguard it from becoming a counterproductive enterprise. Those presuppositions include the divine inspiration of Scripture, its permanence and its basically moral nature, and the centrality and indispensability of the cult. The basic principle here is that Scripture and Midrash both serve positive religious purposes.

I referred earlier to the term *discretion* in relation to the interpretative attention given to the Torah-law. In fact, the term *discretion* is more often used to indicate the interpretative stance that a judge maintains when relating to a law that can be interpreted, or related to any particular judicial case, in more than one way.[13] The interpretative options that a judge has to consider before passing a resolution arena the area in which judicial discretion is enacted. Whatever happens in the mind of the judge, the final verdict shows that more often than not it is the result of an act of personal interpretation. Even if what if formally done is just an act of relating the case at court to the relevant item in the Law, the way this is done is tantamount to creating an interpretation. The various considerations that come into play in that process of interpretation are the equivalent of what we have here called *the midrashic conditions.* In the case of the judge, such considerations include similar precedents, social norms, the ideas and tone of the constitution (or Declaration of Independence), the need to meet the demands of the juridical consensus, and so on. All these are considerations that go beyond the judicial case or the law itself. In the case of the midrashist, by contrast, comparable "midrashic conditions" would embrace formal principles of scriptural exegesis (the *Middot* used in the interpretation of the Torah), social needs, new ideological and political positions, historical requirements, or any current disposition of the community. Moreover, in the case of the interpretation of Scripture there is also the need to meet a certain consensus of opinions maintained and zealously guarded by the social group— even though that consensus may change from group to group, from generation to generation, and from place to place. But as already indicated, everything that happens as a result of applying interpretative discretion goes beyond the lexicological needs of the text itself. It rather enters the domain of the creation of meaning, or of the "midrashic conditions."

The question as to how far one can go in interpretation also deserves some comment at this point; although no simple or direct answer is forthcoming—at least on a theoretical level. One may surely argue that tact and an inner feeling of respect for the conventions of the community are the reasonable borders whose crossing makes an interpretation counterproductive at least, countercultural at worst. Nevertheless, it remains very difficult to tell 'Right' from 'Wrong' in the case of any single interpretation. This is particularly true of scriptural interpretations. What passes for 'correct' in one circle of a culture may be condemned as 'wrong' in another. The phenomenon of Jewish sectarian splits that arise from competing interpretations is a clear proof of our point. What looks like the blessing of interpretation in the eyes of one may, to another, appear to be the curse of confusion and anarchy. In this respect, such distinctions as *Peshat* and *Derash* (the plain and the evocative senses of Scripture, respectively) are often redundant. The 'real *Peshat*' for one side may look like 'bazarre *Derash*' for another. This is particularly the case when, as so often in Jewish history, '*Peshat*' and '*Derash*' become value judgments indicating one's agreement ("this is the *peshat* of the matter") or disapproval ("this is a mere *derash*") in matters that relate to the interpretation of some "rabbinic" issue.[14]

III

As we direct our inquiry forward, I think it advisable to bear in mind some of the major points made so far. The common view has it that because the term *Midrash* is widely associated with the various forms of the rabbinic interpretation of Scripture it should be viewed as a committed, tendentious, or theologically oriented type of interpretation. Therefore if modern analytical forms of interpretation are taken as the model used in any assessment of the midrashic type of scriptural interpretation, the "Midrash" appears as an arbitrary and and prejudiced form of interpretative engagement. What is good for the rabbis and their communities of believers is not of any value for an audience that purports to possess "enlightened" and "critical" modes of interpretation. It should of course be noticed that what is said here about the theological, or engaged, nature of the midrashic activity is equally true of the Christian homily and the Islamic Hadith. In fact, any type of ideologically engaged interpretative undertaking shares the subjective and, in the view of the outsider, somewhat distorting quality of Midrash.

By way of improving on this rather narrow understanding of midrashic activity, I have referred to the interpretative qualities of Midrash within the framework of its "midrashic condition(s)." In so doing, I have tried to make the following points:

1. Midrash should be viewed as a mode of cognition in the same sense as literature, philosophy, or science.

2. Midrash is concerned chiefly with relating, mostly newly created, meanings to Scripture and not with mere exegetical problems.
3. A major concern is with the assessment of those operative factors that help create meaning in relation to the scriptural text.
4. A consideration of specific "midrashic conditions" may be helpful in identifying the various literary, interpretative, and ideational factors that endow a midrashic work (not just comment) with its unique or definitive qualities.

Therefore the unique qualities of *Bereshit Rabba* (the major midrashic compilation composed on Genesis) should be isolated and compared with, say, the *Mekhilta de-Rabbi Yishmael* (the so-called Tannaitic Midrash on Exodus) or the *Sifra* (on Leviticus).[15] For despite the fact that a Midrash in general can easily be recognized on the basis of literary style, general layout, and ideological character, more formal considerations have to be brought into the discussion of the matter. Such considerations should not be ignored by any attentive reader of Midrash, and their investigation are part and parcel of my study of "midrashic condition(s)."

Two further questions also deserve our attention in this theoretical context: What is the typical intellectual milieu particularly conducive to midrashic interpretation? and What are the basic forms of Midrash? These are surely complex matters that deserve more attention than can be given in the framework of a brief essay. Considerable attention has been given to the first question in David Tracy's *Plurality and Ambiguity* (New York, 1987)—though of course, Tracy deals with the moment of interpretation in general and not with rabbinic Midrash. Indeed, Tracy singles out moments of cultural and intellectual crisis as being the pivots around which interpretative moves turn. As we have indicated earlier, interpretation is one of the ways in which spiritual adjustments and changes of behavior are introduced into a Scripture-oriented culture. A scriptural text calls for interpretative attention when it appears to have lost its significative function among a certain group of people.[16] From this perspective, interpretative attention helps the text regain its meaning, relevance, and applicability. Such moments are indicative of historical or intellectual crisis; and so, I contend, interpretation not only helps resolve such crises but enables the scriptural text to maintain its meaningfulness until the next cognitive "break."

Naturally, not every interpretative step that is taken in relation to a scriptural text results from a crisis. Indeed, many people would be reluctant to admit that their quest for (a new) interpretation is the result of such a process. For them, interpretation is at best an intellectual challenge with little or no bearing on the interpretative assumptions received from previous generations. It needs intellectual courage and religious sensitivity to take cognizance of the urge to climb and conquer new interpretative positions. In fact, our main concern here is with just such bold interpretative moves—and not with accidental interpretative insights. It is in the light of this observation that I would like to approach the second question and its concern with the classification (into forms or types) of midrashic interpretation. In this context, I must restrict my attention to but one type of relating to Scripture that comes under the *overall* heading of Interpretation: mythopoesis.[17] To be more precise, I shall focus specifically on the important matter of theophany and shall consider its mythopoetic dimension to be a concern with the divine or angelic modes of theophany, and a personification of nature. Because mythopoesis and myth are closely related and the world of mythology is usually of pagan nature, it has often been contended that mythopoetic material has been expurgated from the Hebrew Scripture. But the matter is not so simple.

Let us turn to an outstanding example bearing on this point: the theophany on Mount Sinai (or Horeb). Were one to judge solely on the basis of the pentateuchal stories found in Exodus 19–20, 31–34 and Deuteronomy 3–4, one might conclude that this theophany was exclusively concerned with the giving of the (Tablets of the) Law. However, matters are not as clear as one could wish; for in a striking number of cases the story of the exodus from Egypt is told without any hint of that important theophany.[18] Moreover, in other instances that theophany (or at least a theophany on Mount Sinai) is even referred to without mentioning the giving of the Law. This is a rather strange state of affairs, to be sure—particularly given the centrality of the Law in Jewish Scripture and tradition. To make some sense of the matter, I shall begin my discussion with instances drawn from the first set of texts.

In Psalms 78 we find a poetic account of the story of the Exodus. Here the wondrous acts of God are told in high pathos. But the event that expectedly crowns all these events (the Sinai theophany) is omitted from the story. Now if in the case of that Psalm one may argue that the Torah (whatever that term may mean in this particular context) is at least mentioned (verse 5), the same cannot be said for other Psalms of this genre (e.g., Psalms 105, 106, and 136). In these accounts, the history of Israel is told with *no* reference to the Sinai theophany. On the other hand, we observe that the word *Sinai* (either as a name of God or of a specific place)[19] is in fact mentioned in Psalms 68—although, to be sure, without any reference to the giving of the Law. In addition, note that when Elijah escapes from King Ahab and seeks refuge on Horeb, the mountain of God (1 Kings 19), he experiences a remarkable theophany. But, in contrast to Moses who had heard there the voice of God speaking the Decalogue, Elijah only heard "a still small voice" (v. 12).

These puzzling but intriguing matters are further complicated by the fact that, at least from a literary point of view, the Decalogue in Exodus 19–20 seems artificially appended to the story of the Theophany. This becomes particularly evident when Exodus 19:25 and 20:1 are read together. "So Moses went down to the people and told them [what?]. And God spoke all these words [= the Decalogue], saying . . ." Exodus 24 adds further difficulties; for now a number of new details are added to the story (the sacrifice for one thing and the details of the vision). Reviewing all this material in a synoptic manner, I would suggest the following conclusions: (1) *Sinai* is the name of the deity who revealed himself on Mount Horeb (cf. Judges 5:5; and compare Psalms 68:9, 18). (2) Initially, that revelation was one in a series of mountain theophanies reported in Scripture. (3) The connection of the Sinai theophany with the Decalogue is explicitly stated in Deuteronomy and pushed to the foreground in Exodus. (4) If the Decalogue was indeed added to an already existing tradition about a Sinai theophany, then it may be argued that this addition has an interpretative function; viz., of giving that ancient tradition a new (possible priestly) slant.[20] In other words, if our brief analysis makes sense, then the collocation of those two traditions indicates the existence of 'midrashic conditions' *even when* technically speaking no formal interpretation is at hand. From this perspective, phases in the crystallization of a religious tradition must also be considered within the larger framework of interpretation.

I should now like to take our consideration of the possible interpretative functions of mythopoesis one step further. In 1 Enoch 1 reference is made to the Sinai-Horeb theophany in the following manner: "The God of the universe, the Holy Great One, will come forth from his dwelling. And from there he will march upon Mount Sinai and appear in his camp emerging from heaven with a mighty power. . . . And there shall be a judgment upon all, (including) the righteous, etc." In line with several theophanies described in Scripture, this one also takes up the subject of divine judgment. Yet what is particularly interesting here is the fact that this apocalyptic type of theophany is explicitly linked to Mount Sinai. We are once again required to ask whether that connection derives from the general model found in Scripture or it has some new polemical overtones. If the latter, then a certain interpretative stance is taken by the writer. In contradistinction to the Warrior-Judge type of theophany and the Decalogue-Sinai theophany, Mount Sinai is conceived by the author of 1 Enoch as *the* place of the *eschatological* judgment. Because prophecy is put in the mouth of Enoch, who lived long before the Sinai-Decalogue theophany, the polemical side of that prophecy may be supposed. It is not necessary here to undertake a discussion of the various motivations that brought about this interpretative act or even its larger import. Our purpose is fulfilled if we have called attention to some of the interpretative aspects of mythopoesis in particular, as well as some of its more general implications for understanding Midrash and 'midrashic conditions.'

IV

The elasticity of interpretative attention suggested by the foregoing mythopoetic elaborations on the Sinai-theophany theme becomes even more evident when the midrashic expositions of talmudic rabbis take the same tack.[21] But before we review their expositions of the Sinai theophany, reference should first be made to Paul's Letter to the Galatians (4:24–25). Here, by means of allegorical interpretation, typology is created in which two types of covenants play the major role: "Now this is an allegory: these women [i.e., Hagar and Sarah] are two covenants. One is from Mount Sinai, bearing children for slavery; she is Hagar. Now Hagar is Mount Sinai in Arabia; she corresponds to the present Jerusalem, for she is in slavery with her children." There is no need to quote the rest of this allegory.[22] Suffice it to say that Sinai stands here (negatively) for the mountain on which the Law was given and the first covenant made (see Exodus 24). No mention is made of the theophany that, as we have seen, played such an important role in ancient Israel. In other words, the concrete basis for any kind of mythopoetic elaboration is removed. We need not wonder why: a christological theologumenon has to be established, and that is done by breaking up the complex tradition about Sinai. In a sense, this is tantamount to an act of midrashic demythologization of the Sinai tradtion. The technique employed is that of the purposeful omission of details; it thus stands in marked contrast with the more common process of Midrash, which is variously marked by the addition of details and their subsequent incorporation into the very text to which they relate.[23]

A particular notable example bearing on our theme is the inclusion of angels in the Sinai theophany. The earliest source known to us in which that happens is the Septuagint to Deut. 33:2: "The Lord came from Sinai . . . he came from the ten thousands of holy ones, *with flaming fire at His right hand*."[24] The italicized words are translated by the Septuagint in the following manner: "on his right hand were his angels with him." The introduction of angelic beings into that verse, not to mention its very application ot the famous Sinai event, certainly adds a new mythopoetic dimension to that theophany. Of related interest is the fact that the appearance of angels is variously found in rabbinic literature. One famous example occurs in the *Pesikta de-Rab Kahana, Piska XII*.22: " 'The chariot of God: two myriads and two thousand angels; The Lord is among them; it is Sinai in holiness' (Psalms 68:18). Rabbi Abdimi of Haifa said: In the study of a Mishnah which is in my possession, I learned that twenty-two thousand ministering angels came down with the Holy One on Mount Sinai . . ."[25] The alleged appearance of angels with God on Mount Sinai evidently amplifies the mythopoetic resonance of that theophany. Its simple aim could have been to add dignity to the royal or divine appearance of God. Yet, in mythopoetic terms, it adds to the numinous quality of the event by increasing the supernatural elements of the story.

By contrast, the angelic presence on Mount Sinai was also used in a polemical context.[26] In his attempt to degrade the Torah in the eyes of the Galatians, Paul writes: "and it [= the Law] was ordained by angels [and not by God] through an intermediary [= Moses]" (Gal. 3:19). A similar claim is made, in a more matter of fact manner, by Stephen: "you who received the law as delivered by angels and did not keep it" (Acts 7:53). In self-defense, Stephen accuses his prosecutors of not obeying the Law by which they want to indict him. That Law, he argues, was given by the angels. A mythopoetic-midrashic point is therefore used here in a way that excludes God from the act of giving the Torah. In Paul's case it is almost certain that he wishes to degrade the status of the Law; Stephen's speech may be interpreted as implying the opposite (viz., that the law of god, given by God, is too sacred to be neglected by His own people). By relegating the Law to the angels, Stephen indicates that it is a law that can be transgressed. It is quite otherwise in the case of a Law given by God himself. Dialectically speaking, to be sure, Stephen also degrades the Judaic Torah: it is nothing but the Law of the angels. It is probably with an eye on refuting just such a line of thinking that the rabbis introduced the subject of an angelic opposition to the giving of the Law of Moses (cf. *b. Shabbat* 88b). Surely if the angels oppose the giving of the Law, they cannot be said to be the ones who have given it to Moses!

To conclude, the introduction of a mythopoetic element—here the angelic participation in the Sinai theophany— into the scriptural story creates a midrashic condition for that story. To begin with, the story is itself viewed in a new light, subsequently the new element becomes a center around which several, and even conflicting, theological statements are drawn. It is not absolutely clear what exactly gave rise to the introduction of that particular mythopoetic element into the biblical account(s) of the Sinai theophany. The linguistic problems that the Septuagint faced in regard with respect to Deut. 33:2 could certainly have been solved in a different way, and not necessarily by introducing mythopoetic material. Moreover, one may even wonder just how that material solves the linguistic problems of the verse. But, once included, this element invested the Sinai story with a special dimension of meaning. It bears repeating that, here as elsewhere, such meaning is not read out of the text but almost literally imposed upon it. The results and consequences are remarkable. Once a new meaning is accepted it is incorporated into the thematic texture of the scriptural text and, one may even say, becomes part of people's conceptualization of the event described (or referred to) by Scripture itself. Once that happens, ever new possibilities are opened for the text and its new setting of meaning. It becomes at once the source of further speculations and the basis of new traditions. In this respect, a midrashic or mythopoetic point becomes the cognitive looking-glass through which a biblical story is viewed and a religious world constructed. This said, our circle of reflection is closed and we return to the beginning: *Midrash is a mode of cognition and the major component in the creation of a religious tradition.*

Notes

1. Of particular interest in this respect are the following three collections of essays: James L. Kugel and Rowan A. Greer, *Early Biblical Interpretation* (Philadelphia, 1986); Geoffrey H. Hartman and Sanford Budick, *Midrash and Literature* (New Haven, Conn., and London, 1986); Robert Alter and Frank Kermode, *The Literary Guide to the Bible* (Cambridge, Mass., 1987)

2. This idea was particularly stressed by G. Scholem. See "The Meaning of the Torah in Jewish Mysticism," in *On the Kabbalah and Its Symbolism* (New York, 1969), pp. 32–86; "Revelation and Tradition as Religious Categories in Judaism," in *The Messianic Idea in Judaism* (New York, 1971), pp. 282–303; "Tradition and New Creation in the Ritual of the Kabbalists," in *On the Kabbalah*, 118–57.

3. This idea will be more fully worked out in a forthcoming book *Midrash and the Midrashic Condition.*

4. Of peculiar value in this respect is Hans-Georg Gadamer, *Truth and Method* (London, 1979).

5. Other categories may equally apply. See, for instance, Michael Fishbane, "Revelation and Tradition: Aspects of Inner-Biblical Exegesis," *Journal of Biblical Literature* 99 (1980): 343–61; *Biblical Interpretation in Ancient Israel* (Oxford, 1985), pp. 6 ff, where D. Knight, *Rediscovering the Traditions of Israel* (Missoula, Mont., 1975) is followed in the distinction between *traditum* and *traditio.* See further, M. Fishbane, *The Garments of Torah* (Bloomington and Indianapolis, Ind. 1989).

6. I. Heinemann has written a series of articles (in Hebrew) discussing the various technical terms used for scriptural interpretation. See *Leshonenu* 14 (1946): 182–89; 15 (1947): 108–15; 16 (1948): 20–28. See also I. L. Seeligmann, "The Beginnings of *Midrash* in the Books of Chronicles," *Tarbiz* 49 (1980): 14–32 [in Hebrew].

7. Still pertinent to the modern study of Midrash is W. Bacher, *Die exegetische Terminologie der Jüdischen Traditionsliteratur* (reprint: Darmstadt, 1965). It is to be lamented that such an invaluable treatise on the various forms of midrashic tech-

nique as Shmuel Waldberg's *Sefer Darkhey Ha-Shinuyim* (Lemberg, 1870; reprinted: Jerusalem, 1970) is totally ignored by students of Midrash. Waldberg shows, inter alia, that many of the forms of midrashic exposition are already well represented in Scripture itself.

8. See Otto Betz, *Offenbarung und Schriftforschung in der Qumransekte* (Tübingen, 1960).

9. I. Heinemann, *Darkhey Ha-Aggadah* (Jerusalem, 1954).

10. Here the writer is at variance with such statements as that of A. Goldberg, "The Rabbinic View of Scripture" in *A Tribute to Geza Vermes* P. R. Davies and R. T. White, eds. (Sheffield, England, 1990) 153–166. Goldberg writes: "Scripture, then, is distinct from what it communicates. What is communicated are things past, while the communication as such is valid and present at any given time." Goldberg assumes that "communication" is already objectively reflected in Scripture, whereas we argue that the "communication" is attributed by the interpreter to the scriptural text. If we distinguish between (1) a historical event, (2) its report in Scripture, and (3) its meaning or message, we may well argue that (a) we have to further distinguish between the original meaning or message of the scriptural report and the meaning or message that the interpreter deems to discover in that report; and (b) if we assume that it is difficult, or even impossible, to find out what the original event exactly was (one's way back to the event is impeded by the scriptural report and the meaning the scriptural writer attributed to that event), then the very act of finding out what the original meaning of that report was likewise becomes an almost impossible task. Consequently, what is left is the license of the interpreter to establish not only the meaning of the scriptural report, but also the nature of (a) the original event and (b) the scriptural version of that event.

11. For a recent and comprehensive study of that subject (including an extensive bibliography), see S. J. Lieberman, "A Mesopotamian Background for the So-Called Aggadic 'Measures' of Biblical Hermeneutics?" *Hebrew Union College Annual* 58 (1987): 157–225. See also S. Lieberman, *Hellenism in Jewish Palestine* (New York, 1962), pp. 47–82: "Rabbinic Interpretation of Scripture." See further W. S. Towner, "Hermeneutical Systems of Hillel and the Tannaim: A Fresh Look," *Hebrew Union College Annual* 53 (1982): 101–35; and I. L. Seeligmann, "Voraussetzungen der Midraschexegese," *Supplements to Vetus Testamentum* 1 (1953): 150 ff.

12. See B. Gerhardsson, *Memory and Manuscript: Oral Tradition and Written Transmission in Rabbinic Judaism and Early Christianity* (Uppsala, 1961). See further, N. Rothenstreich, *Tradition and Reality* (New York, 1972), particularly Chapter 1; "The Meaning of Tradition in Judaism,"pp. 7–18.

13. See the comprehensive study of A. Barak, *Judicial Discretion* (Tel Aviv, 1987)

14. It is worth considering the material adduced by W. Bacher (above, note 7), Part II, pp. 170–73, *s.v. Peshat.*] That material clearly shows that the verbal from *pashat* in Amoraic usage simply signified the exposition of Scripture. No distinctions are suggested between the plain and evocative senses of Scripture. In Tannaitic usage, the term had no interpretative application. See ibid., Part I, p. 162. In a private communication Professor Halivni has pointed out to me the only case in which to the best of his knowledge the interpretative categories of *Peshat* and *Derash* are used as opposites in Amoraic literature: *b. Sanhedrin* 100b.

15. See I. Gruenwald, "The Methodology of the Study of Rabbinic Thought" [in Hebrew], *Milet: Everyman's University Studies in Jewish History and Culture,* ed. S. Ettinger et al., (Tel Aviv, 1985), II, pp. 173–84; J. Neusner, *Comparative Midrash: The Plan and Program of Genesis and Leviticus Rabbah* (Atlanta, 1986). See also the comments of P. Schäfer, "Research into Rabbinic Literature: An Attempt to Define the Status Quaestionis," *Journal of Jewish Studies* 37 (1986): 139–52.

16. In this respect we go beyond the theory of Midrash as developed by D. Boyarin, *Intertextuality and the Reading of Midrash* (Bloomington and Indianapolis, Ind., 1990). Although Boyarin argues that something inherent in the scriptural text gives rise to the midrashic interpretation, we think that what characterizes Midrash is its cognitive functions; that is, the need of the reader to relate to the text. In this respect it becomes an almost irrelevant question whether the scriptural text really "justifies" the midrashic utterance related to it. However, to underatand the literary structure of each midrashic saying it is necessary to state how it reads the quoted scriptural saying.

17. See also the essay by Michael Fishbane, Chapter 4 in this book.

18. See G. von Rad, *Gesammelte Studien zum Alten Testament* (Munich, 1965), pp. 20–33.

19. The etymology and exact meaning of the name *Sinai* has not yet been established beyond doubt. On the basis of the *parallelismus membrorum in* Judges v. 5, it may be suggested that *Sinai* is the name of a deity. In this context it is interesting to compare Judges v. 4–5 and Psalms 19:9. See also F. M. Cross, *Canaanite Myth and Hebrew Epic* (Cambridge, Mass., 1976), 100–2. Cross translated the phrase *zeh sinay* as "lord of Sinai." It is also interesting to notice that in the Hekhalot literature one of the names of God is *zihayon* or *zehayon.* See P. Schäfer, *Konkordanz zur Hekhalot-Literatur* (Tübingen, 1986), I, p. 229. The '. . . *on*' suffix is quite frequent in the formation of holy names in the Hekhalot literature. The *zeh* (or *zih*) will derive from the theophoric *zeh* or *zu* in Scripture, whereas the '. . . *a* . . .' in the middle is enclitic.

20. Although it does not directly bear on our subject, we maintain that the "Decalogistic" Sinai theophany is deprived of the Warrior-Judge elements so characteristic of scriptural theophanies. In this respect, it is indeed endowed with a priestly component: compare Exodus 24 with Deuteronomy 22:10 and Malachi 2:4–9. For a summary of the scriptural idea of theophany, see F. M. Cross, ibid., pp. 147 ff.; M. Weinfeld, "Divine Intervention in War in Ancient Israel and in the Ancient Near East," in *Historiography and Interpretations,* ed. H. Tadmor and M. Weinfeld, (Jerusalem and Leiden, 1986), pp. 121 ff.

21. Of particular relevance are the various midrashic expositions brought under the roof of the words "The Lord is a man of war" (on Exodus 15:3) in *Mekhilta de-Rabbi Yishmael.* See A. F. Segal, *Two Powers in Heaven* (Leiden, 1977), 33 ff.: "Conflicting appearances of God."

22. For a recent and extensive discussion of that passage see H. D. Betz, *Galatians* (Hemeneia—A Critical and Historical Commentary on the Bible; Philadelphia, 1979), 238 ff.

23. See G. W. E. Nickelsburg, "The Bible Rewritten and Expanded," in: *Compendia Rerum Iudaicarum ad Novum Testamentum, Section Two, Vol. II: Jewish Writings of the Second Temple Period,* M. Stone, ed. (Assen & Philadelphia, 1984), 89–156. Al-

though Nickelsburg concentrates on the Apocrypha and Pseudepigrapha, his observations fit in the main into the world of rabbinic Midrash.

24. Angelology in Jewish writings of the Greco-Roman period is the subject of an extensive monograph by M. Mach, *Entwicklungsstadien des jüdischen Engelsglaubens in vorrabbinischer Zeit* (Tübingen, 1992).

25. Following the English translation of W. G. Braude and I. J. Kapstein, *Pesikta de-Rav Kahana* (Philadelphia, 1979), 243.

26. For that aspect in Jewish angelology, see P. Schäfer, *Rivalität zwischen Engeln und Menschen* (Berlin & New York, 1975), *passim.*

2

From Midrash to Mishnah: Theological Repercussions and Further Clarifications of "Chate'u Yisrael"

———————————————————— David Weiss Halivni

I n a previous book,[1] I attempted to demonstrate that the midrashic form of scriptural commentary, in which exegesis is appended to and originally linked with a scriptural citation, predated the mishnaic form, which arranges laws topically without attendant scriptural references. Though this view that Midrash is more ancient than Mishnah was almost universally held in the nineteenth and early twentieth centuries, when debate ensued concerning only the date of the transition from the midrashic to the mishnaic mode, it has lately been subject to more divided opinion.[2] I believe, however, that the antecedence of the midrashic to the mishnaic mode of interpretation is clearly demonstrable through textual analysis and proof from contemporary regalia. Mishnah was excerpted from preexistent Midrash halakhah that already existed in the second century B.C.E. Though the mishnaic form became the dominant vehicle for the transmission of law during the reign of R. Gamaliel the Second at Yavneh, the midrashic sensibility (though not the midrashic form), which insisted that laws be explicitly justified on the basis of scripture or reason, continued to flourish for centuries, embodied within the give-and-take of talmudic argumentation. The formal basis of talmudic discussion remained the Mishnah, but the spirit of the Gemara was thoroughly midrashic.

The very starting point of the Babylonian Talmud, at the beginning of the tractate Berakhot, highlights the dependence of the mishnaic text on previous midrashic efforts as well as the abiding interest on the part of the talmudic rabbis in grounding the Mishnah on a scriptural basis. The justification for the Mishnah's ruling is here made explicit, its apodictic (nonjustificatory) quality tempered. Whereas the Mishnah had begun, "From what time in the evening may the Shema be recited?" the Babylonian Talmud immediately inquires, "On what does the Tanna base himself [that he commences, 'from what time']?" The Talmud answers its own question by stating that "the Tanna bases himself on Scripture where it is written, 'And thou shalt recite them . . . when thou liest down and when thou risest up' [Deut. 6:7]." The obligation to recite the Shema in the first place had to be established before its proper time frame could be clarified. The Gemara was seemingly uncomfortable with a free-floating legal text that seemed to begin *in media res*, unanchored by scriptural support or reference. Thus, though the mishnaic strategy of organizing and classifying law gained ascendancy in the early centuries of the common era, the midrashic connection to Scripture was never fully neglected or severed. Indeed, as I have argued in *Midrash, Mishnah, and Gemara*,[3] the Stammaim (the anonymous redactors of the Talmud) resuscitated and replenished the midrashic method (though not its precise literary form), leaving the apodictic mishnaic mode as an aberration in the overall history of Jewish exegesis.

But the Mishnah, although its preeminence as an exegetical form was shortlived, became the foundation and substratum of all future commentary. Its potency and viability as a carrier of halakhic regulations, initially forged through the influence and prestige of its redactor, R. Judah ha-Nasi, has endured. Study of the Mishnah, soon after its (oral) publication in approximately 200 C.E., became, and remains, a necessary component of Torah education. It is the standard, foundational book of halakhah; yet precisely because of its indisputable authority, its innovativeness and unconventionality have been obscured to many of its readers.

The practitioners of the nascent mishnaic method, however, recognized the need in their own time to justify the transition from the midrashic to the mishnaic way of propounding halakhah. Midrash had earned its prima facie justification through its explicit reliance on and derivation from scriptural verses. Its association with the God-given Torah was natural and apparent. In a postprophetic Jewish world, the apprehension of God's will could be gained only through the correct understanding of His word as embodied in the Torah. Midrash halakhah performed this function of explicating God's message through the medium of the Pentateuchal text. Mishnah, by contrast, was apparently disconnected from Scripture and thus divorced from the traditional channel of authority and authenticity. The legitimacy of and authorization for mishnaic law were simply not self-evident; indeed, its very existence could even have appeared presumptuous. The move from Midrash to Mishnah had thus to be justified by its stewards on theological grounds: if Scripture, at least superficially, was apparently not the wellspring of its halakhic authority, why should the Mishnah be respected or obeyed? Widespread acceptance and approval of the format and content of the Mishnah could be won, or maintained, only if its legitimacy could be rationalized. The move from Midrash to Mishnah was a bold one literarily, with clear ideological resonance, which necessitated that it be accompanied by an equally creative and audacious theological apologetic. If the link to God's Torah were to be made opaque through the mishnaic literary form, in which the opinions of individual rabbis were stated with blunt assertiveness and independence and with minimal reference to scriptural sources, then the link to God had necessarily somehow to be preserved. If the Mishnah's locus of authority and authorization was apparently distinct from that of Midrash, that is, nonscriptural, then what was it?

The attribution of divine source and status to the Oral Law in rabbinic literature is obviously a well-known and well-attested feature of rabbinic theology. Yet the variegated makeup of rabbinic theological conceptions of the revelation of the Oral Law is usually not noted by students of rabbinic literature, who often perceive of those conceptions as homogenous and uniform when in fact they are neither.[4] Not only can the various positions vis-à-vis the revelatory status of the Oral Law be distilled and differentiated one from the other; they can also be stratified theologically. Rabbinic theology in this regard is composed of layers that build on and add to the preceding ones. The stages of rabbinic theology concerning the issue of the divinity of the Oral Law can be shown, moreover, to correspond, or at least to respond, to a particular exegetical dynamic: the transition from the midrashic to the mishnaic mode, and the later reversion to the midrashic form, that we have outlined previously.

I suggest that the theological conceptions of the Oral Law developed by successive generations of rabbis during the talmudic period were molded, at least in part, by the adoption and ascending of the mishnaic method of transmitting halakhah in previous generations. Although, as we have already noted, the midrashic form of scriptural commentary, which accentuated justification and authorization for its rulings, later found even fuller and more sophisticated embodiment within the discursive, argumentational matrix of the Gemara, the challenge posed by the very existence of the Mishnah could not be ignored. In fact, if the mishnaic form had fully displaced the midrashic for good in 200 C.E., the issue of the transition would probably not have been as urgently or acutely felt. But succeeding generations, though beholden to the textual authority of the Mishnah, largely abandoned its literary framework and were instead committed to the midrashic penchant for justification. The divergence of the mishnaic form from the conventional Jewish attachment to Scripture thus had to be retroactively legitimated. And in the process of such legitimation were forged theological claims about the divinity of the Oral Law that were to characterize and define traditionalist Judaism throughout the medieval period and into the modern era. That is, despite the demise of the Mishnah as an exegetical format, the theological impact of its shortlived literary form was enormous. The literary passage from Midrash to Mishnah, which was ultimately not to be determinative exegetically in Jewish history, was indeed, however, decisive and repercussive theologically.

Mishnah Avot was the first attempt to justify the mishnaic form on historical-theological grounds. Scholars[5] have long contented that Mishnah Avot can be divided into several textual strata, with the oldest layer (consisting of 1:1–16; 2:8, 10–14) listing the "chain of tradition" from Moses to the five disciples of R. Yochanan ben Zakkai (accompanied by a triadic statement attributed to each postbiblical member of the chain). This layer was composed by these five disciples (or by their disciples)[6] in approximately the first quarter of the second century, which corresponds to the period a generation after the change-over from the midrashic to the mishnaic exegetical mode. The first-generation Mishnah, redacted during the time of R. Akiva, demanded an enterprising theological justification, and Avot certainly provided one. The rulings of these second-century rabbis were claimed to be traceable back in time to Moses, who had himself received them from God at Mount Sinai. As successors to Moses, these rabbis claimed for themselves equivalent, though derivative, authority. Their legislation, though apparently not dependent upon the Torah Moses had received from God, was nevertheless of divine origin. The first layer of Avot thus served as strategic introduction and warrant for the new exegetical construct known as Mishnah.[7] By staking claim to an alternative but complementary channel of revelatory authority to Scripture, the Mishnah could now lay claim to divinity as explicitly as Midrash had done implicitly. Avot *had* to be explicit and forceful about the Mishnah's divine lineage, because nowhere was it apparent from or dictated by its textual content or form. Indeed, both its content and form militated against such an assumption.

The theological validation for the mishnaic project forwarded by Avot was certainly instrumental in solidifying the acceptability of the first Mishnah at Yavneh. But when the Mishnah of R. Judah ha-Nasi (viz., "Rabbi") was published (orally) in around 200 C.E., the need for justification became even more pressing. Because the Mishnah was by now the focal and supreme text of Jewish learning, Jews may have studied sections of it independently of Avot, its theological preface, and therefore may have been unacquainted with its theological rationale. New efforts toward conceptualizing its theological status were required. Rabbi's Mishnah aspired to supreme halakhic authority, and very quickly nearly earned it. All other Tannaitic opinions, which did not find their way into the Mishnah, were classified as *baraitha*, that is, as external to the main body of mishnaic traditions. Later, the Tosefta, a collection of such *baraithot*, was redacted as a complement to the Mishnah, but its very name bears testimony to its auxiliary and secondary status. But the authority sought by and largely accorded to the Mishnah had not only to be justified but also rationalized. Its virtual splendid isolation from, and virtual substitution for, Scripture had to be made to seem reasonable in the eyes of those who would accede to its claims to jurisdiction. Its ascendancy as the dominant, authoritative halakhic text was, moreover, indeed dramatic and impressive. As the Mishnah seemed not only to displace Scripture, but to dislodge all textual rivals, its attendant justificatory claims became even more comprehensive.

Perhaps the most widely quoted talmudic statement concerning the revelation of the Oral Torah is the one that posits that the entirety of the Oral Law was revealed to Moses at Sinai, including "the comments that an astute student (*talmid vatik*) will someday make in the presence of his teacher."[8] This remark (or a variation of it) is found in two places in the Talmuds and on both occasions, significantly, said in the name of a student of R. Judah ha-Nasi: in the Palestinian Talmud, in the name of R. Joshua ben Levi and in the Bavli, in the name of R. Yohanan. By their time, the Mishnah had become a self-sufficient book of law and the major staple of learning, which could be studied independent of the Torah.[9] Because the Mishnah could also be studied with no substantive impairment without Avot, its introductory accompaniment, the circle of Rabbi's disciples had to be vigilant about its continued ratification by the constituency at large. The legal definitiveness of the Mishnah had to be matched and reinforced by an equally absolute theology. The *talmid vatik* version of the Oral Law revelation motif fit the bill. Indeed, its theological dividend was great, for it became a linchpin of medieval Rabbinate polemics. Its theological audacity and maximalism proved striking and compelling to most Jews.

But, as we stated earlier, this extreme maximalistic conception of the revelation of the Oral Law (embodied in the Mishnah particularly) did not represent a monolithic rabbinic stance. Other, less embracing positions had surfaced as well within the rabbinic community. In *Sifra*, the Midrash halakhah text on the book of Leviticus, it is written that "the Torah, its laws, and their details and explanations, were given via Moses at Sinai."[10] This statement has often been miscast as a companion notion to the *talmid vatik* comment discussed earlier. The two, however, are really rival and not analogous or interchangeable conceptions of the revelation of the Oral Law. And the fact that this statement in *Sifra* is found in a book of Midrash is not coincidental nor incidental to its significance. Its setting within a midrashic context allowed for a more limited conception of revelation. Unencumbered by the same theological pressures and constraints that would later attend the publication and dissemination of the Mishnah, this midrashic statement does not strive for the comprehensiveness and inclusiveness later typified by the *talmid vatik* claim of Rabbi's disciples. Because the justification and authorization for Midrash were more readily apparent than for Mishnah, the theological claims of Midrash did not have to be as far reaching. The statement in *Sifra* was theologically adequate within its midrashic context; at a later time, the Mishnah would require more extensive theological claims.

The statement in *Sifra* posits that along with the explicit laws of the written Torah attendant details and explanations that would make those laws practicable were revealed (orally). It also perhaps seeks to justify extensions of the laws to be yielded through the application of moderate hermeneutical rules. It does *not* claim, as the *talmid vatik* statement later would, that all possible interpretations of the Torah to be learned through human logic (*sevara*) were revealed at Sinai and thus partake of divinity. The *Sifra*'s conception of revelation is more modest and restrained theologically because its exegetical burden is lighter.

Our understanding of this statement of *Sifra* is corroborated by another comment, found at the beginning of *parashat Behar,* on the verse, "the Lord spoke to Moses on Mount Sinai . . ." (Lev. 25:1). The midrashic text here inquires why the Torah would particularly introduce the legislation of the Sabbatical year (*shemitah*) that follows with the specification that God spoke to Moses at Mount Sinai. Why are the laws of *shemitah* different from all other laws in the Torah? The answer given is that just as the laws of *shemitah* are given here in Leviticus in abundant detail (when they had previously been outlined only in principle in Exod. 23:11), so, too, were all the other laws of the Torah, which are only adumbrated in the written Torah, revealed (orally) by God to Moses at Mount Sinai: "just as the laws of the Sabbatical year were given with their general principles and details (*dikdukehah*) at Sinai, so too were all laws given in this way."[11] The laws of *shemitah* are, thus, paradigmatic of all other laws of the Torah and were included in the written Torah with the introductory phrase, "the Lord spoke to Moses at Mount Sinai," to indicate that, for example, the prohibitions concerning the Sabbath, only intimated by the term *melakhah*, were also revealed by God in much fuller detail. These details (*dikdukehah*) reflect the necessary practical apparatus of the law, however, and not all potential theoretical packaging that may ever accompany it (as implied by the *talmid vatik* claim). The clear connection between Scripture and legal application in a midrashic context made this notion of revelation palatable and reasonable. The apologists for the format of the Mishnah, however, needed to be more ambitious and to take the theological notion of revelation a step further, if their exegetical undertaking were not to be perceived as unsubstantiated or unwarranted.

The theological ambition and maximalism displayed by the *talmid vatik* statement of Rabbi's students was extended even further by succeeding generations, for whom the authority of the Mishnah was unquestioned (though its form fell into desuetude). A statement in *Koheleth Rabbah* 5:8 posits that even the postmishnaic additions of the House of Rabbi (*tosaphot*) were revealed by God to Moses, as were the laws regarding proselytes and slaves, *tzitzit*, *tefillin*, and *mezuzot*, all of which, not coincidentally, are not represented in the Mishnah.[12] This statement seeks to embrace postmishnaic legislation within the body of divinely revealed law and reflects the next stage in the developing character of Rabbinic theology concerning the Oral Law, which is related to a particular exegetical dynamic. The activity of Midrash had produced theology that reflected its concerns: the practical application and extension of the laws of the written Torah, through hermeneutic efforts, had to be justified. But such justification could lean comfortably on the midrashic connection to Scripture. The transition from Midrash to Mishnah, however, required a justificatory strategy that forged a new and different source of revelatory authority. Because the exegetical format of Mishnah was distinct from that of Midrash, its theological identity would also have to diverge from the traditional pattern. And the theological path paved by the guardians of the Mishnah would grow ever wider and more encompassing. More and more came to be subsumed under the notion of "*talmid vatik 'atid le-chadesh.*"[13] The transition from Midrash to Mishnah stimulated and animated all Jewish theological conceptions of revelation to follow, despite the fact that the currency of the mishnaic method was relatively shortlived.

We have seen that the Mishnah became imbued soon after its publication with divine status and authority. Its bold liturgical format demanded, or rather elicited, an ambitious theological agenda, one that was quite successfully executed and even amplified on in succeeding generations. But did the Mishnah really perceive itself in the terms in which it was soon theologically packaged? Does the internal evidence of the Mishnah suggest that its redactor intended to claim for his text divine origin? The very existence of *machloket* ("controversy") in the Mishnah indicates that its redactor probably did not intend to claim divine status or divine origin for his text. A divinely related text would presumably display unanimity and uniformity of opinion and not controversy and disputation in its midst. The cataloging of minority opinions in the Mishnah injects its content with a legal ambiguity and logical fuzziness that a supposedly divine text would not accommodate. The Mishnah was intended by its redactor, therefore, to be legally definitive but not textually divine. Yet there is often a gap between authorial intent and reader reception. The Mishnah, though not immediately promulgated or publicized as a divinely revealed corpus of halakhah, very soon gained such an appellation. Because its authority was so quickly and comprehensively established, the Mishnah gained for itself over time an image loftier than that which it originally had sought. We have seen that the developmental history of Rabbinic theology with regard to the revelation of the Oral Torah was actuated in part by the transition from the midrashic to the mishnaic mode of transmitting halakhah. The boldness of this literary change was accompanied by an ever more ambitious and inclusive theological apologetic. Though the supremacy of the Mishnah as an exegetical form did not last long, the theological repercussions of its ascendancy as the authoritative code of Jewish law have been long felt. Theological claims about the extent of the divinity of the Oral Law were, as we have also seen, not uniform. Conceptions of such revelation ranged from the minimalistic, which proposed that only the principles or guidelines of the Oral Law were divinely revealed, to the maximalistic, which asserted that even the nonhalakhic elements of the entire Rabbinic corpus were revealed by God at Mount Sinai. The tradition of the Oral Law as upheld by all within the Rabbinic community, but ascriptions to it of divinity were varied.

Another conception of the revelation of the Oral Law, which is less ambitious than the *talmid vatik* statement, although the two are often thought to be equivalent, and which can be termed the intermediate position, is found in *Midrash Tehillim* 12:4:

> R. Yannai said: The words of the Torah were not given as clear-cut decisions. For with every word which the Holy One, blessed be He, spoke to Moses, He offered him forty-nine arguments by which a thing may be proved clean, and forty-nine other arguments by which it may be proved unclean. When Moses asked, "Master of the universe, in what way shall we know the true sense of a law?", God replied, "The majority is to be followed—when a majority says it is unclean, it is unclean; when a majority says it is clean, it is clean."

In this conception of revelation, which is not quite as inclusive as the *talmid vatik* statement, true learning is *more* than merely rediscovering the given and the revealed. Human participation in the revelatory process itself falls under the rubric of the divine mandate. Humankind must rely upon itself, and not upon God, to fashion a system that is conclusive and categorical from an initial revelation that was purposefully inconclusive and indeterminate.

This statement of R. Yannai, himself a student of R. Judah ha-Nasi, shows that even among Rabbi's circle of disciples there was no unanimity concerning the extent and scope of the revelation of the Oral Torah. R. Yannai apparently accepted the parameters of the conception of revelation embodied within the statement from *Sifra*, that the fundamental details attendant to toraitic commandments, which were necessary for their implementation, were revealed at Mount Sinai. But he implicitly rejected the comprehensiveness of the *talmid vatik* conception of revelation, opting instead for a less grandiose claim about the scope of revelation.

R. Yannai's instinct that the *talmid vatik* position on the scope of the divinity of the Oral Law was not only far reaching; the term *over reaching* was merited and corroborated by even surface historical circumstances and logical realities. The extreme maximalistic conception of the revelation of the Oral Law reflected by the *talmid vatik* statement may have been (and may continue to be) theologically gratifying, but its historical pretensions, when taken at face value, seemed troubling. What, in fact, had happened through time to all "the comments that an astute disciple would someday make in the presence of his teacher?" If already revealed to Moses at Sinai, why were these halakhic insights not in the public domain and tenure of the Jewish people down through the centuries, and why did they seemingly require a second, less publicized "revelation" much later in a rabbinic classroom to become known? Unless we say that Moses kept to himself most of what was revealed to him orally by God at Sinai, these difficulties associated with the *talmid vatik* conception of revelation seem vexing and make this position prima facie problematic. In fact, R. Yom Tov Heller, in the introduction to the *Tosaphot Yom Tov*, argues for precisely that scenario, claiming that the implication of the statement in *b. Megillah* 19b that "the Holy One, blessed be He, showed Moses the minutiae of the Torah" is that God revealed these to Moses for his private edification only and not to transmit them to the people of Israel. If God had intended that Moses indeed convey the bulk of the revelation to the people, the language would not have been "he *showed* Moses" but rather "he *gave* Moses" the minutiae of the Torah. Aside from being a clearly strained interpretation of this talmudic comment, crafted to address the historical problem noted previously inherent in the maximalistic conception of revelation, this suggestion of R Yom Tov Heller is not substantiated by other Rabbinic evidence about the character of Moses as leader. In fact, in *b. Nedarim* 38a, the phrase from Prov. 22:9, "the generous man is blessed," is ascribed to Moses, thus advancing the notion that Moses was munificent and altruistic and thus (for our concern) would not have been parsimonious in sharing God's revelation of the Oral Law with his people. Despite R Yom Tov Heller's ingenuity, a cloistered and dead-end revelation from God to Moses is clearly not what the maximalistic historical conception of the Oral Law is about.

Perhaps a solution to the historical dilemma of the *talmid vatik* conception of revelation is to be found in the suggestion that the laws revealed in massive quantity at Sinai were forgotten over time. This notion is indeed forwarded in *b. Temurah* 16a, which discusses the many laws forgotten by the Jews due to their mourning over the death of Moses. The Rabbis, however, in an effort to substantiate the continuity of the Oral Law tradition, emphasize immediately that these laws were soon remembered and reinstituted. In apparently salvaging the historical durability of the Oral Law, the Rabbis nevertheless did not ensure the logical integrity of the maximalistic conception of its revelation.

A more fruitful approach to tackling this problem is perhaps to be found in the suggestion that it was not simple forgetting but rather sinning on the part of the Jews that led to the need for the progressive "rediscovery" of the Oral Law through time despite its revelation in its entirety by God at Sinai. This idea is captured in the talmudic statement in *b. Nedarim* 22b that were it not for the sinning of the Jews, only the Pentateuch and the book of Joshua would have been necessary for the spiritual well-being of the Jews. The prophetic books would have been superfluous if the Jewish people had only remained faithful to God's word.[14] Sinning, in this reading of Jewish history, is a cause and creator of disjunction, discontinuity, and fragmentation, which can explain as well the historical need for the perpetual disclosure of a one-time and once-and-for-all Sinaitic revelation of the Oral Law. The insights of students through time are necessary to illuminate and rereveal the Torah because sinning on the part of their ancestors had disrupted the flow and stability of the Oral Law tradition. See *b. Eruvin* 54a: "If the first tablets had not been broken (they were broken because of the sin of the Golden Calf), the Torah would never have been forgotten in Israel."

What I have just said pertains to the theological dynamic, occasioned by a correlative exegetical shift, associated with the Rabbinic understanding of the revelation of the Oral Law. The notion of sinning on the part of the Jews discussed previously, which redeems somewhat the theological viability of the maximalistic *talmid vatik* conception of revelation, can be associated even more fruitfully with the revelation of the written Torah. Although a nonmaximalistic theological stance makes the appeal to the idea of sinning an unnecessary one in regard to the issue of the scope of the revelation of the Oral Law, because such a stance is not plagued by similar historical difficulties, the theological problems that riddle the traditional understanding of the revelation of the written Torah make it an attractive and, indeed, indispensable explanation. Much of the detailed regulation of the commandments, later assumed by Rabbinic thinkers to have been revealed at Sinai, was apparently neglected by masses of Jews through the First Temple period. The status of these details as constituent elements of the divine revelation could not have been very firm or widespread. Apparently, during the First Temple period, the conception of the written Torah as the divine constitution was not sufficiently secure as to procure universal obedience to its authority.

Though this is not the occasion to pursue the theme of the divine authority of the written Torah at great length, I will do so in capsule form as a parallel to the preceding discussion of the theological dynamic attendant to the notion of the Oral Law.[15] I have claimed that in the case of the Oral Law, a shift in exegetical and literary strategy occasioned movement on the theological front; in the case of the written Torah, historical realities affected the receptivity of the authority of the written Torah in the community of ancient Israel, which only consequently fostered the theological uniformity of belief in a divinely revealed written Torah that began in the Second Temple period. And, ultimately, modern (traditionalist) theological conceptions of the written Torah must be somewhat adjusted in recognition of these often ignored, or overlooked, historical realities of Judaism's earliest times.[16]

In essence, I have suggested that in cases where *Derash* (the "applied" meaning of a biblical phrase or verse generated through interpretation) seems to depart radically from *Peshat* (the "plain" meaning of a biblical phrase or verse), an act of restoration, and not revision, has taken place. This restoration or rehabilitation of the scriptural text was achieved largely through the efforts of Ezra the Scribe during the early Second Temple period. Therefore, rabbinic *Derash* actually restores the original meaning of the scriptural verse, recovering its divine authorial intention, in places where the text itself had become blemished through the historical process of *chate'u Yisrael* ("the people of Israel sinned"), the sinning of the Jews through idol worship and their consequent neglect of the biblical text during much of the post-Mosaic and First Temple periods.[17] Those occasions when rabbinic *Derash* supplants the *Peshat* of a verse signify that the current text of the verse is faulty and that, in fact, the *Derash* was originally the *Peshat* of the verse.[18]

The notion of faulty text is not new with us. A similar version with regard to a prophetic text is already found in *j. Ta'anit* 4.5 (68c). The concern there is the contradiction between Mishnah Ta'anit 4.6, which states that the city of Jerusalem was breached on the seventeenth of Tammuz, and Jer. 39:2, which states that the event occurred on the ninth of the month. The Yerushalmi resolves the contradiction by positing *kilkul ha-cheshbonot*, inaccurate calculations. This Yerushalmi passage is explained clearly and daringly by the Rashba (1235–1310) in his commentary to *b. Rosh Hashana* 18b (Z. Dimitrowsky, ed.; Jerusalem, 1981, p. 97): ". . . The breaching of the city took place undoubtedly on the seventeenth of Tammuz (the day we fast) . . . , but because of their great anguish (the people) confused the date, made a mistake thinking that the city was breached on the ninth of Tammuz—and the text is written according to the (mistaken) calculation of the people." Practical halakhah, scheduling the fast day, thus follows the actual historical date when the city was breached, whereas the biblical text records the mistaken date of the people. (Incidentally, the paradigm of practical halakhah being more accurate than the text; viz., *Derash* being more accurate than *Peshat*!—lies at the basis of "*chate'u Yisrael*"). From the perspective of history, Jer. 39.2 is faulty.

It should be stated that the acknowledgment of faulty text is no reason for not saying the verse in Deut. 4:44: "And this is the Law that Moses said before the children of Israel," customarily recited when the Torah scroll is lifted up in the synagogue. "This is the Law" could equally refer to the oral restoration, transmitted through Midrash, as it does to the plain meaning of the text. Since the time of Ezra, *Derash* is an integral part of the Law and as such may be subsumed under its nomenclature.

This question, however, is less easily answered when raised with regard to discrepancies between rabbinic and massoretic readings. There are instances in the Talmud (see *b. Kiddushin* 66b and *b. Sanhedrin* 4a) when a halakhah, is based on exposition of a word (or a letter) whose reading disagrees with the reading found in our Torah scrolls.[19] Our reading is halakhically faulty, yet the scribes resisted the temptation already recommended by such an authority as the Rashba in his *responsa* falsely attributed to the Ramban (No. 232) to correct the scrolls in line with the talmudic reading. One has to assume that those who resisted presumed the notion that when Scripture says, "This is the Law," *Law* does not necessarily refer to each and every word of the present Torah scroll.

A by-product of this proposed theory of the faultiness of the scriptural text and the later restorative and corrective activities at the hands of Ezra is that the First Temple period is denuded of halakhic authoritativeness and integrity. The conclusion that during the First Temple period syncretism was prevalent and monotheism therefore unstable is an inescapable one and emerges directly from the scriptural sources themselves.[20] Only beginning with the Second Temple period did the universal belief in the authority, and divinity, of the written Torah emerge. Ezra's generation recognized the sinfulness of the preceding generations and consciously strove to distance itself from the religious trends of its forebears. Legal change in (premodern) Jewish history was accomplished or legitimated in one of two ways: either change occurred unconsciously and imperceptibly over time or else one generation would attempt to reconcile its prevailing customs with the apparent (differing) dictates of a canonical text inherited from the past. That is, they would attempt to rationalize and to justify their practice when it seemed to differ from the textual tradition that should have guided their actions. During the time and within the milieu of Ezra's generation, however, restoration and not reconciliation was the strategy of procuring religious continuity.[21] Ezra did not seek compromise with an immediate past but rather sought revival of a more distant one.

The belief in the divinity of Moses' Torah thus became axiomatic only during the Second Temple period, following on the heels of Ezra's efforts.

The historical reconstruction I have proposed here implies that the text of the Torah that we possess is not immaculate, for although the Torah may be divine in that it was revealed by God, it is nonetheless no longer unblemished, for it was received by and has been affected by humankind. Medieval Jewish philosophers unproblematically assumed the divinity and thus the perfection of our Torah text, but they did not have to contend with such modern ideas as Buber's contentless revelation. The modern Jewish theological agenda must be adjusted to conform to the sensibilities and concerns of historically conscious modern Jews.

R. Joseph Albo's third axiom of faith (after belief in God and Revelation), the inevitability and efficacy of reward and punishment,[22] is, in our time, less in need of emphasis insofar as the modern Jewish orientation towards *mitzvot* is more experiential and less influenced by notions of ultimate divine payback. The faith that the Torah is the legacy of the encounter between God and the Jewish people must instead be reinforced as an axiom of modern Jewish theology, for it has been severely challenged through the rise of the modern consciousness. The belief in the divinity, though not the textual immaculacy, of the Torah and in the authoritativeness of the rabbinic tradition that illuminates it must be replenished. In the modern world that is skeptical of the historicity of revelation, or at least of its substantive content, the more pressing concern of modern Jewish (traditionalist) theology must be to safeguard the authenticity of the midrashic tradition; that is, the content (and not the textual carrier) of revelation. The doctrinal certainty that the text of the Torah is pristine can be dispensed with if assurance can be earned that our understanding of the text, which undergirds our halakhic practice, nevertheless accords with the divine will. Though the divine text itself is no longer perfect, the tradition that attends and clarifies that text is.

What I have proposed may be designated as "historicist" theology, in which humankind—the epitome of historical being—had and has an evolving role in revelation, the essence of Jewish theology. Even the text of the Torah was molded by the realities and burdens of history. The *chate'u Yisrael* period was a necessary historical step toward the acceptance of monotheism by the Jewish people,[23] though it had a debilitating influence on the configuration of the scriptural text.

Now lest I be misunderstood, let me hasten to explain that "*chate'u Yisrael*" does not refer to a point in history distant from the time of revelation exclusively, justifying the question what did the text look like between the giving of the Torah and the sinning of Israel—and hoping to rediscover it archaeologically. "*Chate'u Yisrael*" is thus a metaphor for saying that the revelation did not have much of an immediate effect on the religious life of the people. They more or less thought and behaved as before the Siniatic revelation—that is why forty days after receiving the Torah, they worshipped the Golden Calf; did not observe the basic festivals like Passover or Sukkot (Tabernacles); and, if we are right, neglected to preserve the text. In the long run, however, the effect was enormous. The Torah provided them with the means and potential to transform themselves morally and spiritually—though they did not take full advantage of this until the time of Ezra and the covenant (*'amanah*) recorded in Nehemiah 10.

Moreover, many of the laws of the Torah are incomplete, too general, and in need of interpretation—making it thereby a notch lower in the hierarchy of obligation.[24] God could have given humankind a fully written Torah instead of relying on a human agency to transmit interpretation.[25] He did not do so because he wanted humanity to have a share in the Torah. That share, like anything else human, is historically bound—an inevitable reflection of the human existence in time. Thus, in the case of the written Torah, humankind received a divine product from God and subjected it to human exertion. In the development of the Oral Law, the human was partner to God in the process of revelation. Whereas with the written Torah humanity matured to the acceptance of its authority, growing more comfortable over time with the confirmation of its responsibilities, in the Oral Law humanity was a productive associate from its inception. In the maximalistic conception of the Oral Law encapsulated by the *talmid vatik* statement, revelation is unburdened by time and space. In an historically conscious conception of the Oral Law, in contrast, history is clearly an active ingredient of a developmental process. Even the written Torah was not unaffected by the impermanence and variability that are the inevitable consequences of the march of history.[26]

In sum, the perfection of God does not guarantee the continued perfection of His creation. Revelation is a two-pronged process that necessarily includes a giver (God) and a receiver (the Jewish people) and that bears a legacy in time (the Torah). The giver exists transhistorically, unaffected by the influences of time and space. The receiver, however, exists within history and is vulnerable to all the corrupting and debilitating influences of history. The legacy of revelation—the Torah—also came into being, and continues to persist, within the temporal and physical dimensions of time and space. Though God the creator of the world and give of the Torah is perfect, His creation and His gift are not necessarily so. Indeed, they are, by necessity, subject to the conditions of the physical world because they exist within them. Once the Torah was bequeathed to humankind, it was also exposed to human frailties and constraints. It became part of history.

Appendix

I subsequently realized that the reluctance to embrace *chate'u Yisrael* may stem in part from the popular belief that *nitkatnu hadorot*, the spiritual diminution of the generations, constitutes an essential tenet of Judaism. Accordingly, the closer one lived to the giving of the Torah, the closer one was to the truth. The people of the First Temple, therefore, by virtue of their proximity to revelation possessed a purer, clearer vision of the nature of the Divine and His commandments than subsequent generations—an assumption that *chate'u Yisrael* denies. It claims the reverse: that Judaism did not come into its own until the time of Ezra and his entourage, centuries after the giving of the Torah. Prior to Ezra, prior to the period of the Second Temple, the Jews were either outright idol worshippers or syncretists, neglecting both the observance of the content of the Torah and its precise formulation, the text.

Elsewhere I hope to show that the concept of *nitkatnu hadorot* is not universally accepted in talmudic literature, that consistent voices in Rabbinic writings express contrary sentiments. In fact, one can even argue that the exhortation against anthropomorphism (raised to the level of dogma) is basically a denial of *nitkatnu hadorot*. It endows the later generations with a more accurate, correct conception of the Divine attitudes than that maintained by earlier generations, especially those which immediately followed the giving of the Torah. To the earlier generations, corporality of the godhead was apparently an indispensable article of faith, as attested by the golden calf.

Moreover, Maimonides's (*Guide* III. 32) explanation (rooted in the Midrash) of animal sacrifice as a means of weaning humankind away from idolatry is indirectly extolling later generations over earlier ones. The people who received the Torah came out of Egypt, a place steeped in idolatry (a phrase found several times in the Midrash) and, because of that, needed extra precautions to guard them against relapse, whereas later generations needed no such precautions. To them, the memory of Egyptian idolatry receded into antiquity signifying thereby a lower state of religiosity of the former. (Incidentally, Maimonides's explanation goes beyond "*chate'u Yisrael.*" In the Talmud, "*chate'u Yisrael*" in no way exonerated the sinners, nor does it reduce the iniquitous effect of the sinful act including punishment; whereas Maimonides's explanation implies that God made concessions to the people's sinful behavior almost to the point of forebearing. Moreover, their explanation can be extended to whenever a statement in the Bible collides with an accepted historical or scientific fact, saying that the statement is a concession to the low level of knowledge that prevailed among the people who received the Torah, analogous to the concession made by God to the same people with respect to their religious turpitude. Perhaps this is what lies behind

Maimonides's assertion (*Guide* II. 25) that if Aristotle would have advanced convincing arguments on behalf of the eternity of the world, he, Maimonides, would have accommodated the contrary verses in the Bible accordingly! How? By saying that the contrary verses were a concession to the people's primitive conception of the universe? Or, would he have interpreted the contrary verses midrashically, in a nonliteral manner? All these questions, I hope, will be discussed elsewhere.)

Another possible source of reluctance to embrace *chate'u Yisrael* could be the medieval theory of "consensus" (*ijma*). Medieval scholars of all three monotheistic religions habitually pointed to the universal acceptance of the Bible as proof of the veracity of its content. The consensus theory requires the people who consented to be extraordinarily pious, highly sophisticated, and singularly trustworthy; people who would not err. The concept of *chate'u Yisrael* undermines such confidence in human inerrancy. In fact it singles out the people who lived immediately proceeding revelation and the generations that followed them as religiously underdeveloped, requiring the proddings of prophets along a stretch of several centuries to wean them away from idolatry.

Again, elsewhere I hope to show that the consensus theory was not universally accepted, not even among medieval philosophers, and that instead of basing the veracity of the scripture on consensus, one ought to turn to direct experience (the "experiential") as a validation of the divine nature of the commandments. Experience may not extend to the narrative portion of Scriptures—for that a different mode of justification is needed—but it will provide a more personal, intimate, and firm basis for observance. It will get humanity closer to God.

While a survey of the literature is sufficient to show that *nitkatnu hadorot* was not universally held, that it represents a partisan view, to explore the experiential nature of the commandments is a far greater and more difficult task. It requires a new *ta'amei hamitzvot*, consistently and systematically showing that the observance of the *mitzvot* collectively and individually bring a person closer to God. That makes the later thesis much tougher to prove.

Notes

1. *Midrash, Mishnah, and Gemara: The Jewish Predilection for Justified Law* (Cambridge, Mass.; and London, 1986).

2. Only Isaac Halevy of all earlier scholars, in his *Dorot Ha-Rishonim*, vol. 1, book 3, pp. 292 ff. (Berlin and Vienna, 1923), had claimed that in early times laws were transmitted without references to Scripture. His view and reasoning were generally regarded as polemical and tendentious.

3. *Midrash, Mishnah, and Gemara,* pp. 76–105.

4. See my "On Man's Role in Revelation," in *From Ancient Israel to Modern Judaism: Essays in Honor of Marvin Fox,* ed. J. Neusner, E. S. Frerichs, and N. M. Sarna (Atlanta, 1989), vol. 2, pp. 29–49, for a catalogue of the various rabbinic conceptions of the revelation of the Oral Law and their attendant implications for perceptions of the human component of the revelatory process.

5. See D. Z. Hoffmann, *Die Erste Mischna und die Controversen der Tannaim* (Berlin, 1881–82), pp. 26–27.

6. This oldest link in Avot's chain of tradition does not mention R. Akiva and was probably written during his lifetime. A convention of such lineage records in Rabbinic literature is that the modesty of the author prevents him from including himself in the chain of tradition. The roster of tradents or transmitters usually ends with the teacher(s) of the author, and therefore R. Akiva's name does not appear in this earliest stratum of Avot.

7. For a different dating and for an "external" reason for the chain of tradition in Avot, see Elie Bikerman (Elias Bickerman), "La Chaîne de la Tradition Pharisienne," *Revue Biblique* 59 (1952): 44–54. However, see also W. Sibley Towner, *Hebrew Union College Annual* 53 (1982): 101 ff.

8. *j. Pe'ah* 17a and parallels. Cf. *b. Megillah* 19b, "The Mishnah, too, was given by God"; *Seder Eliahu Zuta* II, p. 171.

9. My view is that the Mishnah was intended as a book of legal rulings (i.e., "pesak") and not just as a mere collection of opinions. See my article, "Mishnahs Which Were Changed From Their Original Forms" [Hebrew], in *Sidra: Journal for the Study of Rabbinic Literature* 5: 86–88, for an account of my understanding of the system of gradations inherent within the Mishnah's legal format. The conception of the Mishnah as a code of definitive law (despite the disputes it houses) rather than as a collection of legal opinions better explains the attribution of divinity to it by its adherents. One is more likely to ascribe divinity to a code of law such as the Mishnah, where one is convinced of its definitiveness and self-sufficiency, than to an "open," incomplete compilation of opinions. The *talmid vatik* comment in the Talmud made by "Rabbi's" students is indicative of such an ascription of divinity to a legal code that is assumed to be conclusive and comprehensive.

10. *Sifra, Bechukotai,* parshah 2, chapter 8 (Weiss ed., p. 112, col. 3). For another conception of revelation, also see, as discussed later, *Midrash Tehillim* 12:4.

11. The same comment here made in the context of the laws of *shemitah* is made concerning the laws of the offering of ordination (*miluim*), etc., in *Sifra, Tzav,* on Lev 7:37. Just as details were spelled out (and made explicit in the written Torah) in regard to these two laws, so, too, in reality, were the practical details of all laws orally revealed to Moses, though they were not explicitly stipulated in the written Torah.

12. J. N. Epstein must be credited with recognizing that the laws of proselytes and slaves, *tzitzit, tefillin,* and *mezuzot* mentioned in the *Koheleth Rabbah* statement were strategically chosen precisely because the Mishnah does not include them, thereby making more inclusive the scope of the divine Oral Law. See his *Introduction to the Text of the Mishnah* [Hebrew] (Jerusalem, 1948), p. 50.

Illuminating in this context is the statement of the Rambam in his *Commentary on the Mishnah, Menahot* 4:1, that the laws of *tzitzit, tefillin,* and *mezuzot* are largely omitted from the Talmud because everyone already knew all the regulations concerning these *mitzvoth*, and therefore there was no need to occupy space with their details in the tractates of the Talmud. This explanation is certainly open to question.

13. A more contemporary example of the extreme maximalism that has come to dominate traditionalist conceptions of the revelation of the Oral Law is the statement of R. Avraham Yeshayahu Karelitz, the "Chazon Ish" (1878–1953), in his *Kovetz Iggerot*, 1:59: "everything written in the Talmud, whether in the Mishnah or in the Gemara, whether in halakha or in *aggadah* (emphasis added), were things revealed to us through prophetic powers (i.e., divinely) . . . and whoever deviates from this tenet is as one who denies the words of our Rabbis, and his ritual slaughtering is invalid and he is disqualified from testimony." The stance of the Chazon Ish takes the notion of revelation implicit within the *talmid vatik* statement to a more dramatic theological pitch than ever before, and this new theological stratum packs practical consequences.

The formulation of the Chazon Ish may well be singularly extreme, but the content is not unprecedented. Already R. Chaim Volozhiner (1749–1821), in his commentary on *Pirkei Avoth* called *Ruah Chaim* (Vilna, 1869), commented on the first mishnah, "raise up many disciples," as follows: "Also when one studies the essentials of Torah and reflects upon them *including the "pilpulim"* ("casuistic arguments")—(through) all of them man becomes attached to God. *For all of them come from Sinai.* Even the comments that an astute student will make was given to Moses on Sinai. He (Moses) brought the Torah down to earth; and God and the Torah are one. He who is attached to the Torah is attached to God (or God is attached to him). May His name be blessed."

The position of the Chazon Ish with respect to *aggadot* is clear theological precedents and precursors, however. The question in *j. Nazir* 56b, 7:2, "*ve-khi hamidrashot amanah hem?* has generated dispute about the status of the nonhalakhic elements of the Talmud. The Riaz (Isaiah ben Elijah di Trani, died c. 1280) is quoted by Joshua Boaz's *Shiltei ha-Gibborim, b. Avodah Zarah* 6a as asserting that this question implies that *aggadot* need not be believed in as matters of faith (in contradistinction to the principles). Menachem ben Judah de Lonzano (sixteenth–seventeenth centuries), in his *Sefer ha-Ma'arikh*, c.v. "sheretz," writes that this nonmaximalistic position of the Riaz is a forbidden one theologically. The debate over the "divinity" of the aggadic portions of Rabbinic literature thus has a long and lively history. It is worth noting that the SHLaH (*Shnei Luchot Ha-Berit*) (Rule Mishnah) and the Chazon Ish (*Iggerot* I:24) both claim that the Mishnah (and the *Shulchan Aruch*, for that matter), by virtue of having been accepted by all of Israel, is endowed with *Ruah Ha-Kodesh* ("holy spirit"), which gives irreversible authority and entitles it to be exposited exegetically in a manner similar to the Bible. (For additional authors, see Y. Spiegel, *Asufot* 4:1990, pp. 23 ff). For midrashic parallels, see S. Buber, in his *Tanchuma*, II, p. 116 (comment on Exod. 34:27).

Ruah Ha-Kodesh is a rung lower than prophecy (see Maimonides, *Mishnah Torah, Yesodei Ha-Torah*, 7, 1). The book as a whole was composed with *Ruah Ha-Kodesh*, while individual laws were revealed to Moses at Sinai.

Even Rabbinic restrictions designed to be a hedge around the law is viewed by some Rishonim (early medieval commentators) as having been given to Moses at Sinai. Thus, the Rabad (1120–1198), quoted also by the Rashba, Ran, and Ritba, tractate *b. Erubin* 15b (in the Ritba, this quotation is found at the beginning of the second chapter), claims "that God revealed to Moses at Mount Sinai all the restrictions that the Rabbis will enact." When God revealed to Moses at Sinai the comments of the astute student—says the Ran (d.1380)—He included among them the future Rabbinic restrictions and told him how the Rabbis will enact them. In a lesser known gloss to Tosaphot *b. Erubin* 4b, still in manuscript, quoted by R. R. Rabbinovicz (*Dikdukei Sofrim*, ibid, p. 11) in the name of R. Yitzchak, it is stated that all Rabbinic restrictions were enacted by Moses "and his court when they descended Mount Sinai." According to the Netziv (1817–1893) in his commentary on the Sheiltot, sheilta 137 (Jerusalem, 1955) p. 140, this is also the view of Maimonides (His attitude to Aggadah, however, is less exalting. See *The Guide of the Perplexed*, III, 43. Compare Otzar heGeonim, B. M. Lewin, *b. Hagigah*, pp. 59–60). See also R. S. Lurya, *Hochmat Shelomo, b. Erubin* 5b. Their position seems to be the most extreme application of the maximalistic approach of revelation for it includes also clearly dated enactments associated with later Rabbis and which are explicitly motivated as hedges around the law.

However, not all Rishonim shared this view. Commenting on the Mishnah Yadaim IV. 3: "I have received . . . as a Halacha given to Moses at Sinai that Ammon and Moab give poormans' tithe in the seventh Year," R. Shimshon of Sens (early thirteenth century) ibid., and the Rosh (1250–1327) at the beginning of the laws of Mikvaot said that it cannot really be a Halacha given to Moses at Sinai since the obligation to give tithe outside Palestine is only rabbinically required. To these Rishonim, all rabbinic restrictions are of Rabbinic origin and cannot automatically be considered as given to Moses at Sinai. This view is also shared by R. O. of Bartinoro (fifteenth century) in his popular commentary to the Mishnah, *Terumot* II, 1.

14. In Rabbinic thought, the prophet is just a messenger of God's word and way and, therefore, in the phrase of *b. Baba Batra* 12a, not as preferable as a scholar. According to this hierarchy, a prophet only redresses, rectifies, and rediscovers, whereas a scholar is creative and productive of new Torah learning. This less than spectacular conception of the role and contribution of the prophet in Rabbinic thought was of course modified in some medieval Jewish philosophy, in which the prophet became the philosopher par excellence.

The nuances of this functional difference between a prophet and scholar are perhaps reflected in the uses of the words *masar* and *kibbel* (or their variants) in *Pirkei Avot*. From Moses to Joshua and through to the men of the Great Assembly, the word *masar* is used, which intimates precise, static, and unyielding transmission. From then on in the historical succession, however, the word *kibbel* is employed, suggesting new and creative contributions to the dynamic of tradition on the part of the scholars mentioned. This difference in terminology, and the attendant implications for conceptualizing the process of revelation and Torah transmission, can perhaps be historically correlated to the notion of sinning discussed earlier. For an interesting discussion of a modern traditionalist understanding of the relationship of prophecy and the Oral Law, see Yaakov Elman, "Reb Zadok HaKohen of Lublin on Prophecy in the Halakhic Process," *Jewish Law Association Studies 1: The Touro Conference Volume*, ed. B. S. Jackson (Chico, Calif., 1985).

15. I refer readers to the fifth chapter of my recent book, *"Peshat" and "Derash": Plain and Applied Meaning in Rabbinic Exegesis* (New York and Oxford, 1991), for a

much more extensive and detailed discussion of the theological-historical theory concerning the text of the written Torah that I merely outline in this essay.

16. The discussion that follows is, in some of its aspects, subjectively theological in character, although it addresses a tension in Jewish theology that is borne of modern critical scholarship. Therefore, what has so far preceded the following discussion has been a scholarly analysis of the development of Jewish theology about the Oral Law; what follows is, in part, my own resolution to a theological problem attendant to the notion of a divine written Torah.

17. The concept of *chate'u Yisrael* is alluded to directly and indirectly in several Rabbinic sources. It is alluded to directly in b. *Nedarim* 22b, "had not Israel sinned, only the Pentateuch and the book of Joshua would have been given to them" and indirectly in *Mishnah Parah* 3:5, which states: "Moses prepared the first red heifer, and Ezra prepared the second, and five [were prepared] after Ezra, [according to] the view of R. Meir; but the sages say, seven [were prepared] after Ezra." According to this historical calculation in the latter text, no red heifers were prepared between the careers of Moses and Ezra—the period that we will claim must be bracketed in terms of halakhic authority and enforcement. This Mishnah thus subtly lends further credence to the conception of this historical epoch as one of ritual carelessness and impurity, and support for the claim that Ezra initiated a process of halakhic reform and renewal.

The most explicit correspondence between sinning on the part of the Jews and changes effected in the text of the Torah during the time of Ezra is claimed in b. *Sanhedrin* 21b–22a, the locus of the axial concept of *chate'u Yisrael*. The fascinating text there reads in part: "It has been taught: Rabbi said: The Torah was originally given to Israel in this [*Ashurit*] writing. When they [Israel] sinned [*she-chate'u*], it was changed into *Ro'atz*. But when they repented, the [*Ashurit* characters] were *re*-introduced." The correlation between halakhic allegiance and scriptural guardianship is here explicitly articulated. A process of textual loss and recovery is bound up with a cycle of halakhic degeneration and regeneration. I, of course, amplify on Rabbi's claim and supplement it with another rabbinic text from *Bemidbar Rabbah* III, 13 (and parallels), a passage that enumerates and explains the presence of the ten *puncta extraordinaria*, or *eser nekudot*, in the Pentateuch and links their existence to Ezra, to fashion my theory about the sequence of halakhic and textual negligence and consequent restoration of the scriptural text during the time of Ezra.

18. Pertinent here is the explanation of Radak (R. David Kimchi, c. 1160–1235), in his introduction to the book of Joshua, of the existence of the *ketiv/keri* discrepancy in many places in the text of the Torah: "During the first exile [in Babylonia], books were lost and were enshrouded in darkness, and sages of the Torah died off." Radak explains that the proper reading of the Torah text was thrown into doubt because of the disruption caused by the burdens of the exile. Radak's explanation of the *ketiv/keri* issue is somewhat similar to my *chate'u Yisrael* explanation of the *Peshat-Derash* dichotomy, but I argue that such forgetfulness must have occurred before the exile. The relatively short duration of the exile militates against assuming that there survived no one who remembered the genuine and traditional reading of the Torah text. The timing of the "forgetting" in my theory is therefore different from that in Radak's: the *chate'u Yisrael* period that led to the faulty scriptural text occurred during the First Temple period; in Radak's

theory, the forgetfulness that resulted in the *ketiv/keri* discrepancy occurred during the exile.

19. For an intelligent summary of the subject, see Y. Maori, "Rabbinic Midrash as a Witness to Textual Variants of the Hebrew Bible," to appear in the *M. H. Goshen-Gottstein Jubilee Volume.*

20. See in relation to this issue, and specifically to the account of the "rediscovery" of a scroll of the Torah during the reign of King Josiah, the very interesting comments in R. Nissim Gaon, *Sefer Megillat Setarim*, ed. S. Abrahamson (Jerusalem, 1965), pp. 348 ff.

21. See Ezra 9:7 for a statement of rebellion against and disavowal of the ways of the previous few centuries and a return to a more distant past.

22. See *Sefer Ha-Ikkarim*, Book 2, ch. 22.

23. See *Peshat and Derash*, p. 224, n. 53, for a parallel made between the historical necessity of the *chate'u Yisrael* period in the establishment of monotheism and Maimonides' explanation of the necessity of sacrifices in the spiritual history of the Jewish people. One could reasonably ask why God put up for so long with the Jews' obduracy in their attachment to idolatry, just as Maimonides asked, and then answered in the *Guide of the Perplexed*, III, 32, why God's spiritual education of the Jewish people had to be so subtle and gradual. As God accommodated human foibles through the stage of sacrifices, so God was patient with the Jews through the *chate'u Yisrael* period of their history and did not forcibly impose monotheism on His people. Spiritual advancement in both cases was an organic and natural progression.

24. Laws that are not explicitly written in the Torah are in some respects treated more leniently than laws that are so written. See R. Asher (Rosh) *ad b. Beitzah* 30a and R. Nissim (Ran) *ad b. Shevu'ot* 23b, s.v. *demokim*.

25. Cf. *b. Eruvin* 21b; *Tanchuma Buber, Ki Tissa*, p. 116; S. Lurya, *Yam shel Shelomo, Baba Kama*, Introduction.

26. The Oral Law can be divided into two categories. Those that serve as definitions of the written text and which are as old as the written text itself (it is inconceivable, for example, that the lawgiver would command "not to do any work on the Sabbath" without specifying what is meant by work) and those that serve as solutions to new problems, which according to the nonmaximalistic view of revelation could be of late origin. The explanation for part of the Law being oral because God wanted humanity to become a partner in the Torah is more appropriate to the former category. The laws of the former category must have been well-established during the giving of the Torah. They were more or less fixed (despite later disagreement as to detail), intolerant of alternatives. They could have been written down and not rely on human oral transmission, but were not done so to make humankind a participant in the Divine Writ, whereas the laws of the latter category had another rationale why they remained oral: to convey the notion that there is no exclusive way of solving these problems, no single established pattern inherently compelling to resolve them. Whatever solution is offered is religiously satisfactory. If the Shammaites, for example, were to have prevailed over the Hillelites their opinion would have constituted normative Judaism. Today we can not follow them because of a later Rabbinic decision rendered against them and not because their opinions are incongruous with the divine will (Kabbalah

has, of course, a radically different orientation on this matter). This topic deserves at least a book-length study. I touch upon it here to alert the reader to this profound problem that has been hardly discussed in modern Jewish theology; namely, why part of the law remained oral.

3

Midrashic versus Other Forms of Jewish Hermeneutics: Some Comparative Reflections

—————————————————————— *Moshe Idel*

I

Modern scholarship abounds in attempts to define and describe the nature of Midrash. Indeed, this evasive *modus interpretandis* fascinates both the younger generation of scholars of Judaica—at least partially because of the affinity between the midrashic mode of interpretation and modern views of literary criticism—the literary critics. Recent trends in modern philosophy (viz., uneasiness with the metaphysical approach, and an attitude that conceives of the text as an entity able to generate more than the author was aware of) have further ensured a vivid interest in the midrashic manner of discourse.

In the present survey I shall depart from earlier efforts to define Midrash from within, and attempt to compare it to other Jewish forms of interpretation. Although I do not aim to draw a firm line between midrashic hermeneutics and other types of Jewish hermeneutics (many of which were well-acquainted with the midrashic approach), I shall nevertheless attempt to point out those features that are important in the early and late medieval types of literature but are either absent or marginal in the Midrash. Thus without denying the recent tendency to close the gap between Midrash and Kabbalah—a tendency I share and regard as most productive—it is important to warn against too simplistic an approach to the relationship between midrashic and kabbalistic hermeneutics.

In the following essay, the midrashic approach to the text will be considered a generic mode of interpretation, rather than a specific attitude restricted to texts written during a certain limited period of time by Jewish authors. The necessity to transcend the common historical periodization is particularly obvious when we recall the existence of nonmidrashic attitudes to the canonic text in some types of Jewish literature composed shortly before the mergence of the classical midrashic literature, as well as during this period. Thus the midrashic approach is fundamentally different from that found in the Qumran scrolls, which is much more historically (viz. eschatologically) oriented;[1] from the *Heikhalot* literature,[2] as we shall see later; and from that of *Sefer Yetzirah*.[3] At the same time, the classical midrashic approach is quite closely related to the later liturgical prayers known as *Piyyut*.[4] By the same token, certain forms of medieval kabbalistic literature, as well as some developments in Polish Hasidism, can be considered as much closer to Midrash than medieval mysticism.[5] Midrash is therefore not only a certain type of literature, but also a certain type of literary activity.[6] As a final consideration at this point it bears noting that midrashic literature is far from being a sure kind of hermeneutical approach. Indeed it seems to me quite plausible that it was also influenced by the "nonmidrashic" *Heikhalot* type of thought.

II

To put the specificity of midrashic hermeneutics into sharp relief, let me compare its concept of the text (the Hebrew Bible) with that found in the *Heikhalot* literature. The following major approaches may be discerned:

1. In midrashic sources, the biblical text is conceived of as being inscribed on the arm or the forehead of God, whose skin serves as the substratum of the primordial Torah, which preexisted the creation of the world.[7] As such, the Torah is divine—though this specifice *epitheton* is not found, as far as I know, in this literature in relation to the Torah. Although these views appear in various midrashic texts, they rather belong to later strata influenced by mystical and magical views.

2. In the talmudic-midrashic literature, the Torah is personified by means of female metaphors.[8] However, in those texts influenced by *Heikhalot* theology, the Torah is described as the daughter of the King (viz., the daughter of God) without resorting to erotic tropes to depict the relation between the Torah and the People of Israel. Thus whereas the ancient Midrash conceives of the text as the "human" counterpart of Israel, be it the bride of the people or of Moses, the *Heikhalot* literature (by describing the Torah as the King's daughter) anchors the canonic text in the divine realm. According

to one striking midrashic text, which reflects the word-view of the *Heikhalot,* the Torah is depicted as sitting in the middle of seven palaces and whoever is interested to see (viz., contemplate) the king (viz., God) is bidden to come and see his daughter.[9]

3. Huge dimensions, similar or identical to those ascribed in the *Heikhalot* literature to God, were also ascribed to the Torah in the Midrash.[10] By doing so, the anonymous authors pointed to the transcendental nature of the text. In this kind of mystical literature, letters and words of the biblical text are envisioned as having huge sizes, whose precise measure can be derived from the numerical value of the respective letters. For example, the divine name *Eheyeh* is described as being twenty-one tens of thousands of parasangs long, because of numerical value of the four consonants that constitute this name.[11]

4. According to another view, found in the *Heikhalot Zutarti,* each and every letter is itself a divine Name.[12]

5. The *Heikhalot* texts evince a vivid interest in cosmogony and cosmology; this concern is marginal in the Midrash and relegated to esoterica in the Mishnah and Talmud.

6. Finally the *Heikhalot* literature operates with the idea of an esoteric level of the idea of an esoteric level of the canonic texts, designated either as *raz* or *sod.* The Midrash, on the other hand, though it never denies such an assumption, does not employ it de facto.

If the first two attitudes to the Torah can be envisioned as hieroglyphic or iconic conception, the next two reflect the atomization or monadization of the text. Moreover, in the former views the external elements are emphasized, with the result that the text is not so much a container or portent of meanings as a revealer of a certain type of form. This transcendence of the semantic nature of the text, in favor of its parasemantic aspect, is closely related to the specific type of theology regnant in the *Heikhalot* literature. Put differently, the anthropomorphic configuration of God that stands at the core of the mystical vision of the ascenders (or the descenders) to the *Merkavah* produced a corresponding conception of the biblical text, which was projected into the supernal realm and partially identified with God or a divine entity.

This exalted status of the text prevented, however, a creative hermeneutics. Indeed, the static nature of the concept of God, so characteristic of this literature, had a direct impact on the exegetical level. A text inscribed on the divine arm, for example, could best be understood and contemplated by emphasizing its formal facets, rather than by reducing it to a portent of a message with a merely human content.

These mystical elements in the *Heikhalot* literature tend to reify the Torah and render it into a transcendental entity that remains, nevertheless, basically similar to the revealed text. It is thus not another Torah that is to be found in the supernal world, but another plane of existence of our mundane Torah, preserving the same sequel of letters and sentences found in the lower world. In other words, it would be strange to assume that other combinations of letters would be conceived as forming the primordial Torah; accordingly, the combinatory approach seems to be negligible in this type of literature.

III

In some circles of Jewish mystics, possible since the second century C.E., a combinatory attitude to language was increasingly articulated. This is especially the case in *Sefer Yetzirah* (edited on the basis of earlier traditions in the sixth century), where the combinations of letters was considered to be the clue to the most profound and fundamental creative processes. Though this combinatory technique is also alluded to in talmudic sources, it takes a central role in this cosmological treatise. As a Jewish treatise, *Sefer Yetzirah* only rarely refers to the biblical text or it verses. Rather language, and more precisely the Hebrew consonants, play the central role in the cosmogony of this treatise. As such, the assumption of the anonymous author seems to be that the free state of the alphabet and all the possible mathematical combinations that may result from the Hebrew letters are imbued with magical powers (which can be precisely related to the nonsemantic nature of those combinations). The Torah would thus be, for author of *Sefer Yetzirah,* a rather limited, historical, and ritualistic condensation of potentialities inherent in the Hebrew alphabet. Though originally indifferent to interpretation, the permutative mood of *Sefer Yetzirah* became, since the Middle Ages, one of the more eccentric approaches to a canonic text—whose orthographic minutae and peculiar shapes of letters have been zealously guarded for centuries. Indeed, the *Sefer Yetzirah* became a prime source for those more radical views that envisioned the Torah as an orderless array of letters—to be combined in order to establish the religiously significant text.[13] The specific order of the letters in the Torah, with its aura of authority and its implicit religious axiology, was regarded with indifference by the creators of this hermeneutical system.

A strongly magical approach to the biblical text is visible in two books that did not attract the attention of modern scholarship: *Shimmush Torah* and *Shimmush Tehillim;* namely, the "Magical Use of the Torah" and "of the Psalms." As magical treatises, these two works rest on the assumption that several biblical verses include, in a hidden manner, the letters of magical Names, and that these can be extracted by different devices (especially the *rashey tevot,* or initial letters, of the words of those verses).[14] Once again, the semantic aspect of the text has been conspicuously disregarded in favor of a nonsemantic approach. It is the power of the hidden order of letters that informs this hermeneutical type, in opposition to the more mystical aspects of the biblical text emphasized by the *Heikhalot* literature. This recombination of the letters does not depend on the combinatory techniques of *Sefer Yetzirah,* but they nevertheless share a very important assumption: that beyond the sacrosanct order of the biblical text it is possible to find a stronger linguistical construction. The plain meaning is sacrificed for the sake of other ideals, mystical or magical, that can be achieved by transcending the regular sequence of letters found in the Bible.

The stronger, eccentric ways of reading the Bible found in the mystical-magical literatures mentioned previously can also be found in the midrashic-talmudic literature. However, in these types of literature they are located at the periphery; whereas, by contrast, in the nonmidrashic literatures just mentioned these eccentric hermeneutics have moved to the center. It is thus not the fixed or clear-cut division between two types of hermeneutics, the semantic-midrashic or eccentric, magical modes, that most distinguishes the different types of ancient Jewish literatures, but rather their relative importance in the respective types of literature.

IV

The Midrash was informed by a theology that has never been presented explicitly. Nevertheless, it is expressly dominated by a personalistic view of God, conceived of as deeply concerned with the human affairs: a changing entity, endowed with power and able to interfere in the course of history. Though similar to the major trends of biblical theology, talmudic-midrashic thought evolved during the hard circumstances of exile, and this lead to the theological identification of God with the vicissitudes of Jewish history. He is no more a God who rules history, as it is evident in the Bible, but rather a God who willingly accepts the tragic *fatum* of his elected people. Indeed, in sharp contrast with the main line of the *Heikhalot* literature, and in even sharper distinction from such works as *Sefer Yetzirah* or *Shimmush Torah* and *Shimmush Tehillim,* God identifies Himself with the fate of Israel, but separates himself from their attempt to examine the Torah.[15] In Midrash, the identification of the Torah with the Divine is marginal; the major assumption is that the authoritative text is an independent entity, to be encountered as a sacred text, which can be interrogated to answer religious questions. This separation between God and Torah notwithstanding, it nevertheless seems that the nature of the hermeneutical enterprise reflects the dynamic nature of God. In lieu of one, frozed type of information that can be extracted from a biblical verse concerning, for example, the unchanging dimension of the divine body of the *Heikhalot* theology,[16] the biblical text now remains open for novel interpretations.

This openness can be explained in more than one way. From our present vantage point, it is precisely the absence of an explicit or systematic theology that enabled a freer, hermeneutical attitude to the text to develop in the Talmud and Midrash. By saying so, I hardly mean or assume that these literary corpora are totally free of theological presuppositions. This certainly make too strong a point. Nevertheless, the absence of treatises that deal with theological matters *stricto sensu*, is not an accident. I thus assume that the midrashists avoided such a theological move on purpose, especially as the strong theological bias of the *Heikhalot* literature and *Sefer Yetzirah* is so evident. On the other hand, the masters of the Midrash also avoided focusing on such parasemantic facets of the texts as *gematria*, shapes of the letters, attribution of huge dimensions to the biblical text, or identification of the Torah with supernal entities. It is the nonmetaphysical approach to the text that enabled the midrashists to maintain its relative openness—a move that is reminiscent of more modern approaches.[17] The text has to stand on its own, and is to open itself to the reader who, for his or her part is not supposed to be deeply indoctrinated by a certain type of theology. The fateful correlation between a certain theology and predictable interpretations of specific texts was circumvented by the midrashists. They sacrificed, so to speak, the mysterious and magical attainment of their contemporaries to remain with an open text—one that can be addressed to a larger community. By remaining faithful to the syntactic and semantic components of the text, the sages of the Midrash were able to communicate messages that could be adapted to changing historical circumstances,[18] and this stands in stark contrast to parasemantic procedures that generated meanings that remained utterly beyond the scope of history and change. Whereas the Midrash is naturally related to the oral, fluid aspects of communication, the mystical and the magical views of the Torah in the Middle Ages were concerned with the unique, unchangeable messages to be extracted by the means of eccentric hermeneutics precisely from the written form of the Torah. To put it differently, intrastructural and hyperstructural reading of the text, found in the mystical-magical literatures, lose contact with common people, and their average consciousness and regular practices. If the Torah conceived of as a huge hieroglyph can be contemplated as if by telescope, concern with the special significance of the separate letters can be compared to the reading of the Torah by a microscope. In both cases, the specific texture of the text vanishes, especially it semantic parts.

Dominated by belief in the unique nature of the elements of language, the Jewish mystics retreated into more formal, schematic, or even atomistic readings than anything we find in midrashic semantics.

Against such telescopic—or microscopic—perspectives, the midrashists read the Torah with regular glasses. These may also distort the text in one way or another, but they do so without exploding its inner syntax. Just as the regular fabric of life is disorganized by contemplative immersion and penetration into the infrastructure of the regular objects, or by indulging in cosmic speculation, so also is the case with respect to textual study.

In fact, special types of consciousness seem to be involved in the mystical and magical interpretations of the Torah: transcending the mundane zone in the case of those who ascend to the *Merkavah;* or the attainment of revelations from the Prince of the Torah, according to another text; or the performance of magical rites related to the use of the divine Names extracted from biblical verses. These were not practices to be preached to the mutlitude; they were much more the attainments of the elite.

Moreover, according to some warning, the best known of them being the legend concerning the four sages who entered the mystical realm of Pardes, it is dangerous even for the elite to indulge in mystical and cosmogonic speculations. Midrash is thus a horizontal type of hermeneutics par excellence, and this helps explain the ethical focus of this literature. Moreover, when dealing with nature, Midrash envisions a lateral encounter with it, not an explanation of its hierarchical emergence from the higher worlds. By contrast, mystical, magical, and philosophical hermeneutics integrated substantial vertical elements into their approach. They thus helped bridge the gap between the supernal and the mundane realms—either by creating an ontological nexus like emanation; by elaborating on the theory of symbol as organically related to the supernal worlds; by describing how to elevate the soul to its source; or by elaborating on the possibility of influencing the heavenly realms magically or theurgically. All these characterize important forms of kabbalistic hermeneutics.

V

Broadly speaking, medieval Jewish hermeneutics as represented by the philosophical, kabbalistic, and Ashkenazi Hasidic literatures drastically deviated from midrashic hermeneutics. The reason for such a bold departure seems to be related to their installment of strong theologies that, as noted, are not characteristic of midrashic literature and thought. Indeed the foregoing types of thought were all profoundly influenced by relatively elaborated theologies, each which impinged their peculiar concerns on the canonic texts. For its part, the midrashic approach reflects a deeply hermeneutical struggle with the semantic aspects of the text, and only rarely allows the impact of rigid extra-textual systems of thought. Though there can be no doubt that the Midrash departs from some biblical ways of thought, it nevertheless remained deeply immersed in the same domain of problems that preoccupied biblical thinking: the myth of exile and redemption, the myth of election, and the deep concern with ritual and ethics. This is not so much the case with respect to the medieval literatures mentioned earlier. More theologically inclined than hermeneutical, they incessantly struggled more with the problem of how to import their respective metaphysical systems into the older texts, than with attempting the embark on a sustained effort of interrogating these texts to discover solutions for their theological quandaries. If midrashic discourse is thus a large scale enterprise engaged in exporting the possible implications of the ambiguous parts of the canon, the superimposition of elaborated theologies (be these Aristoletian, neoplatonic, or theosophic) is characteristic of most of medieval hermeneutics.[19] In due course, the speculative interpreters of the Middle Ages also infused their theologies into the midrashic interpretation of the Bible. To a great extent, these speculative interpretations of medieval Judaism were based on the introduction of some older Jewish techniques that were marginal to the midrashic corpus, to achieve expected results. In fact, both Kabbalah and Jewish medieval philosophy constitute different forms of demystifying and were as much concerned with a comprehensive approach to the Jewish religion as with a verse-centered approach. Paradoxically, in their search for the hidden meaning of the various religious texts, some medieval writers actually helped to establish the idea of the plain-sense of the Scriptures (the *Peshat*), a notion quite marginal to midrashic and talmudic thought.

To go further, I should add that Midrash is not only a verse-centered type of exegesis but an interversal type of hermeneutics as well[20]—one that explores the significance of an obscure, controversial text by means of another obscure, or less obscure, text. Interesting literary achievements of midrashic discourse emerge precisely from the interval created by ambiguities stemming from obscurities in some aspects of various biblical verses.

In the greater intellectual systems of the Middle Ages, the major effort is intercultural. Not only Aristotle, Plato, the Muslim Kalam, but also some other forms of systematic thought were employed by Jewish thinkers to clarify the obscurities of the Jewish tradition, be it biblical or talmudic-midrashic. It seems that only in a few cases one distinct type of medieval literature remained relatively faithful to the midrashic approach; namely, in some forms of Kabbalah. If the more arresting achievements of midrashic interpretation stem from the unexpected results produced by using purely linguistic interpretive techniques, the more speculative interpretations of medieval Judaism were based on the introduction of novel types of interpretations (allegorical or symbolic), or of some older Jewish techniques that were marginal to the midrashic corpus, to achieve expected results. In large part, the speculative approach was intended to clarify the religious mechanism that governs not only perfect human behavior but also divine behavior—thus penetrating into the secrets of the higher worlds. In fact, both Kabbalah and Jewish medieval philosophy constitute different forms of demystifying the divine realm by means of comprehensive explanations. So viewed, midrashic interpretation stands out by contrast as concerned with keeping the higher world a mystery; indeed, most ironically, it is precisely the midrashic approach that prevents any metaphysical discussion of the problem of *unde malum* when the explanation for Rabbi Aqiva's terrible death is the stark: "Be silent, for this is what has arisen in (divine) thought."

The inventiveness of the midrashist is thus deeply rooted in his ability to manipulate the text as a literary work, rather than as a theological artifact; whereas the speculative attitudes envisioned the Bible as essentially a fountainhead of theological truth and only secondarily as a literary creation. Free from systematic theological constraints, the midrashists were able to respond to the same verse in different ways. A theology inclined to emphasizing the divine will—that is, as an ever-changing power that cannot be easily formulated in itself, but whose manifestations are marked in a written document—produced a much more open attitude to the text. Although something similar can be found in some kabbalistic schools, others, like their philosophical contemporaries, were primarily concerned with exposing the one, precise esoteric meaning of the canonic texts. The comparable openness of the Midrash to different theological strands therefore permitted a more creative hermeneutics, and this is also why the modern research has been able to propose relatively comprehensive descriptions of the theologies of the Jewish, medieval speculation whereas the study of midrashic thought still awaits its reconstruction from the different trends embedded in midrashic and talmudic sources.

VI

In what follows I shall try to substantiate my aforenoted view that kabbalistic hermeneutics is, in general, more faithful than others to the midrashic approach. To be sure, there is no question that several kabbalistic schools are as distant from the midrashic approach as the medieval philosophers. Take for example the Provençal Kabbalah and its Geronese repercussions. It would be very difficult to find in the writings of R. Isaac Sagi-Nahor, one of the paragons of the early Kabbalah, anything like the midrashic approach. The dry, monosemic, theosophical symbols and discussions may, perhaps, reflect earlier esoteric traditions, extracted by R. Isaac's predecessors from traditional texts decades before him; but his own hermeneutical approach is very technical. He relates the various elements of the canonic text, the words of the daily liturgy or the sentences of *Sefer Yetzirah*, to the theosophical *termini technici* without any substantial effort to explain the relationship between them. Slightly more hermeneutical is the approach of his student, R. Ezra of Gerona; but his follower, R. Azriel of Gerona, seems to return partially to the way of R. Isaac the Blind, even intensifying the technical use of philosophical terminology. The *Iyyun* literature, whose affinities to R. Azriel of Gerona have been long acknowledged by scholars, is only rarely bothered with interpreting the canonic texts. Somewhat similar to these scholars are the writings of the Ha-Kohen brothers, two important Kabbalists who flourished at the middle of the thirteenth century. They commented on a series of topics, such as the letters of the alphabet and the biblical cantillation-signs, but with one exception never on the canonic texts. For his part, Abraham Abulafia's writings are also deeply concerned with mystical and philosophical issues, but his interest in the midrashic approach is rather slight.[21]

Among the remaining major schools of Kabbalah in the thirteenth century, it would appear that only in the book of *Bahir*, the kabbalistic circle of Nahmanides, and the book of the *Zohar* is there a strong awareness of Midrash as a powerful source of creativity. Thus, in the book of *Bahir*, sometimes referred to as the "Midrash of R. Nehunyah ben ha-Qanah," we can readily isolate some clear cases of midrashic exegesis;[22] and this awareness is also evident in Nahmanides's own writings,[23] and in the commentary on the prayers by his student, Rabbi Yehudah ben Yaqar. Nevertheless, it seems that this awareness and interest gradually disappeared in the writings of Nahmanides's followers, by the late thirteenth century and early fourteenth centuries. In the later Kabbalah, as represented by the Lurianic literature, the midrashic approach is even more diminished, as the use of *termini technici* prevail in an unprecendent manner. Indeed, the more the symbolic approach was attenuated by its absorption into a comprehensive and detailed myth, the less can we expect a midrashic attitude to the interpreted texts.[24]

It therefore seems that only in the book of the *Zohar* is there a conscious and sustained return to the literary genre of the Midrash. This is first of all evidenced by some of the titles found there,[25] and then in a much more significant way by the actual structure of Zoharic discourse. A deep affinity with the rhetorical strategies of the old Midrash is therefore reflected.[26] Add to this the absence of technical terms, the presence of rhetorical locutions, and an implicit theology deriving from interrelated biblical verses, and there are good reasons to regard the *Zohar* as a species of medieval Midrash. Indeed, what seems to be most characteristic of Zoharic theology, and to a certain extent also of other segments of theosophical-theurgical Kabbalah, is the fusion between the static and the anthropomorphic theology of the *Heikhalot* literature, on the one side, and the more dynamic, powerful and personalistic attitude of midrashic-talmudic thought on the other. The static shape of the divine *Shi'ur Qomah* was activated, at least on some levels, by the biblical and midrashic views of God as will and power that can be augmented or diminished.[27] Indeed, the reintroduction of this dynamism into Jewish mysticism had a deep impact on kabbalistic hermeneutics. The processes taking place between the various divine attributes (which are more than the metamorphoses of the divine limbs) allowed for a much more creative and dynamic reading of the Bible—now "midrashically" decoded to reveal supernal processes taking place within the godhead.[28] To the extent that the formal elements of the text remained important in kabbalistic theosophy, they can still be detected in the peculiar emphasis given to the shapes of the Hebrew letters—a topic of real fascination for the theosophical Kabbalists.[29] This correlation is particularly obvious in *Sefer ha-Temunah*, where the author surmises that the alphabet is the real countenance of the divine configuration, referred to as *Shi'ur Qomah*.[30]

The strong presence of highly articulated theologies among the Jews is therefore to be regarded as the major factor in preventing the development of midrashic discourse in Middle Ages. It is therefore both significant and striking that some kabbalistic writings were able to remain closed to midrashic discourse only when they could purport the existence of an elaborated theosophy, expressed in complex or novel nomenclature. Whether the diametrically opposite kabbalistic and philosophic approaches to the canonic texts are the result of a deep spiritual crisis[31] or more variegated and different explanations for the emergence of the new modes of interpreting the texts are perhaps more pertinent, it is obvious that medieval thinkers repeatedly distanced themselves from the nonconstellated thought of the Talmud and Midrash.

The attenuation of the role of kabbalistic theosophical terminology, sometimes by its psychological reinterpretation, enable the Polish Hasidism to regain some of the charm of midrashic discourse. However, even in the case of those Hasidic masters who did not use kabbalistic terminology, it is rather difficult to find a classical midrashic treatment of the texts. The reappearance of orality in Hasidic circles, in the form of sermons delivered by their leaders, was a crucial watershed that contributed toward a certain transcendence of medieval ideological superstructures, as well as the reemergence of simpler and more fluid theologies—informed by a simpler and more flexible hermeneutics.[32] Indeed, it seems that simpler theologies invite a simpler hermeneutical and exegetical approach, whereas more comprehensive and systematical theologies require more complex and eccentric types of exegesis and hermeneutics. Martin Buber was surely correct when he considered Hasidism to be an attempt to deschematize the mystery (viz., religion) that had became ever more schematical and mechanical in the Lurianic Kabbalah.[33]

Notes

1. Cf. C. Roth, "The Subject Matter of Qumran Exegesis," *Vetus Testamentum* 10 (1960):51–65. I do not intend to deny the existence of similarities between Qumran techniques of interpretation and those found in the Merkevah literature (see n. 2) or the Midrash (see M. Fishbane, *Biblical Interpretation in Ancient Israel* [Oxford, 1985], p. 418 and n. 5). However, the emphasis on the eschatological exegesis in Qumran literature is preminent.

2. We can hardly speak about an elaborate hermeneutics in this kind of literature. Though employing *gematria* to extract the precise dimensions of the divine body (see n. 16), the *Heikhalot* authors were relatively indifferent to most parts of the Bible as major sources of inspiration or, alternatively, as texts to comment on. On the other hand, there is a certain degree of similarity between the *Heikhalot* literature and the Qumran fragments. See the recent remarks of L. Schiffman, "Hekhalot Mysticism and Qumran Literature," *Early Jewish Mysticism*, ed. J. Dan (Jerusalem, 1987), pp. 121–37 [Hebrew]; C. A. Newsom, "Merkabah Exegesis in the Qumran Sabbath Shirot," *Journal of Jewish Studies* 38 (1987):11–30; and J. M. Baumgarten, "The Qumran Sabbath Shirot and Rabbinic Merkabah Traditions," *Revue de Qumran* 13 (1988):199–213.

On the elaborate hermeneutics of *Hasidei Ashkenaz*, based also on methods related *to gematria*, see J. Dan, "The Ashkenazi Hasidic 'Gates of Wisdom'," *Hommages à Georges Vajada*, ed. G. Nahon and C. Touati (Louvain, 1980), pp. 183–89; I. Marcus, "Exegesis for the Few and for the Many: Judah he-Hasid's Biblical Commentaries," *The Age of the Zohar*, ed. J. Dan (Jerusalem, 1989), pp. 1–24. Cf. also n. 14, later.

3. On the relative indifference of this treatise to the Bible, see Gruenwald, "Some Critical Notes on the First Part of Sefer Yezira," *Revue des Etudes Juifs* 132 (1973):477; and A. P. Hayman, "Some Observations of Sefer Yezira: [1] Its Use of Sources," *Journal of Jewish Studies* (1984):168–84, esp. 180–181.

4. Cf. A. Mirsky, *Reshit ha-Piyyut* (Jerusalem, 1965), pp. 18–45 [In Hebrew].

5. On this issue, see J. Dan's unpublished article submitted to the conference on eighteenth-century Jewish thought at Harvard University, 1984.

6. This concept is corroborated by the contributions of R. Bonfil and I. Gruenwald to this book.

7. See M. Idel, "The Concept of the Torah in the Heikhalot Literature and Its Metamorphosis in Kabbalah," *Jerusalem Studies in Jewish Thought* (1981):43–45 [Hebrew]; and G. Scholem, *On the Kabbalah and Its Symbolism* (New York, 1969), pp. 48–49.

8. See E. R. Wolfson, "Female Imagining of the Torah: From Literary Metaphor to Religious Symbols," *From Ancient Israel to Modern Judaism: Essays in Honor of Marvin Fox*, J. Neusner, E. S. Frerichs , and N. M. Sarna (Atlanta, 1989), II, pp. 273–78.

9. Ibid., pp. 278–80.

10. Cf. Idel, "The Concept of the Torah," pp. 40–43.

11. Ibid., pp. 39–40.

12. See *Synopse zur Hekhalot-Literatur*, ed. P. Schäfer (Tübingen, 1981), p. 154, no. 364.

13. Cf. Scholem, *On the Kabbalah and Its Symbolism*, pp. 74–75.

14. Idel, "The Concept of the Torah," pp. 27–28, 30, 53–54. See also n. 2, earlier.

15. See D. Weiss Halivni, *Midrash, Mishnah and Gemara* (Cambridge, Mass., 1986), p. 16; and M. Idel, "Infinities of Torah in Kabbalah," *Midrash and Literature*, ed. G. Hartmen and S. Budick (New Haven, Conn., 1986), pp. 141–44.

16. See M. S. Cohen, *The Shi'ur Qomah, Liturgy and Theurgy in Pre-Kabbalistic Jewish Mysticism* (Lanham, N.Y. and London, 1983), p. 93, where Ps. 147:5 is interpreted (by its numerical equivalence) to refer to the size of the divine body.

17. The constellated hermeneutics of the medieval literatures mentioned differs from the disastered approach of Midrash, to use Barthes's concept. G. Hartman drew my attention to the affinity between midrashic hermeneutics and the disastered view of R. Barthes! On this topic, see also the interesting study of D. Stern, "Midrash and Indeterminacy," *Critical Inquiry* 15 (1988):132–61.

18. Compare J. Heinemann, "The Nature of the Aggadah," in *Midrash and Literature* (n. 15), p. 53; S. Rawidowicz, "On Interpretation," *Proceedings of the American Academy of Jewish Research* 26 (1957):91; and M. Rottenberg, *Re-Biographing and Deviance* (New York and London, 1987).

19. On medieval speculative hermeneutics, see Rawidowicz, ibid., F. Talmage, "Apples of God: The Inner Meaning of Sacred Texts in Medieval Judaism," *Jewish Spirituality*, ed. A. Green (New York, 1986), I, pp. 313–55; M. Saperstein, *Decoding the Rabbis* (Cambridge, Mass., 1980); and M. Idel, *"PaRDeS*, Between Authority and Indeterminacy: Some Reflections on Kabbalistic Hermeneutics" (forthcoming), and the studies mentioned in notes 18, 20–21, 24.

20. See J. L. Kugel, "Two Introduction to Midrash," *Midrash and Literature* (n. 15), pp. 91–100, for the concept of verse centerdness; and M. Fishbane, "Inner Biblical Exegesis: Types and Strategies of Interpretation in Ancient Israel," ibid., pp. 19–37, and his *Biblical Interpretation in Ancient Israel* for the reinterpretation of some older traditions by the biblical authors themselves.

21. M. Idel, *Language, Torah and Hermeneutics in Abraham Abulafia*, (New York, 1989), pp. 87–91, 110–11.

22. See J. Dan, "Midrash and the Dawn of Kabbalah," *Midrash and Literature*, pp. 127–39.

23. See. E. Wolfson, "By Way of Truth: Aspects of Nahmanides' Kabbalistic Hermeneutics," *Association of Jewish Studies Review* 19 (1989):103–78.

24. M. Idel, *Kabbalah: New Perspectives* (New Haven, Conn., 1988), pp. 217–18.

25. Cf. *Midrash ha-Ne'elam Midrasho shel Rashbi, Midrash Va-Yehi' Or.*

26. See W. Bacher, "L'Exegese biblique dans le Zohar," *Revue des Etudes Juifs* 20 (1891):32–46, 219–29; and E. Wolfson's contribution to this book, Chapter 8.

27. See Idel, *Kabbalah: New Perspectives*, pp. 156–99, 222–34.

28. Ibid., pp. 230–32.

29. See E. Wolfson, "Letter Symbolism and Merkavah Imagery in the Zohar," *'Alei Shefer, Studies in the Literature of Jewish Thought Presented to Rabbi Dr. Alexander Safran*, ed. M. Hallamish (Ramat Gan, 1990), pp. 195–236; idem, "Anthropomorphic Imagery and Letter Symbolism in the Zohar," *The Age of the Zohar* (n. 2), pp. 147–81 [Hebrew].

30. Idel, "The Concept of the Torah," pp. 70–74; and also Idel, "Infinities of Torah in Kabbalah," p. 145.

31. See I. Gruenwald, "From Talmudic to Midrashic Homiletics," *The Age of the Zohar* (n. 2), p. 259 [Hebrew]; and also Stern, "Midrash and Indeterminacey," pp. 153–54.

32. Hasidic hermeneutics is a domain neglected by modern scholarship. See, for the present, some scanty remarks in M. Idel, "Reification of Language in Jewish Mysticism," *Language and Mysticism*, ed. S. Katz (New York, 1992).

33. *The Origin and Meaning of Hasidism* (Atlantic Highlands, N.J., 1988), pp. 117–19, 133–37, 252–53.

PART II

Ancient Midrash:
Myth, History, and Parable

4

"The Holy One Sits and Roars": Mythopoesis and the Midrashic Imagination

Michael Fishbane

I

Among the historical religions, classical Judaism is often characterized by its apparent break with mythology. Indeed, if one nostrum is widely accepted it is just this: that the foundation document of Judaism, the Hebrew Bible, reflects a primary rupture with the world of myth and mythmaking; and that this break has widened appreciably over the centuries. But such assessments are often based on self-serving assumptions and the restriction of admissable evidence to only part of the stream of tradition. Thus, it is argued that the creation account in Gen. 1, with its schematic structure and implied critique of Near Eastern theomachies, is telling proof of the non-mythological temper of ancient Israel. I am not convinced. Priestly theologies of twenty-five lines or so may have their say; but it is a long way from this to a denial of the mythic imagination overall. Let us simply call to mind that biblical Scriptures are replete with reflexes of a mythic drama which strongly resembles the ancient battle between Marduk and Tiamat (from Mesopotamia) or Ba'al and Yam (their Canaanite counterparts); and that this monotheistic myth remained vibrant throughout the Babylonian exile and long thereafter.[1] Indeed it is quite possible to trace the continuity of biblical accounts of a mythic strife at *Urzeit* and *Endzeit* (like Isa. 51:9 f and 27:1, respectively) well into rabbinic times, and to observe their new variations in the Pseudepigrapha and Midrash. The anthology of mythic theomachies preserved in the Babylonian Talmud (*b. Baba Bathra* 74a–b) is a striking case in point.[2] Assorted details now known from ancient Ugarit resurface in this literary source

60

long after their eclipse or obfuscation in the intervening biblical tradiition.[3] Other aspects of our mythic theme recur in the *piyyuṭim* of the great synagogue poet, Eleazar be-Rabbi Qallir;[4] and some of these survive into the High Middle Ages. Thus Qallir's depiction of Leviathan in a curved form, with the tip of his tail in his mouth,[5] takes on iconographic form in the so-called *Bird's Head Haggadah*.[6] The idea that this primordial serpent encircles with his body the sea that surrounds the world is also preserved, in the biblical commentary of Rabbi David Kimḥi (*ad* Isa. 27:1).[7]

Now the historian of religion is understandably intrigued by this extensive evidence of mythic transformation, and particularly by the creativity of its monotheistic reception. Such a multi-millenial accommodation to mythic types certainly changes the appearance of rabbinic culture for even the most wary. But one must go further, and wonder whether this panorama captures either the more primary or most characteristic aspects of rabbinic mythmaking. By this I mean, first, the movement from natural experience to its mythic dramatization; and then, as a further feature, the mythological reformulation of a received linguistic tradition through exegesis. To explain what I have in mind, let us briefly review two bygone proposals of mythic origins—namely, the theories of Johann Gottfried Herder and Max Müller.

As is well known, Max Müller championed the philological origins of myth. For him, language is the primary process from which myth is derived. Or to put it slightly differently: mythic formulations have their roots in concrete metaphors which have decayed or are misconstrued. And since all linguistic denotation is fundamentally ambiguous, the inevitable "paronymia" of words lies at the source of mythology. Why, for example, are men and stones related in the Greek myth of Deucalion and Pyrrha? Is it not because the words *laoi* and *laas* are assonant? And is not the transformation of Daphne into a laurel to escape the clutches of Apollo made comprehensible once we know that the word *daphnē* means "laurel" in Greek, and that this word can be traced to a Sanskrit cognate meaning the redness of dawn? "Mythology is inevitable," concludes Müller; "it is an inherent necessity of language." And further, "[m]ythology, in the highest sense, is the power exercised by language on thought in every possible sphere of activity."[8]

How different is the romantic perspective of Johann Herder, for whom mythology is primary and language its faded echo. In his prize essay on the origin of speech, he wrote: "As all nature sounds, so to Man, creature of sense, nothing could seem more natural than that it lives, and speaks, and acts. . . . The driving storm, the gently zephyr, the clear fountain and the mighty ocean—their whole mythology lies in those treasure troves, in *verbis* and *nominibus* of the ancient languages; and the earliest dictionary was thus a sounding pantheon."[9] In Herder's view, language itself is a "faded mythology" and not its source; for we first experience the sounds of the "stirring godhead" and only then tell its story.

But for all the pleasure we derive on hearing these mythic genealogies, neither moves us as a comprehensive theory. And yet even if we grant that myth is not *au fond* a philological puzzle, may we not agree that, here and there, verbal assonances or details have inspired mythic narratives? This is no idle query, as it bears decisively on such second-order mythological constructions as the gnostic or rabbinic sort—where such constructions regularly turn on philological forms embedded in a received tradition. On the other hand, even if we grant that myth is not, in all cases, the cultural record of the sounds of nature, are there not some cases where experiences of this sort have produced mythic *topoi*? And so, rather than try to mediate between Müller and Herder on the relative priority of nature and language as the ground of myth, I would rather regard each theory as a typical mode of mythopoesis. The one case allows us to focus on the primary processes of nature which are heard and reported as the acts of the gods; the other, more philological perspective, starts with a given verbal tradition and transforms its polysemy into mythic exploits. Both theories help reveal important modes of the rabbinic mythic imagination. In order to focus the ensuing discussion, I shall restrict my analysis to one aspect of the rabbinic motif of divine sorrow—the roar of God. By this means we shall work our way from nature to myth, and from the mythopoeic exegesis of Scripture in the ancient Midrash to the mythic transformations of medieval Jewish mysticism.

II

Let us begin with a striking *sugya*, or literary unit, found in the Babylonian Talmud (*b. Berakhot* 59a). The context is an elucidation of a mishnah (*M. Berakhot* IX.2), which states: "On [the occasion when one experiences] comets, or *zeva'ot*, or lightning, or thunder, or violent storms, one says—'Blessed [is He] whose power and might fill the world.' " The word *zeva'ot* is the problem; for while it occurs several times in the Bible (e.g., Isa. 28:19), it seems to mean nothing more than "dismay" or some form of personal "quaking"; but has no clear relation to natural wonders. Hence the following discussion:

> What does *zeva'ot* mean? Rav Qatina said: "earthquake" [*guha'*]. Once Rav Qatina was on a trip and passed the home of a necromancer when an earthquake shook. He mused [aloud]: "Might this necromancer know the meaning of this quake?" The latter then called out: "Qatina, Qatina! Don't you know

[what it is]? Whenever the Holy One, blessed be He, remembers His children who are in distress among the nations of the world, two drops fall from his eyes into the Great Sea and His voice resounds from one end of the world to the other— and that is the earthquake." Rav Qatina responded: "[This] necromancer and his explanation are deceitful, for were he correct I would have expected a double tremor [*guha' guha'*]; but this did not occur." But the real reason why Qatina did not acknowledge this interpretation was to prevent the people from being led astray after the necromancer. [Thus] Rav Qatina explained [the phenomenon as]: "God clapping His hands," as is stated [in Scripture], "I, too, shall clap My hands together and abate My anger" [Ezek. 21:22]. Rabbi Nathan explained [it as]: "God groaning," as is stated, "I shall abate My fury against them and be calm" [Ezek. 5:13]. And our sages have explained [it as] "God stamping in the heavens," as is stated, "a shout echos throughout the earth like the sound of those who trample the vats" [Jer. 25:30]. Rav Aha bar Jacob [also] explained [it as] "God squeezing His feet under His Throne of Glory," as is stated, "the heavens are My throne and the earth My footstool" [Isa. 66:1].

This remarkable pericope is composed of several layers of tradition. At the outset, a lexical observation on the meaning of *zeva'ot* is proposed, and reinforced by an episodic encounter between Rav Qatina and a necromancer, who interprets the earthquake as a sign of divine sorrow for the travail of Israel. This lexical explanation is then rejected by the sage, Rav Qatina, in order not to encourage a following for the mantic. This done, a variety of other rabbinical opinions are collected along with prooftexts from Scripture. It would seem that all of the suggestions attempt to account for the earth tremor, and that virtually all of them do so on the basis of an accompanying sound made by God: there is hand-clapping, foot-stamping and groaning, among others. From this perspective, one may suspect that the real purport of the necromancer's explanation is that it was the roaring of God in sorrow that produced the quake, not the two tears, and that the latter was picked upon by Qatina to cavil with the mantic's proposal, as the redactor already hints. Indeed, I would even suggest that the basis of the necromancer's explanation of the roaring voice as the divine cause of earthquakes lies in a folk etymology of the strange word *guha'*. It will suffice here merely to recall that this Aramaic noun derives from the monosyllabic *$\ast g(u)$*, which means "voice" in Ugaritic.[10] The Hebrew verb *hagah* and noun *hegeh* mean "to emit a sound" (cf. Ps. 1:2) and "groan" (Ezek. 2:10), respectively.[11]

But let us not allow lexicography to obscure what is so religiously remarkable about our passage, and that is that a highly rational mishnah, which collects various *mysteria tremenda* of nature and proposes a fixed blessing praising each *tremendum* of God, is explained by later sages and the necromancer in purely mythic terms. That is, earth tremors are presented as the terrestrial expression of a divine pathos. In this way, irrational terrors in the natural world are domesticated and rationalized. Note further that, for all the historical pathos implied in the necromancer's interpretation, he does not invoke a biblical prooftext. This fact underscores the primary aspect of the mantic's mythopoesis, and suggests that the proofs accompanying the views of Qatina and company are the later addition of a redactor. Indeed, if you listen closely you will agree that it is just this voice that dominates the organizational structure of the pericope and provides the hermeneutical rationale for why Rav Qatina rejected the necromancer's reading of the signs of nature.

Taking these several strata of Talmudic evidence into account, I would reconstruct the following ideal-typical stages of mythic progression. In the beginning there were the unnamed and unknowable terrors of nature, which were subsequently mythicized as divine acts. The motivation for such behavior could be entirely ahistorical, as in Rav Aha's view that earthquakes are the effect of God squeezing His feet under His Throne; or they could be passionately historical, as in the view of the necromancer. At a later point, these diverse *mythoi* were linked to scriptural proofs. This development gave the human *dicta* traditional authority, and set the stage for subsequent mythicizations of the sacred text. If the mythopoesis of the necromancer invokes the shade of Herder, mythical elaborations of the literary tradition conjures with the wand of Max Müller.

To appreciate this development, let us turn back to fol. 3b in the same tractate. We find here a more exegetical use of the scriptural text than those noted earlier. Once again the Talmudic discussion is halakhic; but now the topic is the mishnaic *dictum* of the same Rabbi Eliezer that one is permitted to recite the credal prayer of *Shema'* in the evening until the conclusion of the first watch. The later sages queried whether Rabbi Eliezer had three or four evening watches in mind, and thus whether the *terminus ad quem* of the first was four or three hours. The ensuing speculation is terminated by quoting from a non-mishnaic *dictum* of Rabbi Eliezer, who said: "the night consists of three watches, and during each and every watch the Holy One, blessed be He, sits and roars like a lion, as is stated [in Scripture]: 'The Lord roars [*yish'ag*] from on high, and thunders from His holy dwelling; yea! He roars mightily [*sha'og yish'ag*] against ['*al*] His habitation' [Jer. 25:30]."

From the prooftext cited in conclusion, it is clear that the *mythologoumenon* recited at the beginning is based on the threefold repetition of the verbal stem *sha'ag*, "to roar" in the Jeremian prooftext; and it is just this hermeneutical procedure which marks the difference between the *mythos* of Rabbi Eliezer and that of the necromancer, who brings no prooftext and does not specify the time or times of divine pathos. He merely states that "when" or "whenever" the Holy One thinks of His suffering people He cries and groans. One may suppose that just this is the core moteme of the *mythos*, and that the temporal specificity of Rabbi Eliezer is the result of the odd conjunction between a *mythos* (of the divine voice) and a halakhic *logos* (concerning the nightly watches). It may be added that whereas the necromancer's version is historically unspecific, Rabbi Eliezer's *logion* invokes the reality after 70 C.E., when the Temple was destroyed. This is done hermeneutically, by a bold rereading of Jer. 25:30. In its ancient context, this oracle is a prophecy of doom by the God of Israel who roars "from on high . . . against [*'al*] His habitation [*navehu*]. . . against all the dwellers of the earth." It might be suggested that Jeremiah has himself mythicized this doom *topos*, since in Amos 1:2 the prophet announces that the Lord roars from Zion and Jerusalem—i.e., *not* from His heavenly dwelling—that "the pastureland [*ne'ot*] of the shepherds shall lie waste."[12] But Rabbi Eliezer has gone further. For him, the Lord does not roar in anger (against the nations) but in anguish "over" or "because of [*'al*] His [earthly] abode [i.e., Temple, *navehu*]."[13]

By so transforming the particle *'al* from a prepositional ("against") to an etiological ("because of ") sense, and by giving the pastoral word *naveh* a sacral focus, Rabbi Eliezer has dramatically shifted the oracle from prophecy to pathos—from a proclamation of doom to a divine lament evoked by the fate of Israel and the Temple. The deeper cultural dimension of the halakhic discussion is therewith underscored. The Temple in ruins, the sages no longer recall the periods of nocturnal priestly watches in order to fix the upper limit for reciting the evening *Shema'*. This forgotten tradition is then reconstructed by the mythic teaching of Rabbi Eliezer. It is thus not interpretation which saves the myth, as in the well-known passage from Plato's *Phaedrus* (229D ff.), but rather a mythic interpretation which saves history—and gives it new life.

Later tradition pondered the divine roar. In what appears to be an explication of Rabbi Eliezer's *mythos,* the Talmud goes on to note that "Rav Isaac b. Samuel taught in the name of Rav: 'The night is composed of three watches, and over each watch the Holy One, blessed be He, sits and roars like a lion, and says, "Alas for the children [*'oy labanim;* viz., of Israel], on account of whose sins I destroyed My Temple, burnt My Shrine and exiled them among the nations." ' " You will note, first of all, that this version of our tradition presupposes the prooftext from Jeremiah (with the threefold use of *sha'ag*), but has elided it; and that the divine roar gives way to a statement of sympathy and theodicy. God at once averts the justice of His destructive acts and acknowledges its consequences. With this, we have moved considerably from the mythic act of divine sympathy which produces earth tremors (*zeva'ot*) "whenever" the memory of Israel's suffering recurs, to the routinization of divine pathos (expressed thrice daily) and a moralizing reflection. Both developments appreciably weaken the mythic dimension involved.

A further move in this direction is evident in the version of this *mythos* preserved in the name of Rabbi Yose. In this case, the lament, "Alas for the children," (*'oy labanim*) is heard by a traveler who secrets himself in a ruin to pray. By contrast with Rabbi Eliezer's account, the voice here is not God's roar but a divine echo resounding like a cooing dove; and there is also no reference to either earth tremors or priestly watches. Nevertheless, the comment made to Rabbi Yose by Elijah the prophet, that this cooing sound recurs thrice daily during the times of required prayer, does suggest that some mythicizing exegesis (presumably of Jer. 25:30) underlies this account as well—though it has lost its bite. A similarly defanged mixture of myth and morality concludes the pericope, when Elijah goes on to say that "whenever Israel enters synagogues or study houses and answers [the preceptor with the words] 'May His exalted Name be blessed,' the Holy One, blessed be He, moves His head from side to side and says, "Happy is the king who is praised in his palace; so what [woe] then to a father who has exiled his children? And alas for the children [*'oy labanim*] who have been exiled from their father's table!' "

An even stronger example of the theologization and moralization of the *mythos* at hand is found in the Jerusalem Talmud *(Berakhot,* IX, hal. 2, 64a). Here, without any mythic fanfare, the query as to why *zeva'ot* occur is answered legalistically: because of the sin of not properly performing priestly donations.[14] This, it is said, resolves the scriptural contradiction at issue; though an appended opinion states that this is not the "core" of the matter. The old myth is saved by a new etiology of *zeva'ot.* We read: "Whenever the Holy One, blessed by He, looks [down] at the [Roman] theaters and circuses existing in safety, rest and tranquility, while His Sanctuary lies in ruin, He threatens to destroy His world, as {Scripture] says: 'He roars mightily over [*'al*] His Temple;' that is, because of [*bishviyl*] His Temple."[15] In this form, the prooftext from Jeremiah does not support any halakhic decision but provides another mythicizing explanation of the divine pathos which produces earthquakes. The lexical gloss is of considerable interest in this regard, since the explanation of *'al* by *bishviyl* makes it perfectly clear that the divine pathos is self-directed: God roars because of His own ruined Shrine, and not because of Israel's religious loss. Such a conclusion, clearly based on the prooftext from Jer. 25:30, suggests that we rethink the traditions of Rav and Rabbi Yose, in whose name we read that God cries out, "Alas for the children." To do so, we must turn to the medieval reception of our Talmudic *mythos* by various Jews and Christians.

III

In comparing the different versions of God's roar collected in the Babylonian and Jerusalem Talmuds, we have observed a tendency to rationalize or moralize the *mythologoumenon* of earth tremors. I am even tempted to speak of a palpable trend towards demythologization—bearing in mind that the core mythic moteme here (the divine roar) is never directly delegitimized in any of the traditions. Such is not the case, however, among some latter-day readers of the rabbinic texts. For example, when Hai Gaon, the head of the Babylonian academy in Pumbedita in the early eleventh century, answered a *responsum* concerning the tears of God in *b. Berakhot* 59a, he apologized by saying that "it is [merely] a figure of speech [*mashal*]."[16] Similarly, his contemporary in Kairouan, Rabbenu Ḥananel, commented on the same *topos* and asserted that its entire purport is "to demonstrate to Israel that the Holy One, blessed be He, has not abandoned them" and "to strengthen their hearts that they not despair of the redemption."[17] Not satisfied with explaining the figure, Ḥananel attacked the trope directly. "God forbid," he goes on, "[that the text refers to] tears from the eye, but [merely] drops *like* tears." To this docetic rationalization he added the further caveat that there is also no groaning or clapping or kicking by God—but rather that "the Holy One, blessed be He, commands an angel" to do this, in each case. The author of the *'Arugat ha-Bosem* also transmits this position, and sums up the whole with the words, "everything [was done] by an angel."[18]

The Church Fathers were less inclined to literary legerdemain, in these cases, as we can see from the comments of Petrus Alfonsi, a Spanish contemporary of Hai and Ḥananel. In his *Dialogus* with a literary interlocutor, Moises the Jew, Petrus criticizes the "sages" for expounding the "prophets rather superficially" and for ascribing corporeality to God.[19] In a word, "*dicta sunt,*" he says, "*ad litteram solam exponere*"—the Jews expound Scripture in its most literal way.[20] For example,

> they say that once every day He weeps, and two tears drop from His eyes and flow into the Great Sea. . . . This same weeping which they shamefully ascribe to God is, they say, because of the captivity of the Jews, and because of His sorrow they assert that three times a day He roars like a lion and shakes the Heavens with His feet like heels in a press, or emits a sound like a humming dove, and He moves His head from side to side, and says in a lamenting voice: "Alas for Me! Alas for Me! [*heu mihi, heu mihi!*] That I have made My house into a desert and have burned My Temple, and exiled My children among the nations. Alas for the father who has exiled his children, and alas for the children [*heu filiis*] who have been exiled from their father's table!"[21]

This tradition is remarkable in several respects. Not least striking is the fact that, in the very process of criticizing the work of myth of the Jews, Petrus has reworked the various *logia* from *b. Berakhot* 3a and 59a into a continuous mythic discourse. Deleting the various tradents— from the necromancer and Rav Qatina to Rabbi Yose and the prophet Elijah—Petrus has paradoxically provided a *mythos* of even greater force than the Talmudic anthology itself. Added to this is the literary-critical value of his comments; for you will, no doubt, have noticed that the divine lament here is "Woe to *Me*" (*Heu mihi*) and not "Woe to *the children because of whose sins I have destroyed My Temple.*" That is to say, Petrus has articulated a self-directed divine lament and not a theodicy; and it is just this divine reflexivity which appears to be the primary force of the mythicizing reinterpretation of Jer. 25:30. When God roars "over" His Temple, therefore, He laments to Himself "because of" its loss and destruction.

This mythic layer of divine pathos is thus literarily and phenomenologically separate from both the lament over children who have been exiled from their father's table and the rabbinic justification for earthquakes. Its authenticity is confirmed from a Karaite polemic one century earlier (tenth century),[22] in which Salmon ben Yeruḥim confronts his Rabbanite counterparts with their Talmudic "abominations."[23] He first refers to the *mythos* of God roaring thrice nightly, and then adds:

"Rav Isaac ben Samuel ben Martha taught in the name of Rab: 'The night consists of three watches, [and] over each one the Holy One, blessed be He, sits in His Temple and cries for the exile and says, Alas for Me! [*'oy liy*] For I have destroyed My Temple, and burnt My Shrine and exiled My children throughout every land.' "

On the basis of this evidence (confirmed by several manuscript sources)[24] and the Latin rendition of Petrus (taken over by Peter Venerabilis),[25] it stands to reason that we have recovered the original divine lament of our rabbinic *mythos,* and may confidently assume that *'oy liy* ("Alas for Me") was subsequently changed to *'oy labanim* ("Alas for the children") in the later versions of our received Talmud.[26] This change was either the result of a deliberate demythologization of the lament, or, as seems more likely, the direct result of an accomodation to Karaite criticisms. The reading "Alas for Me" is already mentioned in Al-Qirqisani's ninth century polemical treatise *Kitab al-'Anwar* (*The Book of Lights*).[27]

It remains to add that the virulent anti-Rabbanite polemic in Salmon's *Sefer Milḥamot ha-Shem (The Book of the Wars of the Lord)* puts Petrus' own Talmudic reception in a new light; for a comparison of the midrashic *topoi* criticized in chapter 14 of the *Sefer Milḥamot* with the pertinent sections of the *Dialogus* reveals a remarkable concordance between the two.[28] While it is, of course, entirely possible that the arguments of Petrus of Huesca were drawn from the fanatical Benedictine monks from whom he received baptism (before Alfonso I of Aragon); or even that similar religious attitudes may independently produce similar polemical agenda, it is also likely that the Karaites then in Spain served (directly or indirectly) as the tradents of this bill of theological particulars. Let it not be forgotten that the later attacks on the Talmud by another convert, Abner of Burgos, were themselves indebted to a stock of arguments drawn up by Nicholas Donin. This Jewish apostate, who denounced the Talmud to Pope Gregory IX after being excommunicated by the French communities for denying the validity of the Oral Law, provided excerpts of it to the ecclesiastical tribunal for examination. As Y. Baer already observed, the arguments of the Christian inquisitors, when the Talmud was subsequently put on trial (in Paris, 1240) and condemned to be burned, "were substantially the same as those [used] by the Karaites."[29]

IV

I should now like to return to the original Talmudic reading *'oy liy* ("Alas for Me") in *b. Berakhot* 3a, and give one more turn to the mythological wheel. The purpose is to provide a striking variation on our *topos* of divine lamentation (with tears) and earth tremors, and therewith a transition to its hypostatic form in the mystical mythology of the Kabbalah. The place to begin is *petiḥta'* 24 of *Midrash Eikha Rabba*.[30] In the course of a supplemental comment on Isa. 22:12 ("My Lord God of Hosts summoned on that day to weeping and lamenting"), we read:

> When the Holy One, blessed be He, intended to destroy the Temple, He said: "As long as I am [present] in it [viz., the Temple], the nations of the world cannot harm it; so I shall remove My [protective] eye from it and shall swear that I shall have no need of it until the Endtime—and then the enemies shall come [in] and destroy it." Thereupon the Holy One, blessed be He, swore by His arm and put it behind Him (*heḥezirah le-'aḥorav*); as it is written, "He withdrew [*heshiv 'aḥor*] His hand before [*lifney*] the enemy" [Lam. 2:3]. At that moment, the enemies entered the Shrine and burnt it. Once it was burnt, the Holy One, blessed be He, said: "Once again I have no dwelling [place] on earth; [thus] I shall remove My Shekhinah from it and ascend to My first dwelling." . . . At that moment the Holy One, blessed be He, was crying and saying: "Alas for Me [*'oy liy*], what have I done?! I have caused My Shekhinah to dwell below for Israel's sake; and now that they have sinned, I have returned to My first dwelling. Never indeed shall I be a mockery to the nations or a [subject of] derision to humans!"

In this allomorph of the lament motif in *b. Berakhot* 3a, the Holy One cries *'oy liy* as an expression of despair over the destruction of the Temple and the consequent withdrawal of His Shekhinah from the earth. As in the Talmudic variant, the lament is a self-directed statement of loss—though here it is supported with an expression of divine pride and dignity. Another difference between our midrashic text and the tradition of Rav Isaac (in *b. Berakhot* 3a) is that the lament here is a spontaneous outcry at the realization of the destruction, and not a near-liturgical recitation of woe thrice nightly. Indeed in *Eikha Rabba* the divine cry follows a deliberate decision to destroy—dramatically reinforced by an oath to withdraw the protective arm of the Lord. In this form the *petiḥta'* further accentuates the passive-aggressive divine act enunciated in Lam. 2:3, though with one major difference. Hereby the biblical metaphor of withdrawn protection has been literalized and mythicized. The earthly consequence of this divine drama is doom and the ascension of the Shekhinah to the heavenly heights (whence it had gradually descended).[31]

In response to the burst of divine woe (*'oy liy*), the supreme angel, Metatron, volunteers to cry in God's stead. This request is strongly rejected, and God invites the angels with Jeremiah at their head to view, the destroyed Temple. At this sight, the Holy One again bursts into tears and cries: "Alas for Me [*'oy liy*] because of My Abode!" Now God requests Jeremiah to invite the three Patriarchs and Moses to lament, for "they know how to cry." Thereupon, Moses leads the Patriarchs in tears and lamentation; "and when the Holy One, blessed be He, saw them He too turned to keening and crying, and said: 'Alas [*'oy lo*] for the king who succeeded in his youth and failed in his old age.' " With this divine self-deprecation, the pericope ends. Its oblique *'oy lo* recurs in all versions of the tradition. By contrast, the stark pathos of the cry *'oy liy* (twice) is omitted both in *Eikha Zutta* and the *Yalqut Shim'oni*, which depends upon it.[32]

Phenomenologically speaking, *petiḥta'* 24 of *Eikha Rabba* bears comparison with 3 Enoch 48 A (= Schäfer, nos. 68–70).[33] For if the former shows a significant step towards a mythic hypostatization of the divine arm in the context of divine lamentation, this process is all but complete in the Enochian passage. Hereby, God's arm is one of the cosmic mysteries in the Seventh Heaven (along with the source of snow and fire; the heavenly curtain; the holy Names; etc.) shown to Rabbi Ishmael by Metatron, his heavenly guide.

> Rabbi Ishmael said: Metatron said to me: "Come and I shall show you the right arm of the Omnipresent One (*maqom*), which is sent behind [Him] [*nishlaḥat le-'aḥor*] because of the destruction of the Temple. All manner of splendid lights shine from its; and by it 955 heavens were created. Even the

seraphim and ophanim are not permitted to view it until the day of salvation comes."

[So] I went with him; and he took me by the hand, bore me up on his wings and showed it [viz., the arm] to me with all manner of praise, jubilation and psalm—[though] no mouth can [fully] speak its praise, nor in any eye view it because of the extent of its greatness, splendor, glory, honor and beauty. Moreover, all the souls of the righteous who merit seeing the joy of Jerusalem stand beside it, praising it and entreating mercy—saying thrice daily: "Arise, arise! Put on your strength, arm of the Lord" [Isa. 51:9]; as it is written, "He made His glorious arm go at the right arm of Moses" [Isa. 63:12]. At that moment, the right arm of the Omnipresent One would cry, and five rivers of tears flowed from its fingers into the Great Sea, making the whole world quake; as is written, "The earth will split apart, the earth will be rent in ruin; the earth will surely stagger like a drunkard and totter like a lean-to" [Isa. 24:19 f]—five times, corresponding to the five fingers of the great right arm.[34]

In its hypostatic splendor the arm of the Lord is a *mysterium tremendum*, a heavenly mystery in whose might is the salvation to come. Its centrality in the ultimate eschatological drama is indicated both by R. Ishmael's comments and by the prayer of the righteous souls. Indeed, the salvific manifestation of the arm is the subject of the ensuing paragraphs which bring both this chapter and 3 Enoch as a whole to climactic conclusion.[35] As in the preceding *petiḥta*, the *topos* of the divine arm is dramatized here by a midrashic reading of Lam. 2:3–though in 3 Enoch its withdrawal is portrayed as a *post factum* occulation of providential power (*mipney ḥorban*, "because of the destruction"; not *mipney 'oyev*, because of the enemy['s advent]). Moreover, in the Enoch passage, it is the thrice daily evocation of the arm by the righteous which elicits tears. This liturgical ritual in the highest realms stands in stark contrast with the *ex eventu* mourning of God in the *petiḥta*.

A final point of comparison lies in the fact that the lament *topos* in 3 Enoch is not a cry of woe but the silent flow of divine tears through the fingers of the glorious arm. Forming five streams of sorrow that fall into the Great Sea, these tears produce five earth tremors in a manner strikingly reminiscent of Rav Qatina's explanation of *guha'* in *b. Berakhot* 59a. In that passage God roared upon recalling the destruction of the Temple, and His tears fell into the Great Sea. No prooftexts were adduced by the necromancer in support of the divine roar, though we did see how the threefold repetition of the verb *sha'ag* ("roar") in Jer. 25:30 was used to support Rabbi Eliezer's teaching of the nightly watches in *b. Berakhot* 3a. With this in mind, we may now observe that the prooftext from Isa. 24:18–19 provides a similar scriptural support for the teaching of five tremors in 3 Enoch—since the word *'eretz* ("land") recurs five times in that prophetic passage. This midrashic point has been obscured, somewhat, in the transmission of our apocalypse; for the biblical phrase *va-yir'ashu mosedey 'aretz* ("and the foundations of the earth will shake") from Isa. 24:18b has been rendered here *u-mar'iyshot 'et ha-'olam kulo* ("making the whole world quake")—*just before* citing v. 19 and its fourfold repetition of the word *'eretz.*

V

With this hermeneutical refiguring of Lam. 2:3 and the lament of God, we have moved from mythical Midrash (in the *petihta'*) towards a mythopoeic imagination which finds hypostatic realities encoded in Scripture (in Enoch). Indeed, in this shifting upward of the scene of action from a descriptive metaphor to mythic drama and mystic vision, there is a corresponding shift from the *historia sacra* of the Bible to the *historia divina* of Midrash and apocalyptic. An even more dramatic transumption of the *mythos* of divine pathos remains the remarkable achievement of the Kabbalists. Their theo-sophical hermeneutics are a dramatization of hypostatic realities of the bold-est mythic sort. For this, in conclusion, we return to our central *topos* of God's lamentational roar "on behalf of" His destroyed Abode.

In the *Zohar* (III.74b), the combination of the biblical verse from Jeremiah and the lament *topoi* from the Talmud results in highly esoteric hermeneutics. Briefly, its content and character is this. Starting from the stark biblical rule of illicit consanguinity, "You shall not uncover the nakedness of your father or the nakedness of your mother" (Lev. 18:7), Rabbi Simeon bar Yohai de-cides to reveal its secret sense.[36] He begins by citing the verse from Ezek. 11:13, in which the prophet cries "Alas!" (*'ahah*) over the threatened destruc-tion of Israel. On the basis of the orthography of this cry (*'aha = 'aleph-heh-heh*), we are taught that as result of Israel's sins a profound division is effected in the supernal divine Reality—symbolized by the divine Name YHVH, the Tetragram, *yod-heh-vav-heh.* For when Israel sins, the Lower Feminine element of the Godhead (symbolized by the second *heh* in the Tetragram and in the word *'ahah*) is separated from the Palace of the King (symbolized by the letter *vav* in the Tetragram). The result is that the Upper Feminime (symbol-ized by the first *heh* in the Tetragram and in the word *'ahah*) prevents the downward flow of blessing within the diving Totality (*kol*). This teaching of divine disaster is seconded by citing Jer. 25:30, "The Lord roars from on high and gives voice from His holy Shrine, He roars mightily over His *naveh.*" Rabbi Simeon explains the passage as follows: " 'His *naveh*,' precisely; which is the Matrona, and that is certain! And what does He say? 'Alas [*'oy*] that I have destroyed My Temple, etc. "My Temple," [this being the] conjunction with the Matrona.' "

Let me gloss this hermeneutical process. For Rabbi Simeon, the Bible is not a product of ordinary language but the precipitate of divine Speach. This means that its exoteric laws and narratives are but an outer garment of sense, and that, in truth, the Torah is an esoteric teaching about the divine Reality. Thus the law against incest in the book of Leviticus contains a secret warning of the theosophical consequences of human sin, as do the aforementioned prophecies of Ezekiel and Jeremiah. Indeed, when properly decoded, the verbs and nouns of Scripture constitute allusions to hypostatic realities in the divine Realm—where there is a King and a Queen, and a heavenly *hieros gamos* which can be interrupted by sin. In a similar way, the very letters of certain words (like *'ahah*) may symbolize the same theosophical truth. This helps us to understand the remainder of Rabbi Simeon's teaching, which provides a mystical meaning to the content of God's roar (*'oy liy*, "Alas for Me!") as stated in the original Talmudic tradition.

The ensuing explication begins with the mystical philology of the final two components of the cry *'oy*, the letters *vav* and *yod*. The esoteric excursus goes as follows:

We have learned: When the King is separated from the Matrona, and blessings are not to be found, then He is called *vav-yod*. What is the meaning of this designation? It has been taught: The beginning [letter] of the [divine gradation called] *Yesod* [Foundation] is a *yod*, since *Yesod* is a miniscule *vav* and the [gradation called the] Holy One, blessed be He is a majescule *vav*, above [it]; therefore, [this letter *vav*] is written [out for pronunciation] *vav-vav*, [viz.] two *vavs* together, and the initial letter of *Yesod* is *yod*. Now when the Matrona is removed from the King, and the conjunction does not occur through the beginning of *Yesod* [viz., *yod*], the upper *vav* takes the beginning of *Yesod* [which is *yod*], and draws it to itself, and then it is *vay* [viz., *vav-yod*], *vay* for the Totality, the upper and lower [gradations].

The issues involved in this alphabetical arcana require some explication. To begin, it will be recalled that Rabbi Simeon is expounding the meaning of the second two letters (*vav-yod*) of the divine lament *'oy* in *b. Berakhot* 3a. These letters combine to yield the reading *vay*, which, according to an ancient midrashic teaching based on the Greek lament word *vai*, means "Alas."[37] Rabbi Simeon integrates this tradition into his esoteric exegesis, and provides a mystical parallel to the cry *'ahah*. Whereas the letters *heh-heh* of that word symbolize the Upper and Lower Feminine elements of the Godhead, as noted earlier, the letters *vav-yod* of the word *'oy* symbolize the Upper and Lower Masculine elements. When there is harmony in the divine Reality, and a dynamic conjunction between the masculine and feminine dimensions is in effect, these two principles are normally symbolized by the letter *vav*—written *vav-vav*, the first *vav* being the majescule form of it, the second its miniscule version (since, orthographically, the *yod* appears as a diminished *vav*). However, when Israel sins, they cause an interruption in the supernal conjunction so that the Lower Female (the Matrona) is separated from the Upper Male (the King; the Holy One, blessed be He) and he withdraws from her. In this situation, the supernal gradation of *Yesod* (the virile element of the King) contracts from a *vav* to a *yod* (the first letter of the word itself) and is drawn upward to the Holy One (the upper *vav*).[38] The subsequent combination of these two letters, the result of a profound disjunction within the divine Totality, is thus symbolized by the resultant word: *vay*, "Alas."

Rabbi Simeon then goes on to wonder why the lamentation *'oy* (spelled *'aleph-vav-yod*) occurs here, and not its synonym *hoy* (spelled *heh-vav-yod*). His explanation is that the word *hoy* is used "when the matter [involved] is dependent upon repentance and the people do not do so." On such occasions, the divine principle of Repentance, symbolized by the Upper *heh*, draws the letters *vav* and *yod* to her and the word *hoy* is the result. By contrast, when Israel does not repent the King recedes into the divine hierarchy. He then becomes inaccessible to human prayer and absorbed into the divine *absconditus* called *'eheyeh*, which draws the letters *vav* and *yod* to it. The result is the combination of the initial *'aleph* of the divine Name *'eheyeh* ("I shall be;" the divine self-nomination in Exod. 3:14) with the letters *vav* and *yod* of the Tetragram. This produces the more profound lament word *'oy*. It symbolizes both the loss of all hope in repentance and the fateful withdrawal of the flow of divine blessing from all vital conjunctions to a most recessive point in the divine Mind.

The mystical hermeneutics of Rabbi Simeon bar Yohai thus symbolize profound mythic dramas within the Godhead. Put graphically, the supernal *hieros gamos* is a scene of cosmic procreation which is disrupted when the child, Israel, disobeys the will of the Divine Parents and enacts improper liaisons on earth below. Such sin, in this case called "uncovering the nakedness of your father and mother," thus produces a cosmic *interruptus* which causes the Female to separate from the Male, and the Male to withdraw his virile element, so to speak. In this diminished form, the divine Reality cannot be inseminated with blessing and is in a state of woe. Continued failure of the child to repent results in a loss of the nurturant Female and a reabsorption of the vital fluids of divinity into the brain of the supernal *Anthropos*.

In this hypostatic version, the older midrashic *mythologoumena* of divine sorrow have undergone a qualitative shift. A one time historical event of sin, whose consequences are remembered by God with a groan of woe, is transformed into a recurrent cosmic drama in which Israel's sins produce divine disaster. For all that, three lines of continuity between the earlier and later phenomena can be traced. The first concerns the several correlations between myth and history that occur; for what is striking about the midrashic and mystical *topoi* reviewed here is the recurrent nexus between the two. In all cases, historical sin has its reflex or correlation in the divine Realm. A two-tiered perspective is thus envisaged, whereby human acts variously effect a state of woe or lack in the divine. Put differently: (Israel's) history is not dissociated from metahistory but is significantly valorized as its vital catalyst.

The second trajectory that may be traced between the mythic tropes of ancient Midrash and the mystical dramas of Zoharic mysticism is the relationship between divine speech and mundane disaster that may be observed; for whether the divine sound is a wordless roar of sorrow or an explicity cry of *'oy* (with historical or hypostatic significance), there are natural repercussions to God's cry. In one case, the roar results in earthquakes; in the other, divine despair signals doom and the diminishment of earthly blessing. These moments in the natural realm are thus signs of a supernatural response to human action. Irregularities in the world of nature are thus declined as fragments of a divine grammar expressed in the mundane order.

I shall conclude with one more point that serves to link the *mythopoesis* of classical Midrash with its cogeners in later mystical sources. As we have seen, the rabbinic "work of myth" is a deeply hermeneutical process. This holds whether one is dealing with the interpretation of natural processes as reflexes of a divine drama; with the reworking of the Bible through creative philology and semantics; or with the revision of the Midrash itself by means of hypostatic symbolism and linguistic permutations. To appreciate these hermeneutical processes is, therefore, not only to enter the inner-cultural realm of Jewish mythmaking, but to appreciate its protean forms and energy as well. It has been the essential purpose of this discussion to sharpen just this point; and to suggest that, in no small measure, midrashic mythopoesis is and has been a mainspring of the concrete Jewish theological imagination.

Notes

1. Compare Isa. 11:11–16; 27:1; 51:9–11; and Ps. 74:12–14; 89:10–11, among others. Overall, see the seminal contribution of U. Cassutto, "The Israelite Epic," in *Biblical and Oriental Studies* (Jerusalem, 1975), vol. II, esp. pp. 71–102 (originally published in *Knesset* 8, 1943). For some particularly striking correspondences with Ugaritic mythology, see C. H. Gordon, "Leviathan—Symbol of Evil," in *Biblical Motifs, Origins and Transformations,* edited by A. Altmann (Brandeis Texts and Studies; Cambridge, Mass., 1966), pp. 1–9.

2. See L. Ginzberg's *Legends of the Jews* (Philadelphia, 1925), vol. V, pp. 17–18, 26–27, 41–50; and his discussion in *Jewish Law and Lore* (New York and Philadelphia, 1962), p. 63, where he refers to these mythological elements as "faded fragments" of non-Jewish antiquity.

3. See U. Cassutto, "The Israelite Epic," p. 71 ff.

4. See the study of J. Schirmann, *The Battle Between Behemoth and Leviathan According to an Ancient Hebrew Piyyut* (Jerusalem, *1970*), *vol. IV, no. 13.*

5. *Ibid., p. 355, 1.76.*

6. See M. Spitzer (ed.), *The Bird's Head Haggada of the Bezalel National Art Museum in Jerusalem*, Introductory Volume (Jerusalem, 1967), pl.32.

7. For Qallir's statement "He [Leviathan] encircles the Great Sea like a ring," see Schirmann, *The Battle Between Behemoth and Leviathan*, p. 355, 1.77.

8. M. Müller, "The Philosophy of Mythology," appended to his *Introduction to the Science of Religion* (London, 1873), pp. 353–55. See also his *Lectures on the Science of Language*, 2nd series (New York, 1873), pp. 372–76.

9. "Über der Ursprung des Sprache," in *Werke*, edited by Suphan, vol. V, 53 ff.

10. See J. Aistleitner, *Wörterbuch der Ugaritischen Sprache* (Berlin, 1967), p. 63 (no. 612).

11. On the expression *sefer ha-hagu* in CD X.6 and XIII.2, see M. Goshen-Gottstein, *VT* 8, 286 ff. Also cf. Ps. 123:4. with *Q.*

12. A similar tradition recurs in Joel 4:16. The link between a divine roar and earth tremors is made explicit in this passage (note: *ve-ra'ashu*, "will shake"); it is more implicit in Amos 1:2, where a future oracle ("will roar") follows the notice (v. 1) that Amos prophesied two years before the earthquake (*hea-ra'ash*).

13. This understanding of *naveh* is implicit in Exod. 15:13, and explicit in *Mekhilta de-Rabbi Ishmael, Shirata, ad loc.* (also quoting Ps. 79:7). This is also the explanation of the Targum, and is continued by Rashi and Kimḥi.

14. See also the versions in *Midrash Soḥer Tov*, XVIII.12 and CIV, which apparently derive from this Talmudic tradition. Also see next note.

15. I have translated the word *'apiylon* as "threatens," assuming it to reflect the Greek participle *apeilōn* (from *apeileo*, "to threaten punishment"). The form is translated in the *Soḥer Tov* (see n. 14 above) as *biqqesh*, "to decide" (to destroy it, *le-haḥarivo*).

16. B. M. Lewin (ed.), *'Otzar Ha-Geonim: Thesaurus of the Geonic Response and Commentaries* (Haifa and Jerusalem, 1928–43), *Berakhot*, p. 2. R. David Kimḥi apologizes for the expression "roar" in Jer. 25:30 in a similar way, saying that "He roars from on high" is *'al derekh mashal*, "a figurative expression."

17. B. M. Lewin, *Nispaḥim le-'Otzar Ha-Geonim, Berakhot*, 62 f.

18. *Sefer 'Arugat ha-Bosem*, edited by E. E. Urbach (Jerusalem, 1962), III pp. 108 ff.

19. *Dialogus Petri, cognomento Alphonsi, ex iudaeo christiani et Moysi iudaei*, Migne PL CVII, p. 553.

20. Ibid.

21. Ibid., 550–51.

22. According to I. Davidson, *Sefer Milḥamot Ha-Shem* (New York, 1934), p. 3, the work was written before 942.

23. Ibid., ch. 14, p. 108 (11. 5–18).

24. See R. N. Rabbinovicz, *Diqduqei Soferim: Varia Lectionis in Mischnam et in Talmud Babylonicum* (New York, 1976), *Berakhot*, p. 4, n. 5 (MS Munich), and 377 (MS Paris). For other sources, see S. Lieberman, *Shiqi'in* (Jerusalem, 1960; 2nd ed.), p. 70.

25. Migne *PL* CLXXXIX, 622. See the comparison in Lieberman, *Shiqi'in*, pp. 28 ff.

26. The comment of Rashi (eleventh century) on the divine roar in Jer. 25:30, "He [God] mourns [*mit'abbel*] over His Temple" seems to indicate that he also knew the Talmudic reading *'oy liy.*

27. See L. Nemoy's "Al-Qirqisani's Account of the Jewish Sects," *Hebrew Union College Annual* 7 (1930): 352.

28. Thus (op. cit., n.23) Salmon refers to (1) the bodily form of God (the *Shi'ur Qomah*); (2) divine tears and Israel's exile; (3) God wearing phylacteries (cf. *b. Berakhot* 6a); and God's prayer that His mercy overcome His anger (cf. *b. Berakhot* 7a). These topics are all mentioned by Petrus; cf. *PL* CVII, pp. 543, 550–51.

29. *The Jews in Christian Spain* (Philadelphia, 1978), vol. 1, p. 151.

30. S. Buber (ed.), (Vilna, 1899), fols. 13 a–b.

31. For the theme of the gradual ascent of the Shekhinah after Adam's sin, and its descent culminating in the completion of the Tabernacle, see *Pesiqta' de-Rav Kahana* I, p. 1 (Buber, 1b) and *Tanḥuma, Pequdei*, 6; cf. *Genesis Rabba* XIX, p. 7. Hence the ascension after the destruction is a return, as our *petiḥta'* says.

32. See *Midrash Eicha Zutta* (Vilna, 1925), p. 32b, the *Yalqut to Eicha* is appended thereto; see p. 43b (para. 4; in the traditional text, no. 996).

33. *Synopse zur Hekhalot-Literatur*, edited by P. Schäfer, (Tübingen, 1981), par. 34–35 (MSS Munich 40 and Vatican 228, respectively).

34. 3 Enoch 48 A:1–4 = Schäfer, par. 68.

35. I shall discuss this theme and related rabbinic midrashim in a forthcoming study.

36. The prohibition of *'arayot*, so strongly condemned in the Talmud (cf. *b. Sanhedrin* 74a), is given various mystical interpretations in the *Zohar*, see especially the cluster in Zohar III. 74a–75b, and the *Tiqqunei Zohar, Tiqqun* 34 (77b) and 56 (89b). Also cf. *Zohar* I.27b (from *Tiqqunei Zohar*).

37. Cf. *Petiḥta'* to *Esther Rabbati*, VI; *Lamentations Rabba* I.31.

38. For the letter *yod* and its relation to the *membrum virile* and circumcision, see the midrashic tradition recorded in *Tanḥuma* XIII, p. 14, and the clarification in Al-Naqawa's *Menorat Ha-Ma'or*, edited by H. Enelow (New York, 1932), vol. III, p. 470 (Jerusalem, 1961; p. 183). Note the ritual comment in R. Abraham b. Nathan Ha-Yarḥi's *Sefer Ha-Manhig*, edited by Y. Raphael (Jerusalem, 1978), vol. II, p. 579. For a wide-ranging discussion, see E. Wolfson, "Circumcision and the Divine Name: A Study in the Transmission of Esoteric Doctrine," *The Jewish Quarterly Review* 78 (1987): 77–112.

5

The Rabbinic Parable and
the Narrative of Interpretation

————————————————— David Stern

Perhaps the most frustrating feature of Rabbinic literature is its reticence: how little it reveals of the story of its own making, about the situations and circumstances in which its texts originated. An exception to this general rule is the following, rather amusing narrative about one sage's use of the *mashal,* the generic term in Rabbinic literature for the fable and parable:

> Shimeon, the son of Rabbi [Judah], prepared a [wedding] banquet for his son. He went and invited all the sages, but he forgot to invite Bar Kappara. [Bar Kappara] went and wrote on the door [of R. Shimeon's house]: After rejoicing is death. So what value is there to rejoicing?
>
> R. Shimeon asked: Who did this to me? Is there anyone we did not invite? Someone said: Bar Kappara. You forgot to invite him.
>
> R. Shimeon remarked: To invite [Bar Kappara] now by himself would be unseemly.
>
> So [R. Shimeon] went and make a second banquet, and he invited all the sages, and he also invited Bar Kappara. But at every course that was brought in to the guests, Bar Kappara recited three hundred fox-fables. The guests did not even taste the dishes before they grew cold, and the dishes were removed from the table just as they had been brought in. R. Shimeon asked his servant: Why are all the dishes being returned untouched?
>
> [The servant] replied: Because there is an old man sitting there, and at every course he tells fables until the dishes grow cold, and no one eats them.
>
> R. Shimeon went up to [Bar Kappara} and said: What have I done to make you ruin my banquet?
>
> Bar Kappara responded: Do I need your banquet? Did not Solomon say, "What real value is there for a man in all the gains he makes beneath the sun?" (Eccl. 1:3) And what is written after that verse? "One generation goes, another comes, but the earth remains the same forever" (1:4). (*Vayikra Rabbah* 28:2)[1]

Unhappily, this passage tells us nothing about the 300 fox-fables that Bar Kappara recited over every course at R. Shimeon's banquet; in fact, the passage does not bother to record even a single *mashal*, possible because the fables, entertaining as they must have been, were not considered sufficiently "serious" to be preserved in writing.[2] Even so, the passage is revealing, if only for what it suggests about the nature of the *mashal* as a literary form and its function as an allusive narrative with an unspoken message. In Bar Kappara's case, the very act of reciting the *mashal* served an ulterior purpose. It offered him a clever if somewhat nasty means to retaliate against his host for the insult he felt he had earlier suffered.[3]

Admittedly, revenge is an unusual motive for parable making. Elsewhere in Rabbinic literature, several other motives, purposes, and occasions for the *mashal* are depicted. Some sages are reported to have used the *mashal* as an oblique means of expressing political opinions that were too dangerous to be stated openly.[4] Other sages are said to have employed the literary form as an effective weapon for responding to polemical attacks by outsiders (very much the way Jesus is portrayed in the gospels as fashioning parables to argue with the Jewish leaders who oppose him).[5] Still other sages used the parable as a tactful instrument for smoothing over socially awkward or embarrassing situations as well as for praising the dead, either in eulogies or in the course of consoling the grieving relatives.[6] Several sources preserve *meshalim* of this type; one text relates how R. Yohanan b. Zakkai recited two *meshalim* about himself even as he lay in bed dying![7]

The *mashal*'s most frequent occasion, however, was the sermon in the synagogue or the lecture in the Rabbinic academy. Surprisingly, no literary descriptions exist of *meshalim* delivered in these institutional contexts.[8] Still, it seems highly probable that most of the approximately 1,000 *meshalim* recorded in Rabbinic literature were at least intended to be used in these institutions as material for sermons or lessons.[9] It is therefore only appropriate that the most common literary context in which *meshalim* are preserved in Rabbinic literature is that of midrash, the literature of Scriptural exegesis and study. Midrash determined the conventional two-part structure of the *mashal*, consisting of a narrative (the *mashal* proper) and a *nimshal*, the so-called explanation or (as I prefer to call it) application of the narrative. And midrash, too, gave the Rabbinic *mashal* its explicit raison d'être, which was to be an exegetical tool, a device for interpreting Scripture and for arriving at its meaning.

The Rabbis themselves believed that the *mashal* was invented— according to one tradition, by no one less than King Solomon—to reveal the secrets of Torah.[10] To make this very point, the Rabbis recited a *mashal* about the *mashal*:

It is like a king who lost a gold piece in his house, or a valuable gem. Does he not find it by means of a penny candle?

> Likewise: Let not the *mashal* seem trivial in your eyes, for by means of the *mashal* a man is able to understand the words of Torah.[11]

What is trivial about the *mashal* is its fictionality, and this fictionality is legitimated—"saved," as it were—by the *mashal's* exegetical instrumentality. Now we need not accept the Rabbis' estimation of the *mashal's* value—as worth no more than a penny candle—to appreciate their view that the *mashal* is a didactic literary form, a story with a message. But the real object of that message is not exegesis per se; it is an ideology, a world-view—specifically, the idiology of Rabbinic Judaism. The *mashal* is an ideological narrative, and the Rabbis used it, as they used scriptural exegesis, to impress on their audience the validity and authority of their view of the world.[12] And the reason why scriptural exegesis, midrash, was so effective a tool for ideological communication of this kind was because the Rabbis were fully persuaded that their vision of Judaism was God's will for the world as expressed in the Torah.

But why the parable? Why should a fictional narrative have been so effective in communicating an ideological truth? What was it about the *mashal* that made it so attractive to the Rabbis? And how did the parables serve the Rabbis in so many different contexts and occasions?

We can begin to answer these questions by saying that no single explanation or model will comprehensively explain the traits of all *meshalim* in Rabbinic literature (let alone all parables in world literature). In fact, there are at least three separate models for conceptualizing the *mashal,* and these three models lie along a kind of spectrum of parabolic possibilities. Two of the three form the extremities of the spectrum: at one end, the parable as an illustrative or demonstrational narrative; at the other, as a mode of secret or concealing speech. Between these two poles lies a third model, the *mashal* as a rhetorical narrative. As we will see, most Rabbinic *meshalim* happen to fall under this last model (in my view at least); that is, somewhere between the two extreme poles of open illustration and of secret speech. Nonetheless, certain Rabbinic *meshalim* are closer in character to one of the models of the spectrum's extremities; and in the course of the *mashal's* history in Hebrew literature, from the Bible until Agnon (nearly), the parable has been used at different times in conformity with all three models. Each one, accordingly, warrants a brief description before we proceed to our main subject, the Rabbinic *mashal.*

The *Mashal* as Illustration

This view of the literary form sees the *mashal* as a medium for illustrating abstract ideas or beliefs through narrative examples that are concrete, familiar, and thus—this is the primary assumption behind this model—more easily comprehended by an audience that is believed to be inherently incapable of grasping such abstractions on its own and therefore requires the "help" of the parable. Highly influential in New Testament parable-scholarship since the nineteenth century, this conceptualization essentially sees the *mashal* as kind of simile, and explicit figure for likeness and resemblance.[13]

The application of this model to the Rabbinic *mashal* is a complicated matter.[14] There are certainly many instances in talmudic and midrashic texts where the *mashal* is used as an illustration.[15] In *Ber. R.* (1:15), two oft-quoted *meshalim*, attributed to the Houses of Hillel and Shammai, appear as responses to the question, What was created first in the universe, the heavens (according to the House of Shammai) or the earth (House of Hillel)?

> According to the House of Shammai, it is like a king who built a throne for himself, and then made a footstool to go with it, as it is written, ". . . The heaven is My throne and the earth is My footstool" (Isa. 66:1).
> According to the House of Hillel, it is like a king who built a palace; after he built the ground floor, he built the upper stories, as it is written, ". . . on the day when the Lord made earth and heaven" (Gen. 2:4).

As illustrations, these two examples seem at first glance wholly straight forward. Yet in fact they do considerably more than merely illustrate the two Houses' respective views of the order of creation. Each *mashal's* narrative also predicates a different conception of the nature of the created universe and of the God's relationship to it. According to one House, the earth is God's footstool; according to the other, it is His palace.

In literature from the Rabbinic period, one can find other parables of this illustrational kind. But not until post-Rabbinic, early medieval Jewish literature did the use of the *mashal* as an illustration become truly prevalent—initially in the ninth-century composition *Tanna de-Bei Eliyahu,* and even more so in subsequent philosophical works by such authors as Maimonides.[16] For the vast majority of *meshalim* in Rabbinic literature, however, the illustrational model does not offer an adequate description. Most midrashic *meshalim* are far less illustrative than the two examples of the Houses. And even more crucially, the narratives of most *meshalim,* which according to this model are supposed to facilitate and assist their audience in understanding the *mashal's* lesson or its underlying meaning, are actually far more enigmatic and difficult to understand than the *nimshalim* themselves. In these parables, what requires elucidation is the narrative, not the *nimshal* or its lesson. Considered as illustrations, these *meshalim* are horrible failures.

The *Mashal* as Secret Speech

This model, the near opposite of the preceding one, conceives of the *mashal* as a deliberately occluding and concealing mode of language. As such, it resembles the view that identifies the *mashal* with allegory (which is, indeed, what the word *mashal* comes to mean as a technical term in medieval Hebrew). The "allegorical" view itself is first attested in the gospels, in the famous theory of parabolic discourse attributed to Jesus (Mark 4:11–12 and parallels), whereas among modern scholars, it has been most elegantly championed by Frank Kermode, who sees *all* narrative as enigmatic and excluding, having the "property of banishing interpreters from its secret places."[17] For Kermode, the parable is merely a purer, more intense or pristine instance of this general characteristic of narrative.

According to this model, the *mashal* is an intrinsically esoteric form. It is an interpretive shield guarding a secret meaning, separating "insiders" from "outsiders," those who understand from those who do not, and restricting access to its inner comprehension to a select, chosen few.[18] The corollary, often associated with this model of the *mashal,* sees the literary form as one typically used in politically or religiously oppressive situations to express controversial or dangerous beliefs that were better not articulated openly, or could not be, either for political or doctrinal reasons.[19]

The Rabbis themselves would probably have appreciated this conception of the *mashal.* Their own interpretation of Yotham's seditious parable in *Judg.* 9:7–20 treats it as an allegory.[20] And a few other passages in Rabbinic literature corroborate the "secretive" use of the parable. The best example of these is the statement in *Bereishit Rabbah* (22:19), attributed to R. Shimeon b. Yohai, "It is difficult really to express it, and impossible to explain," which prefaces a *mashal* that in effect condemns God for letting Cain kill Abel. But this *mashal* and the few others like it are true exceptions in Rabbinic literature.[21] As a mode of secretive, exclusive discourse, the *mashal* does not emerge in its full shape until the beginning of kabbalistic literature in the early Middle Ages, first in the many enigmatic meshalim preserved in *Sefer Habahir,* and later in the elegant parables found in the *Zohar.*[22] Within Rabbinic tradition, the communicational model for the *mashal* is exoteric, not esoteric. Even where a *mashal*'s message is abiguous or especially subtle and difficult to paraphrase, that message can be "interpreted out" of the *mashal* by any minimally competent reader.

The *Mashal* as Rhetorical Narrative

This model steers a course between the two poles represented in the preceding models; in my view, it is the single one that adequately accounts for *most mashalim* in Rabbinic literature. According to this view, the *mashal* is an allusive narrative told for an ulterior purpose that draws a series of parallels between a fictional story and the actual, "real-life" situation to which the *mashal* is directed.[23] Rather than make those parallels explicit, however, the *mashal* leaves them to its audience to figure out for themselves. This is the inherently hermeneutic character of the form, and no doubt a major reason for the *mashal's* great popularity among the Rabbis. Neither a secret tale with a hidden meaning nor a transparent story with a clear-cut moral, the *mashal* is a narrative that actively elicits from its audience the application of its message—or what we would call its interpretation.

Consider the following mashal from *Vayikra Rabbah* 2:4; its author, R. Berekhyah, was a fourth-century Palestinian sage.

> R. Berehkyah said:
> It is like an elder who had a robe *(ma'aforet)*. He gave his disciple commands, saying: Fold it and iron it and be very careful.
> The disciple asked: My master, O elder! Of all the robes you own, why do you command me only about this one?
> The elder replied: Because that robe is the one I wore the day I was appointed an elder!
> Likewise: Moses said before the Holy One: Master of the Universe! Of all seventy self-ruling nations that you have in the world, you command me only regarding Israel?!
> He replied: For they accepted my sovereignty at Mt. Sinai and declared, "All that the Lord has spoken we will do and we will obey" (Exod. 24:7)

The exegetical occasion for this *mashal,* its prooftext, is Exod. 24:7, which here is understood to be literally an acknowledgment on the part of the people of Israel of *kabbalat 'ol malkhut shamayim*, the acceptance of God's sovereignty. The *mashal's* principal message, however, is not praise of God but of Israel, and that praise is expressed in terms of Israel's uniqueness in God's eyes. Yet this unique status derives, in turn, from the praise, the *doxa*, the special glory, that Israel paid to God—a theme that is raised by the central image in the *mashal's* narrative, the image of the robe. This image, as Saul Lieberman has pointed out, refers to the *ma'aforet*, the special ceremonial robe of office that an elder sage assumed upon appointment.[24] As it is employed in the *mashal*, the image is also a rather bold one, for it suggests that God, too, was not "appointed" to his office until the children of Israel elected Him at Mt. Sinai—a fairly radical theological idea that happens to appear elsewhere in Rabbinic literature.[25] Yet this idea only intensifies the high praise paid to Israel.

The same message of praise informs the exegesis of Exod. 24:7, the *mashal's* prooftext, which culminates the *nimshal* or application of the narrative (the second part of the normative literary form that begins, in the example translated previously, with the word *Likewise*). The full "parabolic" meaning of that exegesis might be paraphrased as follows: even thought the Jews, unlike the seventy gentile nations, do not have an independent or self-ruling political state of their own—a fact that doubtless had a pointed and sad truth for Jews living in Palestine in the fourth century—they are still dearer to God than all the gentile nations because Israel alone accepted God's sovereignty, His law, at Sinai.

Israel's praise in this *mashal* is therefore achieved indirectly through a comparison with the other nations. To that extent, this *mashal* involves a degree of polemic, and if we had to describe its message or theme in a single phrase, we could call it polemicized praise.[26] Most *meshalim* in Rabbinic literature have a comparable rhetorical function. They express thematic messages, but those messages tend to be *phrased* in the terms of either praise or blame, or in a variant of the two: approbation or disapproval; appreciation or disappointment; pleasure or pain. Although praise and blame are not in themselves the *mashal's* meaning, they are its structures of signification, the critical terms in its rhetorical vocabulary. Through praise and blame, the *mashal* communicates its thematic and ideological messages. These messages, though in theory numberless, can in practice be specified rather easily: apologetics; polemics; consolation (often formulated as eulogy, praise of the dead); complaint (blame directed against the *mashal's* addressee, a character usually figuring in the *mashal's* own narrative, for the unfairness of his or her behavior); regret (in which the *mashal's* protagonist reconsiders his or her act of praise or blame); warning (in which the *mashal* anticipates, as it were, its act of blame or praise); and a few others.[27]

In the remainder of this essay, I wish to analyze in detail one *mashal* that, as we shall see, explicitly communicates one message of praise and simultaneously hints at a second message that is closer to blame. The *mashal* is found in *Eikhah Rabbah*, the classical midrash on the Book of Lamentations, as well as in several other sources. Its author, R. Abba bar Kahana, was another fourth-century Palestinian sage. I will first quote the *mashal's* narrative, its *mashal* proper.[28]

R. Abba bar Kahana said:
    It is like a king who married a woman and wrote her a large dowry (*ketubah*). He wrote to her: So many bridal chambers I make for you, so much jewelry I make for you; so much gold and silver I give you. Then he left her for many years and journeyed to the provinces. Her neighbors used to taunt her and say: Hasn't your husband abandoned you? Go! Marry another man.
    She would weep and sigh, and afterwards, she would enter her bridal chamber and read her marriage settelement and console herself. Many years and

days later the king returned. He said to her: I am amazed that you have waited for me all these years!

She replied: My master, O king! If not for the large dowry you wrote me, my neighbors would have led me astray long ago.

The *mashal's* symbolism is nearly all conventional, and does not require elaborate explanation: the king represents God, his consort the people of Israel, the dowry or *ketubah* the Torah.[29] Yet even so, it is important that we not miss the sometimes remarkable use to which these symbols, despite their conventionality, are put in the *mashal.* Consider the helpless consort, a stock figure in some respects but a very unusual character in others. As my wife Kathryn Hellerstein has reminded me, how many other texts in Rabbinic literature— or in ancient literature in general—depict a woman who literally survives through reading or who reads to survive? Or consider the taunts of the neighbors, words that at first glance might appear to be the typical provocations that the wicked neighbors would be expected to use in this kind of narrative genre to arouse the insecurities and fears of a lonely, vulnerable woman. But, in fact, precisely this motif may be the *mashal's* most historically grounded detail. According to Roman law, marriage is by consent, *maritalis affectio,* namely, "the intention to be in the married state." In regard to such intention, the second-century jurist Ulpian specifically discusses cases where husband and wife have lived apart for a long time—exactly as in our *mashal—* and states that if each one has honored the marriage, thay are still married, "for it is not cohabitation which makes a marriage but *maritalis affectio.*"[30] The neighbors in our mashal, however, may be said to raise precisely the opposite possibility: because the king disappeared so suddenly, perhaps he has ababdoned his wife and has no longer been faithful to her. Yet if so, she, the consort, is indeed no longer bound to him in marriage according to the law and would be free to marry another man, as the neighbors encourage her to do. Of course, she refuses this "interpretation" of her husband's absence; however, in the *mashal's* own historical context, the neighbors' "interpretation" may have been the truly more plausible.

As for its rhetoric, the *mashal* is clearly a praise parable. In fact, it is doubled praise. At first, the king praises his wife for remaining faithful to him during the long period of his absence; in response, the consort pays her own praise to the *ketubah* that, she says, gave her the strength to await her husband's return despite her unhappy, isolated situation. That situation is elaborated more fully in the *nimshal:*

Likewise: The nations of the world taunt Israel and say to them: Your God does not want you. He has left you. He has removed His presence from you.

Come with us. We will appoint you to be generals, governors, and officers.

And the people of Israel enter their synagogues and houses of study, and there they read in the Torah, "I will look with favor upon you, and make you fertile . . . I will establish My abode in your midst, and I will not spurn you" (Lev. 26:9, 11), and they console themselves.

In the future, when the redemption comes, the Holy One, blessed be He, says to Israel: My children! I am amazed at how you have waited for Me all these years.

And they say to Him: Master of the Universe! Were it not for the Torah you gave us, in which we read when we entered our synagogues and houses of study, "I will look with favor upon you . . . and I will not spurn you," the nations of the world would have led us astray long ago.

That is what is written, "Were not your teaching my delight, I would have perished in my affliction" (Ps. 119:92). Therefore it says, "This (*zot*) I call to mind; therefore I have hope" (Lam. 3:21).

Our analysis of the *mashal* can begin with its conclusion, the exegesis of Lam. 3:21. In its scriptural context, this verse is spoken by the *gever*, the unnamed male who is both the chapter's protagonist and its speaker. In the chapter's preceding twenty verses, the *gever* has despairingly described how he has been cruelly hunted down and tortured by an all-powerful antagonist whom *we* know to be God but whom the *gever* cannot even bring himself to name. However, in verse 21—the mashal's verse—there is a sudden shift in the *gever*'s lament. For no apparent cause, without any visible motivation, he remembers "this," *zot*, and from that moment on, he begins to recover confidence and regain hope. Now in Lamentations itself, "this"—what the *gever* recalls—is a series of discursive propositions that follow in the subsequent verses. These propositions all concern God's nature—His essential goodness, how His mercies are never spent, how ample is His grace, how good He is to those who trust in Him, and so on—and by recalling then, the *gever* is able to regain hope and confidence.

In the *mashal*, however, the word *zot*, "this," in the verse is interpreted so as to refer not to God but to Torah—specifically to the Torah's promises of redemption, as symbolized in the narrative by the image of the *ketubah* and its promised bridal gifts. To be sure, this interpretation recalls the famous midrash on Deut. 4:44, *vezot hatorah*, "and this is the Torah," which is indeed explicitly quoted in some of the parallel versions of our *mashal*.[31] Yet it is hard to think of another interpretation that could be more revealing of Rabbinic ideology than this one, with its shifting of meaning from God to the Torah as the referent for the demonstrative *zot*. As Alan Mintz has noted, Lam. 3:21 is the pivotal verse in the chapter, the precise moment when the *gever* turns from despair to faith.[32] At precisely this moment, R. Abba's interpretation, with its substitution of Torah for God, virtually sums up the achievement of Rabbinic Judaism in instituting Torah study as the practical and theoretical foundation for Israel's spiritual sustenance in the time of exile, as the replacement for the lost Temple cult, and as the medium of access to the divine will in the aftermath of the Destruction.

This exegesis of *zot* in Lam. 3:21 is only one of several exegetical acts in the *mashal*. In fact, this *mashal* in praise of Torah and its study—in praise of midrash, in other words—is fittingly packed with midrash and with the products of midrash, including references to other *midrashim* and allusions to extra-Biblical *aggadot*. For example, the taunting words that the nations of the world address to Israel in the *nimshal* allude to the famous midrash on Song of Songs 5:9–6:3 found both in the *Mekhilta* (*Shirta* 3, where it is attributed to R. Akiba) and in *Sifre Deut.* (343). Similarly, the verses from Leviticus (26:9, 11), which are cited in the *nimshal*, have a lengthy history of interpretation that can be traced back as early as the Tannaitic collection *Sifra* (*Behukotai* 1:2.5; 1:3.3) where the Rabbis interpreted the verses eschatologically, as blessings to be fulfilled only at the time of the final redemption. And as these verses are invoked in the *nimshal* to comfort the people of Israel, we can assume that R. Abba also intended his audience to understand them as referring to the future redemption (for otherwise the disparity between the dire reality and the promises of the verse would be anything but comforting). As they are cited in the *nimshal*, then, these verses are quoted already in their *interpreted* sense.

Moreover, the *mashal's* central image, the *ketubah*, may itself be an exegetical creation. It is possible that the image derives from a pun on the Hebrew word *vehifreiti*, "I will make you fruitful," in Lev. 26:9, and the Aramaic *parna*, borrowed from the Greek *pherne*, a marriage settlement.[33] This punning etymology would provide a reason for why these particular verses from Leviticus were chosen for the *nimshal*, and it would explain the genesis of the *ketubah* as an image in the *mashal*. And if so, the *mashal* may be said to contain within its narrative the key to its own beginnings as a midrashic act.

Exegesis, though, is not the *mashal's* final intention or its whole purpose. If the verses from Leviticus are to be read eschatologically, as I have suggested, then the narrative in its entirety takes on a new meaning. When the kind, after his lengthy absence, returns to his wife, he may be said—*in narrative terms*—actually to fulfill and realize the promises of Scripture. In other words, the *mashal's* narrative can be seen as dramatizing the coming redemption before its own audience's eyes. The narrative reenacts the scriptural promises. The consolation that the consort is seen to have derived from reading her *ketubah* is thus guaranteed to the *mashal's* contemporary audience. And so, the *mashal* ceases to be simply a parable of praise and turns into a narrative of consolation.

But why should that consolation be necessary in the first place? Why, we might ask, must the poor matron suffer? Why does the king abandon her? Why must she be left alone to her neighbors' persecutions and torments? If her ordeal is a test of faithfulness, why must she submit to such a test when she has done nothing to deserve it?

These questions raise issues that are both theological and historical, and they could be answered accordingly. For our present purposes, however, it will be more appropriate to frame them in narratological terms. In addition to the questions posed above, we might ask, Why does the king suddenly decide to journey to the foreign provinces? Does it ever enter the king's mind that, in his absence, the wicked neighbors will torment his wife and test her? Are the lavish promises he makes in the *ketubah* intended in advance to console her while he is gone? And are his promises sincere? But if they are, then why is he so astonished at her faithfulness? Conversely, if he does not expect the *ketubah* to console his bereft wife, then is there any logical reason for her to remain faithful? Or are his promises disingenuous? Is the king's unexplained absence truly unjustified? Is he perhaps guilty of gratuitous cruelty toward his hapless wife? Is he actually responsible in his own person for the suffering his abandoned wife undergoes in his absence? And why does he finally decide to return?

I have posed these questions not to answer them but to show how all the various doubts contained in them are inevitably raised by the *mashal's* narrative. These doubts point in the direction of a critique of the king's behavior and of the justice of his actions—which is to say, toward a critical interrogation of God and His treatment of Israel. This critique, though never quite explicit in the *mashal*, undercuts the innocent optimism of our earlier "rhetorical" reading of the composition as a praise parable and leads to a second reading of the *mashal*, one closer to complaint than to consolation.

This second reading is connected as well to another anomalous moment in the text, a small but significant discrepancy between the *mashal* and the *nimshal* at a point where their carefully drawn parallels diverge. The *mashal's* narrative, it will be recalled, is related entirely in the past tense: the king journeyed, he returned, he and his wife were happily reunited. At the point in the *nimshal* corresponding to the king's return, however, there is a sudden and unanticipated leap into the future that is signalled by one word, *lemahar.* "*In the future,*" we are told, "when the redemption comes, the Holy One, blessed be He, says to Israel," and so on.[34] For the *mashal's* audience, this discontinuity—between pastness and futurity—can lead only to a single conclusion: genuine consolation, the true fulfillment of the promises in Scripture, will come only at the time of redemption, at the end of history. The return of the king in the *mashal's* narrative was made possible only because fictional narrative, by convention, is narrated in the past tense. But in the realm of historical reality, and as long as that reality—human history—will last, the redemption will always be future. Until it comes to pass, there exist only substitutes for the authentic redemption. Among these substitutes, the foremost is of course the study of Torah, midrash. Yet even study of Torah is not true redemption. It is only a surrogate, a palliative, a band-aid.

In its totality, then, this *mashal* suggests two very different attitudes or meanings that, taken together, produce a message that cannot avoid ambiguity, at least on the interpretive level. To students of literature, the hermeneutical dilemma posed by this ambiguity may be reminiscent of other famous cases of literary ambiguity; Henry James's *The Turn of the Screw*, for example. And as in James's novels, the "solution" to the hermeneutical conundrum posed by this *mashal* lies not in deciding on a univocal reading of the *mashal*—the explicit consolatory reading alone or the implied critique—but in reading both messages simultaneously despite the apparent contradiction between them.

The source of that contradiction and its consequent ambiguity can be explored further. For one thing, its real origins may lie not in the king's behavior but in the consort's. For why, after all, does *she* refuse to question her husband's acts, his loyalty, his faithfulness? Does her insistence on praising the *ketubah* really indicate a need on her part to deny the truth about her husband's cruelty? Is she perhaps constitutionally incapable of seeing how he has mistreated her? Or does she know something that we, the audience of the *mashal,* do not?

Again, these are questions that the *mashal* does not answer, though now not because they are strategically placed in the narrative to intentionally undercut its accepted meaning or its overt message of praise (as with the set of questions raised earlier), but because these questions lie beyond the *mashal's* own ken, the limits of its own comprehension. They are situated precisely at the farthest end of what we might call the *mashal's* theological horizon; indeed, they set its horizon. To appreciate the *mashal,* its audience must take the consort's faithfulness to the king, like Israel's to God, on faith; one cannot question the sincerity of either persona's claim. To be sure, the other ambiguity in the parable—the conflict between the two meanings—persists, and if one were to search for its ultimate cause, it might perhaps be located in the *mashal's* author's own mind, in the unresolved nature of his or her feelings toward God, perhaps in the coexistence of two separate feelings toward God that he could not resolve. But the ambiguity in the consort's mind will not help us understand the *mashal* or its author's mind except to fix the one matter, the one question, that he or she would have found literally unthinkable.

Indeed, rather than try to dissolve the *mashal*'s inner contradiction or search for a psychological or spiritual explanation, one does better to ask, How can the literary form of the *mashal* simultaneously communicate two messages so different and yet related to each other? To answer this question, we must turn to the poetics of narrative in the *mashal* and in particular to two special features of that poetics.

Narrative representation in the *mashal* tends to absolute brevity; in fact, parabolic narrative is often so concise it is like a skeleton or a sketch rather than a fully fleshed-out tale. All but the most necessary details are excluded; and as a result, everything that is said draws the most intense attention. In this concision, the art of narrative in the *mashal* resembles that of the Bible in which, in Eric Auerbach's famous description, virtually nothing is foregrounded whereas the entire background is fraught with meaning. Indeed, this point of resemblance is one of the stronger signs of continuity between the biblical and the Rabbinic literary traditions.

The corollary to this stylistic concision is another characteristic feature of the *mashal*'s narrative poetics; namely, its use of silences, lacunae, omissions, and other intentionally withheld pieces of narrative information, all of which constitute points of discontinuity known, in the technical terminology of narratology, as gaps.[35] Therefore, most of the questions raised earlier about *Eikhah Rabbah* 3:21 relate to gaps in its narrative: to missing links in the story; absent causes or motives; failures at offering satisfactory explanations for an occurence in the plot; contradictions like the discrepancy we noted between the *mashal* and its *nimshal*; and most prominently of all, the discrepancy between its description of God's behavior (as represented in the figure of the king) and our normative conceptions of what God's behavior should be.

Each of these gaps can be described systematically, as I have done elsewhere.[36] But if reading the gaps in the narrative and intepreting their significance constitute the primary hermeneutical activities occupying the *mashal*'s audience, then those activities also have a reflected image within the *mashal* itself. This image is the second feature of the *mashal*'s narrative poetics.

Recent literary theory has familiarized us with the various roles that the reader plays in determining textual meaning. It has also described the different guises through which the figure of the reader can be represented in the fictional structure: the "implied reader," the "narrattee," the "interpretant," and the "interpreting character," a figure who (according to one theoretician) is usually "coextensive with the first-person narrator or the main protagonist of the fiction" and through whom "the author is trying to tell the interpreter [the reader] something *about* interpretation."[37]

In the *mashal,* these various theoretical constructions all coalesce into a figure I call the *implied interpreter:* an idealized character in the *mashal's* narrative who serves as a model for the real interpreter-reader and who guides the latter in the act of reading and interpreting the *mashal's* meaning. Now the implied intepreter is not identical with his or her counterpart in real life. To paraphrase Iser on the implied reader, the implied interpreter is a figure *in the text.*[39] Furthermore, the real addressee will always possess other interpretive resources that he or she will bring to understanding the *mashal:* knowledge of models of coherence (rules of chronology, causality, etc.); of literary conventions (including the stereotyped character of the *mashal's* diction, motifs, and themes); of the hermeneutical conventions of midrash (for example, *kal vehomer, notarikon, gematriyah*). But the implied reader is in most ways an ideal interpreter who possesses all the literary competence needed to understand a *mashal.* As a fictional character, the figure of the implied interpreter literally inscribes the relationship of exegesis and narrative in the *mashal* by joining in his or her single person, or persona, the attributes of both fictionality and interpretation.

To illustrate the implied interpreter's role, we can turn to the *meshalim* already analyzed in this essay. In the first parable from *Vayikra Rabbah* about the elder and his robe, the implied interpreter is less an explicit character than a presence to be inferred from an implied interpretive event, or *scene of interpretation,* in the narrative. The latter is sometimes represented in the form of a recognizable hermeneutical operation like the *kal vehomer,* the argument *a minori ad maius* (from the weaker case to the stronger), or through another kind of identifiable interpretive gesture. At other times, an actual scene is created and represented, as in the *mashal* about the elder. In this case, the elder himself creates a scene of interpretation—by commanding his disciple to do something that the disciple, at least, finds sufficiently extraordinary to require for it an explanation, and then the elder himself becomes the implied interpreter with the disciple as his foil, an interpreter's straight man.

In *Eikhah Rabbah* 3:21, in contrast, the implied interpreter is explicitly represented through the character of the helpless beleaguered consort who consoles herself by reading the promises her absent husband has left her in the *ketubah.* This act, reading the *ketubah,* along with the consort's later explanation (to the king) of its positive effect on her, is about as complete a representation of the implied interpretive event as can be found in any *mashal.* Indeed, in this example, the representation of the implied interpreter may exceed in its significance the interpretation itself. After all, R. Abba bar Kahana could have offered his midrash on the word *zot* as meaning Torah without using a *mashal;* he could have presented it as definition of the demonstrative simply on the basis of Deut. 4:44 (*vezot hatorah*). What the *mashal*'s narrative really contributes is not so much the exegesis of *zot* and not even the dramatization of the fulfillment of the eschatological promises of Leviticus, but a vivid and moving portrayal of the conditions of despair in which the poor abandoned wife finds herself. For it is within these conditions that the *necessity* for the eschatological-consolatory interpretation is born. In presenting this picture of despair and consolation, the *mashal* effectively portrays the history of its own genesis, a narrative of interpretation.

This *mashal*'s narrative is not the only narrative of interpretation to be found in *Midrash*, or even in the *mashal*. But it does sketch the basic lineaments of the story. The narrative invariable begins with a crisis, often marked (as here) by a departure or absence, either literal or figurative. The crisis involves the disappearance not of meaning but of presence (the king's, God's); and it is followed by a growing consciousness on the part of the *mashal*'s characters of the void, the emptiness and irresolution, in which they have been left. If the *mashal*'s narrative reaches a conclusion, the resolution comes through an interpretive event: one that does not aim at discovering meaning in the text but at restoring the absent presence, the guarantor of meaning. Its real aim is the restoration of a feeling of intimacy and relationship with the estranged text, and thereby with God. In this narrative, the purpose that exegesis serves is close to the radical meaning of interpretation as "a presence between," a literal mediator. The act of interpretation, the figure of the interpreter, is primarily a medium of exchange, and the interpreter is most like a translator, one who carries the text across a divide, who negotiates the distance between the text and its felt presence in the reader's life. As *Eikhah Rabbah* 3:21 suggests, interpretation itself is not the end; however, it is the invaluable preparation, the keeper of time before the end.

The narrative of interpretation points to the essential impulse behind the midrashic *mashal:* the desire to represent in and through narrative the special kind of interpretation that midrash constitutes. Yet this representational desire, along with its fulfillment, is predicated on a paradox. Solely by describing the complex, often ambiguous and contradictory nature of human reality, as in the story of a king who abandoned his wife only to return to find her still faithful, were the Rabbis able to give expression to the complexity of their own feelings about God. The *mashal* provided them with the instrument for expressing those feelings.

Notes

1. The text is translated from the critical edition of *Vayikra Rabbah,* ed. M. Margulies (Jerusalem, 1972). For parallels, see *Koheleth Rabbah* 1:3.1, and Margulies's notes *ad loc.* My discussion of this passage, as well as much of the rest of this essay, draws on the far fuller treatment of the Rabbinic *mashal* in my book, *Parables in*

Midrash: Narrative and Exegesis in Rabbinic Literature (Cambridge, Mass., 1991).

2. On Rabbinic fables, see most recently A. Singer's Hebrew article in *Jerusalem Studies in Jewish Folklore*, 4(1983):79–91, and the bibliography cited there. Note as well that the use of 300 for the number of fox-fables Bar Kappara tells is conventional; compare the fox-fable in *Bereishit Rabba (Ber R.)* 78:7, in which its protagonist, a fox, himself recites 300 fox-fables!

3. Note that the Ecclesiastes-like proverb that Bar Kappara writes on R. Shimeon's door is also called a *mashal;* cp. the version of the narrative in *b. Nedarim* 3b.

4. For example, *Ber. R.* 64:9; *b. Berakhot* 61b.

5. For example, *Mekhilta (Bahodesh* 6); *b. Avodah Zarah* 11a and 54b–55a; *b. Rosh Hashana* 17b; and *b. Sanhedrin* 91a.

6. For the *mashal* as a instrument of social politesse: *b. Baba Kama* 60b and 66b; *j. Taanit* 4.5, 66c–d; *b. Taanit* 5b; cp. the story of R. Kahana in *j. Berakhot* 5c. For eulogies, *Abot deR. Natan* A, 14.6; *j. Berakhot* 5b–c;

7. *Semahot deR. Hiyya* 4.1.

8. See, however, the *mashal* of R. Akiba in *b. Niddah* 45a; and *b. Berakhot* 11a for the *mashal* used in the argument between R. Yishmael and R. Eleazar b. Azariah.

9. This is an approximate number based upon the *meshalim* collected by I. Ziegler in his monumental anthology at the back of *Die Königsgleichnisse des Midrasch* (Breslau, 1903) and by R. Johnston in his dissertation, "Parabolic Interpretations Attributed to Tannaim" (1978).

10. *Shir Hashirim Rabbah* 1:8.

11. Ibid.

12. On ideological narrative, see Susan Rubin Suleiman, *Authoritarian Fictions: The Ideological Novel as a Literary Genre* (New York, 1983).

13. See W. S. Kissinger's *The Parables of Jesus: A History of Interpretation and Bibliography* (Metuchen, N. J., 1979). Cp. my critique of more contemporary New Testament scholarship in "Jesus' Parables from the Perspective of Rabbinic Literature: The Example of the Wicked Husbandmen," in *Parable and Story in Judaism and Christianity*, ed. C. Thoma and M. Wyschogrod (New York, 1989), pp. 42–80.

14. For its use in past scholarship about the *mashal*, see Ziegler, *Die Königsgleichnisse* and Tovia Gutmann, *Hamashal Bitekufat Hatannaim* (Jerusalem, 1949).

15. A striking example is in *Ber. R.* 1:1, which portrays God as creator through a description of an architect who builds a palace using a blueprint and an illustration (which symbolize the Torah). In this case, the *mashal* is also about illustration!

16. For example, *Tanna deBei Eliyahu* 18:8. This use of the *mashal* ties in closely with the overall homiletical thrust of the work. For Maimonides, see for one example, *Guide of the Perplexed* Part III, Chap. 51 (The Parable of the Palace).

17. Frank Kermode, *The Genesis of Secrecy* (Cambridge, 1979), esp. pp. 23–47.

18. See J. Bowker, "Mystery and Parable: Mark 4, 1–20," *JTS* N. S. 25 (1974): 300–17.

19. For this view, see David Daube, *Ancient Hebrew Fables* (Oxford, 1973); *The New Testament and Rabbinic Judaism* (New York, 1973), pp. 141–50.

20. *Tanhuma* (ed. S. Buber, Genesis), p. 103.

21. For an additional example, see *Devarim Rabbah* (ed. S. Lieberman), 8:5, p. 110.

22. For example, see *Sefer Habahir* 33 (and compare its Rabbinic model, *Eikhah Rabbah* 2:1) and *Zohar*, II. 99a–b.

23. The definition I have offered is based on W. J. Verdenius, "AINOS," in *Mnemosyne* 15 (1962):389; see also G. Nagy, *The Best of the Achaeans* (Baltimore, 1979), pp. 239, 280–90.

24. Thus Lieberman in his notes to *Vayikra R.* (ed. Margulies), p. 870. Margulies himself differs and defines the *ma'aforet* as a special kind of turban or headdress.

25. See, for example, the other mashal in *Vayikra R.* 2:5, and the remainder of the chapter.

26. Such implied comparative techniques are so common they are virtual conventions of the polemic genre. The most frequent forms are comparisons between two people or things to see who is the most precious (*haviv*), as in *Ber. R.* 30:10 (which compares Abraham and Noah); or the comparison between the one and the many, as in *Tanhuma* (ed. S. Buber), p. 78; or between one person and everyone else, as in *Eikhah R.* 3:24.

27. For apologetic praise, *Eikhah R.* 4:11; apologetic blame, *Midrash Tehillim* (ed. S. Buber), p. 485; for polemic, *Ber. R.* 1:12, and most *meshalim* that begin, "It is the custom of the world," whose purpose is to condemn the pretensions to divinity of the imperial cult; for lament, the parables in notes 6 and 7, as well as *Tanhuma* (ed. Buber; Deut.), p. 13; for complaint, *Eikhah R.* 1:21 and 3:1; for regret, *Ber R.* 5:1; for warning, *Sifre Deut.* 48.

28. The text translated here is that of the Ashkenazic recension of *Eikhah Rabbah;* for the Hebrew, see the critical text I prepared in *Parables in Midrash*, pp. 281–82. Buber's text in his edition of *Eikhah Rabbah*, p. 132, is closest to the Ashkenazic recension, and the text in the Vilna folio edition of *Midrash Rabbah*, p. 26a, is closer to the Sephardic recension (in Parables, p. 283).

29. Note, however, that the *ketubah* in the *mashal* is more like the biblical *mohar* or dowry than the Rabbinic *ketubah;* see Mordechai A. Friedman, *Jewish Marriage in Palestine: A Cairo Geniza Study* (Tel Aviv and New York, 1981), pp. 77, 239–62. In addition to the conventional symbols, note as well that the various motifs used in the *mashal* are nearly all traditional; see my Hebrew article, a much earlier version of this essay, "The Function of the Parable in Rabbinic Literature," *Jerusalem Studies in Hebrew Literature* 7 (1985): 99, n. 33, for discussion of specific parallels.

30. Ulpian, *Digest* 50.17.30; 24.1.32.13; cited and discussed in Susan Treggiari, "Roman Marriage," in *Civilization of the Ancient Mediterranean*, ed. Michael Grant and Rachel Kitzinger (New York, 1988), vol. 3, p. 1345.

31. For more on the interpretation of *zot*, see especially I. Heinemann, *Darkhei Ha-aggadah* (Jerusalem, 1970), p. 188.

32. Alan Mintz, *Hurban* (New York, 1984), pp. 34 ff.

33. I wish to thank Michael Sokoloff for pointing this out to me.

34. In the Sephardic recension, this leap into the future is even more explicit: the verb following *lemahar* is also in the future tense (*kesheyavo*).

35. On gaps, see in particular Meir Sternberg, *The Poetics of Biblical Narrative* (Bloomington, Ind., 1985), especially pp. 186–263.

36. See *Parables in Midrash*, pp. 74–82.

37. The terms quoted are taken from Gerald Prince, "Introduction to the Study of the Narratee," *Reader-Response Criticism*, ed. Jane P. Tompkins (Baltimore, 1980), pp. 7–25; Wolfgang Iser, *The Implied Reader* (Baltimore, 1974); Naomi Schor, "Fiction as Interpretation/Interpretation as Fiction," *The Reader in the Text*, ed. S. R. Suleiman and I. Crosman (Princeton, N. J., 1980), pp. 165–82.

38. See Iser, ibid.

PART III

Medieval Midrash and Exegis:
The Many Ways of *Peshat,*
Remez, and *Sod*

6

The Nature and Distribution of Medieval Compilatory Commentaries in the Light of Rabbi Joseph Kara's Commentary on the Book of Job.*

Sara Japhet

Translated from Hebrew by Jeffrey M. Green

C ompilation, gathering passages from existing works, removing them from their original context, and reassembling them around another subject, thus creating a new text, is a familiar phenomenon found in many literatures. Moreover, the phenomenon of textual interpretation using the method of compilation is also found in the history of exegesis and is widely exemplified by Christian commentaries on Scripture.[1] In the Jewish literary world it is also well exemplified by the compilations of midrashim, which put together the teachings of early and late sages and present them in an order related to the progress of a biblical text.

The presence of this phenomenon in medieval Jewish biblical exegesis was evident from the moment this body of literature began to be studied and discussed. For example, the commentaries on the books of Esther, Ruth, and Lamentations by Jellinek in 1855[2] were immediately recognized as compilations.[3] Further, there are the commentaries on the Torah by the Tosaphists, some of which have been in print since the late eighteenth century, whereas others have remained in manuscript.[4] These were viewed "as a kind of anthol-

*This is an expanded version of an article in Hebrew that is to appear in a jubilee volume in honor of Professor Moshe Goshen-Gottstein. Unless otherwise noted, all quotations from the Bible are taken from the Jewish Publication Society translation.

ogy, for their authors mainly compiled what they had found and heard from their predecessors."[5] However, the use of the term *compilation* to characterize any work implies inherent criticism of the work and depreciation of its value. By its very nature, composition of this sort does not intend to grapple creatively with the written text but rather to cull passages and recombine them. A modern scholar is likely to view such a composition as unoriginal, derivative, and bordering on plagiarism. Therefore, and perhaps for other reasons as well, this literary genre has not been systematically described nor has its place in the history of Jewish biblical commentary been examined. The general introductions that have been devoted to this sphere of literature have not awarded a special place to compilatory compositions and, at most, the matter is mentioned in passing.[6] However, without taking up the question of their evaluation, it is necessary to examine this phenomenon in itself as a legitimate genre of Jewish exegetical literature, to inquire into its origins, to clarify its history, and to determine its place and function in the history of exegesis and literary activity.

We were led to examine the phenomenon of compilatory compositions through a work that did not at first appear to belong to that category at all and that had never been described as such. Moreover, doubts regarding the work's sources and the identity of its author have never been raised. I refer to the commentary by Rabbi Joseph Kara on the Book of Job, a work that has recently been extensively discussed and of which a new scholarly edition has been brought to publication by M. Ahrend.[7] Because our choice of this work may seem somewhat unlikely, we shall first discuss our reasons for choosing it and several aspects of its exegetical character.

I

Rabbi Joseph Kara's Commentary on the Book of Job is marked by certain traits that, to one degree or another, deviate from his other commentaries and that attract the reader's attention on first perusal. We shall mention a number of these traits as the point of departure for our discussion.

1. The first trait, which would seem to be merely external, though its actual significance will become clear later, is the extraordinary length of the commentary. According to Ahrend, it is six times longer than Rashi's commentary on Job, and it is longer than any other known commentary by Kara.[8]
2. Another trait, which at first glance might also appear to be external, though this is not the case, is the presence of hundreds of passages, some short and some long, that are identical to passages

found in other works. According to Ahrend's count, this commentary contains more than 120 passages "which appear both in Rashi's printed commentary and in Rabbi Joseph Kara's commentary on the Book of Job";[9] it has more than 100 passages that are identical with the commentary of Rashbam (Rabbi Shmuel ben Meir) on Job as found in MS Lutzki 778;[10] and it also contains 5 long passages taken from Rabbi Shabbetai Donnolo.[11] This phenomenon, which is surprising and exceptional both in itself and in its details, is unparalleled in Kara's other works.[12]

3. A third trait, with respect to which the commentary on Job also raises grave difficulties, is its position vis-à-vis the Midrash. This position is expressed in various manners: the presence of midrashim in the course of the commentary, the presence of references to midrashic literature such as *Genesis Rabbah, Pesiqta,* and the like, and general statements such as, "this is the literal meaning, and the Midrash is well known" (*zehu peshuto u-midrasho yadu'a*), as well as the use of phrases ordinarily used in midrashic writing.[13] Although Kara's attitude toward the Midrash is complex, demanding detailed examination, nevertheless, this context as well the commentary on Job is a unique phenomenon.

4. An additional trait that departs from everything we know about Kara as an exegete is the extensive reference to linguistic matters that appears in this commentary. All of Kara's commentaries display a certain degree of reference to linguistic matters, mainly semantic discussions, to clarify the meanings of words, phrases, and so forth. What distinguishes the commentary on Job is the relative frequency of such discussions and their exceptional character. For example, they include long discussions of grammatical forms, linguistic analogies, and the like and, in particular, display a considerable broadening of linguistic knowledge and concern, beyond what is generally shown in his commentaries.[14]

5. Kara's commentary on Job contains a large number of expressions and terms that are not typical of his style and found seldom if at all in his other commentaries. Ahrend mentions, for example, a series of terms regularly found in Rashbam but only rarely, or not at all, in Kara, such as "according to the literal meaning of the Bible" (*lefi peshuto shel miqra*), "it is to be interpreted according to its context" (*pitrono lefi 'inyano*), and others.[15]

6. Another peculiar phenomenon are the many instances of rough spots and awkward transitions in the commentary, which especially contrast with the smoothness and clarity generally found in Kara's

commentaries. In these places, the continuity of the commentary may be interrupted, the order of the interpretations may be disrupted, the lemmata may be unnecessarily repeated, and the style may become difficult and unclear, and so on. A partial explanation of these characteristics may be provided by the complex history of the manuscripts and negligent transmission. Nevertheless, their frequency, type, and character make them questionable.[16]

These phenomena belong to various and distinct areas of exegetical activity: the literary character of the commentary, its relation to the sources, its position with respect to the Midrash, its attitude toward the literal meaning of the text, its terminology, the areas of its interest. Together they form a complex array of difficulties that have remained unsolved until now. Approaching these phenomena individually, one might find apparently satisfactory solutions to the separate problems they raise. However, in our opinion these phenomena all belong to a single complex in which they, and others that we have not yet mentioned, are facets of a single structure. The difficulties we have listed are in fact all resolved when we view Kara's commentary on Job from a new vantage point. Before suggesting this solution, however, we shall somewhat expand our discussion of several of the difficulties mentioned previously, primarily the second.

II

We mentioned earlier that more than 100 passages in the commentary are identical, sometimes with very slight changes, to Rashi's commentary on Job in the printed editions.[17] In every one of these passages, Rashi's remarks are included in the unbroken flow of the commentary, without any indication that they are taken from any external source. By contrast, Rashi is mentioned explicitly in five places in the commentary, in various ways; and we shall return to this matter later.[18] As Kara was a younger contemporary of Rashi's and is known to have spent time with him[19] there is no reason to doubt Rashi's influence on Kara, which we would expect to find expressed in his entire exegetical work: the content of the commentary, the methods, the choice of questions and subjects discussed.[20] The relationship between the two scholars may explain Kara's explicit references to Rashi, especially when he differs with him. However, the massive copying of one commentary into a second one is puzzling. It cannot be explained as part of the given structure of influence, and the main difficulty is to determine its motive. It may be assumed that Rashi's commentaries were available to his contemporaries and no less familiar than those of Kara, if not more so. Moreover, their activity within the same geographical area exacerbates this difficulty. Had Kara wished to express agreement with Rashi's commentaries, he could have referred his readers to Rashi himself; and if he wished to include Rashi's ideas and thoughts in his own commentary, it is likely that he would have paraphrased Rashi's main points in his own words. However, repeated, word-for-word copying of passages, without indicating their source, cannot be accounted for in this way. Moreover, even if we concede that authors did not always observe the rabbinical ruling that, "everyone who cites a saying in its author's name brings redemption to the world," can we assume that Rabbi Joseph Kara would have acted in this fashion systematically, without even hinting at it anywhere? And if we add that Kara revered Rashi, this would lead us to expect even more strongly that he would have explicitly stated what he had learned from him, as he does concerning the commentaries of his uncle, Rabbi Menahem ben Rabbi Helbo.[21] Even from the economic point of view this extensive copying is surprising. Parchment, the writing material normally used, was expensive, so why should a commentator have written at length when he was merely copying the words of a contemporary, even one who was senior to him? And, above all, Kara was an independent, creative commentator; and as with all creators, although he was subject to many influences, he approached his task with absolute spiritual independence. Systematic, literal copying is inconsistent with the entire image that Kara projects in his other work.

These questions become more acute when we consider the massive parallelism between Kara's commentary on Job and that of Rashbam. As noted, more than 100 of Kara's interpretations of Job are also found in Rashbam's commentary in MS Lutzki 778.[22] In some instances these parallels are identical, whereas others are close paraphrases of the original. Once Rabbi Shmuel ben Meir is mentioned explicitly, in the commentary to 11:17, to which we shall return. In no other passage is he mentioned, and more significantly, these passages are not presented in a manner indicating that they are taken from another work. The words of Rashbam, like those of Rashi, are completely integrated into the course of the commentary, forming an organic part of it.

The questions that arise from the parallels with Rashi's commentary are particularly pressing here. According to the generally accepted chronology, Joseph Kara was older than Rashbam, and he was apparently his senior colleague. According to the simplistic logic of chronology, Kara's exegetical activity ought to have preceded that of Rashbam, hence it would be impossible for Kara to have copied from Rashbam or even to have been seriously influenced by him. However, lacking precise chronological information, we are unable to determine exactly when Kara and Rashbam wrote their works; and it might be argued that Rashbam's commentary on Job or any other book preceded Kara's commentary on Job, for Rashbam might have composed his commentary as a young man, whereas Kara might have written his in old age. However, even such an assumption cannot explain the massive borrowing from Rashbam so evident in Kara's commentary on Job. Moreover, if Rashbam's commentary had such a great influence on Kara, whether through his written works or through his "interpretations,"[23] why do we find no parallel influence in any of Kara's other commentaries? Ultimately the major question remains unanswered: Why did Kara include entire passages of Rashbam's commentary in his own? Would it not have been sufficient for his readers simply to refer them to that commentary or to present it in brief—if indeed that commentary existed? One way in which Ahrend attempts to account for Kara's massive copying from Rashi is the honor and esteem that Kara felt toward him. Can we also posit a similar attitude on the part of Kara toward Rashbam, who was younger than he? Aside from the difficulty in explaining the phenomenon itself, there is an additional cause for wonder: many of the parallel interpretations found in both Rashbam and Kara refer to the area of language and are characteristic of Rashbam in their exegetical approach, linguistic conception, terminology, and style; and they do not fall within Kara's areas of interest, expertise, or style. Why did Kara quote these interpretations literally, including all their examples, but only in his commentary on Job?

III

All of these puzzling difficulties, which cannot be resolved satisfactorily within the framework of the accepted view of Kara's commentary on Job, can be fully resolved if one takes a different point of departure. That is to say, one must begin with a new understanding of the character and essence of this commentary.

This commentary is generally taken to be a unified and authentic exegetical work, written entirely as we have it by Rabbi Joseph Kara. As Ahrend states explicitly: "The author of this commentary is Rabbi Joseph Kara—and there can be no doubt on this subject."[24] However, this primary and basic assumption must meet the test of criticism. It must not be regarded as self-evident and axiomatic, but rather it must be examined and confirmed in the light of just one piece of evidence: the work itself. To begin this examination, we shall cite a number of passages from Kara's commentary on Job, chosen at random from various points in the work. In citing the passages, we have printed those sections that are literally parallel to Rashi's commentary in bold type, and those that are parallel to Rashbam's commentary in italic. All the rest are unmarked.

A. Chapter 1, verses 1–4.

Verse 1: "Blameless and Upright"—lest you say that he was blameless and upright before other people **but in matters between him and his Creator he was not righteous, therefore it is said, "he feared God."**

Verse 3: *"his possessions were etc."—because in the end everything that he possessed was doubled, therefore the account of his wealth and posession was set down in the beginning.*

"Five hundred yoke of oxen"—that is one thousand oxen. And because they used to drive them in pairs hitched to the plow in yokes as they worked, the Bible used the term "yoke."

"And a very great household"—"shervilia granda" in the vernacular. They are the slaves and maidservants to graze the animals, and so in every place where it mentions the grazing of sheep or cattle, along with that it mentions slaves and maidservants who grazed them, as it is written, "so the man grew exceedingly prosperous."

"Than anyone in the East (qedem)"—of all the men of the east (mizraḥ), for the land of Uz, which is the land of Aram, is in the east of the world, as it is written "Aram from the east (miqedem) and Philistia from the west."

Verse 4: "It was the custom of his sons to hold feasts" . . . this verse is written for you so that you will not wonder when you read about, "one day, as his sons and daughters were eating," etc. and you might wonder what kind of feast it was.

B. Chapter 7, verses 1–2.

Verse 1: "Truly man has a term of service (literally, army) on earth?—a time determined for him to die.

"army"—time; as in "all the time of my service (tzav'i) I wait." Time is called "army" because it has many days, as an army has many men in it. And what gain is there in speaking with iniquity in his tongue? **"And like the days of a hireling"—like someone who has been hired for a year and knows that the days of his hiring will end, so too he knows that the years allotted to him will end,** and how shall I not fear the day of death when my lips shall speak iniquity?

Verse 2: "Like a servant who longs for [evening's] shadows, and like a hireling who waits for his wage"—this is the beginning of the matter; it is not connected to the preceding matter, but to the next one, and this is its meaning: like a slave who looks forward [to the day's end, thinking:] 'when will the evening shadow fall that I may rest from my work?'; and like a hired person who hopes for the wages for his work.

C. Chapter 7, verses 12–16.

Verse 12: "Am I the a sea?"—**that you have set sand to watch him.**

"or the Dragon"—a big fish that you imprisoned in the depths of the sea.

"that you have set a watch over me"—that you ordered: "only spare his life?" give him permission not to guard my soul so that I can die.
Verse 13: "When I think"—this is in the present. When I console myself and say, "my bed (*'arśi*) will comfort me," this is my bed, that I will lie on my bed and rest from my illness.

"My couch will share my sorrow (*śiḥi*)**—my couch at night will suffer my grief a little and I will be able to prevent my talking** (*śiḥi*). It is of no use at all, because you break me in dreams, as he goes on to say:
Verse 14: "You frighten [literally: break] me with dreams," therefore
Verse 15: "I prefer strangulation" [and also] and choose death rather than the existence of my bones.
Verse 16: **"I am sick of"** life for I shall not live forever.
Verse 15: "*strangulation*" (*maḥanaq*)—a noun.
Verse 16: **"let me be"—from doing harm to me, because vanity and few are my days.**

The foregoing passages are a random selection from the commentary and speak for themselves. They draw a clear portrait of a *compilatory commentary* composed of various sections taken literally from different sources and presented sequentially. Occasionally the sequence is coherent, and occasionally the fit is rough, contradictory, and jumpy.

At this stage, and on the basis of our foregoing remarks, it is possible to identify four components of the sections cited earlier: Rashi's commentary on Job and Rashbam's commentary on Job, on the one hand, and "all the rest," which appears to be composed of two components, on the other hand. The latter two components are Kara's commentary on Job and the remarks of the compiler. That is to say, one must make a primary distinction between the compilatory work that is in our possession and that, for lack of another title, we shall continue to call the "Kara Commentary on Job," though in quotes, and the original work by Joseph Kara, his commentary on Job, to which we shall return and discuss later. This general statement regarding the "four components" demands a number of explanatory and qualifying comments:

1. The comparison with Rashi's commentary must be incomplete, as it is based on the edition of "Miqraot Gedolot," and this comparison might be altered to some degree, were there a scholarly critical edition of this commentary. However, given the large number of manuscripts and the lack of fundamental research in this area, we have no alternative.[25]

2. The manuscript containing Rashbam's commentary on Job, Lutzki 778, has not yet been published, and the version has not yet been sufficiently examined. Therefore, we have been cautious in relying

on it. For example, the compiler responsible for our commentary might have possessed a superior and more complete manuscript of Rashbam's commentary, so that additional sections of the "Kara Commentary on Job," which bear Rashbam's characteristic stamp but which do not appear in the Lutzki manuscript, could have been taken from the original Rashbam commentary. Perhaps it will be possible to identify those passages once our ability to distinguish among the components of the work has been developed. In any event, their attribution will always be conjectural.

3. Defining the components of the material that are not parallel to Rashi and Rashbam remains the most problematic task. We stated previously in a general way that there are two components: Kara's commentary on Job and the remarks of the compiler. However, it is by no means easy to identify them with precision. First of all, Kara's original commentary on Job is not extant, so we must reconstruct it, insofar as this is possible, from the present work; and this might lead to circular reasoning. Conversely, there are a considerable number of manuscripts of the present compilatory work, and the differences among them are quite numerous. The oldest and "best" of these manuscripts date from the late thirteenth century, and even the copyists responsible for them "worked quickly, abbreviating and skipping, and they made many errors."[26] This situation forced Ahrend to produce his edition in eclectic fashion, which distances us even further from the "Kara Commentary on Job," and certainly from its sources. Moreover, it seems likely that additional elements have entered this material, such as expansions on the commentary, illustrative verses, remarks of late copyists, and perhaps also sections of works that are no longer extant. Very few of these components are explicitly documented in the work,[27] and the presence of others can be proven by a comparison of the manuscripts,[28] though it is doubtful whether it will be possible to achieve clear and precise distinctions among all of these. This problematic situation is, in itself, a factor in our understanding of the character of the commentary and the phenomenon it represents, but makes it difficult to arrive at a definite identification of the material and to categorize its sources.

Even as we take these comments into consideration and bear in mind the limitations they entail, nevertheless they cannot hide or even blur the character of this work and its goal. Starting from a point of departure that defines the work as a "compilatory commentary," we shall attempt to examine its character and the manner of its composition and to bring out its author's goal and the background of his activity.

IV

A full and precise investigation of the composition of this commentary would be beyond the scope of the present study, and we can offer only a number of guidelines. Our discussion follows two courses: the examination of separate blocs of the text, and the broad survey of the full work. Let us begin, therefore, by examining the author's method in the selected passages we have presented previously.

The author begins his commentary on Chapter 1 with a passage from Rashi's commentary to the words, "Blameless and Upright:" "lest you say that he was blameless and upright before other people but in matters between him and his Creator he was not righteous, therefore it is said, 'he feared God.' " Both the choice of the interpretation and its version are of interest. Rashi's commentary on Job 1:1 does not begin with the passage quoted here but rather ends with it. Rashi begins his commentary with a discussion of the identity of Job and his land or origin, he passes on to other matters, and only at the end of the discussion of verse 1 does he discuss the expression, "blameless and upright." Our author skipped the first, long part of Rashi's commentary and chose instead to discuss Job's origin by means of the commentary of Rashbam on verse 3 (see later). In any event, he chose to begin his commentary with a passage taken from Rashi.

With respect to the wording, the printed editions of Rashi's commentary begin in the middle of the sentence, "but in matters between him and his Creator . . ." and so forth, and the opening sentence is missing. This is not, however, the case with the version cited here, which opens directly with a full sentence, "lest you say that he was blameless and upright before other people but in matters . . ." It is therefore possible that the version found in this work is closer to the original version of Rashi's commentary than that which is found in the printed editions.

The commentary passes from verse 1 to verse 3, taking the comment from Rashbam. In MS Lutzki 778 the commentary on this verse is structured on five lemmata. The first one ("his possessions were") introduces an interpretation of the entire verse, the main thrust of which is an answer to the question of why such a detailed description of Job's wealth was presented.[29] Afterward Rashbam discusses four exegetical details in the following order: "and five hundred yoke of oxen," "household," "wealthy," and "than anyone in the East." The author of the "Kara Commentary on Job" took Rashbam's commentary as he found it, according to its order and its lemmata. However, he did not accept Rashbam's view on the word *'avudah* ("land to cultivate and plow and sow"[30]), but rather he preferred the explanation: "They are the slaves and maidservants to graze the animals." Therefore he interrupted Rashbam's commentary and inserted a different interpretation of the word *'avudah*, which might be that of Joseph Kara. We have seen a similar interpretation in the anonymous commentary brought to publication by Wright, where two opinions are presented: "and this is to mention 'household' following 'cattle' . . . because the owner of cattle could not be without slaves and maidservants and shepherds to drive them, and it did not mention his wealth in land."[31] In the process, Rashbam's short commentary on the word *wealthy* is also dropped. The author passed on directly to the comment on "than anyone in the East," which he also quotes word for word from Rashbam's commentary, and with that he concludes discussion of this verse. It should be noted that, with regard to its meaning, there is no difference between Rashi and Rashbam regarding the word *East*, and both of them interpret it as "Aram." However, the interpretation appearing in our work follows Rashbam and not Rashi in three respects. It appears in the same place in the course of the commentary, it is introduced by the same lemma, and it is copied word for word.

The author takes the commentary on verse 4 from Kara's commentary on Job. Neither Rashi nor Rashbam comment on this verse, and the commentary presented here is entirely in keeping with Kara's exegetical method, in its context, its language, and its wording.[32]

Our author begins the commentary to chapter 7 with that of Kara, as it happens, but after interpreting the first phrase, he presents a remark of Rashbam regarding the word *army*, and finishes it with an additional short sentence. However, the amalgamation is not quite successful. The sequence that emerges is not coherent, and it is evident that the inclusion of the citation from Rashbam has interrupted the original flow. The words, "And what gain is there in speaking with iniquity in his tongue?" are presented after the commentary on *army*, but they are connected to it neither by content nor syntax. Such an interruption is a considerable departure from Joseph Kara's usual style, for his language is normally flowing and the biblical text and his own commentary are organically interconnected. Indeed, if we remove the citation from Rashbam and reconnect Kara's remarks, we find that the subject matter and syntax of the original are quite coherent: "Is there not an appointed time (literally, army) to man upon earth?—a time determined for him to die. And what gain is there in speaking with iniquity in his tongue?" According to Kara's literary perception, 7:1 is a direct continuation of 6:30, and concludes the passage, whereas 7:2 takes up a new matter, as he says: "This is the beginning of the matter, and it is not connected to the preceding matter but to the next one, and this is its meaning."

However, before passing on to the commentary on verse 2, the compiler completes his interpretation of verse 1 with a passage taken from Rashi, which fits the interpretation of *army* as "an allotted time." He added to Rashi's words: "and how shall I not fear . . . my lips shall speak iniquity?" In the latter phrase we have a sudden transition from third person to first person, and it is close in spirit to Kara's commentary. Therefore it might be that Rashi's commentary on "And like the days of a hireling" replaced Kara's original interpretation, leaving Kara's conclusion isolated and incomprehensible.

A somewhat similar technique occurs in the following quoted section, 7:12–16. Rashi's commentary on verse 12 is structured on three lemmata, which, taken together, constitute the entire verse: "Am I the sea—or the Dragon—that you have set a watch over me?" Rashbam, however, relates only to the third of them. The compiler took the commentary on the first two lemmata from Rashi, although taking the third from Rashbam.

In content the commentaries of Rashi and Rashbam on this part of the verse are similar, though Rashi is satisfied by identifying the "watch" with Satan with a mere allusion to Job 2:6. Rashbam, by contrast, quotes the verse explicitly, and significantly, his remarks respond to the stylistic and literary quality of the verse. Because Job's words are expressed as a rhetorical question, "Am I the sea or the Dragon?" Rashbam presents their meaning as a positive desire: "give him permission not to guard my soul so that I can die." The compiler preferred this interpretation to Rashi's version.

In verse 13 Rashi's commentary is concentrated on a single lemma: "My couch will share my sorrow." He makes no comment on verse 14, and his commentary on verse 15 is linked to the lemma, "death to my wasted frame." His commentary on verse 16 hinges on two lemmata: "I am sick" and "let me be." Rashbam's commentary on these verses includes a paraphrase of verse 14 and a few linguistic details in verses 13–15, which are interpreted with great brevity ("when I think," "it will share," "you frighten me," "strangulation"). The compiler, however, passed over Rashbam's commentary on verses 13 and 14 and chose to begin his commentary on verse 13 with Kara's words: "when I think." He interpolated Rashi's commentary within them: " 'My couch will share my sorrow' . . . to prevent my talking." Indeed the secondary insertion of Rashi is immediately evident, for the syntax of the sentence is not entirely clear. In contrast, if we remove the quotation from Rashi, the syntactic continuity of the sentence is clear and excellent: "When I console myself and say, 'my bed will comfort me,' this is my bed, that I will lie on my bed and rest from my illness. . . . It is of no use at all, because you break me in dreams."

Moreover, after the removal of the quotation from Rashi, the commentary on verses 13–15 is shown to be unified and complete, a fitting and coherent interpretation, clearly revealing Kara's method. The commentary is not split up by lemmata but smoothly structured, with the biblical text and the interpreting comments forming a single, coherent unit. The passage also contains expressions that are normally used by Kara to bind his commentary together: "as he goes on to say (*kemo shemefaresh veholekh*)," and "therefore (*lefikhakh*)."[33] The reconstructed commentary of Joseph Kara to verses 13–15 would therefore read as follows:

> "When I think"—this is in the present. When I console myself and say, 'my bed (*'arśi*) will comfort me,' this is my bed, that I will lie on my bed and rest from my illness, it is of no use at all, because you break me in dreams, as he goes on to say: 'You frighten [or, break] me with dreams.' Therefore 'I prefer strangulation' and also choose death rather than the existence of my bones."

After this passage, the compiler once again returns to Rashi's commentary, presenting his interpretation of verse 16 with its two lemmata, but he inserts Rashbam's commentary on verse 15 between them (on the word *maḥanaq*), creating a kind of repetition that is shown by the ordering of the text in the Ahrend edition.

Thus we find that in this passage the compiler took almost all of Rashi's commentary. In verse 12 he preferred Rashbam's commentary for one lemma, and in verse 15 he preferred that of Kara. The compiler took all of Rashbam's commentary on verses 12 and 15, though he did not use his comments on verses 13 and 14. Kara's commentary is represented here by the continuous passage commenting on verses 13–15, in which a unit from Rashi's commentary was inserted. It can be only a matter of speculation as to whether the original Kara commentary also included comments on verses 12 and 16, which were not included in the present work.

These examples are but a small sample of the prevailing phenomenon in the "Kara Commentary on Job," but even this small sample raises several significant points:

1. The compiler who assembled this work removed the names of all the authors he cited. He copied entire passages, word for word, from the works of Rashi, Rashbam, and Kara without mentioning their names and without indicating his sources.
2. Similarly, the compiler indicated nothing at all about himself. He did not identify himself by name, he did not state that he accepts or disagrees with certain teachings, and he generally refrained from polemical remarks.

3. Generally the compiler assembled his commentary as a single, flowing composition; and he attempted to endow it with uniformity. He combined the interpretations that he took from the works that lay before him in as organic a fashion as possible, filling in the gaps in one commentator with remarks taken from another. He generally presented a single commentary on every topic and attempted to avoid repetition. He rarely presents parallel interpretations, that is to say, alternative explanations of a single matter, though these do occasionally appear, introduced by the phrase, "another matter." In those cases the compiler apparently found that the remarks of two commentators were apt, so he decided to present them both.[34] Although the compiler endeavored to achieve coherence and homogeneity, he did not always succeed. This kind of failure is a perennial problem typical of compilatory works, a constant feature betraying the character of the work and the nature of its composition.

V

What is the position of the "Kara Commentary on Job" within the broader phenomenon of "compilations" among the *Peshat* exegesis of Scripture in Northern France? As we noted, this phenomenon has not received scholarly attention; nevertheless, we may examine certain aspects of the question by comparing this work to a number of similar works which clearly belong to this genre. In the compilatory commentaries on the books of Esther, Ruth, and Lamentations,[35] constant, though not full, reference has been made to the sources from which these commentaries are taken, which include Rashi, Rashbam, and Kara. The commentaries on Esther and Lamentations seem to comprise solely the interpretations of Rashbam and Kara, whereas the commentary on Ruth also includes Rashi's commentary, and they are indicated as follows: "Rabbi Shlomo, Rabbi Shmuel, and Rabbi Yossi.[36] By indicating his sources, the author makes his method clear to his reader, though he does not trouble to explain it in an introduction. By contrast, the Hizzekuni commentary on the Torah does not indicate its sources at all while citing them.[37] However, Rabbi Hezekiah ben Rabbi Manoah, the author of this commentary, presents his position regarding this question, as well as his method, in a poem that introduces his work:

And I wandered through many countries to find comments on the Five Books, discovering commentaries of different types, as many as twenty. And, according to my ability, I plucked their best part from them. . . . To find words of precious value and peace, like a column of turquoise, sapphire and diamond. . . . Thus my kidneys advised me, and also my heart filled me . . . to conceal the source of the words.[38]

Although Hizzekuni presents himself to his readers in full pomp and circumstance,[39] the commentaries on Ruth, Esther, and Lamentations are similar to the "Kara Commentary on Job" in that they do not state the names of their author or authors.

We possess only partially the sources of the compilatory commentaries to Ruth, Esther, and Lamentations; and the question of their authenticity has not been entirely resolved.[40] Because of this problem, we shall focus our discussion on the commentary to the Book of Ruth, where indications of the sources are relatively plentiful, and we also possess the complete commentaries of Rashi and Kara.

The comparison between the compilation and its sources shows a clear difference between the attitude of the compiler to Rashi, on the one hand, and to Kara, on the other. The compiler took only a few passages from Rashi's commentary, whereas he borrowed Kara's commentary in full and word for word.[41] Because we do not possess Rashbam's commentary on Ruth, we cannot determine the relative extent of borrowing from him, but in any event the number of his explanations is not great. It therefore seems likely that the compilatory commentary on Ruth is basically an expansion upon Kara's commentary. Its foundations are Kara's full commentary, and it is expanded by the addition of interpretations by Rashi and Rashbam. Similarly, the compilatory commentary on Esther contains the Kara commentary on that book almost in full, with only a few sentences missing.

Seeing this characteristic of the compilatory works on Ruth and Esther, a question arises regarding the "Kara Commentary on Job." Is this work also composed in the same manner? Should we explain its relation to Kara's original commentary on Job similarly? As we do not possess the original commentary, we cannot, of course, answer that question unequivocally, but there can be no doubt that the most extensive component of the "Kara Commentary on Job" is in fact Kara's original commentary. Long sections of the work present Kara's teachings in a single continuous flow, sometimes completely foregoing the principle of compilation. For example, in Chapter 8 we find an uninterrupted, continuous passage that clearly and distinctly reflects Kara's exegetical approach, his language, and his terminology. That chapter includes just one short passage taken from Rashi (on verse 4) and two short passages from Rashbam (referring to verses 6 and 21). This phenomenon is repeated in other chapters, such as 12 and 13, and the reader of those chapters would seem to be on firm footing in attributing these chapters to Kara. However, the work presently under discussion cannot be viewed as a precise parallel with the compilatory commentary on Ruth, and we cannot assume that it contains Kara's commentary in its entirety. The passages included from the commentaries of Rashi and Rashbam are considerable in extent and refer to long passages in the Book of Job. We have seen earlier that the compiler attempted as much as possible to create a continuous and flowing commentary, and he generally avoided presenting parallel interpretations of the same matter. If we assumed that the present work presents Kara's interpretation in its entirety and that the commentaries of Rashi and Rashbam merely complemented and expanded it, then we would have to conclude that, where the other commentators are presented, Kara had nothing at all to say. However, it is more likely that in those cases the author preferred Rashi's or Rashbam's commentary and simply omitted that of Kara. Moreover, if this work did contain Kara's commentary in full, after removing the sections taken from Rashi and Rashbam, we should be left with a perfect sequence, harmonious in all its details, and this is not the case. What remains is lacking in substance, on the one hand, and in continuity, on the other. We are forced to conclude that, despite the prominence of Kara's commentary in this work, it does not include his complete commentary on Job.

The comparison between the compilatory commentaries on Esther, Lamentations, and Ruth and their sources also shows that in general the compiler presented the commentator's words as he found them, juxtaposing them without adding anything of his own. As noted, this practice cannot be completely verified because certain sources are no longer extant, and also because of the condition of the manuscripts that we do possess. Nevertheless, it is evident that the author of the commentary on Esther added nothing of his own, and little more than a few sentences can be attributed to the author of the commentary on Ruth.[42] Was this also the practice followed by the author of the "Kara Commentary on Job," or did he assume a larger role in combining the chosen passages by adding connectives and explanations of his own? Because at present it is impossible to identify the compiler's hand, we cannot answer this question, though it is possible that a more precise examination of the compiler's work could shed light on his personality and methods and thus pave the way to an answer to this question.

Vernacular glosses present a problem in its own right. Kara's original commentary on Ruth, of which we possess a manuscript and the Hübsch edition, does not contain vernacular glosses. By contrast, the compilatory commentary on Ruth, in the passages that are exactly parallel to those in Kara, in the passages that are exactly parallel to those in Kara, contains several vernacular glosses of this kind.[43] How is this difference to be explained? Are we to assume that the vernacular glosses were a component of Kara's original commentary on Ruth, and that their absence in the manuscript and in the Hübsch edition is a result of excision by a later copyist, who was perhaps working outside of France, so that the French glosses were meaningless to him; or on the contrary, should we assume that the manuscript correctly reflects the text of the commentary and that the vernacular glosses were a secondary addition, made either by one of the copyists of Kara's commentary on Ruth or by the compilatory author? This question touches on the general issue of the origin and history of vernacular glosses and is particularly important with respect to anonymous compositions, for vernacular glosses are a primary form of evidence used in determining their origin and date.[44] The "Kara Commentary on Job" is quite rich in vernacular glosses.[45] Some of these are found in the passages parallel to Rashi and Rashbam, though occasionally the same glosses are absent in these passages in their original context, and glosses are even more common in the other parts of the work. Is their source the original Kara commentary on Job? Is it in other works? Are they the compiler's work? Or were they perhaps contributed by later scribes?[46] The issue of the glosses demands a separate discussion, and we can do no more than draw attention to it here.

Another aspect of the manner of this work's composition becomes clear on examination of the placement of the selected passages in the final work. According to the traditional division into sections, the Book of Job is divided into thirty-seven open and closed sections, most of which fit the inner literary structure of the work and its division into speeches.[47] An examination of the structure of the commentary according to the division into sections shows that the compiler clearly preferred to begin the sections with commentary by Rashi and Rashbam and later to pass over to the interpretations of Kara. However, there is no complete consistency or uniformity in this matter. Sometimes the commentary begins with Rashi and continues with Rashbam, sometimes vice versa, and occasionally it opens with one of the two without the other.[48] A dual factor seems to account for variations in the order of the material and deviations from the structural principle: on the one hand, there are the constraints of the sources available to the author, which did not always contain interpretations of the opening verse of a section, and on the other hand, there were constraints related to the material itself and the author's agreement with the commentators whose remarks he chose. Despite this variety and lack of uniformity, a principle of composition seems to be at work here that led to the concentration of material borrowed from the commentaries of Rashi and Rashbam in the beginning of the sections, though not only there. A different principle of compilation is evident in the compilatory commentary on Ruth. Although the work contains Kara's commentary in full, it opens with a passage from Rashbam's commentary and concludes with one from Rashi, and in fact the final words of the work are "The Rabbi Shlomo," which indicates the status and authority of Rashi's and Rashbam's commentaries, although the author is closer in spirit to Joseph Kara, from whom he took most of his work.

VI

A clear, correct view of the genre of the "Kara Commentary on Job"—that is to say, a compilation of passages taken from existing commentaries and not an original work by a single author—necessitates a change in the angle from which this work is to be viewed, but at the same time provides the key for its understanding. Precisely those aspects of the work that had at first seemed puzzling, posing a long series of difficult questions, have now become understandable, even self-explanatory, because of this change in perspective. The expectation of uniformity and inner coherence, on the one hand, and, on the other hand, the desire to discover the exegetical method and literary personality of a single commentator now give way to an examination of the sources of the work, the principles and methods behind their assembly, the spiritual assumptions guiding this kind of literature, and the question of the place of this genre in the history of Jewish exegesis and the historical background against which it was created and flourished.

For example, an issue that has long concerned scholars of Rabbi Joseph Kara has been that of his attitude toward rabbinical literature in general and particularly to Midrash. He is known to have sharply denounced midrashic commentary, saying, "Anyone who does not know the literal meaning of the Bible and who turns himself towards the Midrash is like someone flooded by the rapids of a river and inundated by the depths of the water, who grasps at whatever comes to hand to save himself."[49] Anyone who attributes the "Kara Commentary on Job" to Joseph Kara confronts a grave problem on that score. Not only does this work make relatively frequent reference to rabbinical literature and include midrashim, but it also takes a positive and nonpolemical view of Midrash.[50] However, the moment we define the work as a compilation, this difficulty becomes more apparent than real, for there is no reason to assume that its positive attitude toward Midrash represents Kara. The compilatory author of the commentary also inclines toward literal interpretation, as we see from the character of the work as it stands, but his attitude to Midrash was undoubtedly more moderate than that of Kara. Moreover, the compiler found many of the references to rabbinical literature and Midrash in the commentaries he used, primarily that of Rashi, and references to rabbinical sources thus passed into his work along with the passages he assembled from his sources. Thus, for example, the reader is directed to *Targum Jonathan* on the Prophets three times in this work, and all three of the passages are taken word for word from Rashi.[51] Many of the references to the Mishnah were also introduced into the work with Rashi's commentary, and a detailed analysis of these references shows that, among the references to mishnaic sources, only the affinity with the Ethics of the Fathers is attributable to Kara.[52] The expression, "in the language of the Talmud," which is not common in Kara, is found once in this work (in the commentary on 41:15), in a passage taken word for word from Rashbam's commentary on Job, where the expression "in the language of the Talmud" and similar ones are repeated several times.[53] The only reference in our work to *Avot de-Rabbi Natan* (in the commentary on 31:1) is taken directly and literally from Rashi: "Such was Job's righteousness that he never laid eye on a single woman, . . . as is explained in *Avot de-Rabbi Natan.*"[54]

The foregoing are meant only as examples. Other references to rabbinical teachings and Midrash may derive from another source. The commentary contains only two references to the Jerusalem Talmud: "in the Jerusalem Talmud they say" (37:11), "and thus it is explained in *Genesis Rabbah* and in tractate *Berakhot* of the Jerusalem Talmud" (37:18). The first of these references is erroneous,[55] and both of them are likely to be additions made by the compiler or later copyists. This is doubtless the case with respect to expressions like, "this is the literal meaning, and the Midrash is well known," "the Midrash is common parlance," "its Midrash is in *Baba Batra*," and the like.[56] A precise analysis of all the versions of this work and of its sources is likely to bring us to clearer awareness of the compiler's attitude toward Midrash and rabbinical sources[57] and, in its wake, to a clarification of the various attitudes toward the Midrash among different circles of medieval commentators. However, it is doubtful whether we can learn about the attitudes of the men whose commentaries were collected here, including Rabbi Joseph Kara, from these compilations. The passages of which he is indubitably the author could assist us in answering this question, but the picture will always be a partial one.

VII

We have indicated that among the characteristics typical of the "Kara Commentary on Job" should be mentioned the omission of any indication of the author's names and the effort for maximal integration of the collected interpretations. How then can we explain certain explicit references to early sources and works that are, nevertheless, found in the commentary? Indeed, they are not numerous: Rabbi Menahem the son of Rabbi Helbo is mentioned eighteen times; Rashi is mentioned five times; Rabbi Shabbetai Donnolo is mentioned five times; Rabbi Menahem ibn Saruq is mentioned twice; Dunash the son of Labrat is mentioned four times; Ha-Masoret Ha-Gedolah is mentioned twice; and nine different authors are each mentioned once—Rabbi Saadia, Rabbi Joseph Kara, Rashbam, Eleazar Ha-Kalir, Rabbi Moshe Ha-Darshan; Moshe the son of Rabbi Yehoshua; Rabbi Yizhak the son of Rabbi Meir of Narbonne; Rabbi Eliezer Ha-Gadol the son of Rabbi Yizhak; and Rabenu Kalonymus.[58]

Some of these references were found by the compiler in the commentaries he assembled. One of the two references to Menahem ibn Saruq is an exact quotation of Rashi's commentary to 24:19. Two of the four references to Dunash are taken literally from Rashbam's commentary to Job (28:11 and 30:17), and in the third, to 31:11, the commentary is taken from Rashbam, but the words, "thus Dunash resolved it," are missing in the Lutzki manuscript, though they might have been found in the version used by the compiler. Hence only the fourth reference to Dunash, where he is mentioned together with Menahem, in the commentary to 15:27, is not found in extant versions of either Rashi or Rashbam.

Ha-Masoret Ha-Gedolah is mentioned twice in our commentary: once in a section identical to Rashbam's commentary (29:18), and once in a section taken from Rashi (31:7).[59] Rabbi Moshe Ha-Darshan is mentioned in a passage taken from Rashi (36:1), and Rabbi Eleazar Ha-Kalir is referred to in a long passage drawn from the writings of Rabbi Shabbetai Donnolo, and that is apparently its source. Consequently one may assume that other references, too, the sources of which we are unable to verify, were already present in the text the compiler used. Primary among these is Rabbi Joseph Kara's reference to himself in the first person, which is found in the interpretation of 15:31: "And I, Joseph son of Rabbi Shimon did not hear it in that way, but that is the way it was explained by Rabbi Menahem the son of Rabbi Helbo, my father's brother." This reference is apparently taken from the original commentary on Job by Kara.[60] The numerous other references to Menahem the son of Rabbi Helbo also seem to be taken from Kara's commentary, and in four of them he is indeed called "my father's brother," which is what Kara also calls him in other works of his.[61] Regarding the other men mentioned in this work, we cannot determine whether they were mentioned in Kara's original commentary, in passages culled from other works, or by the compiler himself.

The explicit references to Rashi and Rashbam pose a separate question in their own right.[62] The compiler took hundreds of interpretations from Rashi and Rashbam without mentioning their names at all. Why then are they mentioned in six places? The answer emerges from an examination of the text, in which it is possible to discern three distinct phenomena.

First, four of the five references to Rashi were taken by the compiler with the passages he assembled. In three cases the wording is virtually standard: "I saw in the interpretations of Rabbi Shlomo, . . . and there is a great response to it" (18:2); "thus did I see it in the interpretations of Rabbi Shlomo, of sacred memory, but Rabbi Menahem the son of Rabbi Helbo my father's brother explained it . . ." (22:20); "and I saw it in the interpretations of our Rabbi Shlomo of sacred memory, . . .and that interpretation cannot possibly be . . ." (17:6)—and all three cases conform with the approach of Rabbi Joseph Kara.[63] These three references to Rashi's commentary thus were taken by the compiler with passages from Kara's commentary on Job. Rashi is mentioned in a different fashion in the interpretation of 27:6: "and Rabbi Shlomo the son of Rabbi Yizhak interpreted, . . . but it is not possible to say so." This passage is taken word for word from Rashbam's commentary on Job, including the difference of opinion with Rashi. However, in the Lutzki manuscript it is worded: "and the statement of the *Contairs* (Hebrew, *quntres*) is not possible," in keeping with Rashbam's other references to Rashi.[64] In the work under discussion, however, the reference to the *Contairs* is explicitly identified by the name of its author, "Rabbi Shlomo ben Rabbi Yizhak." With respect to the substance of the issue, however, as before, both the difference of opinion with Rashi and the explicit reference to him are taken from the work used by the compiler, Rashbam's commentary on Job.

Second, Rashi is mentioned in this work once more, at the end of Chapter 7. There a quotation from Rashi's commentary to 6:13–14 is introduced by the words, "And in the interpretation of our Rabbi Shlomo the son of Rabbi Yizhak I found." In contrast to the passages mentioned previously, where Rashi is cited in order to differ with him, here we have a long, word-for-word citation, presented without demurral. The way in which it is presented would seem to parallel the compiler's method, for he also presents the commentators' words as he finds them. However, in contrast to the compiler's approach, this section stands outside the flow of the commentary. It is not cited to interpret 6:13–14 but rather at the end of chapter 7. Moreover, one of the matters clarified by this passage had already been taken directly from Rashi and presented in its correct context, as an interpretation of 6:14: " 'He who withholds kindness from a friend' (RSV)—anyone who prevents pity from his friend and loathes it." Thus it seems that this quotation is a departure both from the methods of Joseph Kara and Rashbam, who mention Rashi briefly in order to dispute with him, and also from that of the compiler, who assembles the passages he has collected in their appropriate place and context, without mentioning their authors. This quotation must therefore be viewed as a late addition to the work made by a copyist.

Third, the sole reference to Rashbam should also perhaps be explained similarly. In the commentary on 11:17 we find the following introductory sentence: "but I saw in the interpretation of Rabbi Shmuel the son of Rabbi Meir, who did not accept his words, but explained it in this way." Afterward there is a long quotation from Rashbam's commentary on Job. In principle this quotation could have been introduced by one of three authors: it might belong to Joseph Kara's original commentary, it could have been added by the compiler of the work, and it could also have been added by a later hand. In his other commentaries Kara neither mentions Rashbam nor responds to him, which is entirely in keeping with the chronological relation between them.[65] Further, as it is certainly not the compiler's practice to name his sources, it seems we must accept Geiger's opinion, that this quotation is a late gloss.[66]

In addition to these references, the Commentary on Job also contains five quotations from the works of Rabbi Shabbetai Donnolo, all of which open in a similar way: "I found in the book of Shabbetai who interprets the Baraita of Shmuel" (9:6), and the like.[67] Ahrend claims that underlying these passages is "One of the characteristic traits of R. Joseph Kara . . . his interest in astronomy and in exegetical speculations which relate to that field."[68] However, in the light of our foregoing remarks, the inclusion of these passages may be attributed to one of three authors: Rabbi Joseph Kara in his original work, the compiler who composed the "Kara Commentary on Job," or some other third hand.

Discussion of this matter is more complex than the references and allusions discussed previously, because it entails several fundamental problems, issues that touch on the development and course of various spiritual currents in medieval Judaism. In the present context we can merely sketch an approach to this issue without discussing it at length. The three outstanding exegetes of the *Peshat* in northern France—Rashi, Kara, and Rashbam— whose work provides the building blocks for the "Kara Commentary on Job," do not mention Rabbi Shabbetai Donnolo even once in their commentaries on Scripture. In contrast, Donnolo is known to have exerted a great deal of influence on the teachings of Ashkenazi Hasidism.[69] The inclusion of sections of his work in the "Kara Commentary on Job" suggests several conclusions: it could indicate the date and origin of the person who included them in his commentary; it provides unequivocal evidence regarding Donnolo's status and influence among the Jews of France and Ashkenaz; it sheds light on one of the ways in which his teaching penetrated various circles of medieval Jewry; and it indicates the way in which various currents prevailing among the Jews of that period joined together and intermingled within a single work.

VIII

In the course of this discussion we have mentioned three outstanding examples, quite different from each other, of compilatory commentaries: the "Kara Commentary on Job," on which we have concentrated; the commentaries on Esther, Lamentations, and Ruth, which were brought to publication by Jellinek from Hamburg MS 37; and the Hizzekuni commentary on the Torah, which can be viewed as an interesting combination of compilation and *"Tosaphot."*[70] However it seems that this was a more extensive phenomenon within the confines of the northern French school, and we can find other exegetical works that belong to this genre, some of which have remained anonymous, whereas others have been named after various authors. Although the question of the unity and cohesion of these works has aroused attention in the past, it has not yet been resolved.[71] In any event, this is one of the directions in which this school developed after reaching its peak in the twelfth century.

A central phenomenon in Jewish spiritual life in the eleventh and twelfth centuries was the strengthening and expansion of biblical commentary in various Jewish centers. Scholars of exegesis have characterized this great renewal by one feature: the innovative shift in exegetical method, a transition from homiletic interpretations (*Derash*) to literal ones (*Peshat*), which is viewed as a true spiritual revolution.[72] The precise essence of this innovation has been widely analyzed and discussed,[73] and there is no need to review it at length. Nonetheless, it should be emphasized that the transition from homiletics to literal interpretation is actually characterized not only by a change in exegetical method but also by an alteration in the literary form of the exegetical works. The collections of midrashim were in fact works of biblical commentary characterized by two traits: they were homiletic interpretations, and they were compilations, anthologies of existing commentary that related to the given text. Literal exegesis of the Bible not only determines a new method of interpretation but also a new way of writing: no longer the collection and assembly of existing material but rather creative composition, which deal directly with the text being interpreted and with the various sources available to the exegete as he works.

In this respect Rashi's commentary is particularly significant. In his exegetical method he found room for both literal interpretation and homiletics, and his explicit statements juxtapose them without any clear preference.[74] Similarly, his own writing is an interesting combination of the two methods we have mentioned. On the one hand, Rashi took many midrashim from ancient sources and presented them in his commentary word for word, sometimes indicating the source and sometimes not, sometimes presenting them as a single interpretation, sometimes combining them with others. That is to say, in his homiletic commentary Rashi continues in the path of compilation. His sources are indeed chosen carefully, according to exegetical considerations, but they are presented in their own words, as found in the sources, or else with slight changes. In contrast, in his literal interpretations, Rashi generally uses his own language and wording as the product of his thought.[75] Rashi's position in the history of exegesis is therefore reflected not only in his method but also in his manner of writing. He stands at the crossroads, on the very turning point.

The independent manner of writing, free of repetition and compilation, took full possession of exegetical creativity with the strengthening and consolidation of the *Peshat* exegesis. The commentators express their views directly, phrasing them themselves, responding to the biblical text, on the one hand, and to the opinions of the Midrash and earlier commentators and grammarians, on the other. In the main area of literal exegesis written in Hebrew, which is to say northern France, this field of activity reaches its peak with the greatest creators of the twelfth century, Rabbi Joseph Kara and Rashbam. However, during that century, and even more so in the thirteenth century, two new developments take shape, branching out from the central trunk. Each of these directions finds expression in its own literary genre, and in both of them we have disciples who continue the work of their masters.

The first direction is that taken in the commentaries on the Torah by the "Tosaphists." This direction proved very fruitful, especially in the thirteenth century, but also afterward.[76] The second direction is exemplified by the compilatory works with which we are dealing here. Although the focus of the Tosaphot was the give and take of discussion, surrounding the central axis of Rashi's commentary, the compilers present the words of the commentators as they found them, without discussion or controversy.

Their goal was to produce a work composed of borrowings that would form a new exegetical continuum. With respect to literary genre these works are not in fact innovative, but with respect to their place in the history of exegesis and their particular method, they have features of their own. In contrast to the compilations of midrashim, they do not combine selections from the midrashic literature, but rather they cull and assemble literal interpretations. Hence they do not cite ancient sources, the *Rishonim*, but rather recent ones, the *Aharonim*. Moreover, these complications are not based on a large number of works, "whatever comes to hand," but rather on a small number of selected authors who employ the same method. In place of the eclecticism that combines many passages according to the order of the relevant verses in the Bible, without striving for inner unity, the compilations apply a method that combines passages chosen from a limited number of sources and assembles them in an exegetical continuum, as coherently as possible. What motivated the creation of these works? The authors of these compilatory commentaries all belong to the "generation of disciples" following the commentators of northern France, a generation that proceeded with its work in the light and shadow of the generation of the "Great Lights." The great commentators of the school of literal exegesis differed from each other in many aspects of their work, but in their combined accomplishments they created a single method, a particular spiritual current in biblical interpretation. These great teachers were regarded as supreme authorities by their disciples, very few of whom attempted to continue their enterprise or innovate after them. The compilatory commentaries express, on the one hand, the self-abnegation of the disciples before their masters, as they stood before an accomplishment that could not be emulated. On the other hand, it also expressed the desire to create a final and authoritative literary canon of literal exegesis. The compilers sought to combine and integrate the choicest and most select of literal interpretations and to erect an inclusive and compelling whole. The method they chose was assemblage, the work of creating a complete and marvelous mosaic, "Words of precious value and peace, like a column of turquoise, sapphire and diamond."[77]

Notes

1. B. Smalley, *The Study of the Bible in the Middle Ages,* 3d ed. (Oxford, 1983), pp. 36, 37 ff. "To study the commentaries of Alcuin, Claudius of Turin, Raban Maur and Walafrid Strabo his pupil, to mention outstanding names, is to study their sources" (pp. 37–38).

2. The commentaries are found in Hamburg MS 37 and were brought to publication by A. Jellinek, *Commentarien zu Esther, Ruth und den Klageliederen* (Leipzig, 1855). These commentaries are also published in some editions of *Miqraot Gedolot.*

3. See Jellinek, ibid.; and also S. A. Poznanski, *Kommentar zu Esechiel und den XII kleinen Propheten von Eliezer aus Beaugency* [Hebrew] (Warsaw, 1913), p. lxxxix.

4. Now see J. Gellis, *Sefer Tosafot Ha-Shalem—Commentary on the Bible* [Hebrew] (Jerusalem, 1982), vol. I, pp. 7–38.

5. Poznanski, *Kommentar,* p. xciii.

6. Poznanski mentions the compliatory commentaries on Esther, Lamentations, and Ruth in his introduction while discussing anonymous commentaries (ibid., p. lxxxix). In the course of his work he often defines certain works as "anthologies" (*yalqutim*), but he does not take note of the phenomenon in general, and his negative attitude is quite evident. M. Greenberg, *Jewish Bible Exegesis—An Introduction* [Hebrew] (Jerusalem, 1983) devotes a short paragraph to the Hizzekuni commentary on the Torah (p. 85). However, he does not define it as a compilation, and he discusses neither compilatory nor anonymous commentaries.

Neither M. Z. Segal, *Introduction to the Bible* [Hebrew] (Jerusalem, 1961), IV, pp. 978 ff., nor E. Z. Melammed, *Bible Commentators* [Hebrew] (Jerusalem, 1975) mention any of these works.

7. M. Ahrend, *Le Commentaire sur Job de Rabbi Yoseph Kara* (Hildesheim, 1978; referred to later as Ahrend, *Kara*). For reviews of this work see M. Sokolow, "Ahrend's Yoseph Kara on Job," *JQR* 72 (1981–82): 153–55; A. Neher, "On the Book of M. M. Ahrend" [Hebrew], *Beit Miqra* 25 (1980): 286–87; E. Touitou, "M. Ahrend, Le commentaire sur Job de Rabbi Yoseph Kara, 1978" [Hebrew], *Tarbiz* 51 (1982): 522–26. See also M. M. Ahrend, *Rabbi Joseph Kara's Commentary on Job* [Hebrew] (Jerusalem, 1988, referred to later as Ahrend, *Commentary*). On the manuscripts of the commentary and earlier editions of it, see Ahrend, *Kara*, pp. 28–32; Ahrand, *Commentary*, pp. 80–84.

8. See M. Ahrend, "The Commentary of Rabbi Joseph Kara on Job and its relationship to Rashi's Commentary" [Hebrew], in U. Simon and M. Goshen-Gottstein, eds., *Studies in Bible and Exegesis, Arie Toeg in Memoriam* [Hebrew] (Ramat Gan, 1980), p. 187 (referred to later as Ahrend, "Rashi"). For a complete list of Kara's commentaries, both those generally acknowledged to be authentic and those held to be reworked by secondary authors, see Ahrend, *Kara*, pp. 180–84.

9. Ahrend, "Rashi," p. 185; also Ahrend, *Kara*, p. 57, and Ahrend, *Commentary*, pp. 24–25.

10. Ahrend, *Kara*, p. 65, Ahrend, "Rashi," p. 187. Although we have not examined this matter systematically, it seems to us that the number of identical passages is even greater. On Rashbam's commentary on Job, see, for the time being, S. Japhet and R. B. Salters, *The Commentary of R. Samuel ben Meir—Rashbam—on Qohelet* (Jerusalem, 1985), pp. 15, 27–30; S. Japhet, "The Commentary of R. Samuel ben Meir on the Book of Job," *Proceedings of the Colloquium, la Culture juive en France du nord au Moyen Age* (Paris, 1990).

11. On Job 9:9; 26:7 and 13; 37:9; 38:31–32; For an analysis of these passages see Ahrend, *Commentary*, pp. 133–44 (Hebrew numerals).

12. See later pp. 101–103 and the notes.

13. The material is presented in detail in Ahrend, *Kara*, pp. 42–43, 52–56; and see also later pp. 115–116.

14. For a partial account of Kara's linguistic knowledge, see M. Littmann, *Josef ben Simeon Kara als Schrifterklärer* (Leipzig, 1886); B. Einstein, *R. Josef Kara und sein Commentar 34 Kohelet* (Berlin, 1886), pp. 41–43; and Ahrend, *Commentary*, pp. 48–42. Einstein examined Kara's linguistic knowledge solely on the basis of the commentary on Job; and Ahrend restricted his investigation to that work from the start. Even according to Ahrend's limited assumption that "some excellent interpretations of grammatical content certainly belong to Rabbi Shmuel ha-Daykan" (i.e., Rashbam) *Commentary*, pp. 27–28, it is doubtful whether Kara's linguistic knowledge may be evaluated on the basis of the commentary on Job.

15. Ahrend, *Kara*, p. 66. Ahrend's list must be augmented. See for the time being, Japhet and Salters, *Commentary of R. Samuel ben Meir*, pp. 28–32.

16. While editing the text of Kara's commentary on Job, Ahrend noted these phenomena and gave expression to them in the edition of the commentary he prepared as part of his doctoral dissertation. For example, he notes there regarding Job 15:5–7, "From all this it is difficult to reconstruct the original version."

However, this point did not receive the same attention in the printed edition of the commentary. As Ahrend notes in his Foreword, this is an "eclectic edition. . . . the critical apparatus and our own commentary have been restricted to a great degree, and the edition was adapted to the format used generally by Mossad ha-Rav Kook in its editions of commentaries by the Rishonim" (Ahrend, *Commentary*, "Foreword," and see also pp. 80–84.

17. Regrettably we do not possess a critical edition of Rashi's commentary on Job; and we must rely on Sokolow's conclusion that Rashi's commentary on Job "is represented faithfully, albiet imperfectly, in the standard printed editions [i.e., *Miqraot Gedolot*]." M. Sokolow, "The Commentary of Rashi on the Book of Job," *World Congress of Jewish Studies* 8 (1981): 143. Ahrend reaches a similar conclusion when he states: "we see no reason to doubt that in general the printed editions of Rashi's commentary represent Rashi's work." Ahrend, "Rashi," p. 186. We have therefore used the edition of *Miqraot Gedolot* without being absolutely committed to that version of the text, assuming that certain details of our work are likely to change in the light of a critical edition.

18. On Job 6:13, which is presented out of place, after the commentary on Chapter 7; and 17:6; 18:2; 22:20; 27:6; and see later, pp. 117–118.

19. For example, see Poznanski, *Kommentar*, pp. xxiv–xxv, Ahrend, "Rashi," p. 184; Ahrend, *Commentary*, pp. 23–24.

20. The question of the contact between Joseph Kara and Rashi also arises in respect to Kara's other works. However, there are significant differences between them in this regard. Littmann, for example, says: "The comparison of the works which come into consideration shows that in most of his commentaries Kara is completely independent, and we only encounter slight use of Rashi's commentary. This is the case in his commentaries on Joshua, Judges, Jeremiah, Ecclesiastes, and Ruth. The commentaries on Samuel and Job are slightly more mixed with Rashi's interpretations. Kara's commentary on Kings is entirely dependent on Rashi's commentary, mainly 2 Kings" (Littmann, *Josef ben Simeon Kara*, pp. 9–10). For that reason scholars have come to contrary conclusions, as we see from the following statements: "In places where he [Kara] does not disagree with Rashi, he quotes him explicitly, but where he wishes to disagree with him, he cites him without mentioning his name" (S. Eppenstein, *Rabbi Yosef Kara's Commentaries on the Former Prophets* [Hebrew] [Jerusalem, 1972], p. 19). In contrast, Ahrend takes the opposite view: "Rabbi Joseph Kara only mentioned Rashi, his 'master,' in his commentary when he wished to disagree with him" (Ahrend, "Rashi," p. 189; Ahrend, *Kara*, p. 30). Eppenstein's conclusion was that "at least to the degree that the younger author can be influenced by the older one, *in the same manner, if not in a more notable fashion, Kara influenced Rashi*" (Eppenstein, ibid., p. 21, emphasis in the original).

21. See later, p. 117 and note 60. It seems that these questions disturbed Ahrend, though he did not relate to all of them explicitly. At the end of his discussion Ahrend expresses a truly paradoxical conclusion: "Indeed Rabbi Joseph Kara was scrupulous to quote teachings in their authors' names. . . . It was his custom to mention everyone from whom he learned even a single word, except for those whose written commentaries lay before his eyes and to which he constantly referred . . . so that he had no need to mention them" (Ahrend, *Commentary*, p. 44). Elsewhere he attempts to justify that approach: "Certainly one should not

reproach Rabbi Joseph Kara for proceeding in this manner, for many of the earlier Jewish sages gave greater heed to the value of their teaching . . . than they made a point of indicating the names of its teachers and their 'copyright' " (Ahrend, *Commentary*, p. 30).

22. This manuscript has not yet been published; and we hope it will be in the near future. For the present, see the studies mentioned in note 10. In this matter one must make an initial distinction between the question of the authenticity of MS Lutzki 778 and the use of Rashbam's interpretations in Kara's commentary on Job. Ahrend doubts the authenticity of MS Lutzki, arguing that "the commentary in the manuscript Lutzki 778 is not that of Rashbam, . . . but rather a compilation of interpretations, . . . among which are also those of Rashbam" (M. Ahrend, "Rashbam's Commentary on Job?" [Hebrew], *Alei Sefer* 5 [1978]: 43; referred to later as Ahrend, "Rashbam"). In our opinion, Ahrend failed to prove his point, and we believe that the work in MS Lutzki is indeed Rashbam's commentary on Job. However, even were we to accept Ahrend's view, the presence of many sections of Rashbam in Kara's commentary on Job, passages that are quite distinctive in content, style, and area of interest, cannot be doubted, as Ahrend himself admits (Ahrend, "Rashi," p. 206; Ahrend, *Kara*, p. 6; Ahrend, *Commentary*, p. 44).

23. Ahrend, "Rashi," p. 187; Ahrend, *Kara*, pp. 68 ff.

24. Ahrend, *Kara*, p. 41. Elsewhere he says: "The commentary is decidedly a creative act which the author stamped with his personality"(Ahrend, "Rashi," p. 189; Ahrend, *Kara*, p. 29), and see also: "The commentary is the independent creation of the commentator to whom it is attributed in all the manuscripts," Ahrend, "Rashi," p. 206.

25. See note 17. In addition to the article by Sokolow mentioned there, see also M. Sokolow, "Rashi's Commentary on Job" [Hebrew], *Gesher* 7 (1979): 125–134; and idem, "Towards Determining the Text of Rashi's Commentary on Job" [Hebrew], *Proceedings of the American Academy of Jewish Research* 48 (1981): 19–35.

26. Ahrend, *Commentary*, p. 84, and on the entire subject see pp. 80–87.

27. As in the long passages from the works of Rabbi Shabbetai Donnolo, see earlier, p. 100, and n. 11, and see also later, pp. 119.

28. In the critical apparatus of the edition Ahrend indicated the differences among the major manuscripts, including the additions and elisions (see note 16). The marginal additions and notes were published separately in an appendix, Ahrend, *Commentary*, pp. 156–60 (Hebrew numerals).

29. On Rashbam's method, which was first to relate to the content of the verse or section in general and only then to relate to the details, see S. Japhet, "The Commentary of R. Samuel be Meir to Qoheleth" [Hebrew], *Tarbiz* 44 (1975): 78–85; and more briefly, Japhet and Salters, *Commentary of R. Samuel ben Meir*, p. 38.

30. See also Rashbam's commentary on Genesis 26:14, "and a large household (*'avudah*)—labor in the fields and vineyards, for 'labor' without any modifier is cultivation of land."

31. W. A. Wright, *A Commentary on the Book of Job* (London, 1905), p. 2. On the identity of the commentator see N. Golb, *Les Juifs de Rouen au Moyen Age* (Rouen, 1985), pp. 246–48. This commentator might have been familiar with Kara's original commentary on Job. He twice refers to it explicitly (in reference to Job 12:21 and 28:18), pp. 38, 82; and Kara's influence on the commentary itself is evident.

32. See Ahrend, *Commentary,* p. 61; G. Brin, *Studies in the Biblical Exegesis of Rabbi Joseph Qara* [Hebrew] (Tel Aviv, 1990), pp. 86–103. It must at the same time be noted that both the principle of "introduction" and the expression, "you should not be surprised" (*'al titmah*) are also found in Rashbam's commentaries. See, for example, Rashbam's commentary on Genesis 1:1.

33. Ahrend, *Kara,* p. 165, no. 10. For an example of the uses of these terms, see his commentary on Ecclesiastes 1, verses 2, 3, 4, 5, 6 and until the end of the chapter.

34. Thus, for example, on 5:3–4, 6:2 (here one commentary is from Rashi and the second from Rashbam); 12:23 (one is apparently by Kara and the other by Rashbam), 15:19–21; and others. The number of parallel interpretations is relatively small, and some of them might have been available to the compiler in the works he used.

35. See p. 122, notes 2 and 3.

36. Thus, for example, in chapter 1 of the compilatory commentary on Ruth, "Rabbi Shlomo" is mentioned in the interpretations of verses 1, 5, 7, and 16. "Rabbi Shmuel" is mentioned in the interpretations of verses 1, 3, 7, 16, 17, 18; and "Rabbi Yossi" is mentioned in the interpretations of verses 1, 3, 8, 15, 17, 18. The following chapters are similar in this regard. These records are not full, but where they are to be found, they are generally accurate. See also Poznanski, *Kommentar,* p. lxxxix.

37. See the remark by Chavel, "the total absence of the names of the authors of the commentaries is very conspicuous," C. D. Chavel, *Hizzekuni, the Commentary on the Torah by Rabbi Hezekiah ben Manoah* [Hebrew] (Jerusalem, 1981), p. 9.

38. Chavel, ibid., pp. 17–18. Nevertheless Hizzekuni frequently mentions Rashi, and this too figures in the introductory rhyme: "and I am not as one refuting the words of our Rabbi Shlomo, but merely as one adding to his words." On the character of this commentary, see Chavel, ibid., pp. 7–10. See also S. Japhet, "The Hizzekuni Commentary on the Torah—on the Nature and Aim of the Composition" [Hebrew], in forthcoming Festschrift for M. Breuer.

39. Hizzekuni presents himself in two ways: explicitly in the introductory rhyme: "The word of the young man Hezekiah, son of Manoah, who speaks here." He also says, "and his name shall be called in Israel Hizzekuni, so that its readers shall remember me through its name." Further, he makes use of the Hebrew acronym *ḥeit-zayin-quf* when he intervenes in the commentary. On the use of that acronym, see J. Offer, "The Hizzekuni Commentary on the Torah" [Hebrew], *Megadim* 8 (1989): 70–73.

40. Kara's commentaries on Ruth, Lamentations, and Esther were brought to publication by A. Hübsch, *Die Fünf Megilloth* (Prague, 1866) from a manuscript in the University of Prague. There are three other editions of his commentary on Lamentations: by Ashkenazi (1849), Buber (1900), and Schönfelder (1887). Rashbam's commentary on Esther is found in S. Z. Heilbert, *Nite Naamanim* (Breslau, 1847), pp. 9–11. On Kara's commentaries on Lamentations, see Ahrend, *Kara,* p. 183. On Rashbam's commentary on Esther, see, for the time being, Japhet and Salters, *Commentary of R. Samuel ben Meir,* p. 16.

41. This fact was clarified fully and in detail by R. Magidov in an unpublished seminar paper, "Rabbi Joseph Kara's Commentary on the Book of Ruth" [Hebrew] (1982).

42. As in the commentary to Ruth 1:13, where the compiler summarizes, while quoting the commentaries of his predecessors on the phrase "debar yourselves from marriage" (*te'agenah*): "Rabbi Shmuel and Rabbi Yossi both said that 'debar . . . from marriage' is connected to 'being abandoned by husbands' . . . but Rabbi Shlomo says that it is a phrase for prohibition." Similarly, the commentary on Ruth 2:7, and elsewhere. The difference of opinion with Rashi in 1:1 could also have been written by the compiler: "and this is not the literal meaning . . . have we not seen that he left because of the hunger?" See Poznanski, *Kommentar*, p. lxxxix. The Aramaic component and the manner in which the disagreement is expressed show that the compiler belonged to the milieu of the Tosaphists.

43. To Ruth 1:21; 2:12, 15 (where there are two vernacular glosses, one of which is an entire sentence), and 19; and 3:8. The commentary on 1:1 also contains a gloss, but it is in a passage apparently taken from Rashbam, though we cannot verify its source.

44. For example, see Poznanski, *Kommentar*, pp. xxxvi, lxxxi, lxxxvii, *et passim*.

45. According to the list compiled by Ahrend, there are a total of 107 vernacular glosses. See the detailed appendix by M. Catane in Ahrend, *Kara*, pp. 120–59, and see also Ahrend, *Commentary*, pp. 145–55 (Hebrew numerals). In the former work all the variants of the vernacular glosses were listed, together with a comprehensive discussion of the phenomenon. In the latter work the matter was presented only in an abridged form.

46. For example, in the commentary on Job 2:8 we find a gloss, "grater," at the end of a passage taken from Rashi, and after it a commentary taken from Rashbam is presented. This would appear to be a clear example of the addition of a vernacular gloss, by either the compiler or a later copyist, but in fact this is not the case. In consulting a representative sample of manuscripts, we found that in three manuscripts of Rashi's commentary on Job, which were chosen at random, the gloss is found in Rashi's commentary on the verse (Parma MS 32; Canzanata MS 53; Escorial MS 4–12). It therefore seems probable that the compiler found the gloss in the commentary by Rashi that he was using.

47. We have examined the division into sections according to the Leningrad MS in the BHS edition. In the poetical part of the book of Job only two section divisions were inserted in places where there is no inner break in the material, and these come after 29:19, and mainly after 31:7. This, however, does not have any real influence on our discussion.

48. See the commentary on 1:1 ff.; 2:1 ff.; 3:2 ff.; 4:1–2; 9:2–3; 11:2–3; 12:1; and so on.

49. The commentary on 1 Sam. 1:17, and see also his well-known remarks on 1 Sam. 1:20; 2 Sam. 12:30; Judg. 5:4; Isa. 5:9; and see Brin, *Studies in the Biblical Exegesis*, pp. 37–39.

50. See, for example, the position taken by Smalley (*Study of the Bible*, p. 151), who points out the lack of consistency in Kara; and also Ahrend's struggle with this problem. Ahrend concludes that Kara rejected homiletics only when there was no factual or conceptual basis for them in the biblical text, but that he viewed it as a complement to the literal interpretation (Ahrend, *Kara*, pp. 9–10, 109–15). Also see Brin's argument, that Kara joined the camp of literal interpreters "in principle" and that he chose to implement his declaration in "key verses," but that in other places "he was willing to compromise," Brin, ibid., pp. 38–39.

51. In the commentaries on 1:20; 15:29; and 36:2. See also Ahrend, *Kara*, p. 53.

52. Ahrend, *Kara*, p. 53.

53. To 1:11, 2:5, 11:5, and others.

54. Ahrend, *Kara*, p. 42.

55. Ibid., p. 43.

56. As in 1:14; 3:3; 10:20; 12:20; 13:12; 14:22; 25:2; and elsewhere.

57. See, for example, the commentary on 26:13. The commentary begins with two passages from Rashbam's commentary on Job, first with the lemma, "By his wind the heavens were calmed," and then to the lemma, "His hand pierced." Separating these two interpretations is a section taken from *Genesis Rabbah* that begins with the words, "and I saw in *Genesis Rabbah* a legend which sounds good to the ear: Rabbi Hanina said . . . " See Ahrend, *Commentary*, p. 66 (Hebrew numerals). It is possible that the inclusion of the Midrash in this place, and also the introduction to it, were written by the compiler.

58. See in precise detail, Ahrend, *Kara*, pp. 43–52, and, more briefly, Ahrend, *Commentary*, pp. 28–29.

59. "Ha-Masoret ha-Gedolah" is not mentioned here in all the manuscripts. See Ahrend, *Kara*, p. 48.

60. Expressions of this kind are also found in other works by Kara, such as his commentary on 1 Kings 8:2, 2 Kings 19:25, Isa. 34:16, Jer. 8:23, and others. See Poznanski, *Kommentar*, pp. xxv–xxviii. It is possible that this indication, as well as the reference to Rabbi Menahem the son of Rabbi Helbo, are what brought later generations to attribute the work to Joseph Kara.

61. See Ahrend, *Commentary*, 15: 31, 22:20, 24:9, 31:1–5, and see also, for example, in Kara's commentary on Judg. 2:15–17; 1 Sam. 1:5, Sam. 23:5, and elsewhere. See S. A. Poznanski, *The Interpretations of Rabbi Menahem bar Helbo on Holy Scripture* [Hebrew] (Warsaw, 1904), p. 9.

62. References to Rashi in the commentary on Job 6:13–14 (after the commentary on chapter 7); 17:6, 18:2, 22:20, 27:6. Reference to Rashbam in the commentary on Job 11:17.

63. See Eppenstein, *Rabbi Yosef Kara's Commentaries*, p. 19: "In those places where Kara rejected Rashi's opinion vigorously, he quotes him with the addition of an indication: 'I found in the interpretations of Rabbi Shlomo of blessed memory,' and sometimes close to quotations Menahem the son of Rabbi Helbo."

64. This is the standard phrase in Rashbam's commentary on Job. See also the interpretation of 8:5–6, 10:16, 11:17, and others. It is also reflected in quotations from this work in *Arugat ha-Bosem*. See Japhet, "Commentary of R. Samuel ben Meir," n. 10.

65. Rozin points out two references to Rashbam in Kara's commentaries: in the commentary on Samuel in the MS of the Theological Seminary of Breslau 104 (D. Rosin, *R. Samuel ben Meir (Rashbam) als Schrifterkläler* (Breslau, 1880), p. 13, n. 4), and on Amos 3:12 (ibid., p. 14, n. 1). However, authorities are generally agreed that this commentary on Samuel was not written by Kara (see Ahrend, *Kara*, p. 181; Poznanski, *Kommentar*, pp. xxvi, lxxvii ff.), and it is also doubted whether the reference in Amos 3:12 is original.

66. A. Geiger, "Beiträge zur jüdischer Literatur-Geschichte" in S. Z. Heilberg, *Nite Naamanim* (Breslau, 1847), p. 19, n. 3. Similarly Geiger believes that the reference to Rabbi Moshe the son of Rabbi Yehoshua is also later, and he conjectures that this author was later than Kara. See A. Geiger, *Parschandata—Die nordfranzösische Exegetenschule* (Leipzig, 1856), Hebrew part, pp. 24–25. Eppenstein believes that the reference to Rabbi Saadia is also late, as he says: "The text here . . . immediately shows that we are dealing with an addition," Eppenstein, *Rabbi Yosef Kara's Commentaries*, p. 13.

67. See note 11.

68. Ahrend, *Kara*, p. 45.

69. See J. Dan, *The Esoteric Theology of Ashkenazi Hasidism* [Hebrew] (Jerusalem, 1968), pp. 18, 22 ff., 30, *et passim* (see the index).

70. See note 38.

71. This group also seems to include the anonymous commentary on Job brought to publication by A. Sulzbach, *Commentary eines Anonymous zu Buche Hiob* (Frankfurt, 1911). This work "is mainly assembled from other commentaries and various books, including some which are not otherwise known." Poznanski, *Kommentar*, p. lxxxv. Other works have also been atributed to Joseph Kara, and scholars are not content with that attribution. For example, the commentary on Samuel in the Breslau Theological Seminary MS 104. See B. Einstein, *R. Josef Kara*, p. 21: "This commentary is . . . certainly not Kara's. . . . It is the work of a compiler who also used Kara's commentary." See also Ahrend, *Kara*, p. 181. This is also true of the commentary on the Minor Prophets in the same MS. See Einstein, ibid., p. 27; and Ahrend, *Kara*, p. 182.

72. See S. Japhet, "Directions of Research and Intellectual Trends in the Study of Medieval Exegesis of Northern France" [Hebrew], in *Newsletter of the World Union of Jewish Studies* 25 (1981): 3–18.

73. For a bibliography on this subject, see, for example, S. Kamin, *Rashi's Exegetical Categorization in Respect to the Distinction Between Peshat and Derash* [Hebrew] (Jerusalem, 1986); B. J. Gelles, *Peshat and Derash in the Exegesis of Rashi* (Leiden, 1981).

74. The best known of these is in his commentary on Genesis 3:8. For a detailed discussion of the methodological statements of Rashi, see Kamin, ibid., pp. 57–110.

75. As an example chosen at random, we offer the passage in 1 Sam. 1:1–6 (as it appears in printed editions). Many midrashim are found in the commentary on these verses, among them verse 1: "From Ramathaim-Zofim—. . . two heights which faced one another" (*b. Megillah* 14a); verse 3: "This man used to go up—an Aggadic Midrash: the way in which he went up one year, he did not go up in another year, to announce it to Israel and so that they would do as he did" (c.f. S. Buber, *Midrash Shmuel* [Cracow, 1893], pp. 42, 44, 45); verse 6: "would taunt her—she would say to her: Have you brought a cloak for your older son and a tunic for your younger son?" (cf. *Midrash Shmuel*, p. 46). The commentary on these verses also includes literal interpretation, such as verse 1: "Elkanah—he was a Levite descended from the sons of Abiasaph the son of Korah. That is his lineage in Chronicles;" verse 3: "This man used to go up—this is present tense, he would go up to Shilo from festival time to festival"; verse 6: "her rival—her husband's wife Penina; against

(*be'ad*) her womb—this is always the meaning of *be'ad*" etc. We also find quotations here from the Aramaic Targum: "And Yonatan translated 'Zophim' (*tzofim*) as from among the disciples of the prophets"; "Ephrati—Yonatan translates it as from the mount of the house of Ephraim."All the interpretations are intermingled with each other.

76. This literary genre has not been systematically studied either. Although Poznanski does devote a rather long chapter of his work to it (*Kommentar*, pp. xcii–cxvi), nevertheless his main concern is identifying the works and determining their dates and origins, on the one hand, and in evaluating their contribution to literal commentary, on the other hand. The new publication of the commentaries of the Tosaphists on the Torah (see note 4) does not refer to this question. On the Tosaphot to the Talmud, see E. E. Urbach, *The Tosaphists: Their History, Writings, and Methods* [Hebrew] (Jerusalem, 1980), pp. 17–31, 676–752.

77. Cf. the opening rhyme in the Chavel edition. pp. 17–19.

7

Maimonides on the Covenant of Circumcision and the Unity of God*

────────────────────────────── *Josef Stern*

Maimonides's explanation of the Mosaic commandments in the *Guide of the Perplexed* is best known for its claim that the many rituals concerned with sacrifices, the Temple, and purity and impurity were all legislated to counteract the idolatrous practices that prevailed among the nations in whose midst the ancient Israelites lived.[1] But for the very reason that Maimonides applied this mode of explanation so systematically and so thoroughly to so wide a range of commandments, it is all the more striking when he did not employ it. One such exception is the commandment of circumcision, which Maimonides addresses in Chapter III:49 of the *Guide,* the last of his chapters on reasons for the Mosaic law.

Maimonides's explanation of circumcision is also anomalous for two other reasons. First, as a rule Maimonides gives one and only one reason or utility for each commandment. For circumcision, however, he gives two. Moreover, he concludes the first of these by calling it "the strongest of the reasons for circumcision," and then adds about the second that it is "also a strong reason, as strong as the first . . . ; perhaps . . . even stronger than the first" (p. 610).[2] Why these two reasons? And why these obviously confusing, apparently contradictory descriptions of their relative strengths?

There is also a second anomaly in Maimonides's explanation of circumcision. His classification of the commandments in the *Guide* generally matches

*I wish to thank Ralph Lerner, Jonathan Malino, and Peretz Segal for extraordinarily helpful critical comments on an earlier draft of this essay. The original stimulus for the thoughts that follow was the *brit milah* of my son Yonatan Avraham. May he grow up to become a full partner in the Abrahamic covenant.

his classification in his legal code, the *Mishneh Torah;* here it does not. In the *Mishneh Torah,* the laws governing circumcision fall in the Book of Love, along with the laws of prayers, blessings, mezuzah, and the writing of the scrolls of the Torah and tefillin. In the *Guide,* however, Maimonides locates circumcision in the fourteenth class of commandments, which contains the laws found in the *Mishneh Torah* in the Book of Women and in the "Laws Concerning Prohibited Sexual Relations," laws concerned with forbidden sexual unions and practices. Why these different classifications in the two works? Furthermore, in the introductory chapter to his explanation of the law in the *Guide* (III:35) Maimonides goes out of his way to tell us twice—once in his description of the ninth class of commandments and again in his account of the fourteenth class—that he has changed his classification of circumcision. Why does he direct so much attention to the change of classification?

My immediate aim in this essay is to resolve these anomalies about Maimonides's explanation of circumcision. However, the real interest of this account is broader than the circumscribed limits of this one commandment. Maimonides's explanation of this commandment, I will suggest, exemplifies a mode of allegorical or parabolic[3] interpretation that he employs not only for the narrative portions of Scripture but also for the commandments and especially for those commandments that appear to be concerned specifically with the human body. The problem these commandments raise for Maimonides, which he then attempts to deal with through parabolic interpretation, concerns the role of the body, or the performance of the commandments, in the achievement of human perfection and the highest form of divine worship, states that Maimonides takes to be essentially intellectual. The problem is not only that the commandments and body do not themselves constitute or belong to this final state. Because of the deep tension in Maimonides's thinking in the *Guide* between form and matter, or the intellect and body, the real problem is whether, and to what extent, the body or the performance of the actions of the Law prevent or hinder the achievement of intellectual perfection.

I

Maimonides's first reason for circumcision, which is of one kind with the other commandments with which it is classified in Chapter III: 49, is to bring about "a decrease in sexual intercourse and a weakening of the organ in question" (III:49:609). And this, Maimonides emphasizes, is aimed at "perfecting what is defective morally" and not, as "has been thought," at "perfecting what is defective congenitally" (ibid.). Here Maimonides is rejecting an explanation of circumcision found first in rabbinic midrash (*Tanhumah,* Tazri'a 5) and then in Saadia's *Emunot VeDe'ot.* In this earlier explanation, the foreskin is naturally superfluous and, because "the perfect thing is one that suffers from neither superfluity nor deficiency," by cutting off this unnecessary part of the body "what is left is in a state of perfection."[4] Maimonides has two reasons for rejecting this interpretation. First, disputing Saadia's "factual" assumption, he explicitly asserts as a matter of common knowledge that the foreskin *is* "useful" for the member and, therefore, hardly superfluous (III:49:609). But second and, more important, throughout the *Guide* Maimonides denies the implication that any natural thing *could* be imperfect. For, as he argued earlier, all natural things, which he identifies with the works of the deity, "are most perfect, and with regard to them there is no *possibility* of an excess or a deficiency" (III:28:335; my emphasis). That is, all natural things are perfect in being equibalanced.[5] But if the natural state of the male organ is already perfect, no commandment could have been legislated to improve on it.

Yet, this natural perfection of the uncircumcised male organ is also the very condition for its moral imperfection. When left in its natural condition, the uncircumcised male organ is a source of "violent concupiscence and lust that goes beyond what is needed" (ibid.); that is, beyond the needs of its natural function, procreation. For the same organ that ensures the survival of the species is also "the faculty of sexual excitement" (ibid.), the source of "abominations" and the part of the person associated with the sense that, Maimonides invokes Aristotle to testify, is "a disgrace to us" (III:49:608). Therefore the natural perfection of the uncircumcised male organ is precisely what makes possible the person's moral imperfection, the bodily desires and acts that the Law opposes.[6]

It is this moral defectiveness of the uncircumcised male organ that, according to Maimonides, the act of circumcision is meant to perfect. But if its natural perfection is its uncircumcised state, how can circumcision morally perfect the person without making him naturally *im*perfect? We now seem to have a geniune tension between one's natural and moral perfection. How does circumcision resolve this?

In his last remark on circumcision, Maimonides contrasts it with the prohibition (in Lev. 22:24) against mutilating the sexual organs of male animals which, he says, "is based on the principle of *righteous statutes and judgments* [Deut. 4:8], I mean the principle of keeping the mean in all matters; sexual intercourse should neither be excessively indulged, as we have mentioned, nor wholly abolished. . . . Accordingly this organ is weakened by means of circumcision, but not extirpated through excision. What is natural is left according to nature, but measures are taken against excess" (III:49:611). Here Maimonides proposes that mutilation of sexual organs is prohibited because it is an extreme that extirpates, or completely eliminates, sexual intercourse. Circumcision, in contrast, is prescribed because it corresponds to the mean, an intermediate state; it prevents excessive indulgence in sex without eliminating it entirely and without demanding complete abstenance.

In referring here to the ethical mean, Maimonides surely assumes that his reader is familiar with his account of the principle in his earlier ethical writings, *Shemonah Peraqim* and *Hilkhot De'ot.*[7] However, there is all the difference between Maimonides's conception of the mean in these ethical writings and here in the *Guide.* In the ethical writings, Maimonides, following Aristotle and Al-Farabi, takes the mean to be the criterion of the virtuous characteristic of the soul, or habit, and only indirectly of the virtuous action. Extremes, both positive and negative, are deplored, and the intermediate characteristic is (almost) always sought. Indeed Maimonides says that the one who always "aims at the mean . . . is in the highest of human ranks."[8] To be sure, he recognizes that the commandments of the Torah do not always cleave to the mean, but where and when they deviate toward one or the other extreme it is only for the sake of curing a prior predilection in the other direction, "to discipline the powers of the body." For the healthy individual, the "goal of the Law is for [him] to be natural by following the middle way" (ibid.).

This is not Maimonides's perspective toward the principle of the mean in this discussion of circumcision or, more generally, in the *Guide.* As he makes clear in Chapter III:8, perhaps his most elaborate presentation of this position, the ideal state with respect to bodily desires and activities, like sex, is not an intermediate state of balance but a state in which we either have no such desires or only the absolute minimum.[9] "All the impulses of matter are shameful and ugly things, deficiencies imposed by necessity" (III:8:434). With sex and the other bodily impulses, what we should seek is not the moderate but "the indispensable," "to reduce [these impulses] to the extent to which this is possible." On the same note, the aim of the commandments and prohibitions concerning sexual unions is not balance but to "make sexual intercourse rarer and to instilling disgust for it so that it should be sought only very seldom" (III:49:606). Here, unlike *Shemonah Peraqim,* nature is not a standard to be sought; rather "the thing that is natural should be abhorred except for necessity" (p. 606), and without "measures," it is clearly implied that the natural "naturally" inclines toward excess. Finally, as an illustration of his ideal type, Maimonides directs us to the figure of Abraham, the biblical originator of circumcision, who will play a central role in the second reason for the commandment. Here, however, Abraham specifically exemplifies the "chastity" for which he is "celebrated" (p. 609) by which Maimonides means not just modest behavior but—as his prooftext, the rabbinic exegesis of Gen. 12:11 according to which Abraham did not even notice Sarah's beauty until he descended to Egypt illustrates—the absence of all sexual impulses.[10] That is, an extreme, not the mean, is Maimonides's ideal according to this first reason for circumcision: the individual who has no *need* of circumcision to restrain his sexual impulses, who by nature is indifferent or oblivious to his bodily impulses, who has sublimated these desires to a point far beyond the "weakening" accomplished by circumcision.

But, if the complete denial, or elimination, of bodily impulses is Maimonides's ideal, he also recognizes that it is only an ideal and not a genuine possibility for any (or most any) humans. Just as one's matter can never be entirely eliminated in the quest for intellectual perfection—for wherever there is form, there must be matter (III:8)—so the male organ cannot be "extirpated through excision" (p. 611). Instead of denial by amputation, the effect of circumcision is an accomodation of the ideal with the necessities of reality.[11] "What is natural is left according to nature, but measures are taken against excess" (p. 611)—and not only natural necessity is respected since the Law itself commands humankind to "be fruitful and multiply." In sum, circumcision does not realize the highest aim but only the best that can be done given the fact that we are creatures of matter; it does not bring the person to the likes of Abraham but only to the best general state for humankind in general.[12] Rather than being a golden standard, the mean exemplified by circumcision attempts to resolve by compromise the tension between the natural perfection and moral imperfection of uncircumcised man.[13]

II

Whereas Maimonides's first explanation of circumcision is the moral perfection of the individual, his second reason for the commandment focuses on the community rather than individual and on its theoretical, or intellectual, rather than practical good.

> According to me circumcision has another very important meaning, namely, that all people professing this opinion—that is, those who believe in the unity of God—should have a bodily sign uniting them so that one who does not belong to them should not be able to claim that he was one of them, while being a stranger. For he would do this in order to profit by them to deceive the people who profess this religion. Now a man does not perform this act upon himself or upon a son of his unless it be in consequence of a genuine belief. For it is not like an incision in the leg or a burn in the arm, but is a very, very hard thing.
>
> It is also well known what degree of mutual love and mutual help exists between people who all bear the same sign, which forms for them a sort of covenant and alliance. Circumcision is a covenant made by Abraham our Father with a view to the belief in the unity of God. Thus everyone who is

circumcised joins Abraham's covenant. This covenant imposes the obligation to believe in the unity of God: To be a God unto thee and to thy seed after thee. This is also a strong reason, as strong as the first, which may be adduced to account for circumcision; perhaps it is even stronger than the first. (pp. 609–610)

According to this explanation, circumcision serves two functions. First, the mark differentiates those within the community or religion who profess the unity of God from those outside who do not share this belief. Second, it creates the distinctive sense of community among its members that constitutes the Abrahamic covenant. Let me take up these two functions in turn.

As a means of communal differentiation, the sign of circumcision works in two directions. In the passage just quoted, it excludes foreigners who claim to belong to or who attempt to join the community for some improper ulterior motive, say, to marry Jewish women or profit financially. Now, the suspicion that the would-be convert has an ulterior motive for wanting to become a Jew is frequent in the literature, and insofar as the first step in the procedure leading to conversion is always to eliminate such a motive, one might even say that there is a presumption of one.[14] However, already by the Rabbinic period, the court eliminated such an ulterior purpose by verbal examination. In our passage Maimonides seems to be proposing that in ancient Israel this may have been a function of the act of circumcision itself: the very requirement that the would-be convert must undergo circumcision— or its anticipation insofar as it was imagined to be "a very, very hard thing"—was meant to filter out the insincere and improperly motivated.[15] But on this view circumcision would not be a *part* of the conversion ritual so much as a *preliminary* to it.[16]

Circumcision may also function to differentiate members of the community in the other direction: not by preventing outsiders from improperly joining but by keeping members of the community from *exiting*. This role of circumcision emerges elsewhere in Maimonides's writing, in both the *Guide* and the *Mishneh Torah* in the course of explaining the scriptural prohibition that "No uncircumcised [man] shall eat of the [paschal lamb]" (Exod. 12:48). In the *Guide*, Maimonides reports in the name of the Sages that the reason for this injunction was that "during their long stay in Egypt" the Israelites had ceased circumcising themselves "with a view to assimilating themselves to the Egyptians" (*Exodus Rabbah*, XIX, cited in III:46:585); therefore, when the Law prescribed both the Passover sacrifice and the necessary condition that the individual and his family offering the sacrifice must be circumcised, all the Israelites circumcised themselves—"and *the blood of circumcision* mingled with *the blood of the paschal lamb* because of the great number of men who had just undergone circumcision . . ." (ibid.) Now, this powerful last image may suggest in addition that the mass circumcision in Egypt, like a sacrifice, was meant to atone for the Israelites' failure to circumcise themselves during the interum. However, the more basic point of the passage is that, because the mark of circumcision makes an individual physically distinguishable as a member of the Jewish community, it thereby prevents him from assimilating, or abandoning his communal identity. During the Hellenistic period, as is well known, individuals deliberately attempted to circumvent this differentiating effect of circumcision by stretching their foreskin, a fact to which the Talmud (*j. Pe'ah* 1.1) alludes and to which Maimonides also refers in the *Mishneh Torah.*[17] In this passage, Maimonides reads this differentiating function of circumcision already into its Mosaic legislation in Egypt. The ancient Israelites in Egypt became the first Hellenized Jews.[18] Therefore, at the first critical juncture in their national differentiation from the Egyptians among whom they had until then attempted to efface their identity, the Israelites were made to be circumcised precisely to ensure that, once distinct, they remained that way.

In the *Mishneh Torah* Maimonides makes a similar point but with a different emphasis.[19] Here he explains that the origin of the requirement that Gentiles undergo circumcision for conversion to Judaism is that the ancient Israelites entered the divine covenant through circumcision, a fact he infers from the same biblical injunction of Exod. 12:48. In this context, he takes the Passover sacrifice to exemplify the "new" Mosaic covenant and circumcision not as a precondition specifically for the sacrifice but as part of the process of entry into, or conversion to, that covenant. But here, too, Maimonides implies that the "new" covenant, and circumcision as part of a rite of passage into that new covenant, were necessary precisely because the Israelites had assimilated with the Egyptians. "*Moses* circumcised [the Israelites] because they had all, with the exception of the Tribe of Levi, abrogated [*bitlu*] the covenant of circumcision [*brit milah*] in Egypt" (my emphasis).[20] Here circumcision is not just one among other particular commandments the Israelites had ceased to perform. By ceasing circumcision, the Israelites annulled or abolished a *covenant*: they surrendered their identity as a distinct community. And having abrogated the previous (Abrahamic) covenant through assimilation, nothing less than a new covenant fathered by Moses was necessary. Hence, Maimonides emphasises that it was Moses who circumcised the nation, just as the obligation of circumcision falls on the father of the uncircumcised infant according to Mosaic law.[21]

In the original passage in III:49, however, it is not the community as defined by the Mosaic law that is differentiated by the mark of circumcision but the community described as "Abraham's covenant," all "those who believe in the Unity of God," a group that would seem to be more inclusive. Furthermore, as a "bodily sign" the mark of circumcision "unites" all those who believe in the unity of God precisely because it "imposes [on them] the obligation to" adopt that belief. And, finally, its differentiating function is subordinated to its other main function—to bring about "mutual love and mutual help" among members of the community and "forms for them a sort of covenant or alliance." Indeed, because Maimonides uses the phrase "mutual love and mutual help" to characterize friendship throughout the chapter (see, e.g., III:49:601), one might say that the leading purpose of circumcision is to create a general bond of friendship among those who perform it. But in order better to understand how it does this, it will help first to examine the role of friendship in the explanation of another commandment in the same class, the prohibition of harlotry.

Maimonides's first reason for the prohibition of harlotry (Deut. 23:18) is to preserve clear "lines of ancestry" (p. 602) and not, surprisingly, sexual restraint (which is instead its second reason). This may strike us as especially odd inasmuch as harlotry is Maimonides's prototype for the pursuit of sexual satisfaction as an end in itself and its prohibition is the first commandment Maimonides addresses in the fourteenth class whose general reason is to "bring about a decrease of sexual intercourse . . . as far as possible" (III:35:538). But as it turns out, these reasons are not unrelated. Knowledge of one's ancestry is necessary, Maimonides argues, because the family, or tribe, realizes the mutual love, support, and "fraternal sentiments" that characterize friendship in "their perfect form" (p. 602); only by knowing one's lines of ancestry will one, then, acquire these attitudes that are "the greatest purpose of the Law" (p. 602). But what most undermines these sentiments of friendship is the unlimited pursuit of sexual desire, exemplified by harlotry that destroys the fabric of the family. Therefore, Maimonides presents these two— the family as a model of friendship and harlotry as a model of sexual indulgence—as if they were contradictory alternatives. Commandments that deny the one he takes ipso facto to affirm the other and vice versa. For this reason, Maimonides opens this chapter devoted to diminishing sexual desire with an explanation oriented toward strengthening its complement, the ideal of friendship. For what he sees as the true alternative to a life governed by impulses of matter is not a life of ascetic denial but one directed at the love characteristic of friendship.

The same type of explanation applies to circumcision. According to its first reason, the commandment diminishes the desire for and pleasure of sexual intercourse; according to its second, it creates a community of people giving mutual love and help to each other, namely, friendship. Here also, because Maimonides imagines the way of life that aims at sexual satisfaction as the rival to that which aims at friendship, he presents these two purposes of circumcision as complementary halves. The ritual of circumcision makes possible a community founded on friendship *by* diminishing the sexual impulses of its individual members.

There is also a second connection for Maimonides between friendship that achieves its most perfect form in the family and the covenant of circumcision. When he describes the community circumscribed by circumcision and distinguished by its belief in the unity of God as "Abraham's covenant," Maimonides's choice of Abraham—rather than Israel or Moses—is determined by more than the fact according to the Torah that Abraham was the first to perform circumcision. For Abraham was also the ancestor of Ishmael, or the nation of Islam. And in the Islamicate world in which he lived, Maimonides obviously knew that Jews were far from being the only, or the largest, group observing the rite of circumcision. Furthermore, elsewhere in his writings Maimonides unequivocally states that Muslims (in contrast to Christians) are pure monotheists who believe in the unity of God.[22] Thus the followers of Islam satisfy all three of Maimonides's criteria for membership in the covenant he describes as *Abraham's covenant,* a term that is not, then, meant to be coextensive with any other term specifically for the Jews, such as the *people of Israel* or *the Mosaic covenant.* And not only are the Abrahamic and Mosaic covenants extensionally different; what they "mean," the obligations they respectively demand, are also different.[23] Hence, in this explanation of the commandment, circumcision does not function to differentiate the Jews from other communities; instead it cuts across the traditional national and religious divisions to unite all those who are circumcised and monotheists within a new covenant. But at the same time, this new covenant, outwardly marked by circumcision and inwardly by belief, is not opposed to or even separate from natural groupings like the family; it would be more correct to say that it selects one set of ancestral relations over others. It cancels, or plays down, the role of the more immediate ancestors—Israel and Ishmael—to unite all their descendents directly under Abraham, the remote ancestor. Similarly, the "degree of mutual love and mutual help that exists among those people who bear the sign of circumcision" should not be viewed entirely apart from Maimonides's conception of the degree of mutual love and help that is to be found in a family united under a common ancestor. On the contrary, because the artificial mark of circumcision coincides with the natural line of Abrahamic ancestry, the two complement and mutually reinforce one another.

We see a similar attempt to elevate circumcision from the status of a single Mosaic commandment to that of an essential criterion of an autonomous Abrahamic covenant in the *Mishneh Torah.* At the very end of the "Laws of Circumcision," Maimonides praises the significance of circumcision "in connection with [which], thirteen covenants were made with Abraham the Patriarch" in contrast, he adds, to the commandments of the Mosaic law that are described in Scripture in connection with only three covenants.[24] There, too, he contrasts the two figures of Abraham and Moses with respect to their performance of circumcision. Abraham, "perfected" by circumcision, is presented in the strongest positive light; Moses, who failed to circumcise his own sons and was almost struck down for it on his return to Egypt, is cited, negatively, as an example of the severity of transgressing the commandment. Here, in other words, circumcision, as the identifying commandment of the Abrahamic covenant, is presented as if it were the equal of the entire Mosaic law.

Of course, in using circumcision to reinterpret the notion of covenantal community to include Muslims, Maimonides was well aware of the fact that he was opposing the received Rabbinic position concerning the status of circumcision among Gentiles. In the *Mishneh Torah,* he therefore goes to considerable lengths in order to justify the legal consequences of his new conception of the Abrahamic covenant. He writes as follows:

> Circumcision was commanded to Abraham and his descendants only; as it is said "You and your offspring to come" (Gen. 17:9). The offspring of Ishmael are excluded, as it said: "For it is through Isaac that offspring shall be continued for you" (Gen. 21:12), and Esau is excluded because Issac said to Jacob: "May He grant the blessing of Abraham to you and your offspring," from which we can infer that he alone is the descendant of Abraham who upholds his law [*dato*] and his righteous way. And they are the ones who are obligated to be circumcised.
>
> The sages said: The sons of Keturah who are the descendants of Abraham who came after Ishmael and Isaac are obligated to be circumcised. However, because the descendants of Ishmael have today become intermingled [*hit'arvu*][25] with the descendants of Keturah, all of them are obligated to be circumcised on the eighth day, even though they are not executed for it [i.e., for failing to do so]. ("Laws of Kings," X, 7–8).

Maimonides's reasoning in these two *halakhot* is a tour de force. In the first, he presents the received Rabbinic position, which legally excludes Ishmaelite, or Muslim, circumcision.[26] The one novel point Maimonides adds to the talmudic discussion is his "inference" that authentic Abrahamic lineage is to be determined only in terms of the person's faithfulness to Abraham's way of life. In its immediate context, this criterion is clearly used to exclude Christianity, or Esau. However, in light of what we have already seen in the *Guide,* it might also be understood by implication to include

Islam, which does uphold Abraham's monotheism. In any case, having explicitly excluded the Ishmaelites, or Muslims, from the obligation of circumcision in the first *halakhah,* Maimonides overturns this decision in the second. What in the Talmud is merely an individual opinion he now cites as the view of "the sages" in general that, because the descendants of Keturah, the second wife of Abraham (Gen. 25:2), are obligated to be circumcised and because the Ishmaelites have assimilated with them over time—with the result that we cannot now distinguish Ishmaelites from Keturites—all Ishmaelites are now also obligated to be circumcised.[27] To be sure, he recognizes that there is no legal force to this obligation. But what stands out in these passages is Maimonides's drive to find some legal strategem to legitimate Ishmaelite, or Muslim, circumcision. He cannot simply equate the Muslim practice with the Mosaic commandment without openly contradicting the Rabbinic tradition. He must also preserve a distinction among the descendants of Abraham between Ishmael, the Muslims, and Esau, the Christians. Therefore, he invents a new invisible legal category of Abrahamic descendants, the children of Keturah, whose only function in practice is to ground the unenforcible "obligation," or legitimacy, of Moslem circumcision as a religious commandment of Abrahamic origin associated with belief in the unity of God.[28] With this legal fiction, in other words, Maimonides institutionalizes in the Mosaic law as codified in the *Mishneh Torah* the idea conceived in the *Guide* of an Abrahamic covenant to which everyone circumcised belongs, including Moslems.[29]

To summarize, we have now seen two important ways in which Maimonides develops his notion of the Abrahamic covenant in terms of his idea of familial friendship or love. But, in one other respect, he distinguishes the love engendered by circumcision, on the one hand, and the love found among family members and, in particular, parental love, on the other. This is a difference between them as kinds of love that are, furthermore, potentially in conflict or competition: for the one to be realized, the other must be suppressed or, at least, circumvented.

This difference, and tension, between the two kinds of love can be glimpsed first in Maimonides's explanation of the particular condition that circumcision be performed on the eighth day after birth. This requirement, I should note, needs some special explanation to begin with because it prima facie conflicts with Maimonides's claim that the covenant into which one enters by circumcision "imposes the obligation to believe in the unity of God." If circumcision signals such an obligation, the proper time for the ritual should be adulthood when the person has the mature intellectual faculties to acknowledge it.[30] Therefore, to explain away this discrepancy, Maimonides offers "three wise reasons," the third of which concerns us. According to this reason, the Law commands circumcision when the child is a newborn because "the imaginative form that compels the parents to love it" is not yet so "consolidated" at that age that it would induce them not to perform the circumcision. In other words, because parents' love is a function not of their faculty of reason but of the imaginative faculty which "increases through habitual contact and grows with the growth of the child, . . . if [the child] were left uncircumcised for two or three years, this would necessitate the abandonment of circumcision because of the father's love and affection for it" (p. 610).[31] Here, then, the Law recognizes that its aim—the covenantal love brought about through circumcision—may be resisted by the imagination-based love of the parent; out of love, the father may refuse to circumcise his child. In reaction, the Law does not attempt to deny or eliminate that parental love; once again, "what is natural is left according to nature." Instead the commandment is designed to exploit the imaginative faculty when it is at its weakest. By requiring circumcision in the first days of the child's life, the Law attempts to anticipate and circumvent the developed parental love that would exclude the covenantal love created by circumcision. As God did not lead the Israelites into Canaan through the land of the Philistines in His "wily graciousness and wisdom" (III:32:524ff.), so here the Law reflects a "wise reason" (p. 610) which reins in the imagination by cutting off its power of resistance before it matures.

This tension between the parents' love for their child and the love of the covenant created by circumcision is based on a more fundamental difference between them. The love of the parent, as already mentioned, is based in the imagination; the mutual love engendered by circumcision has its basis in the intellect. To be more exact, both what constitutes the ground of the Abrahamic covenant and what makes it a divine covenant is the content of the intellectually cognizable belief shared by the community that it communicates.

To appreciate this intellectual character of the Abrahamic covenant, it should be noted, to begin with, that nowhere does Maimonides describe Abraham's covenant as a covenant *with* God or *between* humans (or a nation) and God. Instead he says that the "mutual love and mutual help [which] exists *between people* who all bear the same sign . . . forms *for them* a sort of covenant and alliance" (p. 610, my emphasis). In other words, the covenant is a relation entirely among humans. This characterization is a direct consequence of Maimonides's metaphysics. For a covenant between God and humankind would entail the existence of a relation between God and creatures—and this Maimonides has already demonstrated to be impossible because relations hold only among members of the same species and there is no species common to God and anything else. Instead the Abrahamic covenant is an entirely natural, human relation constituted by the sentiments of mutual love and mutual help that exist among all the people who bear the sign of circumcision.

What, then, makes this covenant divine? Not the identity of one of its partners but rather its content: the fact that the covenant of circumcision was instituted "with a view to the belief in the unity of God" and that it "imposes the obligation to believe in the unity of God: *to be a God unto thee and to thy seed after thee* [Gen. 17:7]" (III:49:610). Here, it should be noted, Maimonides quotes only the second half of the biblical verse. He omits its first half in which God describes "My covenant between Me and you and your offspring to come," and he omits it, I would suggest, because it expresses the very kind of objectionable metaphysical relation he has demonstrated to be impossible. Instead, then, of interpreting the second half of the verse as expressing God's half of the pact, Maimonides takes it as expressing the content of the belief that makes the covenant divine.

In this interpretation, the covenant of circumcision follows the example of the Mosaic law as a whole. For what distinguishes the Law according to Maimonides, and what makes it a *divine* law, is that it aims not merely at what he calls the "soundness of the circumstances pertaining to the body" but also at the "soundness of belief" or "correct opinions with regard to God." Now, these "sound beliefs" and "correct opinions" that the divine law communicates are not what Maimonides elsewhere in the *Guide* describes as the "perfection of the soul," or "having an intellect in actu"; that is, apprehension of intelligibles or knowledge through demonstration (III:27:511). Such perfection, Maimonides makes clear, is achieved only through full intellectual apprehension of everything that can be known, it contains only intelligibilia but no "actions or moral qualities," and it "is the only cause of permanent preservation," that is, immortality. The sound beliefs that constitute the "welfare of the soul" are rather beliefs held on the basis of tradition or authority, beliefs that the Law does not present in a scientific, demonstrative form but only "in a summary way" and sometimes in the form of parables (III:27:510). Rather than conferring perfection themselves, these sound beliefs create an ideal environment for the intellectual community in which the capable individual can achieve perfection.[32] And this goal, Maimonides argues, is what makes the law that inculcates these beliefs divine.

Similar remarks hold for the divine covenant, or community, created among all the individuals who undergo the experience of circumcision. The bodily act of circumcision "imposes" the intellectual obligation to believe in the unity of God, but simply having this belief does not yield intellectual perfection. What circumcision does bring about is a community all of whose members hold (at least) this one obligatory belief that, for those who can engage in demonstration and scientific inquiry, can then be transformed into the kind of apprehension that does constitute intellectual perfection. So, although the performance of circumcision does not itself lead to intellectual perfection or "permanent preservation," it does create a covenant, or community, whose end is not merely the moral or political well-being of its members, the soundness of their bodies, but also their intellectual well-being, the soundness of their beliefs. And, as in the case of law, such a covenant, or community, is therefore divine.

One question, however, has remained unanswered throughout this account. Suppose that all individuals who are circumcised mutually love and help each other and, thereby, form a covenant among themselves. And suppose also that this covenant requires of its members that they believe in the unity of God. Still, one wants to know, exactly what is the connection between circumcision and belief in the unity of God? The former is clearly meant to be an outward bodily sign of the inner state of the believer, but why this sign—this act and mark on this part of the body—for this particular belief? Of all the parts of Maimonides's story, this is certainly the most enigmatic, if only because he tells us *nothing* explicit in answer to the question. It is not difficult, of course, to imagine various ways in which the highly suggestive act and sign of circumcision might be taken to symbolize this belief as well as countless other themes of the Law.[33] But the plain fact is that Maimonides makes no attempt to read any such symbolism into this ritual—or indeed any other commandment or sacred object or act. On the contrary, the reader senses genuine antipathy on his part to all such hermeneutics.[34]

Rather than look for ways in which circumcision might be taken to symbolize belief in the unity of God, let me suggest two other possible nonsymbolic connections. The first of these is in virtue of the fact that circumcision is *Abraham's* covenant; that is, because of the identity of its progenitor. For Abraham is portrayed not only as the first person to practice circumcision but also, in Maimonides's writings, as "the first to make known the belief in Unity" (III:24:502). In both the *Mishneh Torah* and the *Guide,* he is described as the first philosopher who "claimed . . . that speculation and reasoning had come to him indicating to him that the world as a whole has a deity" and that He is one, knowledge that he then conveyed to the people "through speculation and instruction" (I:63:152–53).[35] Of course, Maimonides's emphasis that Abraham himself came to these truths through his own speculative reasoning, rather than through divine revelation, is not only to inform us of a contingent fact about how *he* happened to discover them. As he explains elsewhere, demonstrative intellectual apprehension of these two propositions—the existence and unity of the Deity—is equal in epistemic status to their knowledge by way of prophetic revelation.[36] Therefore, Abraham's speculative knowledge of these truths is equivalent to, though autonomous of, their prophetic knowledge by way of the later Mosaic revelation, and to describe belief in them as an obligation of the Abrahamic covenant is to ground that obligation in the intellect as opposed to prophetic revelation, a ground shared by all rational creatures and not only the particular members of Mosaic covenant.[37]

This relation between circumcision and belief in the unity of God by way of the figure of Abraham at best explains, however, why *we* might draw such a connection. It does not explain why Abraham himself, as it were, would have taken circumcision "to be a covenant . . . with a view to the belief in the unity of God." Let me, therefore, offer a second conjecture about their relation. In a number of passages in the *Guide*, though not in III:49, Maimonides refers not to the Unity of God but to the Unity of the Name of God.[38] The source of this description is unquestionably Gen. 21:33, a verse that serves as Maimonides's invocation at the beginning of each of the three books of the *Guide* but that Maimonides also cites specifically to describe Abraham who, he says, arrived at his belief in the unity of God by speculation, which he then proclaimed *"in the Name of the Lord, God of the world"* (II:13:282; cf. also III:29:516). However, the key to the explanation we are seeking is, I think, the following description of the Patriarchs who are said to have given all their efforts to "spread the doctrine of *the unity of the Name in the world* and to guide people to love Him" (III:51:624). Here Maimonides appears to *identify* God and His Name. Now, by *the Name of God*, Maimonides tells us in I:61, he means not just any description or singular term for the deity but specifically the underived and simple tetragrammaton that indicates God's absolutely simple and incomposite essence.[39] Only the tetragrammaton, the name that is truly one, simple, and incomposite, names the One. Or, in slightly different terms, because of a correspondence, or equivalence, between the unity of the Name of God and the unity of God, the Name names the deity. This is not to say that the unity of the Name of God itself names the unity of God. But because the tetragrammaton signifies God in virtue of their "common" unity, in contexts (like the passage just quoted) in which the unity of God is at issue one can equally well speak of the unity of His Name. The one can stand in place of, or represent, the other.

Now, this connection between the unity of God and that of His name is significant in our present context because according to various midrashim with which Maimonides was almost certainly familiar the mark of circumcision is itself correlated with the divine name. Most notably, in the *Midrash Tanhuma*, God is said to "have placed His name on [the people of] Israel in order that they may enter the Garden of Eden. And what is the name and the seal that He placed on them? It is [the name] *Shaddai*. The *shin* He placed on the nose, the *dalet* in the hand, and *yod* on the [place of] circumcision."[40] Although this passage emphasizes the name *Shaddai*, which God is said to have sealed on the people of Israel, it is clear that the real point of the "seal," the mark that ensures entry into the Garden of Eden, is the imprinting of the letter *yod* on the male organ, for the letter *yod* is itself an abbreviation of the name of God, that is, the tetragrammaton.[41] That is, the mark of circumcision is an inscription of the tetragrammaton on the human body. Now, as we have seen, for Maimonides the significance of the Name of God, that is, what makes it the *name of God*, is not a function of the word as such but of the notion it signifies, namely, His essence which is His unity.[42] What I would therefore propose is that, if Maimonides indeed used this midrash as a source, he may well have interpreted the connection it draws between the mark of circumcision and the Name of God, not as a connection with the word, but as a connection with the notion it signifies, the essence or unity of the deity. Like the way, according to the midrash, in which God places, or inscribes, His name on the place of—and through the act of—circumcision, Maimonides says that by the act of circumcision the notion signified by the divine name is "placed" on the person in this sense: the obligation is "imposed," or placed, on the person to believe in the notion of the unity of God. The mark of circumcision does not symbolize the belief but, like a legal seal, it represents the covenant, the power that is the source of the obligation to believe in the unity of God.

III

With this explication of Maimonides's two reasons in the *Guide* for the commandment of circumcision, we can now return to our opening questions: Why these two reasons? Why the openly contradictory and confusing remarks about their relative strengths as reasons? And why the different classifications of the commandment in the *Guide* and *Mishneh Torah*? I shall take up these questions in turn.

The presentation of multiple reasons for commandments is not characteristic of Maimonides's general approach to explaining the Law in the *Guide*, but it is characteristic of his general method of interpretation of prophetic works. In the Introduction to the *Guide*, he tells us that the greatest source of misunderstanding of prophetic texts is the failure to recognize all of their meanings. In particular, the ordinary reader fails to realize that these texts contain parables "not explicitly identified there as such" (I:Introduction:6), and that these parables possess, in addition to what we might call their "vulgar," or literal, meaning, two other kinds of meaning, an external meaning and an internal meaning. In contrast to the vulgar meaning of scriptural verses that express beliefs that *no one* should ever hold, beliefs like the corporeality of God, both the external and internal meanings express kinds of wisdom; that is, beliefs that *should* be adopted. The difference between the external and internal meanings of a parable is a function entirely of their content, not in their respective intended audiences or their forms of presentation (e.g., whether the meaning is explicit or concealed). To be more specific, as Maimonides explains in his interpretation of the Rabbinic parable of "apples of gold in settings of silver" (ibid.:11), the external meaning of a parable "contains wisdom that is useful in many respects, among which is the welfare of human societies" whereas its internal meaning "contains wisdom that is useful for beliefs concerned with the truth as it is" (ibid.:12), That is, the external meaning of a parable communicates moral and political wisdom, the beliefs necessary for the moral and political welfare of a community, whereas its internal meaning communicates theoretical wisdom, the beliefs necessary for its intellectual welfare.[43]

Just as Maimonides proposes that these two levels of meanings—in addition to their literal, vulgar meaning—characterize textual parables, so I want to propose that, in addition to their vulgar reason, he recognizes two additional levels of *reasons* for certain commandments—we might call them *parabolic commandments*—and among them is circumcision.[44] Thus the vulgar, or literal, reason for the commandment of circumcision is that it is meant to perfect a natural or congenital defect of the male organ—which, as we saw, Maimonides emphasizes is a purpose because of which the commandment was not legislated and for which it should never be performed. But in addition he proposes an external reason and an internal reason for the commandment. The explanation that circumcision morally perfects the individual by inculcating moderate sexual restraint is its external reason because it explains the commandment as a means of realizing the moral or political welfare of the society. The second of Maimonides's own proposed reasons— that circumcision "obligates" belief in the Unity of God—is its internal reason: it communicates to, or "imposes" on, the community a belief that is necessary, if not sufficient, for its intellectual welfare and for the perfection of its individual members. In short, Maimonides's multiple reasons for circumcision perfectly fit his model of parabolic interpretation.

Seeing Maimonides's two reasons as a two-layered parabolic explanation of circumcision may also throw some light on his confusing remarks about the relative inportance and strengths of the two reasons. For his description of the relative values of the external and internal meanings of a parable in terms of the figure of "the apple of gold in settings of silver" suffers from a similar kind of equivocation. First he tells us that "the external meaning ought to be as beautiful as silver, while its internal meaning ought to be more beautiful," like gold to silver. But then he adds that the external meaning should give some indication to the observer of what is to be found in the internal meaning, suggesting that it already contains some of the gold of the latter. So, when seen from a distance, it looks like an apple of silver, already something very valuable; but when seen from up close and scrutinized with great attention, it becomes clear that it is of gold. Similarly, Maimonides begins by saying that his first reason for circumcision is "the strongest of [its] reasons"—especially in contrast to its received, and popular, vulgar reason— even though the second, he concludes, may indeed be as the strong; hence, as strong as the strongest of its reasons, and even stronger than the first. In other words, his first reason is silver but the second is gold.

Finally, let me turn to the problem of classification. Why does Maimonides classify the commandment or circumcision in the *Mishneh Torah* in the Book of Love, rather than in the "Laws Concerning Prohibited Sexual Relations" in the Book of Women among whose laws he classifies it in the *Guide*? Maimonides's commentators have not been the only ones who have found the reason for this change obscure. Maimonides himself acknowledges its irregularity in his Introduction to the *Mishneh Torah*, where he finds it necessary to comment on his classification of this commandment, hence, in need of some special justification. The reason he offers is that he includes it in the Book of Love among the "commandments that are constantly performed and that we are commanded to perform in order to love God and to keep Him regularly in mind" because circumcision is "a mark in their flesh to remember God at all times even when the person is not wearing phylacteries or fringes." Now, most interpreters of Maimonides have focused on the themes of regularity and constancy that enter into this explanation.[45] But, more obviously, what all these commandments have in common is that they lead to love of God and serve as a constant reminder of Him. Moreover, at the end of the Book of Knowledge Maimonides tells us explicitly what such love of God consists in: "One only loves God with the knowledge with which one knows Him. According to the knowledge will be the love."[46] That is, what all the commandments in the Book of Love have in common is that they all lead to knowledge of God; that is, they communicate true beliefs about Him. But this is exactly the function of circumcision according to Maimonides's second reason. Hence, I would suggest that it is because of the belief in the unity of God that it "obligates" the members of its covenant to accept, and the intellectual welfare that it thereby makes possible—that is, because of its second reason— that Maimonides classifies circumcision in the Book of Love in the *Mishneh Torah.*

In the *Guide*, however, Maimonides's classification of circumcision among the laws of prohibited sexual relations would seem to correspond to his first reason: that circumcision restrains the man's sexual appetite and thereby contributes to his moral perfection. Why should this reason determine its classification in this text? The reason for this choice, I would suggest, lies in Maimonides's comment, earlier in his account of reasons for the commandments, that he "shall give reasons for the [biblical] text according to its external meaning" (III:41:567). As I have argued elsewhere, what Maimonides means by *external meaning* in this context is not the vulgar, or literal, meaning of the biblical text but its parabolic external meaning, the external meaning (or reason) of the verse (or commandment) when recognized to be a parable; that is, its moral-political significance.[47] Following the external meaning of the commandment of circumcision, it should therefore be classified, as indeed it is, among the laws governing sexual relations whose purpose is moral perfection.

If the story I have told is correct, then at least one aspect of the explanation of the commandment of circumcision, its classification, is determined in the *Guide* by its external meaning, its moral or political significance, and in the *Mishneh Torah* by its internal meaning, its intellectual or theoretical significance. This, to be sure, may appear to reverse a widely held view of the relation between the two works according to which the *Mishneh Torah* is a book written for the community at large, or the common run of men, and the *Guide* for the philosophical elite. But this position is much too simple and crude. Both the external and internal meanings of Scripture, or reasons for its commandments, are kinds of wisdom (in contrast to their vulgar meaning-reason) and, therefore, the subject matter of philosophy. And neither of these kinds of wisdom furthermore, seems to correspond to any particular brand of audience. What seems to be the real moral of my story is the unity of Maimonides's corpus of writings, the degree to which his two greatest treatises (as opposed to his running commentaries) complement each other, and the extent to which especially the *Mishneh Torah* depends for its full understanding on the argumentation provided in the *Guide*.[48]

Finally, given the analysis we have presented of the relation between Maimonides's two reasons for circumcision, it follows that he explains, or interprets, this commandment as a philosophical parable. But that does not mean for Maimonides that the commandment has any less halakhic significance. To explain a commandment as a parable is not to explain away its legal necessity or obligatoriness. What Maimonides's shift to the parabolic mode of interpretation does reflect is his attitude toward the body or, more generally, matter, which he takes to be an ineliminable obstruction both to concentration on and apprehension of God.[49] That is, one's body not only has no active role to play at the highest level of divine worship; the very fact that one is a creature of matter may indeed prevent one from attaining such heights. Therefore, any verse or, even more so, commandment concerned specifically with the body or a bodily function—such as, sexual intercourse, eating, or defecation—is necessarily problematic for Maimonides. For the performance of all such commandments focused on the body lead one away from rather than toward the deity. With each of these commandments, Maimonides therefore attempts to show that within its bodily subject matter there exists a more abstract form (or forms), an object of the intellect, expressing the practical and theoretical perfections of humanity. The aim of the philosophical interpretation of Scripture is to strip off its outermost matter to reveal this inner form.

Notes

1. On this account, see my "The Idea of a Hoq in Maimonides' Explanation of the Law," in S. Pines and Y. Yovel, eds., *Maimonides and Philosophy* (Dordrecht, 1986), pp. 92–130; and my "On an Alleged Contradiction Between Maimonides's *Mishne-Torah* and the *Guide of the Perplexed*" [Hebrew], *Shenaton Ha-Mishpat Ha-Ivri* (Annual of the Institute for Research in Jewish Law, The Hebrew University of Jerusalem), 24–25 (1988–90): 283–298.

2. All references to the *Guide* are to Shlomo Pines's translation, *The Guide of the Perplexed* (Chicago, 1963). Parenthetic references are to part, chapter, and page. Note that one cannot appeal to Maimonides's use of contradictions in this case, as these apparently inconsistent claims are blatantly explicit.

3. I use these two literary terms interchangeably; a more exact characterization of the kind of interpretation involved will be discussed later.

4. *'Emunot VeDe'ot*, trans. J. Kafih (Jerusalem, 1970–71), III, X, 7; S. Rosenblatt, trans., *Book of Doctrines and Beliefs* (New Haven, Conn., 1948), p. 177.

5. See II:39:380 and III:49:605, especially Maimonides's use of Deut. 32:4 as prooftext both for the "consumate perfection" of nature and the "consumate justice" of the commandments.

6. See also Maimonides's citation in this context of *Genesis Rabbah* LXXX.

7. See *Shemonah Peraqim*, (*Eight Chapters*, Introduction to *Avoth*) in Maimonides's *Commentary* on the *Mishnah*, Chapters I–IV; and *Mishneh Torah Hilkhot De'ot*, Chapters 1–3. For an English translation see Raymond L. Weiss and Charles Butterworth, trans. and ed., *Ethical Writings of Maimonides* (New York, 1975).

8. *Shemonah Peraqim*, IV.

9. I discuss this chapter and theme at great length in a forthcoming monograph, *Excrement and Exegesis: A Case-Study of Maimonidean Philosophical Allegory.*

10. See *b. Baba Bathra* 16a; compare Rashi, Gen. 12:11.

11. On a related role of accomodation in Maimonides's explanation of the institution of sacrifices, see my "The Idea of a Hoq," pp. 111–113.

12. See, however, *Mishneh Torah* "Laws of Circumcision" 3:8, based on *M. Nedarim* 3. There, too, the kind of perfection to which Maimonides refers would appear to be moral rather than congenital or natural, although the figure of Abraham seems to be used to exemplify something closer to the mean. On the use of the term *tamim* (perfect) in the sense of the mean, see also *Guide* II:39:378–381. Maimonides's conception of the mean appears, however, to shift from the *Mishneh Torah* to *Guide;* for discussion, see the references cited in note 13.

13. For a similar interpretation of the ethics of the *Guide* and of the mean, seen now Herbert Davidson, "The Middle Way in Maimonides' Ethic," *Proceedings of the American Academy for Jewish Research* 54 (1987):31–72. Although it seems to me still open whether Maimonides intended this conception of the mean to hold for all characteristics of the soul, I am almost entirely in agreement with Davidson's description of Maimonides's position in the *Guide*. I would disagree, however, at least in part with his explanation for the shift in Maimonides's view from *Shemonah Peraqim* and *Hilkhot De'ot* to the *Guide*. As I argue at greater length in *Excrement and Exegesis* (see note 9), this shift is simply one dimension of the ways, according to Maimonides, in which matter comes to be an obstruction both to apprehension of and concentration on God. On the latter, see now my "Maimonides in the Skeptical Tradition," forthcoming.

14. See "Laws of Forbidden Sexual Intercourse," pp. 13, 14.

15. Compare Maimonides's later statement, among his reasons for why circumcision is performed in childhood, that "a grown-up man would regard the thing, which he would *imagine* before it occurred, as terrible and hard" (III:49:610, my emphasis), and therefore, may well not perform it.

16. Maimonides's source for this interpretation may be the biblical story (Gen. 34) of Shechem the son of Hamor who, after raping Dinah, agrees along with his people to be circumcised in order to unite with the Israelites. Note, however, that this story may undercut the claim that circumcision is a good test of the would-be convert as the text suggests that the motive of the Shechemites is to marry the Israelite women and profit from the association. Furthermore, instead of preventing outsiders from deceiving the community, circumcision is primarily used in that episode by Jacob's sons to deceive the outsiders. It is also not clear from the passage in our text how Maimonides wishes us to contrast circumcision and "an incision in the leg or a burn in the arm." Are the latter meant to be idolatrous practices, like the mourning gashes of Leviticus 21? Does Maimonides emphasize this difference to circumvent a possible parallel between the two?

17. See "Laws of Circumcision" 3:8 ("Whoever nullifies the covenant of our ancestor Abraham and retains his foreskin or stretches it, even if he possesses knowledge of the Torah and practices good deeds, has no portion in the World to Come"), based on *Mishnah Avoth* 3, 11. Maimonides's use of the Rabbinic phrase 'World to Come' in this *halakhah* may refer to membership in the community of Israel, following his use of the phrase in his "Introduction to Heleq," or it may refer to the immortality of soul. In the latter case, Maimonides's negative formulation of his *halakhah* may be significant because circumcision is at best a necessary but not sufficient condition for the kind of perfection that could yield immortality, or "permanent preservation" (III:27:511).

18. This midrashically based depiction of the ancient Israelites in Egypt is, of course, in sharp contrast to other midrashim that emphasize the degree to which they had attempted to preserve their distinct identity throughout their Egyptian captivity, e.g., by preserving their distinct names and clothing.

19. "Laws of Forbidden Sexual Intercourse," pp. 13, 1–3, based on *b. Keritot* 9a.

20. Ibid., 13,2.

21. To be sure, the two covenants are not entirely distinct; the Levites, from whom Moses is descended, are said not to have ceased to practice circumcision, continuing the Abrahamic covenant. Similarly, in "Laws concerning Idolatry," 1:3, Maimonides states that throughout their sojourn in Egypt the Levites, unlike the rest of the Israelites, never engaged in idolatry. Thus the Mosaic covenant builds on the Abrahamic rather than simply replaces it. I return to the contrast between the two covenants later.

22. For Maimonides's opinion that Muslims believe in the unity of God (and deny idolatry or polytheism), see his letter to Obadiah the Convert, in R. Moses b. Maimon, *Responsa*, ed. Jehoshua Blau [Hebrew] (Jerusalem, 1958), Responsum #248, Vol. II, pp. 725–28; and in *Letters of Maimonides*, ed. Isaac Shilat [Hebrew] (Jerusalem, 1987), pp. 238–41. For his view that Christians do not truly believe in divine unity, see *Guide* I:50:111 where Maimonides says that "the Christians [who] say: namely, that He is one but also three, and that the three are one" "resemble" the one "who says in his words that He is one, but believes Him in his thought to be many," although emphasizing that what he is concerned with is "what we should believe" rather than "what we should say." Likewise, see Maimonides's *Commentary on the Mishnah, Avodah Zarah* 1:3 where he explicitly calls Christians idolators. On the contrast between Muslims and Christians, see also Maimonides's responsum to the students of R. Ephraim, in Blau, #149, pp. 284 ff; and in Shilat, pp. 215 ff. For further discussion, see David Novak, "The Treatment of Islam and Muslims in the Legal Writings of Maimonides," in W. Brinner and S. Ricks, eds., *Studies in Islamic and Judaic Traditions* (Atlanta, 1986), pp. 233–50; Lawrence Kaplan, "Maimonides on Christianity and Islam," *L'Eylah* 22 (1986): 31–34; and now Eliezer Schlossberg, "The Attitude of Maimonides Towards Islam" [Hebrew], *Pe'amim* 42 (Winter 1990): 38–60. (Thanks to Menahem Kellner for bringing this last article to my attention.) To avoid a possible misunderstanding, I should add that my remarks in the text are not meant to suggest that Maimonides's comprehensive attitude toward Islam was uniformly positive. As Schlossberg shows, his attitude toward Islam as a historical reality, especially in light of its treatment of the Jews, was quite negative and surely much more critical than the idealized view depicted in the text.

23. For a similar distinction, see now Menachem Kellner, *Maimonides on Judaism and the Jewish People* (Albany, N.Y., 1991), Chapter 9. Kellner calls the two communities *Jews* and *Israel* but in many respects his distinction is identical to mine.

24. "Laws of Circumcision," 3:9; based on *b. Nedarim* 31b.

25. As Michael Fishbane pointed out to me, the pun here on *hit'arvu*, or intermingled, and *'aravim*, Arabs, cannot be accidental.

26. For further discussion of this *halakhah*, see *b. Sanhedrin* 59b. Note, as Maimonides emphasizes in his opening sentence, that circumcision was never commanded to the Noahides at large but only to Abraham and his descendants. Therefore, circumcision might be classified specifically as an Abrahamic law to be distinguished both from the seven Noahide laws and the Mosaic commandments. For an opposing view, see, however, Maimonides, *Perush Ha-Mishnayot (Commentary on the Mishnah), Hullin*, 6:6 (based on *b. Makkot* 23b) where he writes, in illustration of the principle of a law "proscribed from Sinai,"that "we do not circumcise because Abraham circumcised himself and the members of his household but because God commanded us, through Moses, to become circumcised as had

8

Beautiful Maiden Without Eyes: *Peshat* and *Sod* in Zoharic Hermeneutics

Elliot R. Wolfson

I

Scholars who have discussed the hermeneutical posture of thirteenth-century Spanish Kabbalah in general and that of *Zohar* in particular have usually subscribed to the view that one controlling factors in kabbalistic exegesis is the distinction between the exoteric meaning, the *peshat*, or *sensus litteralis*, and the esoteric, that is, the mystical or kabbalistic interpretation, the *sensus spiritualis*. The Torah is thus depicted as possessing an external and internal dimension, the hidden meaning and its revealed, literal counterpart. Correspondingly, the method of interpretation itself is characterized by this set of polarities, *nigleh* and *nistar*, the exoteric and esoteric. It should be noted, parenthetically, that with respect to this issue, scholars have also called attention to the fundamental similarity between the hermeneutical posture of philosopher and Kabbalists, for both assumed a twofold sense in Scripture, the literal and hidden meaning, the latter corresponding respectively to either philosophical or mystical truths.[1]

It is generally thought, moreover, that the hierarchical view implied by this dichotomy was expanded further by Spanish Kabbalists in the latter part of the thirteenth century by means of the well-known conception of the fourfold scheme of interpretation that eventually received the name *pardes*, an acronym for *peshat* (literal), *remez* (allegorical), *derashah* (homiletical), and *sod* (esoteric). Inasmuch as the history and development of this notion has been discussed by various scholars, I will not enter into a lengthy discussion about the origin of this structure or a detailed analysis of each of its components.[2] My focus rather is on the question of hierarchy of meaning that this structure implies and whether this is an appropriate characterization from the particular vantage point of the Kabbalists' understanding of Scripture.

From a certain perspective it is indeed valid to view this fourfold structure in an hierarchical way. This does not imply, however, that the kabbalistic exegete himself progresses in some linear fashion from the plain sense, to the homiletical, then to the allegorical, and, finally, penetrating the ultimate meaning of Scripture, the mystical.[3] Indeed, it is unlikely that any Kabbalist, especially in the period under discussion, would have considered these different layers of meaning as absolutely distinct. It is nevertheless plausible to suggest that for the Kabbalists the four senses of Scripture are to be arranged in some hierarchical manner, the literal sense occupying the bottom rung and the mystical the highest. After all, whatever the external influence on Jewish exegetes that may have fostered the articulation of four levels of meaning, there existed four well-defined exegetical methods that corresponded to each of these interpretative categories.[4] In that respect it is necessary to emphasize what should be an obvious historical factor: the four layers of meaning must be understood in their proper literary or textual context. Hence, precedents for literal interpretation are to be found not only in the classical Rabbinic texts but especially in the Andalusian and Franco-German traditions of scriptural exegesis; midrashic interpretation had a long history stretching from the formative period of Rabbinic thought to the late Middle Ages; allegorical or tropological forms of interpretation were employed to a degree in Rabbinic literature and highlighted by medieval Jewish philosophers; and an evolving theosophic system existed that could be, as indeed it was, applied exegetically by the Kabbalists. From this vantage point it is entirely correct to view the stratification of the four layers of meaning in an hierarchical way.

Two important claims for the understanding of kabbalistic hermeneutics follow from the hierarchical approach. First, the literal meaning is assigned a secondary value with respect to determining the "true" meaning of Scripture, which is thought to consist of allusions to processes occurring in the divine world. Words of Scripture, kabbalisticly interpreted, become *figurae* or *signa* of the supramundane, divine reality. Second, the dichotomy between the external and internal sense may lead one to the conclusion that, for the Kabbalist, the *peshat* can obscure the true meaning of the biblical text, the *sod*. Expressed in slightly different terms, the mystical interpretation, much like the philosophic according to Maimonides,[5] is thought to arise out of a sense of conflict between the literal meaning of Scripture and theosophical truth.[6] The mystical reading of the biblical text thus supplants the literal sense. This viewpoint has been most emphatically articulated by Gershom Scholem who set out to explain how the mystic approach to Scripture embraces simultaneously a conservative and revolutionary attitude:

> But even where the religious authority of the same sacred book is recognized, a revolutionary attitude is inevitable once the mystic invalidates the literal

meaning. But how can he cast aside the literal meaning while still recognizing the authority of the text? This is possible because he regards the literal meaning as simply nonexistent or as valid only for a limited time. It is *replaced* by a mystical interpretation.[7]

It must be noted that on another occasion Scholem remarked with respect to the *Zohar* that its author "remains closely bound to the Scriptural text. Often an idea is not so much extrapolated and projected into the Biblical word but rather conceived in the process of mystical reflection upon the latter."[8] In yet another context Scholem commented that the critical effort "to determine whether the Biblical text inspired the [mystical] exegesis or whether the exegesis was a deliberate choice" may be "too rationalistic a view" to evaluate the creativity of the mystic, for the "thought processes of mystics are largely unconscious, and they may be quite unaware of the clash between old and new which is of such passionate interest to the historian."[9] Although in these two instances Scholem does acknowledge that, from the internal, uncritical perspective of the mystics themselves, kabbalistic ideas may be thought to spring from the scriptural text, it is clear that his general orientation was to deny that concern with the literal sense figured in any prominent way in kabbalistic exegesis. In the final analysis, according to Scholem, kabbalistic hermeneutics is based on a radical dichotomy of the hidden and revealed meanings. Thus, after describing the assumption of theosophical Kabbalists that the Torah is a *corpus symbolicum* of the hidden divine reality revealed in the *sefirot*,[10] Scholem concludes that "this method of interpretation has proved almost barren for a plain understanding of the Holy Writ."[11] In yet another passage Scholem observes that, although the author of the *Zohar* advances examples of four layers of meaning, the literal, homiletical, allegorical, and mystical, only the fourth matters to him, for the first three methods "are either taken from other writings or, at the most, developed from ideas not peculiar to Kabbalism. Only when it is a question of revealing the mystery of a verse—or rather one of its many mysteries—does the author show real enthusiasm."[12] We may conclude, therefore, that, according to Scholem, genuine interest in problems of *peshat* does not figure prominently in zoharic—and, by extension, kabbalistic—hermeneutics.

Such a view has been shared by other scholars as well; here I will mention two others, Wilhelm Bacher and Isaiah Tishby, whose remarks are focused especially on the case of the *Zohar.* Although Bacher acknowledged that the method of literal interpretation, *peshat,* played a significant role in the *Zohar,*[13] it was clearly his opinion that, for the author of this book, the literal sense is superseded by the various other levels of meaning, including the internal, mystical sense. "Le sens littéral simple est, pour lui, le degré inférieur de l'interprétation biblique; c'est le *sens multiple* de l'Ecriture qui est le fondement de son systéme, et c'est à la doctrine du sens multiple de la parole de l'Ecriture qu'il emprunte la justification des mystères qui y sont contenus."[14] For Bacher, therefore, the literal is quite distinct from the esoteric. A similar view is taken by Isaiah Tishby. After reviewing the critical passages in the *Zohar,* where there is a critique of those who accept only the literal meaning of Scripture, Tishby remarks that the "author of the *Zohar* concluded from the doubts that undermined the literal meaning of Scripture that the 'Torah of truth' was to be found in the internal part of the Torah, which is concealed by its external form."[15] Elsewhere Tishby notes that, for the author of *Zohar,* "there is no comparison as to worth between the revealed meaning of Torah and the hidden meaning. The external significance of the Torah relates primarily to existence in the physical world, whereas the internal significance is connected with the system of the Godhead."[16] To be sure, Tishby is careful to note that the *Zohar* does not reject the literal meaning nor does it attack those rabbis who confine themselves to the study of Torah in its literal sense as we find, for example, in the case of the anonymous author of *Ra'aya' Mehemna'* and *Tiqqune Zohar.*[17] Judged from the kabbalistic perspective, the value of *peshat,* together with the other forms of exegesis, *derashah* and *remez,* is that it functions as an aid to uncover the inner mystical truth.[18] In its essential nature, however, the literal sense does not reveal anything of the esoteric matters that preoccupy the mind of the Kabbalist, and indeed may impede the attainment of such knowledge.[19]

It is my contention that this scholarly approach prevents one from understanding one of the basic assumptions that underlies the hermeneutical stance of the *Zohar* and its unique conception of a text: insofar as the Torah represents not only the intention of the divine author but the configuration of the divine structure or form,[20] it follows that the *sensus litteralis* comprehends all the senses of Scripture, exoteric and esoteric. That is, the *sensus spiritualis* is part of the Bible's signification inasmuch as it is intended by the divine author.[21] The *Zohar* does not simply reject or denigrate the more normative literal-historical-grammatical understanding of *peshat* but operates with a theological conception of peshat that assumes that the Torah, the divine image, comprehends the mystical meaning in its most elemental and ideogrammatic form. The hidden and revealed, therefore, are not distinct spheres of meaning from the vantage point of the divine author or the Kabbalist who has penetrated the innermost depths of Torah, an experience compared in the *Zohar* and other kabbalistic sources to sexual union.[22] Scholars who have discussed zoharic hermeneutics in the past have not adequately taken into account the positive conception of the *peshat* operative in the *Zohar.* Yet, precisely this conception provides us with the zoharic notion of text, and, by extension, meaning. In a sense the kabbalistic conception, expressed especially by the *Zohar,* reverts to the conception of *peshat* that emerges from Rabbinic writings where it signifies authorial intention,[23] as determined through an authoritative teaching, rather than the simple or literal meaning, connotations that become standard in the medieval exegetical tradition.[24] That is, from the vantage point of the Rabbis, *peshat* designates the scriptural verse in its appropriate context, which, in turn, may be illuminated by literal or midrashic explanations. The simple or plain meaning, therefore, is one but not the only aspect of *peshat*, the semantic unity of the text.[25] The question of the zoharic conception of *peshat* thus lies at the center, and not the periphery, of a discussion on the hermeneutical principles and strategies of the *Zohar*. A key issue in determining this conception is the relationship between *peshat* and *sod* that I will investigate in detail in the remainder of this essay.

II

Before discussing the role of *peshat* in zoharic hermeneutics, it is of interest to consider several sources that provide some more background for the position adopted by the *Zohar*. I begin with the hermeneutical posture espoused by Naḥmanides (1194–1270). It can be shown from any number of sources that Naḥmanides subscribed to the view that Scripture has an inner and outer dimension,[26] or, as he put it in one context, "the verses of Scripture are true literally and figuratively,"[27] or again, "the Torah makes explicit and alludes."[28] One passage is particularly striking in that he distinguishes three senses to a scriptural text (the example is Prov 31:10), viz. the literal (*melitzah*), the figurative (*mashal*), and the esoteric (*sod*).[29] That Naḥmanides considered all these levels to be contained within the text of Scripture is most evident from his interpretation of the rabbinic dictum, "a biblical verse does not lose its literal sense," *'ain miqra yotzei midei peshuṭo*,[30] in his notes to the second principle in the introduction to Maimonides's *Sefer ha-Miṣvot*. Reacting to Maimonides's claim that the Rabbis occasionally derived laws from Scripture without any textual basis, and thereby denied their own principle stated previously, Naḥmanides emphasized that with respect to biblical interpretations connected with halakhic matters the verse does not lose its literal sense because all these interpretations "are contained in the language of the text" (*kullam bilashon ha-katuv nikhlalim*). Naḥmanides goes on to contrast his own conception of *peshat* with those "who lack knowledge of the language"—or, according to another reading, the "language of those who lack knowledge"— and the Sadducees, that is, the Karaites. It seems likely that by the first Naḥmanides intends those who would limit the literal sense to that which is established on purely philological and historical grounds. Such a group, like the Karaites, would fail to see the polysemous nature of Scripture. For Naḥmanides, by contrast, "the text contains everything . . . for the book of God's Torah is complete, there is no extra word in it nor any lacking, everything was written in wisdom."[31] Scripture thus comprises both the literal and figurative meaning, the external and internal sense:

This is the meaning of their dictum, "a verse should not lose its literal sense;" they did not say, "a verse is only according to its literal sense." We have rather the interpretation [of the verse] together with the literal sense, and it should not lose either of them. On the contrary, Scripture must bear everything, and both are true.[32]

I do not mean to suggest that Naḥmanides rejects the idea of *peshat* in the more restricted connotation as the *sensus litteralis*. On the contrary, from his comment that there is both *midrash* and *peshat*, it is evident that he accepts the standard medieval conception of *peshat* as the historical, grammatical, and philological meaning. What is crucial for Naḥmanides, however, is that this notion of *peshat* is itself contained in a broader conception of a scriptural text that comprises all meanings including the mystical.[33] As Bernard Septimus has pointed out, Naḥmanides advanced the Andalusian tradition of *peshat* "by broadening the conception of interpretation" to include Rabbinic—halakhic and aggadic—as well as kabbalistic modes of explanation.[34] For Naḥmanides, then, the term *peshat* denotes the textual reality that comprises the literal and midrashic—and under the rubric of midrashic the Kabbalist includes the mystical—explanations. The same point is made by another thirteenth-century Kabbalist from Castile, R. Jacob ben Jacob ha-Kohen: "[The principle] 'a verse should not lose its literal sense' always applies to all the Torah; the literal sense (*ha-peshat*) is the root, the homiletical the branch (*ha-midrash*), and everything is true."[35]

It is this notion of the text as comprehending the external and internal meanings that, in my view, provides the underlying principle for Naḥmanides's repeated claim that the contextual meaning of certain biblical texts can be comprehended only through knowledge of the esoteric lore. In the vast majority of cases Naḥmanides keeps the literal and kabbalistic meanings distinct, treating the latter like an added dimension that enhances our understanding of Scripture but that nevertheless should not be confused with the plain sense. It is thus that Naḥmanides often alerts the reader to the fact that he is divulging esoteric matters by the introduction, *'al derekh ha-'emet*, "by way of truth." On occasion, however, Naḥmanides relates a kabbalistic explanation without identifying it as such. Furthermore, a significant number of examples in his commentary indicate that he entertained the possibility that the simple, plain, or contextual meaning was comprehensible only in terms of kabbalistic truths. Various scholars have discussed this phenomenon as it appears in the Torah commentary of Naḥmanides.[36] In a paper on Naḥmanides's kabbalistic hermeneutics I have argued that one can distinguish two typologies wherein this convergence is operative: in some instances the literal and mystical meanings overlap because there is only one textual dimension corresponding to one reality outside the text, whereas in other instances there is an overlapping meaning, but the text allows for two levels, exoteric and esoteric, which correspond to two levels of reality, the mundane and the divine.[37] This exegetical posture challenges in a fundamental way the notion of an interpretative hierarchy applied universally and without qualification by the Kabbalists. Not only is it the case that the literal sense does not always obscure the hidden signification, but the latter in some instances alone provides the key to read the text contextually. It is some such conception that underlies Ezra of Gerona's remark in his introduction to his commentary on Song of Songs to the effect that biblical exegetes do not understand certain sections of Torah for they are based on the wisdom of Kabbalah.[38] That is to say, the esoteric meaning is not ancillary, but rather is necessary for the very comprehension of the plain sense of the scriptural text. To put the matter epigrammatically, *sod* is the depth of *peshat.*

It is instinctive to compare Naḥmanides's hermeneutic with that of Jacob ben Sheshet, an older contemporary Geronese Kabbalist, though apparently belonging to an independent circle.[39] To begin with, it is necessary to mention, as was done already by Scholem, the obvious contrast between the two Kabbalists with respect to their stated positions regarding the nature of Kabbalah.[40] Naḥmanides for his part described Kabbalah as a body of received tradition that must be transmitted orally from teacher to student and that cannot be comprehended by human reasoning or supposition.[41] The point is made in various contexts in Naḥmanides's writings, but for the sake of comparing his view with that of Jacob ben Sheshet I will cite the following passage from his "Sermon on Ecclesiastes," for it focuses on the mystical reasons for the commandments, precisely the principal concern of ben Sheshet:

> With respect to these matters and others like them one cannot understand their truth from one's own mind (*mida'at 'atzmo*) but only through tradition (*be-kabbalah*). This matter is explained in the Torah to whoever has heard the rationale for the commandments through a tradition (*ta'am ha-mitzvot be-kabbalah*) as is fitting. This refers to one who has received from a mouth which has received, going back to Moses, our teacher, [who received] from God.[42]

Jacob ben Sheshet, in diametrically opposite terms, expressed the viewpoint that one can, indeed from a religious perspective must, innovate kabbalistic interpretations (or, more specifically, mystical rationales for the commandments) in order to propagate and glorify the Torah. This is epitomized in succinct fashion in the following directive offered by Jacob ben Sheshet in

Sefer ha-'Emunah ve-ha-Biṭṭaḥon: "Know that the words of the rabbis, may their memory be for a blessing, are the words of the living God and they should not be contradicted, but it is a commandment for every sage to innovate [interpretations] of the Torah according to his ability."[43] To cite a second example from the same work: "For in every matter a person can give his own explanation from his mind, and there is nothing deficient in this."[44] Elaborating on this theme in another work, *Sefer Meshiv Devarim Nekhoḥim,* Jacob ben Sheshet writes:

> I know that there may be some among the pious and sages of Israel who will blame me for I have written the reason for two or three commandments in the Torah, which may be an opening for one to give a reason for many other commandments by way of wisdom. I can bring a proof that every sage is capable of offering a reason for every commandment whose reason is not explicitly stated in the Torah.[45]

That the innovation is to be considered no less authoritative than a received idea is emphasized in Jacob ben Sheshet's bold claim with respect to his view that the meaning of the tetragrammaton, as the Torah in general, varies in accordance with its vocalization:[46] "If I had not innovated it from my heart, I would have said that it is a law given to Moses at Sinai."[47] One should not, however, conclude from these comments that Jacob ben Sheshet was not the recipient of kabbalistic doctrine transmitted orally; on the contrary, on more than one occasion he reports having received traditions in just such a manner, as, for instance, from R. Isaac the Blind.[48] Moreover, it is evident that Jacob ben Sheshet did not think that the wisdom of Kabbalah was exhausted by his own innovative views or even by those he received.[49] The fact of the matter is, however, that he does maintain, *contra* the explicit claims of Naḥmanides, that kabbalistic explanations can be adduced through the exercise of one's own powers of discernment and scriptural exegesis. Although I myself have challenged the standard characterization of Naḥmanides as "reserved"[50] or "conservative"[51] Kabbalist, arguing that he is not merely the recipient of a limited corpus of secrets but rather expands the range of kabbalistic secrets through a consistent and innovative hermeneutical posture vis-à-vis Scripture as read often through the lenses of Rabbinic *aggadah* (including in this category the kabbalistic teatise, *Sefer ha-Bahir*),[52] it still is evident that the distinction between Naḥmanides's and Jacob ben Sheshet's understanding of the kabbalistic enterprise must be upheld. Even if Naḥmanides is up to much the same task as Jacob ben Sheshet, his insistence that Kabbalah is a received tradition is instructive and must be set against the overtly innovative orientation of Jacob ben Sheshet.

Having delineated in clear fashion the essential difference between Naḥmanides and Jacob ben Sheshet, it is necessary to draw one's attention to a basic similarity in approach between the two. It emerges from a few places in the latter's writings that he shared the hermeneutical assumption expressed by Naḥmanides to the effect that the *peshat* of the verse can overlap with the *sod*, indeed that occasionally the most appropriate way to comprehend *peshat* is through *sod*. One passage in particular is noteworthy for interpreting the Rabbinic dictum, "a verse should not lose its literal sense," Jacob ben Sheshet employs language that is remarkably close to that of Naḥmanides in his notes to Maimonides's *Sefer ha-Miṣwot*, which I cited previously[53]:

From all the matters that I have written you can understand that there is no event in the world that does not have a force above which appears to be a paradigm (*dugma'*) or image (*dimyon*) [of that which is below]. Therefore, when you find something in the words of our rabbis, blessed be their memory, or in the words of the Torah, or one of the reasons for the commandments, or the [speculation] of one of their rewards, do not think in your heart that it is said with regard to the lower matter. Rather it is said with respect to the supernal [matter] which corresponds to the lower. Regarding that which is written in the Torah, our sages, blessed be their memory, already said, "a verse should not lose its literal sense." Inasmuch as it says "a verse should not lose [its literal sense]," but not that Scripture is interpreted [only] according to its literal sense, we learn that even though the Torah has seventy aspects,[54] none of them can deny the *peshat*, and perhaps the *peshat* is one of the seventy. Thus, no sage has permission to offer an interpretation which contradicts the *peshat*, for the rabbis, blessed be their memory, have said ["a verse should not lose its literal sense"].[55] [Concerning] the *peshat* there are commentators who say that the verse is missing four or two words, or half of it is extra and unnecessary; yet, Scripture is as it is. In truth, there are many verses to which we must add a word or two in order to understand their *peshat*, but this is not due to a deficiency in Scripture but rather our deficiency, for we do not comprehend the holy language [Hebrew] except as it compares to the language in which we are immersed in the exile because of our sins.[56]

Like Naḥmanides, then, Jacob ben Sheshet maintains that the principle of the Rabbis is that a verse should not lose its literal sense, not that a verse is to be interpreted only in accordance with its literal sense. A careful scrutiny of Jacob's writings, a project beyond the confines of this essay, would reveal, moreover, that, like Naḥmanides, he too has extended the meaning of the word *peshat* so that the simple meaning (often rendered through the prism of Rabbinic interpretation) can itself constitute the esoteric signification. The positive role accorded the *peshat* meaning is based on the hermeneutical principle articulated in the beginning of the preceding citation, the principle that served as the cornerstone of biblical exegesis for the theosophic Kabbalists: events later are to be understood in terms of their supernal patterns or images in the sefirotic pleroma. Biblical narrative and law, therefore, themselves are to be interpreted as symbolic of this upper realm. Just as in the ontic sphere the mundane has its correlate in the divine, and the latter is only known through the former, so on the textual plane the esoteric or mystical signification is apprehended only through the exoteric or literal-historical-grammatical meaning. Discerning the *peshat*, therefore, enables the exegete to interpret the scriptural text kabbalistically. In the final analysis, for Jacob ben Sheshet, as other theosophic Kabbalists of his time, the Torah in its mystical essence is identical with the divine name.[57] This identity underlies his claim, alluded to earlier, that the unvocalized Torah scroll admits of multiple meanings just as the tetragrammaton allows for a multiplicity of vocalizations, each engendering a different vehicle for kabbalistic intention during prayer. Yet, despite Jacob ben Sheshet's claim that the meaning of each and every word of the Torah changes in accordance with its vocalization, the fact is that there is one text whose ideogrammatic form represents the shape of the divine. This principle underlies Jacob ben Sheshet's claim against the commentators who on occasion derive the *peshat* by adding or detracting words from Scripture: the written text is as it is—nothing more nor less! This understanding of "Scripture as it is" provides the basic element in Jacob ben Sheshet's conception of *peshat*, that is, the "text" that encompasses the multiple levels of meaning. The Rabbinic stricture against negating the *peshat*, therefore, does not preclude either rabbinic, especially aggadic, or kabbalistic interpretations. On the contrary, it may happen that the kabbalistic interpretation is itself the *peshat*, or put differently, the *peshat*, when properly understood, allows one to comprehend the mystical sense of Scripture.[58] This view is affirmed as well in an anonymous text, attributed to Naḥmanides, called the "Treatise on the Inwardness of the Torah." This text, prima facie, espouses an extreme form of the hierarchical view by clearly distinguishing between the literal sense (*derekh peshat*) and the internal sense (*derekh penimi*), which is identified further as the inner soul (*neshamah penimit*) of Torah.[59] The author even criticizes those who would limit their understanding of Torah to the literal sense and urges the reader to believe that alongside the literal meanings are deep secrets in Scripture.[60] He insists, moreover, like Jacob ben Sheshet,[61] that the Torah scroll is not vocalized because any received vocalization would limit the meaning of the verses in a set and fixed way.[62] In spite of his emphasis on the potentiality for infinite interpretability, the author is careful to note that all meanings "are contained within the simple verses of Scripture (*pishatei ha-miqra'*), and all of Torah acts according to this literal sense (*peshat*)."[63] For those who can comprehend the inner soul of Torah, it is evident that the *sensus mysticus* is comprised within the *sensus litteralis*.

What has been stated with regard to Naḥmanides, Jacob ben Sheshet, and the anonymous Kabbalist can, in my view, be transferred to other mystic exegetes as well. To appreciate the way in which the theosophic Kabbalists, especially in the formative period of kabbalistic literary history, looked at Scripture it is necessary to grasp the dynamics of kabbalistic interpretation with respect to the fundamental issue of the relationship between *peshat* and *sod*. The position of the theosophic Kabbalists in general, and that of the authorship of the *Zohar* in particular, is put into sharp relief when compared with the view of Abraham Abulafia, leading expounder of the ecstatic kabbalah in the second half of the thirteenth century. In his detailed discussion of the seven exegetical methods of Abulafia, Moshe Idel has pointed out that the *peshat,* according to Abulafia, is oriented toward the masses who cannot comprehend truths on their own accord. The literal sense thus serves a pedagogical purpose, transmitting the tradition in order to educate the masses to perform good deeds, to submit to the authority of the law, and to inculcate truth in accordance with the level of their comprehension.[64] Although Abulafia pays lip service to the Rabbinic dictum, "a verse should not lose its literal sense," it is clear that for him there is a radical dichotomy between the literal and mystical, the exoteric and esoteric.[65] A typical statement of this is found in his *'Or ha-Sekhel* in the following passage:

> Even though we have alluded to the hidden matters, the verses should not lose their literal sense. Insofar as there is nothing compelling us to believe that this is an allegory and should not be [understood] according to its literal sense in any manner, we should initially believe the literal sense as it is. . . . Afterwards it should be interpreted as much as it can withstand according to the hidden way, for all that which is interpreted according to what is hidden instructs about a deeper wisdom and is more beneficial to a person than the exoteric teaching. The exoteric is written to benefit the masses who have no analytic skill to distinguish between truth and falsehood, but this will not benefit the knowledgeable person who seeks felicity unique to the rational faculty.[66]

The negative view of *peshat* emerges with clarity from Abulafia's understanding of the mystical dimension of the text. This mode of interpretation, focused as it is on reading the text as a string of separate letters that make up the different divine names, is, as Idel has aptly put it, a "text-destroying exegesis."[67]

The theosophic exegete, by contrast, would maintain the equal validity and necessity of the literal meaning. Indeed, the insight of the mystical illumination is such that there is an awareness that the esoteric is inseparable from the exoteric and, in the last analysis, a full appreciation of the one is dependent upon the other. The point is well-made by Menaḥem Recanati: "In every place in the Torah that you can elevate the [meaning of] a particular narrative (*ha-ma'aseh*)[68] or commandment to an entity higher than it [i.e., the *sefirot*], you must elevate it . . . provided that you do not say that the matter is not as it is in its literal sense."[69] The necessity to preserve the literal meaning together with the esoteric emphasized by the Kabbalists resonates with the following claim in an anonymous passage, presumably written by someone of Ashkenazi extraction, interpreting the statement attributed to R. Ḥanina bar Papa in *b. 'Eruvin* 65a: "He whose wine is not poured in his house as water is not in the category of blessing":

> The Torah is compared to water and to wine,[70] i.e., the Torah in its literal sense is compared to water and the hidden sense to wine, for the numerical value [of the word wine, *yayin*] is [that of the word] secret [*sod*], as it says, "The wine enters and the secret comes forth."[71] That is to say, when one has learnt the mysteries of Torah which are compared to wine as the literal meaning of Torah is compared to water, then the wine pours forth like water, i.e., its mysteries together with the literal sense. In such a case there is certainly a sign of blessing![72]

The concurrence of *peshat* and *sod* from the perspective of the kabbalistic reading is made in the following statement of Isaac of Acre:

> I have seen the truth of the revealed and hidden secret (*sod nokhaḥ ve-nistar*) in many verses and in prayers and blessings. The one who believes only in the hidden (*nistar*) is in the category of the heretics, and these are the foolish of the philosophers who philosophize and are dependent upon their speculations. They are wise in their own eyes, for they have no knowledge of the ten *sefirot belimah* which are the name of the Holy One, blessed by He. Their faith is evil and deficient, for they act negligently with respect to prayer and blessings and make light of all the commandments. The one who believes solely in the external (*nokhaḥ*) are the foolish of the traditionalists (*ha-mequbbalim*), for it is inappropriate to separate the Holy One, blessed be He, and His name. It is certainly the case that the Holy One, blessed be He, is His name and His name is the Holy One, blessed be He. Thus the ten *sefirot belimah* are the boundary without boundary[73] . . . through them one can comprehend the secrets of the *haggadot* and the establishment of the words of the rabbis, blessed be their memory, "a verse should not lose its literal sense."[74]

Interestingly, Isaac of Acre classifies the philosophers as those who neglect the literal sense and believe only in the hidden, that is, the inner or allegorical meaning, a claim well known from other kabbalistic sources as well.[75] The traditionalists, on the other hand, believe only in the revealed sense and lack knowledge of the hidden meaning that is focused on the sefirotic world. The truth, one may presume, lies with the one who heeds both the revealed and the hidden meanings. Indeed, as Isaac says, it is only through knowledge of the *sefirot*, the *nistar*, that one can both comprehend the aggadic texts and fulfill the injunction of the rabbis that a verse does not lose its literal sense (*peshat*).

III

If we turn at this juncture to the *Zohar*, we will find that here too the notion of *peshat* is such that it comprehends within itself the *sensus mysticus*. This assumption underlies the hermeneutical strategy of the *Zohar* to discover in every minute detail of Scripture an allusion or symbol pointing to the hidden world of God. Far from being an impediment or obstacle to the mystical sense, therefore, the *peshat* (understood in its expanded sense) provides the key for unlocking kabbalistic truths. From the vantage point of zoharic hermeneutics the internal, mystical dimension of Torah, the *nistar*, is not concealed but rather revealed by the external form or garment, the *nigleh*. Indeed, biblical interpretation in the *Zohar* can be characterized as a form of hyperliteralism,[76] for the very words of Scripture are transformed into vehicles for God's self-revelation[77] inasmuch as the letters are, to use the expression of the anonymous author of *Sefer ha-Temunah*, "the true image, as it is written, 'he beholds the image of the Lord' (Num. 12:8), and this is the secret of the name of the Holy One, blessed be He."[78] This is the force of the repeated identification in the *Zohar* of God's name and the Torah: the verses of Scripture refer to intradivine processes in the sefirotic realm inasmuch as the latter is said to be constituted within the name that is the Torah.[79] In contemporary semiotic terms the matter may be expressed as follows: the symbolic transformation of Scripture undertaken by the zoharic authorship is dependent on such a close reading of the conventional textual signs that this mode of anagogic interpretation engenders a kind of literalism whereby the gap between levels of discourse (as that between ontological spheres) is closed. The kabbalistic interpretation proffered by the *Zohar* thus necessitates, in Betty Roitman's telling expression, a "return to the text" for through the kabbalistic reading scriptural words "become elements of a lexicon and present themselves as independent syntagms of greater or lesser length, each of which functions as the statement of a semantic equivalence."[80]

To be sure, I do not deny that in some of the most important statements in zoharic literature affirming the diverse interpretative layers of Scripture the hierarchical view is evident. Thus, for example, there is the well-known metaphor employed in *Midrash ha-Ne'elam* on the book of Ruth, which compares the Torah to a nut: just as the nut has three external shells and a kernel within, so too the words of Torah have four types of meaning, the literal sense (*Ma'aseh*),[81] and the homiletical (*Midrash*), the allegorical (*Haggadah*),[82] and the mystical (*Sod*).[83] In another context the *Zohar* at first notes that every verse can be interpreted according to three senses: literal (*Peshat*), homiletical (*Midrash*), and mystical referred to as the "supernal wisdom" (*hokhmah 'ela'ah*). The Torah is then described by the metaphor of the tree whose different parts are said to correspond to various types of meaning: literal, homiletic, allegorical, numerological, mystical, and halakhic.[84] Moreover, on several occasions the *Zohar* speaks of the Torah as being like the name of God in terms of being both hidden and revealed,[85] and in at least one place it is emphasized that the revealed meaning is appropriate for human beings whereas the hidden is reserved for God, though R. Shim'on ben Yoḥai was granted permission to reveal the secret truths.[86] The hierarchical approach is evident as well in one of the more dramatic and imaginative sections in the *Zohar* wherein the author describes the adventures of the fellowship of R. Shim'on in the most wondrous and fantastic terms. They are said to be in a garden, which is described further as the place from which one enters the world-to-come. After having fallen into a deep sleep, they are aroused by an angelic voice. The narrative then unfolds three successive stages of revelation, each reaching higher limits than the previous one. The first entails an encounter with "masters of Scripture" (*marei miqra*), the second with the "masters of Mishnah" (*marei mathnitha*), and the third with "masters of *aggadah*" (*mareihon de-aggadah*).[87] From the context it is evident that each group reveals deeper matters, culminating with the masters of *aggadah* who are described as possessing "faces illuminated like the light of the sun . . . for they see each day the light of Torah as is appropriate." The comrades are not given permission to enter into the place where the masters of *aggadah* are located, presumably because their teachings are too esoteric. What is significant for our purposes is the hierarchical ordering of interpretative postures implicit here: Scripture, Mishnah, and *aggadah,* the latter, I suggest, being identical with kabbalistic meaning.[88]

Perhaps the passage that is most hierarchical in nature is the one that distinguishes four levels of meaning to the scriptural text: the narrative that is the garment, the laws that are the body, the mystical secrets that are the soul, and the innermost secrets—to be revealed only in the messianic future—that are the soul of the soul. These four are said to correspond respectively to the following ontological graduations: the heavens, Shekhinah, *Tif'eret*, and *Keter*.[89] The wicked are those who say that the Torah consists only of narratives and therefore look at the garment, the *peshat*,[90] but not the body that consists of the laws and commandments. From the context it would appear that the wicked are Christian exegetes who are viewed as literalists in the sense that they look at and accept only the narrative of Hebrew Scripture insofar as it serves as the background for their own Scripture. They, however, do not consider the body underneath the external garment, for they explicitly reject the biblical laws as interpreted in the Rabbinic tradition.[91] The righteous, by contrast, know how to look at the Torah see what lies beneath the garment. It is essential to note that the body is correlated with the Shekhinah as well as the commandments, two themes that find expression elsewhere in the zoharic corpus.[92]

A careful examination of the key passages that suggest that the literal meaning hides or envelopes the mystical truth will demonstrate, however, that this is from the perspective of only the uninitiated or unenlightened. Indeed, the process of mystical enlightenment or illumination consists precisely of the fact that the *ba'al ha-sod* sees the inner light (the esoteric matter) shine through the external shell (the literal sense) of the text. Perhaps this is nowhere more evident than in the following account:

> The Holy One, blessed be He, enters all the hidden matters [or words] that He has made in the holy Torah, and everything is found in the Torah. The Torah reveals that hidden matter and immediately it is cloaked in another garment wherein it is concealed and not revealed. Even though the matter is hidden in its garment, the wise, who are full of eyes (*malyan 'aynin*), see it from within its garment (*ham'an lah mi-go levushah*). When that matter is revealed, before it enters into a garment, they cast an open eye (*pekihu de'ayna*) upon it, and even though it is immediately hidden it is not removed from their eyes.[93]

The disclosure of that which is hidden within the Torah occurs through the outer garment in which it is cloaked. This is the force of the claim that the wise, who are "full of eyes," *malyan 'aynin* (I return to this image later), see the concealed matter form within the garment, *ham'an lah mi-go levushah*. The function of the garment, paradoxically, is to concomitantly conceal and reveal: the secret is hidden from everyone by the garment but it is only from within the garment that the secret is revealed to the wise.[94] The plausibility of this interpretation is supported by the famous parable of the beautiful maiden and her lover, which immediately follows the passage just cited. In this parable the maiden, who symbolizes the Torah, is said to disclose four levels to her lover, the mystic, in a gradual process of unveiling: the first stage corresponds to the level of literal sense (*Peshat*), the second to homiletical or midrashic interpretation (*Derashah*), the third to allegory (*Haggadah*), and the fourth to the mystical or esoteric. The last stage is not given a specific name but is described as the maiden revealing herself "face to face" (*'anpin be-'anpin*) to the lover and disclosing "all her hidden secrets and hidden ways."[95] When the mysteries or secrets of Torah are revealed to the mystic, he unites with the Torah and is called *husband of Torah* and *master of the house*, epithets that signify that this union is of an amatory nature. In the moment of unification the maiden says to the lover:

> Do you see the allusion that I alluded to at first [i.e., the initial disclosure which corresponds to the literal sense]? So many secrets were contained in it. Now he sees that nothing should be added or taken away from those words [of Scripture]. Then the *peshat* of the verse is [revealed] as it is, not a single word should be added or deleted.[96]

At the end of the process, when one comprehends the mystical essence of Torah and thus unites with her in an intimate relation akin to sexual union, then, and only then, does the plain sense of the verse become comprehensible. Traditional commentators on the *Zohar* have realized the full implication of this passage: mystical enlightenment culminates with a reappropriation of *peshat*,[97] here understood as the text as it is, to use the terminology of Jacob ben Sheshet, which comprises all senses of Scripture, including the *sensus mysticus*.

The inclusion of *sod* within *peshat* is highlighted as well in the following statement of Moses de León in one of his Hebrew theosophic works:

> Those very stories [in the Bible] are the secret of God, and they are included in the wisdom of His thought, the secret of His name. When a person removes the mask of blindness from his face, then he will find in that very story and literal sense (*ha-ma'aseh*)[98] a hill of spices[99] and frankincense.[100] Then his blind eyes will be opened[101] and his thoughts will gladden, and he will say, "Whoever you are, O great mountain" (Zech. 4:7), exalted, "where you hid on the day of the incident"[102] (1 Sam. 20:19), as I explained in the book that I composed called *Pardes*. I called it by the name *Pardes* in virtue of the matter that is known, for I composed it in accordance with the secret of the four ways [of interpretation], according to its very name [as alluded to in the saying] "Four entered the *Pardes*,"[103] i.e., *peshat, remez, derashah, sod*, this is the matter of *Pardes*. I explained there these matters pertaining to the secret of the narrative and literal sense written in the Torah, to show that everything is the eternal life and the true Torah, and there is nothing in all the Torah that is not contained in the secret of His name, may He be elevated.[104]

In this passage de León mentions his use of the fourfold method of interpretation, but insists that all levels of meaning, including the literal narrative (*sensus historicus*), are contained in the secret of the name that is mystically identified with the Torah. It may be concluded, therefore, that the *peshat* itself comprehends the *sod*. This last point is brought out in a striking fashion in another zoharic passage that serves as the preamble to the *Sifra di-Ṣeni'uta* ("Book of Concealment"). In the middle of that passage a parable is given to describe the fate of one who is occupied with the study of *Sifra di-Ṣeni'uta*, a process referred to, on the basis of the description of R. Aqiva in the famous legend of four who entered *Pardes*, as "entering and existing." Such a person is compared to a man who lived in the mountains and knew nothing of life in the city. This man sowed wheat and ate the kernels raw. One day he went to the city and was given bread, cakes kneaded in oil, and fine pastry made with honey and oil. At each interval he inquired about the ingredients used to make the item he was consuming and was told in each case wheat. After having received the last item, he proclaimed: "I am the master of all these (*marei dikhol 'illayn*), for I eat the essence (*'iqra*)[105] of them all which is wheat."[106] The one who successfully studies the "Book of Conceal-ment" is thus compared to the mountain man who eats the essential ingredi-ent used in making all the different items, viz., wheat. There seems to be in this parable a self-awareness on the part of the author of *Zohar* that the *Sifra di-Ṣeni'uta* somehow represents the kernel of zoharic theosophy whereas other parts, perhaps especially the *'Idrot,* are further elaborations that are compa-rable to the various baked goods in relation to the wheat.[107] It is evident, moreover, that wheat functions here as a symbol for Torah, a well-known motif in classical rabbinic literature[108] in general and thirteenth-century kabbalistic sources in particular.[109] Of especial interest is the talmudic expres-sion, "masters of wheat," *marei ḥitya,* for those who have mastered the sources.[110] That the *Zohar* is probably drawing on this image is strengthened by the fact that the *Sifra di-Ṣeni'uta* is composed of five chapters, which perhaps are meant to call to mind the five books of the Torah; that is to say, this part of *Zohar* is structurally parallel to the Pentateuch.[111] Furthermore, it is possible that the wheat, bread, cakes, and fine pastry allude to the four levels of interpretation, literal, midrashic, allegorical, and mystical.[112] The wheat, there-fore, symbolizes the literal sense of Torah,[113] its essence or most basic ingredi-ent, which is at the same time, as the *Zohar* points out, the principle (*kelala*),[114] i.e., that which comprises within itself all the other levels. The movement of zoharic hermeneutics may be thus compared to a circle, beginning and ending with the text in its literal sense. For the *Zohar* the search for the deepest truths of Scripture is a gradual stripping away of the external forms or garments until one gets to the inner core, but when one gets to that inner core what one finds is nothing other than the *peshat,* i.e., the text as it is. To interpret, from the perspective of the *Zohar,* is not to impose finite meaning on the text, but to unfold the infinite meaning within the text. A description of the interpretation process as a form of appropriation by Paul Ricoeur is, I believe, particularly apt in characterizing the convergence of *peshat* and *sod* in the *Zohar:* "Appropriation . . . is the recovery of that which is at work, in labour, within the text. What the interpreter says is a re-saying which reactivates what is said by the text."[115] By decoding the text in light of sefirotic symbolism the theosophic Kabbalist recovers that which is at work within Scripture, at least as viewed from his own perspective.

It is of interest to consider at this juncture the following description of Moses Cordovero (1522–1570), for he has combined the negative attitude toward *peshat* characteristic of *Ray'aya Mehemna* and *Tiqqune Zohar* with a more positive orientation of the main body of the *Zohar.*

> A person must remove the garments from the Torah and break her shells in order to comprehend her depth and her hidden spirituality.[116] . . . They must without doubt strip the Torah from all of her shells . . . then they will understand without any external garment. This is the secret of the Torah that the Holy One, blessed by He, will create in the future. . . . All her shells will be broken and the inner core of the Torah will be comprehended. . . . The kabbalistic secret is clothed in the literal sense for one cannot know how to expound it except by way of the literal sense, as if one said Abraham was a merciful man [i.e., from the attribute of *Ḥesed* or mercy], and his going to Egypt [symbolizes] his descent to the shells. . . . In this manner one cannot speak of Kabbalah without it being mixed with the secret of the literal sense and corporeality.[117]

Cordovero thus begins with a description of the necessity to break the shell of the literal sense, to remove its garment, in order to comprehend the inner core or mystical essence of Torah. The denuded Torah, without shell or garment, characterizes the state of affairs in the messianic age. The Torah in the preredemptive state must have these shells or garment. There is little doubt that with respect to this negative view of *peshat* Cordovero was influenced by the formulation of *Ra'aya Mehmena* and *Tiqqune Zohar.*[118] In the second part of the passage, however, Cordovero insists, in line with the main body of *Zohar,* that the esoteric meaning can be comprehended only through the literal sense. *Sod,* therefore, is clothed in *peshat,* and the only way to apprehend the former is through the latter.

What is perhaps an even more succinct presentation of the hermeneutical orientation of the *Zohar,* which I would term as the retrieval of *peshat,* is contained in the following statement of Moses Ḥayyim Ephraim of Sudlikov (c. 1737–1800), grandson of Israel ben Eliezer, Ba'al Shem Tov (1700–1760):

The secret of *teqi'ah, teru'ah, teqi'ah* is [to be explained] by [the rabbinic idiom] "a verse should not lose its literal sense." That is, initially a person must study and comprehend the literal sense. Afterwards he should expand to [the comprehension of] the various lights and secrets of the Torah. And after that from the power of interpretation he should return and come [to an understanding of] the true literal sense (*ha-peshat ha-'emet*). This is [the significance] of *teqi'ah, teru'ah, teqi'ah*. At first there is the *teqi'ah* which instructs about the literal sense (*ha-peshat*), i.e., a straight sound (*qol pashuṭ*).[119] Afterwards there is a *teru'ah*, which contains the letters *torah 'ayin*, i.e., the [Torah] is interpreted in seventy [the numerical value of *'ayin*] ways. And afterwards a *teqi'ah*, to return to the true literal sense.[120]

In the case of the *Zohar* one finds precisely the kind of "mystical literalism"[121] described by the Hasidic master that is predicated on the notion that the esoteric sense is contained within the literal, an insight apprehended by the mystic who returns to the literal sense, that is, the true literal sense, *ha-peshat ha-'emet*, only after interpreting the text in its multiple aspects. The literal sense is a cover hiding the mystical light only for the unenlightened; the mystic, by contrast, sees that light through and within the cover. The rejection on the part of the *Zohar* of a purely literal reading of biblical narrative does not imply a bifurcation of meaning between *peshat* and *sod*, but only a failure to understand the inherent mystical dimensions of *peshat*.[122] That is, even the *peshat* contains *sod*, and one who looks at the *peshat* without knowledge of the supernal realm cannot truly understand *peshat*. This, I believe, is implied in the following passage: "Even though the narrative of the Torah or the [literal] account (*'ovda'*)[123] goes out from the principle of Torah (*mikelala de'oraitha*) [i.e., the realm of divine emanations that in their collectivity are the Torah in its supernal form] it does not go out to instruct about itself alone but rather to instruct about that supernal principle of Torah (*kelala 'ila'ah de'oraitha*)."[124] The function of the literal-narrative meaning is to instruct the reader about the supernal Torah, the divine pleroma. Without such knowledge the Torah in its purely literal fashion is not even comprehended. This is the force of the mystical understanding of the *sensus litteralis* presented in the *Zohar*. Thus, in one of the contexts in which the *Zohar* emphasizes that the Torah, like the name of God, is hidden and revealed, the focus is an interpretation of "And she [Tamar] sat down at the entrance to Enayim" (Gen. 38:14).

R. Abba said: This section proves that the Torah is hidden and revealed. I have looked through the entire Torah and have not found a place that is called *petaḥ 'enayim.* Rather all is hidden and it contains a secret of secrets. . . . What is *petaḥ enayim?* [The word *petaḥ* may be gathered from what] is written, "he [Abraham] was sitting at the entrance of the tent" (Gen. 18:1). It is also written, "and the Lord will pass over the door" (Exod. 12:23), and "Open the gates of righteousness for me" (Ps. 118:19). [The word] "eyes" [signifies] that all eyes of the word are looking upon this opening.[125]

It is obvious, then, that the hidden meaning of the expression *petaḥ 'enayim* refers to the fact that it functions as a symbol for the last of the divine gradations, Shekhinah, the opening to which all eyes are turned.[126] The kabbalistic signification, therefore, is the sole meaning that the term has for the Zohar; it does not represent a deeper meaning set over against a more straightforward literal meaning for, indeed, no "actual" place corresponds to that name.[127] The interpretation of the *Zohar* is based on a particular reading of the verse found in several Rabbinic sources,[128] though the statement in *Genesis Rabbah* 85:7 is that which most closely resembles the language of the *Zohar:*

Rabbi said: We have reviewed all of Scripture and we have not found a place which is called *petaḥ 'enayim.* What, then, is *petaḥ 'enayim?* This is to teach that she cast her eyes to the opening to which all eyes are cast. And she said: Let it be Your will that I should not leave this house empty handed.[129]

Like the midrashist the Kabbalist begins from the assumption that there is no actual place known by the name *petaḥ 'enayim.*[130] Therefore, the simple meaning of the biblical expression must be sought elsewhere. The explanation in the midrashic compilation attributed to Rabbi, that is, Rabbi Judah the Prince[131]—which itself is intended as an explication of *peshat* and not interpretative layer superimposed on the text—that this refers to the "opening" to which all eyes are cast, that is, a figurative characterization of God,[132] is appropriate and transformed by the *Zohar* into a theosophic symbol. That is, this opening is none other than the divine Presence, the last of the *sefirot,* which is often characterized in theosophic kabbalistic literature as the gateway or openness through which one enters into the sefirotic pleroma. Hence, the *peshat* here is comprehensive only in light of the *sod,* though the formulation of the latter is based on the midrashic (and decidedly nonmystical) reading. In this case, therefore, the claim that the Torah is hidden and revealed should not be construed as an affirmation of dual meaning in the text, but rather that the revealed meaning is itself comprehensible only in light of a hidden signification or symbolic correspondence. In this respect, the *Zohar* follows Naḥmanides and Jacob ben Sheshet who, as I mentioned earlier, affirmed that on occasion the mystical meaning alone provides and adequate explanation for the *peshat.* To take another illustration from the *Zohar:*

> R. Shim'on said: If people only knew the words of Torah then they would comprehend that there is no word or letter in the Torah that does not contain supernal, precious secrets. Come and see: it is written, "Moses spoke and God answered him with a voice" (Exod. 19:19). It has been taught[133]: what is [the meaning of] "with a voice"? With the voice of Moses. This is correct, the voice of Moses precisely (*dayka'*), the voice to which he was attached and through which he was superior to all other prophets.[134]

In this particular example the kabbalistic recasting of the midrashic reading is offered as the *peshat* of the verse, the plain meaning. Hence, the voice through which God responded to Moses is, as reflected already in the midrashic interpretation, the voice of Moses, but in the *Zohar* the latter is transformed into a symbol for one of the *sefirot,* viz., *Tif'eret,* the gradation to which the earthly Moses is attached.[135] The transformation of the midrashic into the kabbalistic is noted by the author of *Zohar* by his use of the expression *dayka'* in connection with the phrase *voice of Moses,* which I have rendered as precisely. This term is used in many contexts by the *Zohar* to emphasize the kabbalistic intent[136] of the given passage as, for example, in the following:

> It has been taught[137] [concerning the verse] "For on this day atonement shall be made for you to cleanse you of all your sins" (Lev. 16:30). It should have been [written] "this day" (*ha-yom ha-zeh*). But it says "on this day" (*ba-yom ha-zeh*) precisely (*dayka'*), for on that day the Holy Ancient One is revealed to atone for everyone's sins.[138]

The pretext here is a presumed problem with *peshat*—a repeated phenomenon in the *Zohar* to which I will return later on—which is answered by stressing that the precise form of the biblical text instructs the reader about a mystical process. It will be noted that the same role is played by the word *mamash,* which served already as a technical term in Rabbinic literature to denote that a given biblical expression should be understood in its factual or real sense and not in some imaginative, figurative, or allegorical way.[139] In the *Zohar* the word *mamash* can designate that a specific term is to be understood in its kabbalistic signification.[140] Thus, for instance, one reads:

> He began to expound again and said: "From my flesh I will see God" (Job 19:26). Why [is it written] "from my flesh" (*u-mibesariy*)? It should have been "from myself" (*u-me'atzmiy*). Rather, from my flesh literally (*mamash*)! And

what is it? As it is written, "The holy flesh will pass away from you" (Jer. 11:15), and it is written, "Thus shall My covenant be marked in our flesh" (Gen. 17:13). It has been taught: whenever a person is marked by the holy sign of that covenant, from it he sees the Holy One, blessed be He. From it literally (*mamash*)![141]

This is a striking example of the hyperliteralism that characterizes the zoharic reading of Scripture. By means of the technique of *gezerah shavah*, the linking of seemingly disparate contextual fields based on identity of expression,[142] the Zohar determines that the occurrence of the word flesh (*basar*) in Job 19:26 must be explained as denoting the *membrum virile;* hence, it is from the phallus that one sees God.[143] The meaning of this is clarified by the mystical notion, itself rooted in earlier midrashic modes of thinking, that the sign of the covenant of circumcision is a letter inscribed on the body.[144] In that sense it can be said that one sees God from the very flesh on which the sign of the covenant has been inscribed.

Another example of the hyperliteralism of the *Zohar* may be gathered from the following passage: "The first tablets were inscribed from that place [*Binah*]. This is the secret of the verse, 'incised on the tablets' (Exod. 32:16). Do not read 'incised' (*ḥarut*) but rather freedom (*ḥerut*).[145] *Ḥerut* indeed (*mamash*)—the place upon which is dependent all freedom."[146] Utilizing the midrashic reading of the biblical expression *ḥarut* as *ḥerut*, the *Zohar* renders the plain sense of the verse as referring to the *sefirah* which is designated by the term *ḥerut*, the ontic source of all freedom, that is, *Binah*, which is the source as well for the tablets of law, the subject of the verse in question. On occasion the *Zohar* uses both of these expressions together, *mamash* and *dayka',* to note that the literal meaning is comprehensible only in terms of the kabbalistic significance.[147] To cite one pertinent example:

> R. Judah: Israel did not come close to Mount Sinai until they entered the portion of the Righteous One [*Ṣaddiq*, i.e., the ninth emanation or *Yesod*, Foundation] and merited it. From where do we know? It is written, "On that very day they entered the wilderness of Sinai" (Exod. 19:1). "On that very day" indeed (*mamash dayka'*)! And it is written, "In that day they shall say: This is our God; we trusted in Him [and He delivered us]" (Isa. 25:9).[148]

The kabbalistic explanation that Israel approached Mount Sinai only after having entered the divine grade of *Yesod*, or *Ṣaddiq*, is derived from the literal expression, *ba-yom ha-zeh*, "on that very day," for the word *zeh*, the masculine, demonstrative pronoun, is one of the standard symbols for this particular *sefirah*.[149] Further support for this reading is adduced from Isa. 25:9 where the demonstrative *zeh* is again used, as read by the theosophic exegete, as a name of this attribute of God. The kabbalistic truth is, in the last analysis, revealed to a careful reader of the text in its most elemental sense through the rabbinic hermeneutical technique of *gezerah shawah*.[150]

That the implication of the expressions *dayka'* and *mamash* is to signify the convergence of *peshat* and *sod,* such that the determination of kabbalistic meaning is channeled through the linguistic signification of the terms in the given utterance,[151] can be seen unambiguously from the following passage:

> R. Shim'on said: it is written "And new moon after new moon, and sabbath after sabbath" (Isa. 66:23). Why is the one [new moon] compared to the other [sabbath]? Everything amounts to one gradation, the one coupled with the other. The happiness of the one is not found in the other except when the Holy Ancient One is revealed; then the happiness of all [is found]. It has been taught: "A psalm. A song, for the sabbath day" (Ps. 92:1), to the sabbath day literally (*mamash*)! This is a praise which the Holy One, blessed be He, utters. At that time the happiness is found and the soul is increased for the Ancient One is revealed and the union is set. Similarly, when the moon is renewed the sun illuminates her with the happiness of the light of the Ancient One above. Therefore this sacrifice [offered on the New Moon] is above so that everything will be ameliorated and happiness will be found in the world. Thus [it is said] "they should bring a sacrifice for me," the word [*'al*] precisely (*dayka' millah*). It has been taught: it is written, "A burnt offering for sabbath in addition to the regular burnt offering" (Num. 28:10). One must focus one's mental intention higher than the rest of the days. Thus [it is written] specifically (*dayka'*) "in addition to [i.e., *'al*, which can be read as the preposition atop or over] the burnt offering." It has been taught: [with respect to] Hannah it is written, "she prayed to (*'al*) the Lord" (1 Sam 1:10). [The word] *'al* indeed (*dayka'*), for children are independent on the holy *mazzal* (i.e., *Keter* or the Holy Ancient One.]₁⁵² . . . There is no word or even a small letter in the Torah that does not allude to the supernal wisdom, and from which are suspended heaps of secrets of the supernal wisdom.[153]

In this highly compact passage the *Zohar* draws various mystical conclusions by effectively overliteralizing the verses under discussion. In particular, attention is paid to what would appear to be a rather innocuous word, the proposition *'al* that, when read kabbalistically, is decoded as a sign for the uppermost aspects of the divine. Having determined the meaning of this term it is then possible to link together disparate textual units—in this case derived both from biblical and talmudic sources—by means of the technique of *gezerah shavah*. What would appear from the outside as an obvious imposition of an external and autonomous system upon the biblical text is in fact presented as the precise and literal meaning of the relevant verses. Therefore the concluding statement is to the effect that every word, indeed every letter, of Scripture alludes to a supernal secret. In the case of the *Zohar* we might say, inverting the instructive phrase of one scholar, *peshat* is "deep midrash,"[154] if we understand by the latter a reference to theosophic symbolism.

Another, an by far the most frequently employed, term in the *Zohar* to mark the convergence of *peshat* and *sod* is the word *vada'y*. With respect to this usage it must be noted that the *Zohar* is again drawing on Rabbinic literature, wherein this word, like *mamash*, functioned as a *terminus technicus* to underscore or emphasize the factual or sensible meaning, the *peshat* as it came to be called in Amoraic sources, of a certain expression in contrast to a nonliteral or figurative connotation.[155] At least three different nuances can be discerned in the zoharic usage of the key term. It is used to emphasize the actual or real meaning,[156] to mark a kabbalistic symbol,[157] or to signify the convergence of the exoteric (literal) and esoteric (symbolic) meaning,[158] I will mention only a few examples of countless possibilities found scattered throughout the landscape of the *Zohar*. From a purely statistical perspective the examples I will give are somewhat arbitrary in that they reflect only a very small portion of the passages that could have been cited. However, by calling attention to the limited cases where this exegetical device is used, I hope minimally to focus scholarly attention on an important, but neglected, phenomenon in zoharic hermeneutics. It is my intention, moreover, that the typologies established here will be tested, refined, and applied in other studies in the future.

Let me begin with the following zoharic interpretation of Esther 8:15:

> Mordecai went out before the king in royal attire [*levush malkhut*, literally, in the garment of royalty], the garment of royalty indeed (*vada'y*) [i.e.,] the image of that [supernal] world. . . . R. Shim'on said: how sweet are these words, fortunate is my lot. I know that the righteous in that world are clothed in the garment called the garment of royalty, and indeed so it is.[159]

The expression *levush malkhut*, understood in its literal sense from the vantage point of the *Zohar*, signifies the luminous garment that derives from the Shekhinah, the divine attribute also called by the name *Malkhut*. The verse informs us, then, that when Mordecai went before the king he was cloaked in just such an aura, which is construed as an image of the garment of the righteous in the sefirotic realm. There is here no second meaning for the expression *levush malkhut*, but rather its plain meaning indicates the mystical notion. Another way of putting this matter is that the literalism of the text instructs the reader about the esoteric doctrine. The same approach is apparent in the zoharic interpretation of the verse, "When the men of the place [of Gerar] asked him [Isaac] about his wife, he said, 'She is my sister" (Gen.26:7):

This is similar [to the incident of] Abraham,[160] for the Shekhinah was with him and his wife, and on account of the Shekhinah [the statement] was uttered, as it is written, "Say to wisdom, You are my sister" (Prov. 7:4). Therefore he was strengthened and said "She is my sister." By both Abraham and Isaac it was certainly appropriate, for in the verse it is written, "My sister, my darling, my faultless dove" (Song of Songs 5:2). Thus it was indeed (*vada'y*) appropriate for them to say "She is my sister."[161]

Troubled by an obvious problem that has engaged the interest of biblical commentators through the ages regarding Isaac's (as Abraham's) overt deception, the *Zohar* provides an explanation that accounts for the *peshat* but only by reference to a kabbalistic secret. The connotation of the word *sister* in the account of Abraham and Isaac is Shekhinah, a usage attested in the two other biblical verses—when read kabbalistically as well—cited in the preceding passage. The *peshat*, when so understood, removes the problem of lying entirely for both Patriarchs referred to the divine Presence and not their respective spouses. Even though the *peshat* offered by the zoharic reading ignores the continuation of the verse itself, it is evident that the kabbalistic explanation of the word *sister* is indeed presented as the plain meaning of the idiom in this context.

Let me cite another example to illustrate the point:

R. Ḥiyya began to expound, "the glory of God is to conceal the matter, the glory of kings is to search out the matter" (Prov. 25:2). "The glory of God is to conceal the matter," for a person does not have permission to reveal secret matters for they have not been given permission to reveal matters that the Ancient of Days concealed, as it is said, "that they may eat their fill and cover that which the Ancient One [concealed]" (Isa. 23:18).[162] "To eat their fill," up to that place wherein they have permission [to reveal] and no more. Thus it is said, *ve-limekhaseh 'atiq*, verily (*vada'y*) that which the Ancient One (*'atiq*) covers.[163]

The author of the *Zohar* follows here the reading of the verse from Isaiah attributed to R. Eleazar in the Talmud (*b. Pesaḥim* 119a): "What is the meaning of *li-mekhaseh 'atiq*? That which the ancient of Days (*'atiq yomin*) has concealed. And what is that? The secrets of Torah." The midrashic reading is accepted by the *Zohar* as the *peshat* of the verse, signified by the usage of the *terminus technicus vada'y*. In the case of the *Zohar*, moreover, the talmudic reference is transposed in light of sefirotic theosophy, for the word *'atiq* designates the first of the divine gradations, though already in the Talmud the word *'atiq* has a specific theological reference. In this case as well, therefore, We have an instance where the *peshat* of a verse is rendered by its esoteric meaning. That the word *vada'y* serves as a kind of signpost to designate that the plain sense of the biblical expression is to be rendered by its sefirotic correlation is repeatedly stressed in the *Zohar*, as for example:

> Why is it written, "Her ways are ways of pleasantness" (Prov. 3:17)? [R. Eleazar] said to [R. Ḥiyya]: How foolish are people of the world, for they do not know how to consider words of Torah, for the words of Torah are the way to merit that pleasantness of God, as it is written, "Her ways are ways of pleasantness." The ways of pleasantness (*no'am*) indeed! What is this pleasantness? As it is written, "To gaze upon the beauty (*no'am*) of the Lord." It has been taught that the Torah and its ways derive from that Beauty. . . . Thus, it is written, "Her ways are ways of pleasantness, and all her paths peaceful."[164]

From the vantage point of the Kabbalist, then, the expression *darkhe no'am*, the ways of pleasantness, refers to the gradation in the sefirotic pleroma out of which the Torah, itself a designation for the *sefirah* of *Tif'eret*, emerges. In that sense the expression should be taken quite literally for the ways of Torah are the ways of pleasantness; that is, pleasantness being the ontic source for the Torah.

The exegetical function that the author of the *Zohar* assigned to the word *vada'y* as marking the overlapping of exoteric and esoteric signification can also be seen from the following passage:

> What is [the meaning of what is] written, "So he [Moses cried out to the Lord, and the Lord showed him a piece of wood (*'etz*)" (Exod. 15:25)? The word *'etz* is nothing but the Torah,[165] as it is written, "She is a tree of life (*'etz ḥayyim*) to those who grasp her" (Prov. 3:18). And the [word] Torah is nothing but the Holy One, blessed by He. R. Abba said: the [word] tree is nothing but the Holy One, blessed He, as it is written, "For man [is] the tree of the field" (Num. 20:19,[166] the tree of the field (*'etz ha-sadeh*) indeed (*vada'y*), i.e., the tree of the field of holy apples.[167]

Using the ancient midrashic formula to derive semantic meaning from a specific expression, "the word *X* is nothing but *Y*,"[168] the author of *Zohar* sets out to show that the reference to the piece of wood in Exod. 15:25 refers to God or, to be more precise, the aspect of God that corresponds to the Torah and is called the Holy One, blessed He; that is, *Tif'eret*. The first view achieves this by two steps: first, by following rabbinic exegesis and specifying that the word tree (or wood) signifies Torah; and second, that the word *Torah* denotes the Holy One, blessed be He. R. Abba, by contrast, reaches the goal with one step: the word *tree* itself denotes the Holy One, blessed be He. This is proven from the verse, "For man [is] the tree of the field," which is read the tree of the "field of holy apples"; that is, the Shekhinah. The tree that is in the field of holy apples is *Tif'eret,* also designated as the anthropos.

From the perspective of the zoharic authorship, then, the word *vada'y* can signify that the literal sense of Scripture is to be sought in its kabbalistic meaning. That this is so may be seen clearly from one final example:

> "The Lord spoke to Moses and Aaron, saying: This is the ritual law that the Lord has commanded" (Num. 19:1–2). R. Yose began to expound: "This is the Torah that Moses set before the Israelites" (Deut. 4:44). Come and see: the words of Torah are holy, supernal, and sweet. . . . For he who is involved in [the study of] Torah it is as if he stands each day on Mount Sinai and receives the Torah. . . . The comrades have thus taught: Here it is written "this is the ritual law" (*zo't ḥuqqat ha-torah*) and [in the other case] it is written "and this is the Torah" (*ve-zo't ha-torah*). What is the difference between these two? This concerns a supernal mystery and thus have I learnt: "This is the Torah" to show everything in one unity, to contain the Community of Israel [Shekhinah] within the Holy One, blessed be He [*Tif'eret*] so that everything will be found as one. Therefore [it is written] "and this is the Torah." Why is there the additional *vav* [in the word *ve-zo't*]? As it has been said, to show that everything is one without any separation. [The word] *ve-zo't* [signifies] the principle (*kelal*) and the exception (*perat*) as one, the masculine and feminine. Thus [it is written] "And this is the Torah" indeed (*vada'y*)! But the word *zo't* without the additional *vav* [signifies] "the ritual law" (*ḥuqqat ha-torah*) indeed (*vada'y*), and not the Torah, i.e., the law of the Torah and the decree of the Torah. . . . Thus [it is written] "and this is the Torah" literally (*mamash*), [signifying] one complete unity, the containment of the masculine and feminine, the *vav* and the *heh* [the word] [signifies] the *heh* alone, and thus [it is written] "this is the ritual law."[169]

Ever a close reader of the biblical text, the zoharic authorship here heeds the distinction between the two expressions, "and this is the torah" (*ve-zo't ha-torah*), on the one hand, and "this is the ritual law" (*zo't ḥuqqat ha-torah*), on the other. The former expression when decoded (perhaps encoded would be the more appropriate word) kabbalistically alludes to the unity of the feminine and masculine aspects of the divine, Shekhinah and *Tif'eret,* signified respectively by the words *zo't* and *torah,* whereas the latter refers exclusively to the feminine aspect designated as *zo't* as well as *ḥuqqat ha-torah.* The verse "and this is the torah" is thus being read as: this, *zo't,* that is, Shekhinah, is one with the torah, that is, *Tif'eret.* By contrast, the verse "this is the ritual law" is read as follows: this, *zo't,* that is, Shekhinah, is the ritual law, *ḥuqqat torah,* both terms designating the same potency of the godhead. The former verse, therefore, unlike the latter, is a statement that proclaims the divine unity, understood in its particular kabbalistic nuance. This point is related by the kabbalistic interpreter to the additional *vav* in the former case, *ve-zo't*, a letter that signifies the union of male and female. In the last analysis, therefore, the kabbalistic reading is indicated by the very orthography of Scripture, which constitutes the *peshat* in the extended sense of the term.

The centrality of the role of *peshat* in zoharic hermeneutics can be ascertained as well from the many instances in the *Zohar* wherein a problem with the simple meaning serves as the basis for a kabbalistic truth that, when exposed, illuminates the verse. Suffice it here to mention a few examples to illustrate this phenomenon. In one passage the claim of the *Zohar* that every word of Scripture has a secret is based on a problem with the literal meaning of Exod. 2:6, "When she [the daughter of Pharaoh] opened it, she saw that it was a child, *va-tiftah va-tir'ehu 'et ha-yeled*. The obvious problem, reflected in any number of medieval biblical exegetes,[170] is why the word, *va-tir'ehu*, which contains the verb (saw) and the direct object (him), is followed by another direct object of the same verb, the child, *'et ha-yeled*. This problem in *peshat* serves as the springboard for the mystical imagination of the author of *Zohar*, who notes that the extra letters in the word *va-tir'ehu*, the *heh* and *vav*, which symbolize the attributes of Shekhinah and *Tif'eret*, were inscribed on the infant Moses. This kabbalistic interpretation is based in part upon the following statement in *b. Sotah* 12b: " 'When she opened it, she saw that it was a child.' It should have been written *va-tir'eh* (she saw) [instead of *va-tir'ehu*, she saw him]. R. Yose ben Ḥanina said that she saw the Shekhinah with him." Interestingly enough, in his commentary to the relevant verse the eleventh-century exegete, R. Solomon ben Isaac of Troyes (Rashi), cites this talmudic interpretation as the midrashic one after he offers what he considers to be the *peshat* viz., the direct object *the child* (*et ha-yeled*) modifies the prior expression *she saw him* (*va-tir'ehu*). From the perspective of R. Yose ben Ḥanina, however, the midrashic explanation is itself the *peshat* of the verse. Scripture should have used the verbal form *va-tera'* followed by the direct object *'et ha-yeled*. The seemingly superfluous expression, *va-tir'ehu*, therefore, is interpreted as a reference to the Shekhinah. According to the opinion of some later Ashkenazi authorities, the reference to the Shekhinah is derived from the two extra letters in the word *va-tir'ehu*, the *heh* and *vav*, for these letters make up one of the names of God, *ho*.[171] Thus, for instance, Judah ben Eliezer (twelfth and thirteenth century), writes: " 'When she opened it, she saw that it was a child.' R. Solomon ben Isaac (Rashi) explains that she saw the Shekhinah with him. This is derived from the fact that it is not written *she saw* (*va-tera'*) but rather *she saw him* (*va-tir'ehu*), and this [the extra letters *heh-vav*] is the name of the Holy One, blessed be He."[172] Similarly, in the Torah commentary stemming from the circle of R. Judah ben Samuel the Pious, though erroneously attributed to Eleazar ben Judah of Worms, one finds the following formulation: " 'She saw him' (*va-tir'ehu*) should be read as she saw *ho* (*heh-vav*), she saw the light of the Shekhinah."[173] The *Zohar* continues this line of interpretation, but, in accordance with its own theosophic conception, distinguishes between the *heh* and *vav* referring, as was said earlier, to Shekhinah and *Tif'eret*. Although the kabbalistic explanation given carries one far from the *sensus litteralis* in any conventional manner, it is instructive that the mystical exegesis begins with a textual difficulty on the *peshat* level.

Another example of this phenomenon occurs in the zoharic interpretation of "The Lord appeared to Abram and said to him, 'I am El Shaddai' " (Gen. 17:1). The *Zohar* raises a question on the use of the particular divine name, El Shaddai, in this context. This question has been posed by most of the standard medieval biblical commentaries, including, for instance, Rashi, Abraham ibn Ezra, Nahmanides, and Obadiah Sforno. It is clear, then, that the query of the *Zohar* must be understood within this context. The response of the *Zohar* involves a complicated kabbalistic exegesis that will illuminate this particular usage in terms of a mystical signification. That is, circumcision effects a change from the demonic realm, symbolized by the word *shed,* to the divine, represented by *Shaddai* or the last of the *sefirot,* the Shekhinah. The two words, *shed* and *Shaddai,* share the same consonants with the exception of the *yod* in the latter, the letter that corresponds to the sign of the covenant, *'ot berit;* that is, the sign of circumcision. After having been circumcised Abraham can be called *tamim,* which the *Zohar* renders in accordance with the Targum, *shalim;* that is, perfect. Such a person is blessed by Shekhinah as is further attested by the verse, "May El Shaddai bless you" (Gen. 28:3). The kabbalistic exegesis is propelled by and returns to a concern with the literal sense of the text.

One can discern the same process in the following passage:

> "Elohim blessed Noah and his sons" (Gen. 9:1). R. Abba began to expound, "It is the blessing of the Lord that enriches, and no toil can increase it" (Prov. 10:22). "The blessing of the Lord" (*birkat YHWH*) is the Shekhinah, for she is appointed over the blessings of the world, and from her the blessings go out for everyone.[174]

According to the zoharic reading of Gen. 9:1, the Shekhinah, last of the ten gradations, blessed Noah. This is highlighted by the mystical exegesis of Prov. 10:22 where *birkat YHWH* is deciphered as a technical name for the Shekhinah. The point of the passage is that the verse in Genesis can be understood only when one is aware that Elohim is a name of the Shekhinah, the source of blessing. This is *peshuṭo shel miqra;* that is, the plain meaning of the text; no other sense would serve as an outer shell or covering hiding the inner meaning. On the contrary, the text allows for only one meaning, the proper deciphering of which belongs in the hands of the enlightened Kabbalist. Thus, in the continuation of this passage the *Zohar* explains the semantic shift from the use of the name YHWH in "Then the Lord said to Noah, Go into the ark etc." (Gen. 7:1), to Elohim in "Elohim blessed Noah and his sons" (Gen. 9:1): "As it is said, the master of the house grants permission for one to enter, and afterwards the wife tells one to exit. One enters at first with the permission of the master and in the end leaves with the permission of the wife." When the allusions are properly decoded it turns out that the tetragrammaton corresponds to the masculine potency, *Tif'eret*, and Elohim to the feminine Shekhinah. The kabbalistic symbolism allows the zoharic authorship to account for a subtle shift in the text concerning the various divine names, an issue that has continued to provide grist for the mill of biblical scholarship. In this connection it should be noted that the *Zohar* often pays careful attention to the different names of God as they appear in the Bible inasmuch as they are a reference to particular *sefirot*. To take what may be considered a rather typical example of this phenomenon: "R. Eleazar said the Shekhinah was speaking with [Abraham] for through this gradation the Holy One, blessed be He, was revealed to him, as it is written, 'I appeared to Abraham, Isaac, and Jacob in the name El Shaddai. [R. Shim'on] said to him: So it certainly (*vada'y*) is!'" In these cases it is unequivocally the case that the very *peshat* of Scripture can only be comprehended by way of kabbalistic explication.

Another typology that can be discerned in the *Zohar* concerns the interpretation of a verse wherein a problem with the literal sense functions as a stimulus for the kabbalistic interpretation. In these cases, unlike the ones previously discussed, the assumption is not that the *peshat* is the *sod*, but only that concern with the *peshat* serves as the pretext to develop the esoteric reading. An example of this may be seen in the following:

> Come and see, it is written, "This shall be (*ve-hayita zo't*) to you a law for all time" (Lev. 16:34). It should have been [written] "this shall be for you" (*ve-hayita lakhem*) [i.e., without the article *zo't*. What is the import of the word "this" (*zo't*)? For it is said a law for all time (*ḥuqqat 'olam*). In every place [the expression] "a law for all time" (*ḥuqqat 'olam*) is called the decree of the king, for all laws enter into that place and it seals them as one who seals everything in a treasure. "A law for all time" indeed (*vada'y*)! In that [grade referred to as] *zo't* is inscribed and engraved all its hidden and concealed matters.[175]

Beginning with an ostensible problem at the level of the simple meaning, the *Zohar* is able to interpret the seemingly extra word as a cipher for a deep mystical truth. The word is not superfluous, but rather indicates to us the kabbalistic significance of the whole verse: the law referred to is not simply the rituals specified for atonement on Yom Kippur, but it is a mystical symbol for the last of the gradations. In this case, and countless others that I could have cited, the literal sense does not entirely overlap with the mystical. The issue rather is that the latter is derived by a probing of the former. It is precisely such a strategy that fills the pages of the *Zohar*, the Kabbalist exegete heeding each and every word of Scripture, maintaining the divinity and ultimate significance of the text as it is in its received form.

In sum, it may be concluded that the scholarly consensus that the interest in *peshat* in the *Zohar* is secondary and unrelated to the internal meaning, must be corrected. From three distinct vantage points it can be argued that concern with the literal sense is essential to zoharic hermeneutics. First, the *Zohar* is operating with a theological conception of the *sensus litteralis* such that it is thought to comprise within itself all senses of Scripture, including the mystical. Second, numerous examples in the *Zohar* indicate that the authorship of this work accepted the view that in certain cases the *peshat* of a verse is comprehensible only in terms of *sod;* that is, the kabbalistic meaning is not a supplementary one but is rather the exclusive sense of the text. Third, the search for the esoteric meaning in *Zohar* often begins with a standard problem of reading the verse contextually. While the mystical imagination carries the *Zohar* beyond the reaches of the literal meaning in any exact sense of the term, from the perspective of *Zohar* itself, by removing the external coverings, one opens up the text to see it as it is in its most basic form, viz., a self-revelation of God. Discovering *peshat;* for the authorship of the *Zohar* means discarding the outer layers that conceal the inner light or soul of the text. Those who look only at the *peshat,* without knowledge of what lies beneath, do not in the end really understand even the *peshat;* that is, they have no text. In that sense the act of reading (i.e., interpreting) is constitutive not only of meaning but of the text itself.

This point is depicted in a profound way in one of the parables spoken by the mysterious elder to R. Yose: "Who is the beautiful maiden who has no eyes, and whose body is hidden and revealed; she goes out in the morning and hides during the day, adorned in ornamentations that are not."[176] From the continuation of this section it is evident that this maiden symbolizes the Torah who stands before her lover. Thus we have a striking contrast between the description of Torah as the maiden without eyes and the mystic exegete who, as I noted earlier in another context, is referred to as the "wise one full of eyes."[177] The force of the latter expression is clear enough as may be gathered, for instance, from another passage in *Zohar* where the mystics are characterized as "masters of the eyes (*marei de'eynin*) who know with their mind and contemplate the wisdom of the Master.'[178] This last description reflects a shift in the epistemological focus characteristic of the *Zohar* from the auditory to the visual as the essential modality by which gnosis of the divine is gained.[179]

But what does it mean to say of the Torah that it has no eyes? Yehuda Liebes has suggested two possible meanings: the first that it is invisible and the second that it has no aspect or color. The former explanation fits well into the context for, as has been pointed out already, the maiden is described as hiding and revealing itself in progressive stages before the lover. That is, the Torah is invisible to all but the Kabbalist who knows how to "see"; that is, interpret, her. The difficulty with this explanation is a philological one, for the actual expression is that the maiden has no eyes. This implies that she cannot see, not that she cannot be seen. It thus seems to me more likely that the second explanation is the correct one. That the word *eyes* has the connotation of colors, aspects or characteristics is attested already in biblical[180] and Rabbinic[181] usage.

Specifically, in terms of kabbalistic precedents mention should be made of Isaac ben Jacob ha-Kohen's statement to the effect that Tanin, the intermediary between Samael and Lilith in the demonic realm, corresponding to *Yesod* on the side of holiness, is described as having no eyes; that is, no characteristic.[182] In the case of the zoharic parable I would suggest, moreover, that this description of the maiden indicates that the parabolic image is operative simultaneously on two planes, the hermeneutical and the ontic. That is to say, the maiden symbolizes not only Torah but the divine grade to which the latter corresponds, viz., the Shekhinah.[183] Indeed, it can be shown from other passages in the *Zohar* that the Torah is identified as the feminine persona of God, the Shekhinah, a conception rooted in the older aggadic motif concerning the female image of the Torah,[184] even though according to a widely attested conception in thirteenth-century Kabbalah the Written Torah corresponds to the masculine and the Oral Torah to the feminine. It is the case, moreover, that the Shekhinah is often enough described as that which has no form, or color of its own but only that which it receives from above. The maiden without eyes, therefore, signifies that the text in and of itself is "blind," without sense; whatever meaning the text has is imparted to it by the open eye (*peqiḥu de-'eyna'*) of the reader in the same manner that the Shekhinah assumes the forms that she receives from the *sefirah* of *Yesod*, the *membrum virile* in the divine organism. The interpreter thus stands in the position of the masculine *Yesod* when confronting the text, which is likened to the female Shekhinah, and the interpretative relation is essentially erotic in its nature.[185] The mystic, full of eyes, gives sense to the eyeless text by his bestowing glance, a glance that bestows by disclosing that which is latent in the text. The constitution of meaning in the hermeneutical relationship underlies the task of reading according to the *Zohar.* Paradoxically, this act of bestowal is characterized as an appropriation of that which the text reveals from within its concealment. This is true for all levels of meaning, only at the end of the process, when the mystic stands face to face with the text, is the text finally disclosed.

In the final analysis, the rejection on the part of the *Zohar* of a purely literal reading of biblical narrative does not imply a bifurcation of meaning between *peshat* and *sod*, but only a failure to understand the inherent mystical dimensions of *peshat.* That is, even *peshat* contains *sod*, and the one who looks at the plain meaning without knowledge of the supernal realm cannot truly understand the plain meaning. The relation between esoteric and exoteric levels of meaning is very much reflected, as Idel has noted, in the respective ontology of the given Kabbalist.[186] Hence, the ontological assumption that the corporeal world symbolically reflects the divine, a common feature of theosophic Kabbalah, in the realm of exegesis generates a positive attitude toward *peshat* and its relationship to *sod*. This positive attitude is even more pronounced in the case of the *Zohar*, where the pantheistic tendencies are evident.[187] That is, all reality is said to form one continuous chain so that there are no radical breaks. It follows that entities in the realm are but final links in this chain. Analogously, the literal sense comprises within itself the esoteric truths. The *peshat* therefore, is not a shell that is to be broken or a garment to be discarded, but rather a veil to be penetrated so that through it one can behold the mystical insight—in the words of the *Zohar*, to see the secret matter from within its garment. The attitude of *Zohar* toward the written text of Scripture had an enduring influence on the kabbalistic tradition, which unfolded for several hundred years after its appearance. Thus, for example, the noted Kabbalist, Ḥayyim Vital (1543–1620), who in his programmatic introduction to the *Sha'ar ha-Haqdamot* launches, on the basis of Zoharic passages drawn mainly from *Ra'aya' Mehemna'* and the *Tiqqunim*,[188] a sharp critique of those who adopt a literalist approach toward the Written and Oral Torah, in one place underlines the inherent necessity of the *peshat* and its organic relation to the *sod* or inner meaning:

This too [the attribution of physical characteristics such as wings to the angels] will be a wonder in the eyes of the literalists, and they will think that in this too there is form, and the matter is not [to be taken] according to its literal meaning. They do not understand that the literal sense (*peshat*) and the symbolic (*remez*)[189] are one thing like the soul and the body, for the one is the image and likeness of the other. If the soul would change its limbs from the limbs of the body, of necessity the former could not be clothed in the latter. A small vessel cannot contain a larger one; and if the latter goes inside the former, it cannot go inside with all its parts. In this manner the literal meaning of Scripture (*peshatei ha-torah*) must be like the soul of the Torah and its inwardness (*nishmat ha-torah u-penimiyutah*) for the body is the image of the soul. It is also necessary that the inwardness be something spiritual, for if not it would have no need to be clothed, as [it follows from] the way of the literalists who explain the beginning of the Torah.[190]

From this passage we can understand the thrust of Vital's attack on the literalists. He does not oppose the study of *peshat* but what he does reject is the study of *peshat* divorced from any consideration of *sod*. In his view the literal and the symbolic meanings are one organic unity in a relationship like that of the soul and body. Just as there is a morphological resemblance between soul and body enabling the former to be clothed in the latter, so too there is correspondence between the literal and esoteric textual levels. The hidden signification is clothed in and ultimately known through the literal. The view expressed here confirms the posture of the *Zohar* that I discussed at length in this essay.

The implicit principle of zoharic hermeneutics is rendered explicitly by subsequent Kabbalists, such as R. Isaiah ben Abraham Horowitz (ca. 1565–1630), known as *ha-SheLaH ha-Qadosh*, the "holy Shelah," based on the initials of his major work, the *Shene Luḥot ha-Berit* ("Two Tablets of the Covenant"). Commenting on the relation of the hidden (*nistar*) to the revealed (*nigleh*), the Shelah writes:

The revealed is the hidden, i.e., the revealed is the disclosure of the hidden and its dissemination. It follows that the revealed is the hidden. Thus it is with respect to matters of the Torah: the revealed is not an independent matter in relation to the hidden, in accord with the view of the masses who hold that the hidden way is separate and the revealed way separate. This is not the case, but rather the hidden evolves [through a chain] and is revealed. To this the verse alludes, "Like golden apples in silver showpieces is a phrase well turned" (Prov. 25:11). That is to say, just as the silver approximates the gold but it is on a lower level, so is the revealed in relation to the hidden.[191]

Although in the continuation of this passage the Shelah approvingly refers to Maimonides's interpretation of the verse from Proverbs in the introduction to the *Guide of the Perplexed*, the fact is that the position he has articulated reflects that of the *Zohar* with respect to the essential correspondence of the two levels of meaning. Just as ontically the external (the material world) is the manifestation of the internal (the spiritual realm of the divine emanations), so textually the exoteric meaning (the literal sense) is the externalization or disclosure of the esoteric (the mystical sense). There is thus a complete identification of the esoteric and exoteric so that any potential conflict between the two is resolved: the religious proscription to study talmudic disputes (*havayot 'Abbaye ve-Rava*) is itself included in the mandate to study mystical matters (*ma'aseh merkabah*).[192]

I conclude with one final example, a statement of R. Shneur Zalman of Lyady (1745–1813), founder of Ḥabad Ḥasidism, which likewise reflects the hermeneutical orientation of the zoharic authorship and indicates to what an extent the latter had a profound influence on the shaping of subsequent Jewish mystical conceptions about the text and its multivalent levels of meaning:

> Thus [Scripture] is called *miqra'*, for one reads (*qore'*) and draws down the revelation of the light of the Infinite (*'Ein-Sof*) by means of the letters[193] even if one does not understand anything. . . . This is not the case with respect to the Oral Torah which is clothed in wisdom, and therefore if one does not understand one does not draw down [the light]. With respect to the Written Torah, however, one draws down [the light] even if one does not understand . . . since the source of the emanation (*meqor ha-hamshakhah*) is above wisdom. . . . Thus the Written Torah is called *miqra'*, for they read and draw down [the emanation] by means of the letters. . . . Included in the study of Scripture is also the study of *aggadot*, for most of the *aggadot* are on verses [in Scripture] and few are homiletical. Moreover, they are not comprehended and are thus considered to be in the category of Scripture. Included in Scripture is also the study of the inwardness of Torah (*penimiyut ha-torah*), for the midrash of *Zohar* is one the verses of Torah. Moreover, in the study of the secrets of Torah one only comprehends the reality (*ha-metzi'ut*) [of the divine] from the chain [of emanation] and not from the essence [or substance] (*ha-mahut*) [of God]. Therefore it is not the same as Mishnah or Talmud through which one comprehends the essence of His wisdom (*mahut hokhmato*).[194]

Shneur Zalman thus distinguishes between study of Scripture and Kabbalah, on the one hand, and Mishnah and Talmud, on the other. Whereas by means of the former one comprehends the reality of the divine as expressed in the chain of emanation rather than from God's own essence, the latter enables one to comprehend the essence of God's wisdom as clothed on those levels. Most important for our purposes, Shneur Zalman includes study of kabbalistic secrets within the parameters of Scripture that, in its most fundamental sense, entails the mere reading of the text, for esoteric wisdom is largely based on the delineation of the inwardness (*penimiyut*) of the verses of Scripture, epitomized by *Zohar*. Against the background of the continuous chain of emanation, the Written Torah in its elemental form, that is, the very letters of the

Torah scroll, is to be viewed as the final garment of the light of the *'Ein-Sof*. By simply reading the letters of Torah, therefore, even without the slightest comprehension, one can draw down light from the Infinite.[195] In that sense there is a complete appropriation of the mystical claim that the Torah, in its literal sense, is the name of God:

> "Take to heart these instructions with which I charge you this day" (Deut. 6:6). This is the Written Torah, *miqra'*, from the verse "They shall serve you to summon (*le-miqra'*) the community" (Num. 10:2), said with respect to the trumpets, for this is the expression of calling (*qeri'ah*) and gathering (*'asefah*). Thus all the Torah is the names of the Holy One, blessed be He. By means of this [Scripture] one reads and draws down the light of the Infinite from above to below.[196]

Though embellished with its own particular terminology, the statements of Shneur Zalman are a faithful depiction of the attitude of the *Zohar* itself toward the text of Scripture. Indeed, the repeated claim in the *Zohar* that the Torah is the name of God affirms that in its literal sense—determined by the Massoretic orthography—Scripture comprises the mystical significations. By means of the open eye the wise one will see the inner light in and through the very garment that at the same time conceals it from the purview of everyone else.

Notes

1. See I. Tishby, *The Wisdom of the Zohar*, trans. D. Goldstein (Oxford, 1989), vol. 3, pp. 1077–1082; F. Talmage, "Apples of Gold: The Inner Meaning of Sacred Texts in Medieval Judaism," in *Jewish Spirituality from the Bible Through the Middle Ages*, ed. A Green (New York, 1986), pp. 313–355.

2. See W. Bacher, "Das Merkwort PRDS in der jüdischen Bibelexegese," *Zeitschrift für die alttestamentliche Wissenschaft* 13 (1893): 294–305; P. Sandler, "Li-Ve'ayat PaRDeS we-ha-Shiṭah ha-Merubba'at," in *Sefer Auerbach* (Jerusalem, 1955), pp. 222–35; G. Scholem, *On the Kabbalah and Its Symbolism* (New York, 1969), pp. 53–61; A. Van Der Heide, "Pardes: Methodological Reflections on the Theory of the Four Senses," *Journal of Jewish Studies* 34 (1983): 147–59; Talmage, "Apples of Gold," pp. 319–21.

3. See especially the article of Van der Heide referred to in the preceding note.

4. A similar point has recently been made by M. Idel, "PaRDeS Between Authority and Indeterminacy: Some Reflections on Kabbalistic Hermeneutics" (typescript). I thank the author who made a copy of his paper available to me.

5. See A. Altmann, "Maimonides's Attitude Toward Jewish Mysticism," in *Studies in Jewish Thought*, ed. A. Jospe (Detroit, 1981), p. 203: "the unsettling realization that there are contradictions between the literal meaning of Scripture and

philosophical truth. . . . drives Maimonides to develop his theory of the layers of esoteric and exoteric meaning." One could argue that even for Maimonides the conflict between the literal reading and the figurative is applicable only when the text is taken at face value as understood by the philosophically unenlightened. That is to say, the external meaning is, when properly understood, to be read figuratively. This indeed is the purport of the bulk of the first part of the *Guide of the Perplexed*, which consists of the lexical chapters treating various terms in Scripture, many of which suggest on the superficial level an anthropomorphic conception of God.

6. See G. Scholem, *On the Kabbalah*, p. 33.

7. Ibid., p. 13 (author's emphasis).

8. G. Scholem, *Major Trends in Jewish Mysticism* (New York, 1954), p. 205.

9. *On the Kabbalah*, p. 33.

10. See *Major Trends*, p. 209.

11. Ibid., p. 14.

12. Ibid., p. 210.

13. W. Bacher, "L 'Exégèse Biblique dans le Zohar," *REJ* 22 (1891): 41–45.

14. Ibid., p. 35.

15. Tishby, *The Wisdom of the Zohar*, vol. 3, p. 1083.

16. Ibid., p. 1085.

17. See ibid., pp. 1090–1092; and the recent analysis in P. Giller, "The Tiqqunim: Symbolization and Theurgy" (Ph.D. thesis, Graduate Theological Union, 1990), pp. 106–9. Even in the case of this Kabbalist, however, it can be argued that the denigration of the literal sense is directed at those who would affirm the exoteric meaning at the expense of entirely ignoring the esoteric; see Giller, ibid., pp. 125–6. See, e.g., the representative statement in *Tiqqune Zohar* 43, ed. R. Margaliot (Jerusalem, 1978), fol. 82a: "*BeReShIT*, there is a dry place (*'atar yavesh*, the consonants of the word *bereshit*). . . . Thus is one who causes the kabbalah and wisdom to be removed from the Oral Torah and the Written Torah, and he causes that no one will be occupied with them. For they say that there is only *peshat* in the Torah and the Talmud. Such a person is surely like one who removes the spring from the river and the garden." Ibid., 69, fol. 114a: "Woe to those foolish people whose hearts are closed and whose eyes are closed, concerning whom it is said, 'They have eyes but they do not see' (Ps. 115:5) the light of the Torah. They are animals who do not see or know anything but the straw of Torah which is the external shell and its chaff. . . . The sages of Torah, the masters of secrets, throw away the straw and chaff, and eat the wheat of Torah which is within. The twenty-two letters of the Torah are the numerical value of the word wheat (*Ra'aya'*)." (Concerning this numerology, see note 109. See, by contrast, *Zohar* 3:275b [*Ra'aya' Mehemna'*] wherein the leniencies of *halakhah* are described as the straw of Torah and the restrictions as the wheat; both together are contrasted with the secrets of Torah.) Cf. *Zohar Ḥadash*, ed. R. Margaliot (Jerusalem, 1978), fol. 118b (*Tiqqunim*): "R. Shim'on began to expound: Woe to those people whose hearts are closed and whose eyes are shut, for they do not pay attention to the various secrets hidden in the Torah. They desire only to eat the straw of the Torah which is the literal sense (*peshat*), the garment of the Torah, but they do not taste the kernel that is within." See also *Tiqqune Zohar* 19, fol. 38a. The claim I have made with regard to the

author of the *Tiqqunim* and *Ra'aya' Mehemna'* can also be applied to Ḥayyim Vital's discussion in the introduction to the *Sha'ar ha-Haqdamot* (Jerusalem, 1909), 1a–4d, which is based largely on the revelant passages discussed or mentioned in this note. See discussion later and the text cited in note 189.

18. See Tishby, *The Wisdom of the Zohar*, p. 1089.

19. See Talmage, "Apples of Gold," p. 314, who notes in passing that the exoteric sense, the *nigleh*, "may impede, as is suggested in the mystical classic the *Zohar*."

20. See Scholem, *On the Kabbalah*, p. 39; Tishby, *The Wisdom of the Zohar*, pp. 1080–81; M. Idel, "The Concept of Torah in the Hekhalot and Its Transformation in the Kabbalah" [Hebrew], *Jerusalem Studies in Jewish Thought* 1 (1981): 49–58.

21. My formulation is indebted to the description of St. Thomas Aquinas's hermeneutics in J. Preus, *From Shadow to Promise: Old Testament Interpretation from Augustine to the Young Luther* (Cambridge, 1969), p. 54. See also H. de Lubac, *Exégèse Médiévale les quatre sens de l'écriture*, second part, vol. II (Paris, 1964), p. 160. For a different interpretation of Aquinas, see A. Funkenstein, *Theology and the Scientific Imagination* (Princeton, N.J., 1988), pp. 55–56, 219, n. 14. See also the description of the symbolist mentality in M. Chenu, *Nature, Man, Society in the Twelfth Century* (Chicago, 1968), pp. 110–11: "Consideration of sacred history involved a biblical interpretation which took literal history (*littera*) as the basis for continuous reference to supra-historical realities figured in terrestrial events . . . the very nature of the Judaeo-Christian revelation posits an ongoing interrelationship among things that underlay this hermeneutic approach . . . it was the extent and the forms taken by the application of the principle that produced a generalized typology and so determined the scriptural symbolism common to the Middle Ages." It follows, according to Chenu's analysis, that allegorical readings of Scripture which destroyed the literal sense of the text are contrary to the nature of symbolism; see ibid., p. 117.

22. See Y. Liebes, "The Messiah of the Zohar" [Hebrew], in *The Messianic Idea in Jewish Thought: A Study Conference in Honour of the Eightieth Birthday of Gershom Scholem* (Jerusalem, 1982), pp. 135–45, 198–203; M. Idel, *Kabbalah: New Perspectives* (New Haven, Conn., 1988), pp. 227–28; E. Wolfson, "Circumcision, Vision of God, and Textual Interpretation: From Midrashic Trope to Mystical Symbol," *History of Religions* 27 (1987): 207–13; idem, "The Hermeneutics of Visionary Experience: Revelation and Interpretation in the Zohar," *Religion* 18 (1988): 323–24; idem, "Female Imaging of the Torah: From Literary Metaphor to Religious Symbol," in *From Ancient Israel to Modern Judaism Intellect in Quest of Understanding: Essays in Honor of Marvin Fox*, ed. J. Neusner, E. S. Frerichs, and N. M. Sarna (Atlanta, 1989), vol. 2, pp. 295–98, 302–5.

23. I owe this formulation to David Weiss Halivni who uses it, however, to describe "the peshaṭ of a halakhic text." See his *Peshaṭ and Derash: Plain and Applied Meaning in Rabbinic Exegesis* (Oxford, 1990).

24. See especially R. Loewe, "The 'Plain' Meaning of Scripture in Early Jewish Exegesis," *Papers of the Institute of Jewish Studies London* 1 (1964): 140–85.

25. See S. Kamin, *Rashi's Exegetical Categorization in Respect to the Distinction Between Peshat and Derash* [Hebrew] (Jerusalem, 1986), pp. 31–32.

26. See *Sefer ha-Miṣvot le-ha-RaMBaM we-Hassagot ha-RaMBaN*, ed. Ch. D. Chavel (Jerusalem, 1981), p. 45.

27. Ibid., p. 44.

28. Commentary to Num. 3:1. See also introduction to Torah commentary, ed. C. D. Chavel (Jerusalem, 1984), p. 4. On the use of the word *remez* in Naḥmanides, see E. Wolfson, "By Way of Truth: Aspects of Naḥmanides' Kabbalistic Hermeneutic," *AJS Review* 14 (1989): 164–65.

29. See *Kitve Ramban*, ed. C. D. Chavel (Jerusalem, 1982), vol. 1, p. 180. In my earlier study, "By Way of Truth," pp. 128–29, I interpreted this passage in a somewhat different manner, arguing that in this context Naḥmanides used the word *mashal* synonymously with *meliṣah*, both referring to the literal or external sense. After reconsidering the passage, however, it seems that the word *mashal* here, as elsewhere in Naḥmanides' *ouevre*, denotes the figurative or parabolic sense. Cf. Ezra of Gerona's introduction to his *Perush le-Shir ha-Shirim* in *Kitve Ramban*, vol. 2, p. 480.

30. *b. Shabbat* 63a; *b. Yevamot* 11b, 24a. This principle has been the focus of much scholarly discussion. For representative treatments, see I. Frankel, *Peshat in Talmudic and Midrashic Literature* (Toronto, 1956), pp. 71–77; B. Gerhardsson, *Memory and Manuscript: Oral Tradition and Written Transmission in Rabbinic Judaism and Early Christianity* (Copenhagen, 1961), p. 66; Loewe, "The 'Plain' Meaning of Scripture," pp. 164–67; Kamin, *Rashi's Exegetical Categorization*, pp. 37–43.

31. *Sefer ha-Miṣvot*, p. 44.

32. Ibid., p. 45. For a different understanding of Naḥmanides's statement, see Kamin, *Rashi's Exegetical Categorization*, p. 38.

33. See A. Funkenstein, *Theology and the Scientific Imagination* (Princeton, 1988), p. 215, who considers Naḥmanides as an example of the maximalist approach that sees "the whole body of science and theology . . . epitomized in the Bible." The task of the interpreter is thus to decode that which is contained in the biblical verses. Funkenstein's statement that "Ramban . . . went as far as to claim that the philosophical translation actually constitutes the simple, literal sense of the Scriptures, while allegory is the mystical, kabbalistic dimension of understanding, in which the whole Scripture is nothing but a continuous name [of] God," is to me problematic.

34. B. Septimus, " 'Open Rebuke and Concealed Love': Nahmanides and the Andalusian Tradition," in *Rabbi Moses Naḥmanides (Ramban): Explorations in His Religious and Literary Virtuosity*, ed. I. Twersky (Cambridge, 1983), p. 18.

35. *Perush Mirkevet Yeḥezqel le-R. Ya'aqov ben Ya'aqov ha-Kohen mi-Qastilyah*, ed. A. Faber (M.A. thesis, Hebrew University, 1978), p. 46.

36. See Septimus, " 'Open Rebuke and Concealed Love'," p. 21, n. 37; D. Berger, "Miracles and the Natural Order in Naḥmanides," in *Rabbi Moses Naḥmanides*, p. 112, n. 19. See the following note.

37. See Wolfson, "By Way of Truth," pp. 129–53.

38. *Kitve Ramban*, vol. 2, p. 479.

39. See M. Idel, "La història de la càbala a Barcelona," *Curs La Càbala* (Barcelona, 1989), pp. 59–74; idem, "Naḥmanides: Kabbalah, Halakhah, and Spiritual Leadership," paper delivered at the conference on Mystical Leadership, Jewish Theological Seminary of America, 1989. It is difficult to date Jacob ben Sheshet's career with any precision, though Scholem surmises that he was writing around 1240. See G. Scholem, *Origins of the Kabbalah* (Princeton, N.J., 1987), p. 251.

40. Scholem, ibid., p. 380.

41. This understanding of Naḥmanides has been most fully worked out by M. Idel, "We Have No Kabbalistic Tradition on This," in *Rabbi Moses Naḥmanides,* pp. 53–71; see also idem, *Kabbalah: New Perspectives,* p. 215.

42. *Kitve Ramban,* vol. 1, p. 190.

43. *Sefer ha-'Emunah ve-ha-Biṭṭaḥon,* in *Kitve Ramban,* vol. 2, p. 364. In several contexts Jacob ben Sheshet notes that the kabbalistic reason he offers reflects his own opinion in contrast to something he has received either orally or from an authoritative text; see e.g., pp. 361, 368, 385.

44. Ibid., 378.

45. *Sefer Meshiv Devarim Nekhohim,* ed. G. Vajda (Jerusalem, 1968), p. 83. The passage is already cited, with a different rendering, in Scholem, *Origins,* p. 381.

46. See *Sefer Meshiv Devarim Nekhohim,* pp. 107–8; *Sefer ha-'Emunah ve-ha-Biṭṭaḥon,* p. 370; Joseph Gikatilla, *Sha'are Ṣedeq,* printed in E. Gottlieb, *Meḥqarim be-Sifrut ha-Qabbalah* (Tel-Aviv, 1976), p. 154; Menaḥem Recanati, *Perush 'al ha-Torah* (Jerusalem, 1961), 40b. For a discussion of these sources, see M. Idel, "Infinities of Torah in Kabbalah," in *Midrash and Literature,* ed. G. H. Hartman and S. Budick (New Haven, Conn., pp. 146–47, 150.

47. *Sefer ha-'Emunah ve-ha-Biṭṭaḥon,* p. 370; cf. Idel, "We Have No Tradition," p. 68, n. 58; idem, "Infinities of Torah in Kabbalah," p. 146. The innovative posture of Jacob ben Sheshet appears later on in Recanati; cf. *Sefer Ṭa'ame ha-Miṣwot* (Basel, 1581), 3a, 4b.

48. See, e.g., (a) *Sefer ha-'Emunah ve-ha-Biṭṭaḥon,* p. 357: "Thus I have heard from the mouth (*shama'ti mipi*) of the Hasid, R. Isaac the son of the great R. Abraham, may his memory be for a blessing, who said in the name of his father"; (b) p. 362: "Thus I have heard this formulation (*shama'ti zeh halashon*) in the name of the Hasid, R. Isaac the son of the great R. Abraham, may his memory be for a blessing"; (c) p. 364: "Thus I have heard from the mouth of the sage, R. Joseph the son of Samuel, may his memory be for a blessing" [cf. *Sefer Meshiv Devarim Nekhohim,* pp. 193–96]; (d) p. 380: "Thus I have received from the mouth (*kibbalti mipi*) of R. Isaac the Frenchman, blessed be his memory" [cf. p. 396; on the identity of this figure, cf. Scholem, *Origins,* p. 251)]; (e) p. 401: "Thus I received in the name (*kibbalti bishem*) of the Hasid, R. Isaac the son of the great R. Abraham, may his memory be for a blessing"; (f) p. 409: "Thus I have heard this formulation in the name of the Hasid, R. Isaac the son of the great R. Abraham, may his memory be for a blessing." Cf. *Sefer Meshiv Devarim Nekhohim,* p. 82.

49. See, e.g., ibid., p. 369.

50. Scholem's word; see *Origins.*

51. The term employed and popularized by Idel; see "We Have No Kabbalistic Tradition on This."

52. See "By Way of Truth," especially pp. 103–29, 153–78.

53. As already noted by Chavel in his edition of *Sefer ha-'Emunah ve-ha-Biṭṭaḥon,* p. 379, n. 1.

54. Cf. *Numbers Rabbah* 13:16.

55. Cf. *Sefer Meshiv Devarim Nekhohim,* p. 180.

56. *Sefer ha-'Emunah ve-ha-Biṭṭaḥon,* p. 379.

57. See ibid., p. 418.

58. See ibid., pp. 390–91, 402.

59. See G. Scholem, *Peraqim le-Toledot Sifrut ha-Qabbalah* (Jerusalem, 1931), p. 113.

60. Ibid., pp. 112, 113–14.

61. See note 46.

62. Scholem, *Peraqim*, p. 115.

63. Ibid.

64. M. Idel, *Language, Torah and Hermeneutics in Abraham Abulafia* (Albany, N.Y., 1989), pp. 83–87.

65. See ibid., pp. 73-77.

66. MS Vat. 233, fols. 43a–43b.

67. *Kabbalah: New Perspectives,* pp. 207–8.

68. The same word is employed in *Midrash ha-Ne'elam* for the literal sense, and its Aramaic equivalent is used in the main body of the *Zohar.* See notes 81, 98, 123. On the word *ma'aseh* in Amoraic literature to denote narratives, see W. Bacher, *Die Exegetische Terminologie der Jüdischen Traditionsliteratur* (Leipzig, 1899), Vol. 2, *Die Bibel- und Traditionsexegetische Terminologie der Amoräer,* p. 116.

69. *Sefer Ta'ame ha-Miṣwot* (London, 1963), 2a.

70. Cf. *b. Ta'anit* 7a.

71. *b. Sanhedrin* 38a; *b. 'Eruvin* 65a.

72. MS Oxford 352, fol. 189b.

73. This expression reflects the language of Azriel of Gerona. See his *Sha'ar ha-Sho'el* [*Perush 'Eser Sefirot*] in Meir ibn Gabbai, *Derekh 'Emunah* (Jerusalem, 1967), 2b.

74. MS Guenzberg 775, fol. 50a.

75. See Isaac of Acre, *Sefer Me'irat 'Enayim,* ed. A. Goldreich (Jerusalem, 1981), pp. 58 ff. where he cites the text criticizing the philosophers from Jacob ben Sheshet's *Sha'ar ha-Shamayim.* See the editor's comments on pp. 409–14, and especially 414, n. 16 where he cites the relevant passage from *'Oṣar Ḥayyim.*

76. See D. Matt, *Zohar, The Book of Enlightenment* (New York, 1983), p. 31.

77. See Idel, "Infinities of Torah," p. 151.

78. Printed in *Sefer ha-Malkhut* (Casablanca, 1930), 6b. For an analysis of this motif from the vantage point of the *Zohar,* see E. Wolfson, "Anthropomorphic Imagery and Letter Symbolism in the Zohar" [Hebrew], *Jerusalem Studies in Jewish Thought* 8 (1989): 147–81.

79. See note 20.

80. B. Roitman, "Sacred Language and Open Text," in *Midrash and Literature,* pp. 171–72.

81. See note 68.

82. See F. Talmage, "The Term 'Haggadah' in the Parable of the Beloved in the Palace in the Zohar" [Hebrew], *Jerusalem Studies in Jewish Thought* 4 (1985–86): 271–73.

83. *Zohar Ḥadash,* 83a.

84. *Zohar* 3:202a.

85. Cf. ibid., 1:234b; 2:230b; 3:71b, 73a, 75a, 98b.

86. Ibid., 3:159a.

87. Cf. ibid., 162a–b.

88. The relation of *aggadah* to Kabbalah is one of the critical questions in assessing the role accorded the theosophic doctrine within the system of normative Judaism (i.e., the Judaism determined by the Rabbinic corpus) by medieval Jewish mystics. This question has been the focus of various scholarly accounts. For a review of the issue from the particular vantage point of Naḥmanides, cf. Wolfson, "By Way of Truth," pp. 153–78. It must be noted that Kabbalists related the word *haggadah* to the Aramaic root *nagad,* i.e., to stretch, to draw or pull, to flow. They thus localized the discourse of haggadah in the divine gradation characterized by these verbs; viz., the *sefirah* of *Yesod,* which corresponds to the *membrum virile* in the divine realm. As such *Yesod* is the locus of haggadah and *sod,* esoteric gnosis; indeed, in some sense the two are identical. See E. Wolfson, "Circumcision, Vision of God, and Textual Interpretation," pp. 205–15. See also the telling remark of Moses Cordovero, *Zohar 'im Perush 'Or Yaqar* (Jerusalem, 1989), vol. 17, p. 144.

89. *Zohar* 1:152a. Cf. the formulation of Isaac of Acre, *Sefer Me'irat 'Enayim,* p. 110: "The words and letters [of Torah] . . . are like the garment of a person . . . the plain meanings and the commentaries are the body, the true Kabbalah and the great powers and secrets . . . are the soul, and this is [the import of] the verse, 'From my flesh I will see God' (Job 19:26)."

90. The identification of the *peshat* as a garment is quite common in kabbalistic literature where the word is related to the verb *pashat,* i.e., to remove one's garment. The noun, *peshat,* derived from the verb, *pashat,* is understood as the object that is removed, i.e., the garment. An interesting exception to this rule is to be found in Elḥanan ben Abraham ibn Eskira, *Sefer Yesod 'Olam,* MS Guenzberg 607, fols. 10a–b, wherein the *peshat* is described as the material substratum that receives the different forms as garments: "We must understood the matter concerning the *peshat* properly and thoroughly. . . . The word [is derived from] the language 'he removed his clothing,' for it takes off a matter and puts on a matter. And this is their saying, 'a verse should not lose its literal sense,' for the matter is permanent and the forms change. The written Scripture is like the matter and the forms are taken off and put on, but it endures."

91. For a similar critique of the Christian reading of Scripture, see Judah Barzillai, *Perush Sefer Yeṣirah,* ed. S. J. Halberstam (Berlin, 1885), p. 77. See also F. Talmage, "R. David Kimḥi as Polemicist," *Hebrew Union College Annual* 38 (1967): 219–20, who cites a passage in which RaDaK accused Christians of their literalism connected to the anthropomorphic conception of God. On the other hand, as Talmage points out, RaDaK on occasion accuses Christians of being extreme allegorists who deny the literal meaning of the legal portions of Scripture. Cf. M. Simon, *Vetus Israel* (Paris, 1948), p. 181.

92. On the relation of Shekhinah to the body (*guf*), see Y. Liebes, *Peraqim be-Millon Sefer ha-Zohar* (Jerusalem, 1976), p. 178, n. 33; on the identification of Shekhinah as the locus of *miṣvot,* see E. Wolfson, *The Book of the Pomegranate: Moses de León's Sefer ha-Rimmon* (Atlanta, 1988), pp. 18–19, n. 35, and 59–62.

93. *Zohar* 2:98b.

94. That the garment is a locus ov vision is attested as well in the continuation of the zoharic passage (ibid., 99a): "That elder began to expound: 'Moses went inside the cloud and ascended the mountain' (Exod. 24:18). What is this cloud? It is as it is written, 'I have set My bow in the cloud' (Gen. 9:13). It has been taught that the bow sent its garments and gave them to Moses, and by means of that garment Moses ascended to the mountain, and from it he saw what he saw and delighted in all." Cf. ibid., 229a. On the theme of the garment as the locus of vision or esoteric knowledge, see D. Cohen-Alloro, *The Secret of the Garment in the Zohar* [Hebrew] (Jerusalem, 1987), pp. 69–74.

95. Ibid., 99a.

96. Ibid., 99b. For a slightly different interpretation of the expression used here, *peshatei di-qera'*, see Tishby, *The Wisdom of the Zohar,* p. 1085.

97. See, e.g., the views of Moses Cordovero and Abraham Galante cited in A. Azulai, *'Or ha-Ḥammah,* vol. 2; pp. 125a–b.

98. The same term employed to connote the literal sense in *Midrash ha-Ne'elam*. See note 68.

99. Cf. Song of Songs 8:14.

100. Cf. ibid., 4:6.

101. Cf. Isa. 35:5

102. The Hebrew expression used here is *yom ha-ma'aśeh,* which may reflect the previous use of the word *ma'aśeh* in this passage, denoting the literal sense of the biblical narrative.

103. *b. Ḥagigah* 14b and parallels.

104. *She'elot u-Teshuvot le-R. Mosheh de Le'on be-'Inyene Qabbalah,* in I. Tishby, *Studies in the Kabbalah and Its Branches* [Hebrew] (Jerusalem, 1982), pp. 56, 64. Cf. *Sefer ha-Mishqal,* ed. J. Wijnhoven (Ph.D., Brandeis University, 1964), pp. 49, 105.

105. Cf. *Zohar* 2:257b, where Mishnah is described as "the secret which is within for one learns there the essence of everything" (*'iqra di-khula*).

106. Ibid., 2:176a. Cf. ibid., 61b–62a, where various levels of food are distinguished, and that designated specifically for the "comrades engaged in Torah," i.e., the Kabbalists, is the "food of the spirit and soul," which is said to derive from the second gradation, supernal Wisdom.

107. For an alternative explanation of this passage, see Liebes, "How the Zohar Was Written" [Hebrew], *Jerusalem Studies in Jewish Thought* 8 (1989): 17–18.

108. See note 110. The more frequent symbol for Torah in rabbinic literature is bread. Cf. *Siphre ad Deuteronomium,* ed. L. Finkelstein (New York, 1969), 45, p. 104; *b. Shabbat* 120a; *b. Ḥagigah* 14a; *b. Sanhedrin* 104b; *Numbers Rabbah* 13:16. Cf. the expression "the leaven of the Pharisees," in Mark 8:15; see also Matthew 16:11–12 and Luke 12:1. For a later use of bread as a symbol for Torah study, see Maimonides, *Mishneh Torah, Hilkhot Yesode Ha-Torah,* 4:13; *Guide of the Perplexed,* vol. I, p. 30. On bread as a symbol for the Oral Law, see *Zohar Ḥadash,* 50b. See also *Zohar* 3:33b (*Piqqudin*).

109. Cf. Wolfson, "Anthropomorphic Imagery," p. 155, nn. 33–34. To the sources mentioned there, see also *Zohar* 3:188b (*Yenuqa*) where the wheat is identi-

fied as the Shekhinah that comprises the twenty-two letters within herself; and cf. *Tiqqune Zohar,* 69, fol. 114a.

110. *b. Berakhot* 64a (already noted by Matt, *Zohar,* p. 203); *Shir ha-Shirim Rabbah* 7:3 (where wheat refers more specifically to the cultic laws in Leviticus).

111. Cf. the anonymous commentary on *Sifra di-Ṣeni'uta* from a student of Isaac Luria, published in *Zohar ha-Raqi'a* (Jerusalem, n.d.), fol. 119a; and the commentary of Elijah ben Solomon, the Gaon of Vilna, on *Sifra di-Ṣeni'uta* (Jerusalem, 1986), 1a.

112. Cf. Matt, *Zohar.*

113. This stands in marked contrast to *Tiqqune Zohar,* 69, fol. 114a, where the wheat is associated with the inner essence of Torah apprehended by the mystics as opposed to the straw or chaff, which is identified as the literal meaning. Cf. *Zohar* 3:272a (*Ra'aya Mehemna*).

114. *Zohar* 2:176b.

115. P. Ricouer, *Hermeneutics and the Human Sciences,* ed. and trans. J. B. Thompson (Cambridge, 1981), p. 164.

116. Cf. Hayyim Vital in his introduction to *Sha'ar ha-Haqdamot* (Jerusalem, 1909), 1b: "When [the Torah] is in the world of emanation it is called kabbalah, for there it is removed from all the garments which are called the literal sense (*peshat*) from the expression 'I had taken off (*pashṭti*) my robe' (Song of Songs 5:3), for [the literal sense] is the aspect of the external garment which is upon the skin of a person, sometimes spread (*mitpashet*) over him, and this is the essence of the meaning of the word *peshat.*" See, however, *Sha'ar ha-Miṣvot* (Jerusalem, 1978), p. 83 [*Peri 'Eṣ Ḥayyim,* ed. Meir Poppers (Jerusalem, 1980), p. 356], where Vital speaks of the containment of all four subjects, Scripture, Mishnah, Talmud, and Kabbalah, within the world of emanation insofar as the latter compromises within itself all that which is below it in the chain of being. Still, it is evident from the context that Scripture, the Written Torah, belongs most properly to the lowest of the four worlds, the world of *'Asiyah,* whereas the three aspects of Oral Torah—Mishnah, Talmud, and Kabbalah—belong respectively to the remaining three worlds, *Yeṣirah, Beri'ah,* and *'Aṣilut.*

117. *'Or Yaqar* to *Ra'aya Mehemna* (Jerusalem, 1987), 15:87.

118. See note 17.

119. Cf. *b. Rosh Hashanah* 26b.

120. *Degel Maḥaneh 'Efrayim* (Brooklyn, N.Y., 1984), 87b.

121. Cf. Matt, *Zohar,* pp. 31, 253.

122. Cf. *Zohar* 1:163a; 3:149a–b, 152a.

123. The Aramaic *'ovda* parallels the Hebrew *ma'aseh* used in *Midrash ha-Ne'elam* on Ruth for the literal meaning; see note 68.

124. *Zohar* 3:149a.

125. Ibid., 71b–72a.

126. Cf. ibid., 14a.

127. Cf. the interpretation of Isa. 5:1 in *Zohar* 1:95b–96a.

128. Cf. *j. Ketubot* 13:1 (ed. Venice, 35c); *j. Soṭah* 1:4 (16d), attributed to R. Ḥiyya; *Tanḥuma,* ed. S. Buber, Wayeshev, 17, 93b–94a, in the name of R. Joshua ben Levi.

129. *Genesis Rabbah,* ed. Theodor-Albeck (Jerusalem, 1965), p. 1041.

130. See, by contrast, the comment of Rav reported in the name of R. Ḥanin in *b. Soṭah* 10a.

131. The attribution to Rabbi is found in *j. Ketubot* 13:1, but in the other sources the attribution varies. See references in note 128.

132. See, especially, the wording of the version in *Midrash Aggadah,* ed. S. Buber (Vienna, 1894), p. 92: " 'And she sat down at the entrance to Enayim' (Gen. 38–14). We reviewed all of Scripture and did not find a place where was *petaḥ 'enayim.* Rather this [expression] is to teach that she cast her eyes upon the one (*bemiy*) to whom all eyes are cast. And she said before the Holy One, blessed be He, Let it be Your will that I do not leave this entrance empty."

133. *b. Berakhot* 45a.

134. *Zohar* 3:265a.

135. Cf. ibid, 3:7a.

136. To be sure, there are instances where the word *dayka'* does not signify a kabbalistic meaning, but rather a more straightforward midrashic sense. See, e.g., *Zohar* 1:133b in connection with the interpretation of the verse, "Abraham willed all that he owned to Isaac" (Gen. 25:5).

137. Cf. *Zohar* 2:185b.

138. Ibid. 3:68b.

139. Cf. W. Bacher, *Die Exegetische Terminologie der Jüdischen Traditionsliteratur,* Vol. 1, *Die Bibelexegetische Terminologie der Tannaiten,* pp. 49, n. 1, 105; Vol. 2, p. 113; Loewe, "The 'Plain' Meaning," pp. 170–72.

140. See, e.g., *Zohar* 2:61b; 3:73a,188b. In other contexts the word *mamash* signifies the nonfigurative, though not necessarily kabbalistic, meaning. See, e.g., *Zohar* 1:133a, where the verse, "Isaac then brought her [Rebecca] into the tent of his mother Sarah" (Gen. 24:67), is interpreted in terms of the tradition that Rebecca was in the actual image (*diyoqna' mamash*) of Sarah. Thus the verse reads "the tent of his mother Sarah" (*Sara 'imo vada'y*). On this use of the term *vada'y,* see note 156. See also *Zohar* 3:160b where we find the expression *mitqashri ba-Qadosh Barukh Hu mamash* which must be rendered "they were bound to the Holy One, blessed be He, in actuality. The *Zohar* also employs the term *bagufa'* to denote the sense of actuality as opposed to a figurative or metaphorical sense. Cf. Liebes, *Peraqim,* p. 182, n. 45.

141. *Zohar* 1:94a.

142. For background on this hermeneutical principle, see S. Lieberman, *Hellenism in Jewish Palestine* (New York, 1962), pp. 58–62.

143. See E. Wolfson, "Circumcision, Vision of God, and Textual Interpretation," p. 206.

144. I have studied this motif in depth in "Circumcision and the Divine Name: A Study in the Transmission of Esoteric Doctrine," *Jewish Quarterly Review* 78 (1987): 77–112.

145. Cf. *m. 'Avot* 6:2; *b. 'Eruvin* 54a.

146. *Zohar* 3:6b.

147. Cf. ibid., 2:62a.

148. Ibid., 61a.

149. On the interpretation of demonstrative pronouns in kabbalistic literature and its relation to midrashic precedents, see B. Roitman, "Sacred Language and Open Text," pp. 159–75, especially 165 ff.

150. The potential randomness of the hermeneutical technique of *gezerah shavah* is already evident from the statement of the Rabbis to the effect that a person should not adduce a *gezerah shavah* on his own (*p. Pesahim* 6:1, 33a; *b. Niddah* 19b). See Lieberman, *Hellenism in Jewish Palestine*, p. 61; Loewe, "The 'Plain' Meaning," pp. 152–53, n. 79. See ibid., pp. 164 ff., where the author suggests that the Amoraic formula, "a verse does not its literal sense," originating in Pumbeditha, was employed "to counter exorbitant deductions from identity or close analogy of expression (*gezerah shavah*)."

151. My formulation here is deliberately lifted from Roitman, "Sacred Language and Open Text," p. 167, who however takes the opposite position when describing the kabbalistic system of textual exposition: "Most important, this determination of meaning is not channeled through the linguistic signification of the terms in the utterance. Anagogic interpretation of this kind is dependent on a code which is not linguistic in the sense of natural language, although it integrates in its system certain linguistic elements not actualized in the discourse." In my opinion the system of exposition operative in the main body of *Zohar* functions precisely in the way which Roitman denies, viz., the symbolic encoding of the biblical text—what she calls the *anagogic interpretation*— is indeed dependent on the determination of meaning of the relevant terms (*parole*) in terms of normal modes of discourse (*langue*). Roitman herself reaches a similar conclusion; see pp. 171–72 (partially cited in note 80).

152. Based on the passage in *b. Mo'ed Qaṭan* 28a to the effect that one's children, livelihood, and sustenance are dependent on fate (*mazzal*) and not merit (*zekhut*). In the interpretation of the *Zohar* the word *mazzal* designates either *Keter* or, according to the more recondite doctrine of the '*Idrot*, one of the aspects of the upper *parsuf,* the '*Arikh 'Anpin* or '*Atiqa' Qadisha'.*

153. *Zohar* 3:79b.

154. See W. Braude, "Midrash as Deep Peshat," in *Studies in Judaica, Karaitica and Islamica Presented to Leon Nemoy on His Eightieth Birthday,* ed. S. R. Brunswick et al. (Ramat Gan, 1982), pp. 31–38.

155. Cf. Bacher, *Die Exegetische Terminologie,* Vol. 1, pp. 48–49; Vol. 2, p. 60; Loewe, "The 'Plain' Meaning," pp. 170–72.

156. Here (as in the next two notes as well) I will cite only a sampling of the relevant sources: See *Zohar* 1:8b, 10a, 45a, 63b, 87a, 91a, 95a, 108a, 110b, 133a (cited in note 92), 142a, 153b, 175a, 192b, 219a, 221b; 2:4a, 10a, 44b, 47b, 48a, 49b, 62a, 66a, 146a, 183b, 187b, 225a, 243a, 247b; 3:6b, 77a, 98b, 147b, 163b, 239b. This particular usage is prevalent in *Ra'aya' Mehemna'* and *Tiqqune Zohar* as well. See, e.g., *Zohar* 3:28a (*Ra'aya' Mehenmna'*), 264b (*Ra'aya' Mehenmna'*); *Zohar Ḥadash,* 31c (*Tiqqunim*).

157. See *Zohar* 1:74a, 86a, 96a, 132b, 158b, 247b; 2:65b, 148b, 189b; 3:103a, 148a, 173b, 174a.

158. See *Zohar* 1:50b, 82b, 85b, 93a, 105a, 145a, 191b, 196b, 240a, 245b, 249a; 2:33a, 121b, 127b, 148b. It must be noted that Kabbalists prior to the generation of the *Zohar* already employed the expression *vada'y* to render the simple meaning in

terms of a mystical truth. Thus, for example, this usage is found in a passage of Ezra of Gerona, alluded to briefly by Jacob ben Sheshet (See *Sefer ha-'Emunah ve-ha-Biṭṭaḥon*, p. 377) and cited more extensively by Menaḥem Recanati (*Perush 'al ha-Torah* [Jerusalem, 1961], 48d). The same usage is found in Joseph Gikatilla and Moses de León's Hebrew writings. See *Sha'are 'Orah*, ed. J. Ben-Shlomo (Jerusalem, 1981), Vol. 1, p. 149, n. 3.

159. *Zohar* 3:170b.

160. Cf. ibid., 1:82a.

161. Ibid., 140b.

162. I have translated the expression, *ve-limekhaseh 'atiq*, according to the reading of the *Zohar*, which follows that of *b. Pesaḥim* 119a. The more literal rendering of this expression is "clothe themselves eloquently."

163. *Zohar* 3:175b.

164. Ibid., 2:57b.

165. *b. 'Arakhin* 15b.

166. I have translated the verse in light of the zoharic reading and not as an accurate rendering of the literal sense.

167. *Zohar* 2:60a–b.

168 Cf. Lieberman, *Hellenism in Jewish Palestine*, pp. 49–51.

169. *Zohar* 3:179b.

170. See, e.g., commentaries of Solomon ben Isaac (Rashi), R. Samuel ben Meir (Rashbam), Abraham ibn Ezra, and Obadiah ben Jacob Sforno on the relevant verse. See also Naḥmanides on Exod. 36:5.

171. See, e.g., commentary of Rashi to the Mishnah in *b. Sukkah* 45a, s.v., *'aniy va-ho.*

172. Cited in J. Gellis, *Tosafot ha-Shalem* (Jerusalem, 1987), vol. 6, p. 42.

173. *Perush ha-Roqeaḥ 'al ha-Torah*, ed. C. Konyevsky (Bene Beraq, 1980), vol. 2, p. 14.

174. *Zohar* 1:70b–71a.

175. Ibid., 3:69a–b.

176. Ibid., 2:95a.

177. The image of being covered with eyes is used in Ezekiel to describe the wheels (*'ofanim*) of the chariot; see 1:18, 10:12. This very image is used in Hekhalot texts where, however, the *'ofanim* designate a distinct class of angels. See P. Schäfer, *Synopse zur Hekhalot-Literatur* (Tübingen, 1981), section 40. Cf, ibid., section 29, where the angels in general are said to be full of eyes. See ibid., section 12, where God is said to have set 365,000 eyes in Metatron, who is the transformed Enoch. And ibid., section 33, where the angel Kerubiel is described by this image, as well as section 41, where the image is applied to Serapiel. See also ibid., section 246, 596; *Masekhet Hekhalot*, in *Bet ha-Midrash*, ed. A. Jellinek (Jerusalem, 1967), Vol. 2, p. 43. In *Hekhalot Rabbati* we read about the eyes in the robe (*ḥaluq*) of God; see *Synopsis*, section 102. Cf. MS Oxford-Bodleian 1610, fol. 46a, where a tradition is cited in the name of the *ba'ale merkavah* to the effect that God is filled with eyes from inside and outside. I have not yet located a text from ancient Jewish mystical speculation that describes the mystic himself as full of eyes nor have I located in

Rabbinic literature the notion that a sage or exegete is so described. See, however, Philo, *Questiones et Solutiones in Exodum,* III, 43, where the soul is said to be "all eyes" so that it may "receive lightning-flashes" of illumination. This is related to a motif repeated on a number of occasions by Philo concerning God's implanting eyes in an individual so that he will be able to see God. See G. Delling, "The 'One Who Sees God' in Philo," in *Nourished with Peace: Studies in Hellenistic Judaism in Memory of Samuel Sandmel,* ed. F. Greenspahn, E. Hilgert, and B. Mack (Chico, Calif., 1984), pp. 33–34.

178. Zohar 2:235b (*Tosefta'*).

179. Cf. Wolfson, "The Hermeneutics of Visionary Experience," pp. 317 ff., especially 321, 340–41, n. 86.

180. Cf. Num. 11:7, and see Maimonides, *Guide of the Perplexed,* III.2.

181. See, e.g., *m. Shabbat* 1:6.

182. Cf. G. Scholem, "Qabbalot R. Ya'aqov we-R. Yiṣḥaq ha-Kohen, *Madda'e ha-Yahadut* 2 (1927): 262–63. This source was already suggested by Liebes, *Peraqim,* p. 190, n. 78. See also Ṭodros Abulafia, *Sha 'ar ha-Razim,* ed. M. Kushnir-Oron (Jerusalem, 1989), p. 65.

183. See Liebes, ibid., who cites this interpretation as that of later Kabbalists but rejects it as the intended or contextual meaning of the *Zohar.* But see the following note.

184. Cf. Wolfson, "Female Imaging," pp. 295–97. To the sources mentioned there one should add *Zohar Ḥadash,* 55c–d (*Midrash ha-Ne'elam*).

185. See the references given in note 22.

186. Cf. Idel, *Kabbalah: New Perspectives,* pp. 208 ff.

187. Cf. Scholem, *Major Trends,* pp. 222–24, 241; idem, *Kabbalah* (Jerusalem, 1974), pp. 147–48; J. Ben-Shlomo, "The Research of Gershom Scholem on Pantheism in the Kabbalah," in *Gershom Scholem: The Man and His Work* [Hebrew] (Jerusalem, 1983), pp. 22–23.

188. See note 17.

189. For this usage of the word *remez* in kabbalistic sources, see Wolfson, "By Way of Truth," pp. 164–65, n. 188.

190. *Sha'ar Ma'amere RaZa'L* (Jerusalem, 1898), 8d.

191. *Shene Luḥot ha-Berit* (Amsterdam, 1648), 3a.

192. See ibid., 16a–b; and J. Katz, *Halakhah and Kabbalah* [Hebrew] (Jerusalem, 1984), p. 98 (in Hebrew).

193. The notion that the letters of the Torah serve as a conduit to draw down the light of the Infinite is a commonplace in Hasidic literature, serving ultimately as the background for the notion of Torah study as a contemplative act. See J. Weiss, *Studies in Eastern European Jewish Mysticism* (Oxford, 1985), pp. 56–68. For a comprehensive discussion of the earlier kabbalistic sources for this magico-mystical conception, which influenced the Ḥasidic formulation, see M. Idel, "Perceptions of Kabbalah in the Second Half of the Eighteenth Century," *Jewish Thought, An International Journal of History and Philosophy* 1 (1991), sect. IV. See note 195.

194. *Liqquṭe Torah* (Brooklyn, 1984), *Va-Yiqra',* 5b–c.

195. Elsewhere in his writings Shneur Zalman characterizes Torah study as a vehicle by means of which one unites with the light of the Infinite (*'or 'Ein-Sof*) insofar as the Torah itself is the very expression of the divine will and wisdom rather than something ontically distinct from God. Cf. *Tanya* (Brooklyn, 1979), I, 9a–10a, 29a–b; IV, 145a (in that context he distinguishes between two goals of Torah study, both rooted in Lurianic thought as transmitted by Vital, to redeem the holy sparks from the demonic shells and to unify the forces above by drawing down the light from the Infinite); and the recent discussion in Naftali Lowenthal, *Communicating the Infinite: The Emergence of the Habad School* (Chicago, 1990), pp. 59–60.

196. *Liqquṭe Torah, Wa-Etḥanan,* 12c.

9

Proverbs, Figures, and Riddles: The *Dialogues of Love* as a Hebrew Humanist Composition

Arthur M. Lesley

> To understand a proverb, and a figure;
> the words of the wise
> and their riddles.
> —*Proverbs 1:6* [1]

The *Dialogues of Love* by Yehuda Abravanel has attracted more attention from historians of Jewish philosophy than its influence on later Jewish thought deserves. Written in the form of a literary dialogue between a man and a woman on the subject of love, the work promiscuously juxtaposes obscure and intricate cabalistic secrets with allegorical interpretations of classical myths, criticism of earlier Jewish Bible commentators, and corrections to statements in Plato's works. The mystagogy, fastidiousness, and frivolity evidently are all equally intentional, but to what purpose and for what audience? And is this what we are to expect from a father bereaved by the kidnapping and forced conversion of his son, from the learned son of the noble leader of the Spanish exile? The work has puzzled historians, seeming as it does simultaneously to raise and contradict expectations that we have of both late medieval Jewish philosophy and Renaissance thought.[2] Some of the perplexity that the text provokes can be dispelled by clarifying a few of the assumptions which make Yehuda Abravanel's manner of commenting on biblical texts appear so strange to those who are familiar with medieval Jewish philosophy.

The first unfamiliar assumption, the one that defines the genre of the *Dialogues,* is that radically incompatible kinds of discourse can be integrated into a single text, to make significant statements about the relations of the individual,

God, and the world. The *Dialogues of Love* combines a variety of discourses that had not previously been juxtaposed in a single text: the full curriculum of Maimonidean philosophy, neoplatonism based on an acquaintance with authentic texts of Plato, astrology, Spanish Kabbalah, classical mythology, the entire body of Midrash and Jewish Bible commentary, and humanist rhetoric. Rhetoric and dialectic were the kinds of discourse that can contain all the others and refine them, and the genre of this particular text is literary dialogue.

A second assumption, that the divinely revealed text of the Hebrew Bible and the accompanying oral tradition that Judaism transmits are the origin of all human truth, accounts for the centrality of biblical commentary in the work and the unusual comparative method of that commentary. Although Jews, Christians, and Muslims all had long asserted the priority of revelation, in the fifteenth-century texts and the *Dialogues*, it is constantly being tested with evidence. Because revelation is the source of all knowledge, texts that differ with Jewish teaching can nevertheless be harmonized with it and may even supply an understanding of revelation that Jewish scholars have not previously recognized. The world's inconceivable diversity can be given order only through reference to God, who is known through the Bible. Abravanel's method of referring to unaccustomed kinds of texts ultimately confirms the originality, sufficiency, and perfection of the written and oral revelation that the Jews possess. The comparative method, which treats all other opinions as corrupted versions of the original revelation, produces new understandings of the received text, not only confirmation of received Jewish interpretations.

The strangeness of the *Dialogues* is evident, then, on the largest scale, that of composition, and on the intermediate scale, in the manner of carrying on the discussion through comparison. The ways that Yehuda uses one of the smallest units of the argumentation, the *mashal*, or metaphor, also deviate from expectations of medieval Jewish philosophy. At the beginning of the *Guide of the Perplexed*, in his remarks about the "parable," *mashal*, Maimonides defines the terms of discussion of the relation between reason and revelation, philosophical truth and biblical expression. The *Dialogues* diverges from Maimonides's priorities in a way that is distinctive to the late fifteenth century.

Mentioning these three assumptions that underlie the book already suggests why the work aroused a sufficiently hostile reaction among Jewish Maimonideans to retard its influence on Jewish thinkers. When the currents of Jewish thought that launched the work receded and it was preserved for quite different reasons by a European audience, it became for historians like a ship stranded far from the coast, curious evidence of how far inland the sea once reached.

I

The earliest documented reaction to Yehuda Abravanel's *Dialogues of Love* appears in a letter that Saul Cohen Ashkenazi sent to Yehuda's father, Isaac Abravanel, in Venice, in 1507. After surveying the breadth and depth of Yehuda's learning, Saul damns with faint praise what he considers to be Yehuda's misuse of his Averroistic philosophical learning:[3]

> Please bring these obscure questions of mine to the attention of your dear son, my brother, the exalted, most elevated and sublime universal sage, Rabbi Yehuda, may God preserve him, if he happens to be there. He will restore my soul and provide for my old age if he answers my inquiries. For I have heard it said that Yehuda rises laudably from study to study, along the ascending path to the wisdom of philosophy and its roots, in whatever language and writing, and in exposition of the greatness of the Commentator's statements, arguments and demonstrations. And after these things he draws himself along a marvelous path, precious with learning, and utters ancient riddles (*hiddot*), to understand fable (*mashal*) and eloquence (*melitsa*), that are available to every adherent of a divinely revealed religion (*kol adam elohi torani*).

As an Averroist Maimonidean, Saul Cohen has sketched the ascending course of studies that brought Yehuda to the eminent rank of commenting on Averroes, and then implies that he is slumming by concerning himself with riddles, fables, and eloquence. Yehuda's capacity for the highest studies contrasts with his preoccupation with lowly ones. Further, as the addressee of Elijah del Medigo's polemical *Examination of Religion* (1491), Cohen implies that Yehuda has mingled subjects, philosophical investigation, and study of Scripture, which ought to be scrupulously separated. As Del Medigo wrote in the *Examination*, "I do not think the words of the Torah are explained through the method of philosophy, nor does the former [Torah] need the latter [philosophy]. . . . Moreover, no one would think me in error because in my philosophic works I deal with the philosophers according to their methodology."[4] Del Medigo's and Cohen's attitude, which has been characterized as "a moderate double-truth theory,"[5] clearly would lead them to disapprove of the *Dialogues of Love*. Cohen's words also recall the unfavorable comparison of the Christian Gospels with the Hebrew Bible, in Joseph Albo's *Book of Roots* (ca. 1415):[6]

> The moral instruction in the Gospels and the teaching of right conduct are expressed altogether in the form of parables (*meshalim*) and dark sayings (*hiddot*), which is not appropriate for a law. For it is hard to get at the meaning of anything expressed in the form of parable and metaphor (*hiddah*

umashal). . . . A statement expressed in the form of a parable or allegory (*hiddah o mashal*), like the prophecies of Zechariah, has not the perfection it ought to have, for it needs explanation, and may bear different meanings. This is why Ezekiel complained because his prophetic messages took the form of parables (*meshalim*): "Ah Lord God! They say of me: Is he not a maker of parables (*memashel meshalim*)" (21:5), indicating that this was a defect. And God then spoke to him in plain words.

Plain words, which express the plain meaning of the biblical text, are preferable because common people, who need to benefit from their lesson, can easily understand them.

Nevertheless, *meshalim*, variously understood as "parables," "fables," "stories," "metaphors," "proverbs," "examples," or "allegories," were, of course, not suspect in themselves to Jewish philosophers. Following Maimonides, they acknowledged that the *mashal* was useful for teaching both the masses and the elite at the same time: for the masses the *mashal* gave a comprehensible form to truths they could not otherwise understand. For the elite, the *mashal* hinted at a *nimshal*, an inner meaning, truths that rational argument could demonstrate. The masses would take the evident sense of the *mashal* as a sufficient lesson from the biblical narrative, and philosophers would take the *mashal* as a hidden reference to the *nimshal*, which they understood to refer to some stage in the process of perfecting the human intellect. The *mashal* was considered to be a rhetorical figure, which was persuasive for the common people, but served only as an illustration or an allusion for philosophers.

Maimonides's *Guide of the Perplexed*, which was intended to dispel the embarrassment of philosophically trained Jews at "uncertain terms and the parables" in the Bible that appeared to contradict philosophic truths, discusses the two ways in which the Hebrew Bible uses the figurative language of the *mashal*.[7] Maimonides distinguishes simple statements from parables and the external from the internal meaning of parables; finally, he distinguishes between parables in which there is a word-for-word correspondence between the vehicle and the tenor of a metaphor and parables in which a whole story corresponds to a single philosophical statement. The account of Jacob's ladder, in Gen. 28:12–13, exemplifies parables in which each word has a distinct internal meaning. Proverbs 7:6–21, warning against the harlot, is an example of a narrative that alludes to only one philosophic statement. He then instructs his readers:

You should not inquire into all the details occurring in the parable, nor should you wish to find significations corresponding to them. For doing so would lead you into one of two ways: either into turning aside from the parable's intended subject, or into assuming an obligation to interpret things not susceptible of interpretation and that have not been inserted with a view to interpretation. The assumption of such an obligation would result in extravagant fantasies such as are entertained and written about in our time by most of the sects of the world, since each of these sects desires to find certain significations for words whose author in no wise had in mind the significations wished by them. Your purpose, rather should always be to know, regarding most parables, the whole that was intended to be known.[8]

The consequences of distinguishing the two kinds of parables are apparent in the introduction to his two-page philosophical commentary on the Song of Songs of Joseph Ibn Kaspi (ca. 1279–ca. 1345):[9]

> I have no doubt at all that this book [the Song of Songs] belongs to the second kind of parable [*mashal*] that the *Guide* mentions at the beginning of his book. Not every word in it adds something to the intended meaning [*nimshal*]. Not every word in the parable refers to the subject of the allegory [*nimshal*], just as is demonstrated by the passage that he mentions [Prov. 7:6–21], which also deals with a lover and a beloved, the subject of this whole book. The subjects of the two books, however, are not equivalent. That story [in Proverbs] is a parable of the adhesion of natural matter and form. This story [the Song of Songs] is a parable of the conjunction of the Agent Intellect with human reason, which is divided into four kinds, the most noble of which is the emanated intellect. . . . And therefore the most precise [reference] is that he gave the name, "thou fairest among women" [Song 1:8] to the most precious faculty and called the pleasant lover the active intellect. He also intended, however, to refer to the entire rational soul, as is necessary for our parable at several places in this book.

Kaspi's practice illustrates the philosophical-allegorical method of interpreting a biblical text. The philosophical interpreter supplies the *nimshal,* the inner sense, to the *mashal* of the sacred text and afterward may disregard the details of the text if seeing no connection between them and that inner sense. In his *Gevia' Kesef,* Ibn Kaspi shows how philosophical allegorization can be applied to statements of any kind, because all figurative statements may serve as *meshalim* for the philosophical *nimshal:*[10]

> The world of Separate Intelligences, or if you will, the universe of the Intellect, or the universe of the Intelligences, consists of Him, blessed be He, His court and His attendants, as our Sages said. This category is divided, according to our conception, into three components, when described in terms of cause and effect, as Abu-Nasr (Al-Farabi) said (when he described them as) "the Primary One, the Secondary Ones, and the Active Intellect." You should

know that it was from this that in ancient times there first emerged a belief in the Father, the son, and the Spirit. Only later was that belief transformed into something else.

Kaspi has here turned Christian theological terms into mere metaphors for what he considers to be a demonstrably true statement about ultimate reality. Such metaphors, *meshalim*, can be taken from any kind of discourse. There is formally no difference between this procedure and the allegorization of pagan myths that Yehuda Abravanel performs so strikingly in the *Dialogues*.

Jewish Bible interpretation by the fifteenth century was divided into several schools. Philosophers would find biblical confirmation of the basically static relationships of physics, metaphysics, and ethics that the Aristotelian system presented. Theosophic Kabbalists would integrate words, verses, names, and other aspects of the text into a dynamic set of correspondences and other relationships among the ten *sefirot* and their dependencies in lower worlds.[11] All schools of Jewish Bible interpretation would agree on the revealed perfection of the received Hebrew text, and all made use, in distinct ways, of the scheme of multiple senses that is familiar from Christian interpretation. Nevertheless the contrast between philosophic allegorization and rhetorical-kabbalistic allegorization is stark—as also is the difference between Kaspi's two-page commentary on the Song and Alemanno's five hundred. Alemanno's vigorous emphasis on the literal sense appears to be even stronger than Yehuda Abravanel's. It makes varied rhetorical analyses of the *mashal*, as well as multiple internal senses—philosophic and kabbalistic.

Yehuda Abravanel multiplies different allegorical senses. For example, he analyzes the story of Perseus, son of Jupiter, who killed the Gorgon and, after his victory, flew away through the ether, which is the highest heaven. Abravanel gives five levels of interpretation to the story.[12] (1) the historic, Perseus killed Gorgo, a tyrant; (2) the moral, the prudent man destroyed vice and ascended to heaven; (3) the natural allegory, the human mind overcomes earthliness to understand heavenly truths; (4) the heavenly allegory, celestial nature detached itself from corruptible things to attain immortality; (5) the theological allegory; the angelic nature destroyed its corporeality and rose to heaven.

The application of new rhetorical methods to biblical interpretation and the readiness to examine texts more minutely for hidden meanings other than philosophical allegories led to greater emphasis on the first kind of parable that Maimonides defined. In the foreword to the commentary on Proverbs, *Yad Avshalom*, Isaac Arama (ca. 1420–1494) surveys three kinds of discourse in which the prophets practiced exemplary eloquence (*leshon limmudim*):[13]

The first is rhetoric (*melitsa*), in which not only one meaning is intended, whether the utterance is simple or profound, light or grave, like most of the matter in the words of Torah and the language of the prophets. We cannot explain why the degrees of simplicity of the rhetoric or its profundity vary from passage to passage. The second is poetry (*shira*), in which two meanings, one explicit and one implicit, are actually intended, not only the explicit. Examples of this are, "Out of the eater came forth food" (Judges 14:14) and "The trees went forth . . . " (Judges 9:8) and such riddles as those of Ezekiel and Zechariah. The third is fable (*mashal*), for which there is an obvious and a hidden sense, but although the hidden sense is primary, the external sense is not devoid of importance. This is the case with many subjects in the divine Torah, the obvious sense of which is marvelously useful for bodily life, whereas beneath its wings there are many precious, internal pearls, which are useful in satisfying souls. . . . In each of these three modes, the obvious sense is a metaphor for the hidden sense, and the two combined are good.

Arama's determination not to accept Maimonides's distinction between the two kinds of *mashal* is obvious. Similarly, commenting on the Song of Songs, Alemanno, who otherwise admired Kaspi, considered his simple philosophical allegorization of the Song, which has been cited previously, erroneous in content and methodologically careless about the plain meaning of the text.[14]

I am making these propositions not only about the general topic of the Song, but also about the specific details, because, just as Nature cannot be understood in general, apart from an understanding of its specifics, because everything is contained in the specifics; so it is true in poetic and other compositions, that their general sense is composed of their particular details. What wise man worthy of the name would let words drop accidentally from his mouth and not fastidiously employ the poetic or other arts? . . .

Consequently, our conception is not like that of many, who say about poems and stories that are copious in words that it is better to disregard the speeches and story, whether they are understood or not. These people then fashion wings for the story to fly to heaven and earth and everywhere, as their allegorical sense, without paying any attention at all to the meaning of the details of the story . . .

It was otherwise, however, in the conception of the early commentators, who were like messengers always saying, "The literal sense of the scriptural verse is never to be disregarded." . . .

As Abu Hamid said in his *Divine Lights*, neither the inner nor the outer meaning of a verse must be considered exclusively. The error of the "spiritualists" ["internalists"] was to look with a blind eye at one of the two worlds without knowing how to balance them. Denial of secrets is the opinion of the boor, the pursuer of the inner is oversubtle, but whoever combines them is perfect. . . .

> We, therefore, shall first show the simple meaning of the words of this song and afterwards teach its secrets and allegories

Fifteenth-century Bible commentators did not merely make commentaries more copious and interpretations more ingenious. They paid more attention to the internal meaning of external textual details and to finding a more varied and complex internal meaning for the text. This was the way in which the received texts were interpreted to support a philosophical-kabbalistic interpretation. The distinction of the *Dialogues* among such commentaries is its explicitness and its presentation in the genre of dialogue. The conditions that made possible such a combination of form and content resulted from various developments that occurred during the fifteenth century.

II

During the fifteenth century, Jewish learning underwent substantial change. Deterioration in the political circumstances of Jewish settlements, particularly on the Iberian peninsula, made rebuilding and sustaining Jewish communities that had collapsed, institutionally and morally, under fractionalized elites and external attacks into the necessary task of Jewish leaders. Christian polemics, notably in public disputations, frequently alleged that Jews concentrated so much on studying Talmud that they were ignorant of all else, even the divinely revealed text of the Bible. Fractious Jewish elites gave ineffective leadership, and once traditional leadership collapsed, it was difficult to reestablish any leadership.[15]

> Jewish communal leadership . . . was faced by a clearly theological challenge: how to defend Judaism in the face of the attacks of the Church, how to define who a Jew was in the face of the converso problem, and how to strengthen the faith of those Jews who stood firm in their Judaism, despite the pressure of the Church and the temptation represented by the conversos . . . the traditional communal/halakhic leadership (the "halakhic Maimonideans") was forced by the circumstances . . . to embark upon a clearly theological endeavor despite the fact that it had little innate interest in purely theological . . . questions.

Jewish scholars, notably the circle of Hasdai Crescas (d. 1412), responded in several ways. Because preserving and restoring Jewish communities depended on recreating communal religious identity, scholars formulated principles of Jewish faith for the masses.[16] The "theological endeavor" included adapting to Jewish teachings the theology of Thomas Aquinas, which made theology and its ancient sources in prophetic revelation superior in reliability and rank to those of philosophy.[17] As the Hebrew Bible and Kabbalah established truths beyond those that reason could prove, all Jewish scholarship could be founded on study of the Hebrew Bible.[18]

In the introduction to his grammar book, *Sefer Ma'aseh Efod* (1403), Isaac ben Moshe Halevi, called Efodi or Profiat Duran, presented an educational program for restoring the unity of Jewish communities that based all studies on the Hebrew Bible. According to this program, philosophers, talmudists, and Kabbalists were to derive the principles of their special disciplines from study of the Hebrew Bible, which ordinary Jews would also study. Efodi's program postulated, as Yehuda Halevi and St. Bonaventure both argued, that all disciplines are derived from the Bible.[19] The contention rebuts the Christian claim that the Jews neglected all learning, including the Bible, in favor of the Talmud, and therefore had lost their claim to divine election. The Bible, when studied in Hebrew, as the Jews' distinctive sign of election, in opposition to the community that relied on the Latin translation. Efodi's Hebrew grammar book was meant to enable Jews to regain an immediate understanding of divine revelation and demonstrate their direct connection with their heritage of revelation.

All human knowledge was originally made known through God's revelation, in Hebrew, to Adam and, most fully, to Moses and the later prophets. Solomon's reign attests to the completeness and sufficiency of this learning and to the fact that other nations learned parts of this revealed truth from the Jews, although adding some inaccuracy to it. This contention was central to Efodi's educational program and is fully expressed by one of his early sixteenth-century disciples, Abraham Farissol:[20]

> And if in these times, because of our sins we have been exiled from our land, nevertheless, God's word is exclusively among us. . . . And also on the awesome day at Mount Sinai, He crowned *us* with the entire Torah, which includes all sciences: natural, logical, theological, judicial and political, from which the whole world has drunk. . . . There were and currently are found among us all the high sciences, both new and old, which reached us through the potency of the prophets and from the words of the Torah, which is perfect in all the ways that perfection is possible, containing everything, including interpretation of the rhetorical expressions and speech and all of the true science of the holy kabbalah, which a man may merit to know only in the language of our holy Torah. Indeed, where else could all the other peoples and languages receive any sciences that were not already ours? For all the sciences are stolen from us! For most of the science of their language is from Greece and Chaldea and their sciences were translated into them from others.

As a consequence of the punishment of exile, and as a punishment of its own, the Jews had lost the arts and sciences and were able to preserve only

the Written and Oral Torahs, the canonical texts of revelation—the Bible—
and the reliable, unbroken tradition that supplemented and interpreted those
texts: the legal, homiletic, and mystical teachings found in the Mishnah, in
Midrash, in Talmud and Kabbalah. Jews possessed all that was necessary for
proper behavior and happiness, as well as the knowledge necessary for personal immortality. Proper understanding of the ancient, canonical texts, however, required understanding the words, references, assumptions and lines of
reasoning of the ancients. Jews needed, then, to recover all that was recover-
able of the revealed ancient wisdom, in order to restore continuity with the
past.

To identify lost learning, such as music, architecture, and mathematics,
Jews would have to be able to show that it was mentioned in the Bible and
Rabbinic texts, or find evidence there that the Hebrews knew the original
form of the modern nations' arts and sciences. Jews also recovered ancient
Jewish texts that Jewish tradition forgot because they were not written in
Hebrew, most notably the Greek writings of Philo and Josephus and the
Letter of Aristeas. Reliable testimony of non-Jewish authorities also could
show that Jews had practiced a discipline and had even taught it to non-Jews.
They could discern, in noncanonical and non-Jewish works, learning that
either conformed to Jewish teaching, or at least did not contradict it, and
therefore was acceptable for use.

To be acceptable, an item needed either to be assimilable as a linguistic
or conceptual equivalent to what was already canonical. These Jews could
incorporate one of these "recovered" items of ancient Jewish wisdom into
received Jewish learning through a thought process that resembles loan-
translation. Like a translator, these scholars would find approximate equivalence between the new item and something in one of the kinds of discourse
that were already canonized within Jewish scholarship: philosophy, Kabbalah,
talmudic study, Midrash. Once this was done, they could adopt the contemporary practice of the discipline among the nations, as long as it did not
contradict other canonical statements.

The *Dialogues of Love* is a work that performs this process repeatedly in its
discussions; it reduces any manner of alien saying into a version of the pre-
sumedly original wisdom, revelation as it was recorded in the written text of
the Hebrew Bible and in the oral tradition.

By explaining all innovation as recovery of a lost part of the original
Jewish heritage, these Jews were screening themselves from the all-too-fre-
quent explanation of modern historians, that they were "borrowing" or ac-
cepting foreign "influences." Indeed, they used whatever they "recovered" as
a means of combatting Christian, humanist conversionist arguments. At the
same time, the belief that revelation to the Jews had included all human

wisdom meant, in effect, that nothing human need be considered alien to a Jew.

By recovering the texts, disciplines, and information that they lost in exile, Jews could restore continuity with preexilic Judaism of Second Temple times. This parallels the goal of the humanist movement, to restore continuity with classical antiquity, through Augustine or Cicero. But the attitude of Hebrew humanists to the intervening generations of tradition was quite different from that of the classical humanists. The Jews asserted their continuity with the chain of tradition and their immediate predecessors and blamed exile for any discontinuities, whereas the humanists contrasted the superiority of classical literature and times with the errors and perversities of recent generations of scholars, such as scholastic Averroists.

In addition to making the Hebrew Bible into the fundamental text for Jewish study and Hebrew the basis for Jewish learning, *Ma'ase Efod* completed the integration of European Jewish learning into the Latin, rather than the Arabic, framework.[21] Efodi proposed to reorganize Jewish study of the language arts, by adopting the Latin classification, the *trivium* of grammar, rhetoric, and poetry, instead of the classification of the "logical" arts, poetry, rhetoric, sophistry, dialectics, and demonstration, that Jews had received from the Arabic philosophic tradition. The Latin classification gave greater importance to rhetoric than the Arabic classification. Coincidentally, at exactly the same time Latin rhetoric was being reformulated by the Italian humanists, through recovery of ancient texts, into a powerful practical art of language, for both interpretation and composition. The practice of writing Hebrew in imitation of the ancient biblical text, under the guidance of rhetorical analysis provided by Cicero and Quintilian, produced a Jewish counterpart of European humanism, a Hebrew humanist movement.[22]

Rabbi Yehuda Messer Leon asserted the antiquity in Hebrew, and therefore the acceptability, of the newly available art of rhetoric.[23]

> When I studied the words of the Torah in the way now common amongst most people, I had no idea that the science of Rhetoric was included therein. But once I had studied and investigated Rhetoric . . . out of treatises written by men of nations other than our own, and afterwards came back to see what is said of her in the Torah and the Holy Scriptures, . . . I saw that it is the Torah which was the giver.

Hebrew writers followed the main tendencies of the schools of rhetoric in contemporaneous Latin and Italian. The repertoire of genres of Hebrew writings from Italy between about 1450 and 1650 reflects an overall strategy of rhetorical imitation, based on Latin and vernacular rhetorical theory and practice, which were applied to a Hebrew canon of generic models. Jewish writers adapted these genres to Hebrew by adding an important step to the humanist procedure of imitating classical models: assuming that the Hebrew Bible, because of its antiquity and presumed divine origin, contained the original models for all classical genres, Hebrew writers would identify the presumed biblical model for the classical genre and then imitate that original. This procedure, which may be called *biblical classicism*, gave Hebrew writers quite specific guidance for stylistic choices and amplified the acceptable range of subjects and compositional features that would be permissible for a given genre. Biblical classicism served both to "illustrate" Hebrew, which in Italy served for several decades almost as a Jewish vernacular, and to reaffirm the claims of Hebrew to priority and superiority among the ancient languages. Rhetorical study served the renewed interest in addressing a wider audience than the elite and classified and analyzed the available kinds of discourse.

The most important innovation in Yehuda's *Dialogues* is in the manner of interpreting the biblical text. His ways of interpreting, at the same time, biblical passages and pagan myths demonstrate the intersection of new Hebrew rhetoric with the established Jewish philosophical and kabbalistic traditions of interpretation. The emergence of rhetoric in fifteenth-century Jewish writing contrasts strikingly with earlier attitudes toward the discipline.

Medieval philosophers considered theological discourse to be of the same rank as rhetoric, which for them was a minor division of the art of logic, which cannot prove assertions to be true or independently attain truths. Theology and rhetoric were useful only politically, to persuade the masses to obey the law, to keep peace in society, and certain essential dogmas, in order to attain immortality.[24] When Alfarabi defined the relation between philosophy and theology, he strongly disparaged theology:[25]

> Since religion teaches theoretical things through representation and persuasion, and those who adhere to it will know only these two methods of instruction, then it is obvious that the art of theology which is subordinate to religion will only be conscious of persuasive things and will not show the soundness of any matter pertaining to religion except through persuasive methods and arguments. . . . Persuasion only comes about through premises which are preferred at the beginning of reflection and are well known, and through enthymemes and examples; in general, through rhetorical methods . . . Therefore, the theologian limits himself . . . to that which is common according to the beginning of reflection. He has this in common with the multitude.

The elitist stance of Maimonidean philosophers persisted right through into the sixteenth century. Saul Cohen and Elijah del Medigo, late fifteenth-

century Averroistic Maimonideans, called on communal authorities to sup-
press teaching anything to the masses that they could not study according to
the rules of the appropriate disciplines. Most particularly, they opposed teaching kabbalistic explanations of reasons for the commandments and condemned public exposition of theological concepts in rhetorical form that was
practiced by a group of thinkers that became prominent in the fifteenth
century, first in Spain and then in Italy. Yohanan Alemanno and Yehuda
Abravanel belonged to this group, along with other scholars, such as Yehuda
Messer Leon, Isaac Abravanel, Isaac Arama, and Abraham Bibago. Knowing
the grounds for Cohen's and del Medigo's opposition, Yehuda nevertheless
chose to write the *Dialogues of Love.*

IV

The most important and innovative comparisons with the Bible that Yehuda
makes in the *Dialogues* are with Plato's works, so that Sofia can say, "I am
pleased to see you making Plato mosaic and one of the Kabbalists."[26] This was
Yehuda's strategy of defense against Christian use of Plato in polemics. Marsilio
Ficino (1433–1499), the outstanding translator and interpreter of Plato's
Greek writings in Florence and leader of a circle of eminent thinkers,
reinterpreted Plato to solve both philosophical and Christian theological
problems.[27] "Platonism appeared to Ficino to be a kind of propaedeutic to
Christianity, so that it seemed practicable to develop in a Christian direction
the religious motifs that it contained." In Florence between May and July
1485, a religious debate took place between two Jews, probably Elijah del
Medigo and Abraham Farissol, and a Jewish apostate, Flavius Mithridates. As
Ficino reminds Domenico Benivieni,

> You were also present at the debates which took place frequently and which
> are still taking place in the home of Giovanni Pico della Mirandola, who is
> venerated above others; where Elias and Abraham, Hebrew physicians and
> peripatetics, spoke at length against Guglielmus of Sicily. They contend that
> the prophetic oracles do not refer at all to Jesus, but were spoken with some
> other meaning. They turn them all in a different direction, so far as they are
> able, wresting them from our hands, nor does it seem that they can easily be
> refuted unless the divine Plato enters the debate, the invincible defender of
> the holy religion.[28]

Although Jewish scholars had long known, through Arabic, of eight works
by Plato, either by name or in heavily interpreted paraphrases,[29] the Jews who
were associated with Ficino's circle in Florence were the first to encounter

authentic texts of Plato and use of his writings for Christian polemics. These Jews would have been the first to rebut such arguments. Elijah del Medigo, who was Pico's consultant on Hebrew philosophy from 1482 to about 1486, refers to contemporary interest in Plato in the Hebrew translation of his Latin commentary on Averroes's *De Substantia orbis*, also from 1485.[30] Del Medigo quotes Themistius to deride Plato's manner of argumentation, saying that he did not complete the discussion of any topic, wrote elliptically, and put riddles (*hiddot*) into his dialogues, which anyway say little that is valuable. He goes on to note that poets and rhetoricians of his own time have taken to expounding platonic teachings, for which "they use the demonstrations of Aristotle to explain the riddles of Plato." These thinkers, including Giovanni Pico, are investigating Plato because they think that there is truth in every type of wisdom. Del Medigo's characterization of Christian Platonism could easily be directed against Jewish Platonism. He, in opposition, intends his writing to defend the philosophical writings of Averroes.

The same quotation from Themistius' commentary on Aristotle's *On the Heavens* is also found in the notebooks of Yohanan Alemanno, Pico's Jewish consultant from 1488, who apparently was the first Jewish thinker to try to adapt Florentine Platonism as an apologetic strategy for Judaism.[31] Another entry in Alemanno's notebooks, from near 1500, names ten of Plato's books, in Italian, and adds brief descriptions that closely resemble Ficino's own.[32]

Alemanno, under the influence of Pico and the Florentines, was the first Jew to attempt to use Plato to reconcile Jewish thought, including Kabbalah, with Aristotelian philosophy, against Christian polemics. The apocryphal traditions that Plato had studied with Jewish teachers, even with the prophet Jeremiah in Egypt, and equally apocryphal Arabic testimonies that Plato confessed himself unable to comprehend the depths of Jewish religious teaching, made Plato initially attractive to include within a Jewish synthesis. Considered as a late-coming foreign student, Plato could, if properly understood, serve as a confirmation of the revelation that Jews consider themselves to possess and to be transmitting. Alemanno did not, however, systematically compare Plato's texts with Jewish texts, as Yehuda Abravanel did.

V

The book that was published in 1535 as the *Dialogues of Love* is incomplete. Not only is a promised fourth dialogue, explaining the effects of love, not written, also missing is the kind of introduction with which early sixteenth century compositions in any of the possible original languages of the dialogues, Italian, Latin, Spanish or Hebrew, would have begun. All the dialogues that sixteenth-century writers took as examples, whether by Plato, Cicero, Yehuda Halevi, or Castiglione, have an introductory statement of the topic or circumstances, but these *Dialogues* do not. These *Dialogues* are not, then, the complete work that its author intended. Reconstructing the introduction to the work, in the categories that were available to the author, clarifies Yehuda Abravanel's intentions for the work.

By the late fifteenth century in Italy, the Hebrew introduction, like the scholastic or humanist introduction, would be based on the form of the *accessus ad auctores.* Originally an introduction to school commentary on an ancient author, the *accessus* was a series of six to eight questions that served to define the work.[33] A draft of Alemanno's commentary on the Song of Songs contains such an introduction:[34]

> The things with which commentators customarily open his (*sic*) books, which are altogether eight: The intention of the book. Its usefulness. Its rank. Its parts. Its relation. The manner of study carried on in it. And what its name tells about it. And who is the one who left it. The intention refers to what the book is intended to inculcate in us. Its usefulness refers to the use that results from acquiring these ideas. Its rank indicates whether it is first or second or last among other books and other knowledge. Its parts refers to the parts into which that investigation ought to be divided, primary and secondary, large and small. Its relation refers to its relation to other ideas, whether it is a propaedeutic to something else, or vice versa. The manner of study refers to the manner in which the ideas known through it will be explained, whether by image or proof, and this by evidentiary proof or syllogistic. What its name indicates about it, is the name of the book, which indicates its character. The name of the author, indicates the wisdom of the author, which is obvious from the mere mention of his name, because of the fame of his wisdom.

If Yehuda's introduction had survived, most likely in such a form, the author's name would not have been a surprise, although the name of the book would not necessarily have been *Dialogues of Love.* The manner of study practiced throughout the *Dialogues* is to compare a statement in a biblical passage with statements that are taken, variously, from astrology, philosophy, Plato, Kabbalah, Midrash, and earlier Jewish Bible commentary. Yehuda pays close attention to phrasing and the fine distinctions between verses, and he uses several forms of philosophical allegorization. Each discussion is completed when the statements that have been brought from the various other texts have been traced to, or harmonized with, the biblical text. This manner of argumentation applies practically the assumption that the divinely revealed Hebrew text of the Bible is the original form of all truths that humanity can know. The more diverse the statements that can be treated as derived from the biblical passage, the stronger the confirmation that Judaism is the only legitimate continuation of the original divine revelation. In choosing a genre in which to bring together his diverse texts, the most important question for the overall composition, Yehuda would have been able to draw upon Hebrew and Latin literary precedents, especially as they were understood by the Hebrew humanists. Vernacular, Latin, and Hebrew writers on rhetoric all discussed the genres of writing that were appropriate to philosophical discourse. The art that permits comparison of heterogeneous texts is rhetoric, and the art that evaluates contradictory statements is dialectic. At the intersection of the two disciplines is the literary dialogue.

In a way that plausibly anticipates Yehuda's choice of the form of his composition, Alemanno surveys the available genres of didactic writing from each discipline of the linguistic arts, in ascending order of the veracity of their statements. He then considers exemplary works from genres of each discipline. The examples are taken from Jewish writing and the products of human art and reason, from other nations:[35]

> Usage in expounding speculative truth follows several manners:
> 1. If in poetic and gnomic fashion: like the prophets, who were accustomed to expounding deep truth that was to be obeyed, as in Moses' Song of the Sea, the Song of Songs and others, as well as many written by the philosophers.
> 2. Rhetorical narrative, in which very deep matters are discussed, as in the narratives of the Torah and prophets and the other wise men, such as al-Ghazzali, whose book is almost entirely narrative and lacking in demonstrations.
> 3. One of the dialectical modes in which are mingled refutations, as the writings of the early philosophers, according to al-Farabi and Averroes.
> 4. One of the dialectical modes in which veracious demonstrations are mingled, as was done in the time of Plato and the time of the Tannaim [Rabbis from before 200 C.E.], as Shem Falaquera wrote in *Reshit Hokhmah.*
> 5. In demonstrative, deductive fashion, as Aristotle and his disciples wrote.

"Poetic and gnomic discourse" (1) includes biblical poetry and, by extension, other ancient kinds of poetry. Among these are the poets, such as Ovid, whose mythological "lies" are mentioned in the *Dialogues*: the myths of the *Metamorphoses* and their later Italian retellings.[36] Alemanno's "rhetorical narratives" (2) include biblical and foreign histories, as well as other stories, fables, and parables. "Dialectical discourse which includes argument and refutation" (3), as are found in the early philosophers, sounds like a reference to a hypothetical stage in the development of philosophy, perhaps based on accounts of the ancient sophists. Alemanno might consider literary dia-

.

logues to fit into this category. The "dialectical mode which includes veracious demonstrations," (4) for which Plato's dialogues and Rabbinic discussions in the Mishnah and Talmud serve as paradigms, seems to be the closest that Alemanno might have come to the *Dialoghi*. "Demonstrative and deductive exposition" (5) about logical, metaphysical, or physical topics refers to scholastic philosophy, based on the systematic university studies that were derived from the works of Aristotle.

Historians of Jewish philosophy have taken Yehuda Halevi's *Kuzari*, another Jewish philosophical dialogue, to be the model for the genre of the *Dialogues*, but it is mistaken to expect to find a single precedent for this innovative composition. Rather than one model, the practice of writing in the genre of the dialogue best explains the form of the apparently anomalous work. Medieval Hebrew debates which discussed philosophical topics for a popular audience should be recalled, such as Shem Tov Falaquera's *Book of the Seeker* and *Epistle of the Debate*. In late fifteenth-century Italy, the dialogues of Plato and Cicero and new humanist dialogues in Latin and the vernaculars were also available to Jews. The best explanation of the genre, however, is found in Torquato Tasso's influential *Discourse on the Art of the Dialogue*, from near the end of the sixteenth century.[37]

> [T]he dialogue is an imitation of a discussion, made in prose for the benefit of civil and speculative men. There are two kinds of dialogue: one deals with choosing and avoiding; the other is speculative and takes for the subjects of its debates matters that touch on truth and knowledge. In both, one imitates not only the disputation but also the characters of those who are disputing, and in both one employs a style that is sometimes highly ornamented and sometimes very pure, as befits the subject. . . . There are . . . two chief kinds of imitation: one of action and active men, and the other of speeches and men who reason.[38]

Tasso agrees with those who divide "imitations of discourses into three kinds. One of these can be performed on the stage and can be called *representative*, for it introduces characters—just as comedy and tragedy do—and lets them do the reasoning *dramatikos*. Plato and Lucian use this method in their dialogues. Another kind, however, cannot be staged because the author speaks in his own voice and, like a historian, narrates what this character says and what that one replies. These discussions can be called *historical* or *narrative*, and it was this kind that Cicero generally wrote.[39]

The dialogue is principally defined by the plot, the subject of the discussion, which determines the overall shape of the text, the opinions expressed and the characters who express them, and the style.

Discussions can be directed toward contemplative matters or toward actions; if they are directed toward actions, they deal with choosing and avoiding, if toward contemplative matters, with knowledge and truth. Accordingly, some dialogues ought to be called civil and moral, while others should be called speculative. Because a large number of the Platonic dialogues are speculative, and because the subject of debate in almost all of them is infinite, they seem entirely unsuited to the stage.[40]

The *Dialogues of Love*, as is appropriate for the confrontation with Plato's writings, is a speculative dialogue. Because "the writer of a dialogue . . . occupies a middle ground between poet and dialectician," dialecticians, who specialize in argumentation through questioning, ought to write dialogues. Here is Yehuda Abravanel's rebuttal to Saul Cohen's charge that writing dialogues is a waste of a philosopher's training.

In the fifteenth and sixteenth centuries, Jews, like Christian investigators of the *Prisca Theologia*, sought greater certainty in ancient texts than modern philosophy could provide. The antiquity of a belief was sufficient to make it worth considering as a gnomic truth, a *mashal*, or riddle that contained deep wisdom. The Jewish philosopher's task, in opposition to the Christian philosopher, was to show the Jew's possession of the original, revealed form of all kinds of wisdom. Paradoxically, the antiquity of that original wisdom was confirmed by the existence of ancient variants of it, which the philosopher would sift with dialectical skill. The comparative historical perspective became integrated, for the first time, into biblical commentary, which was simultaneously theology for the whole community. Yohanan Alemanno, Abravanel's older colleague, asserted the educational superiority of ancient opinions, "the words of the wise and their riddles," over the obscurantism of the classical Jewish philosophers:[41]

It is clearly true that a person cannot gain true and necessary wisdom unless he ascends, day by day, month by month and year by year, from modern science to the ancients' wisdom, both near and remote, so that he knows and understands them truly; not only the opinions of Aristotle and Plato and those more ancient among the gentile sages, but also the doctrines of the most ancient sages, such as the Amoraim and Tannaim, the prophets, and our teacher, Moses, peace be upon him, and the partiarchs of the world, such as Abraham, Enoch, Methuselah, Seth and Adam, as far as it is possible to know their opinions and doctrines. The reason [for teaching this] is that the wisdom of the ancients, particularly the wisdom of the Hebrews, is not like the wisdom of the moderns: the [ancient] wisdom is knowledge compressed into a few decisive words about the essence of existence, as well as the principles and details of the sciences, without leaving the slightest doubt in anyone's mind. Their knowledge is about the essence of things and the core of the sciences—not doubts and husks and superficialities like the knowledge of the modern gentiles, all of whose knowledge is derived from weak syllogisms and proofs that remain dubious in people's minds, because of the many arguments that support contrary interpretations, until there is not one of these moderns who knows something and is persuasive about it in his speech, or even persuaded in his heart and thoughts. He is only a believer-nonbeliever, someone who swerves right and left, at one time saying this, and at another, that. Such is not at all the case with the words of the prophets and their disciples, all of whose words are true in the heart of those who know them.

Notes

1. This translation of Proverbs 1:7 combines the two Jewish Publication Society versions: in the 1917 edition, the terms are *proverb, figure,* and *dark saying;* and in 1982, *proverb, epigram,* and *riddle.*

2. Julius Guttmann, *Philosophies of Judaism,* trans. David W. Silverman (New York, 1966) pp. 294–95. Shlomo Pines, "Medieval Doctrines in Renaissance Garb? Some Jewish and Arabic Sources of Leone Ebreo's Doctrines," *Jewish Thought in the Sixteenth Century,* ed. Bernard Dov Cooperman (Cambridge, Mass., 1983), pp. 390–91. Colette Sirat, *A History of Jewish Philosophy in the Middle Ages* (Cambridge, 1985), pp. 407–10.

3. Saul Cohen Ashkenazi, *She'elot haRav Shaul Cohen* (Venice, 1574), 2v.

4. M. David Geffen, "Faith and Reason in Elijah del Medigo's 'Behinat Ha-Dat' and the Philosophic Backgrounds of the Work," Ph.D. dissertation, Columbia University, 1970, p. 82, n. 46.

5. M. David Geffen, "Insights into the Life and Thought of Elijah del Medigo," *PAAJR* 41–42 (1975): 69–86.

6. Joseph Albo, *Sefer Ha-'Ikkarim. Book of Principles,* ed. and trans. Isaac Husik, 5 vols. (Philadelphia, 1946), vol. 3, p. 222.

7. Maimonides, *The Guide of the Perplexed,* trans. Shelomo Pines (Chicago, 1969) p. 12. For a survey of the texts and approaches of philosophers and Kabbalists in the twelfth to the fourteenth centuries, see Frank Talmage, "Apples of Gold: The Inner Meaning of Sacred Texts in Medieval Judaism," *Jewish Spirituality from the Bible through the Middle Ages,* ed. Arthur Green, *World Spirituality: An Encyclopedic History of the Religious Quest,* vol. 13 (New York, 1988) pp. 313–15.

8. *Guide,* p. 14.

9. Joseph Ibn Kaspi, *Hatzotzrot Kesef,* in *Asarah Klei Kesef,* ed. Isaac Last (Pressburg, 1903) vol. 1 (reprint ed. Jerusalem, 1969), pp. 183–84.

10. Basil Herring, *Joseph Ibn Kaspi's "Gevia' Kesef." A Study in Medieval Jewish Philosophic Bible Commentary* (New York, 1982), p. 136.

11. Moshe Idel, *Kabbalah: New Perspectives* (New Haven, Conn., 1988), pp. 200–49; Gershom G. Scholem, "The Meaning of the Torah in Jewish Mysticism," *On the Kabbalah and its Symbolism* (New York, 1965), pp. 32–86.

12. Leone Ebreo, *The Philosophy of Love (Dialoghi d'Amore)*, trans. F. Friedeberg-Seeley and Jean H. Barnes (London, 1937), p. 111.

13. Rabbi Yitzhak Arama, *Sefer Mishlei im Perush Yad Avshalom*, (Cracow, 1858–59), p. 1.

14. Yohanan Alemanno, *The Desire of Solomon*, British Museum MS. Or. 2854, fol. 99r–108r.

15. Menachem Kellner, *Dogma in Medieval Jewish Thought. From Maimonides to Abravanel* (Oxford, 1986), p. 81.

16. Kellner, ibid.

17. Hava Tirosh-Rothschild, *Between Worlds. The Life and Thought of Rabbi David ben Judah Messer Leon* (Albany, N.Y., 1991), pp. 114–21, 139, 185 ff.; idem, "Maimonides and Aquinas: The Interplay of Two Masters in Medieval Jewish Philosophy," *Conservative Judaism* 39 (1986): 54–66.

18. Shaul Regev, "The Rationalist-Mystical Trend in Fifteenth-Century Jewish Thought" [Hebrew], *Jerusalem Studies in Jewish Thought* 5 (1985): 155–89.

19. Rabbi Yehuda Halevi, vol. 2, p. 66: "so too are all these branches of knowledge ordained for the knowledge of Sacred Scripture; they are contained in it; they are perfected by it; and by means of it they are ordained for eternal illumination. Wherefore all our knowledge should end in the knowledge of Sacred Scripture . . ." *Saint Bonaventure's De reductione artium ad theologiam. A Commentary with an Introduction and Translation*, ed. and trans. Sister Emma Thérèse Healy (Saint Bonaventure, N.Y., 1955), pp. 28–29.

20. Profiat Duran, *Sefer Ma'aseh Efod* (Vienna, 1865; reprint ed. Jerusalem, 1970), p. 8; *Sefer Magen Avraham*, chapter 23, cited in David B. Ruderman, *The World of a Renaissance Jew* (Cincinnati, 1981): p. 77, n. 44. Translated from Ruderman, "Abraham Farissol: An Historical Study of His Life and Thought in the Context of Jewish Communal Life in Renaissance Italy," Ph.D. dissertation, Hebrew University of Jerusalem, 1975, p. 113.

21. *Sefer Reshit Hokhmah leRabbi Shem Tov Falaquera*, ed. Moritz David. (Berlin, 1862; reprint ed. Jerusalem, 1970), pp. 35–41.

22. Hava Tirosh-Rothschild, "In Defense of Jewish Humanism," *Jewish History* 3 (Fall 1988): 32–57; Arthur M. Lesley, "Jewish Adaptation of Humanist Concepts in Fifteenth- and Sixteenth-Century Italy" *Renaissance Rereadings. Intertext and Context*, ed. Maryanne Cline Horowitz et al. (Urbana and Chicago, 1988), pp. 51–66.

23. Judah Messer Leon, *The Book of the Honeycomb's Flow*, ed. and trans. Isaac Rabinowitz (Ithaca, N.Y., 1983), p. 145.

24. Maimonides, *Guide*, I.71, I.34, I.35.

25. Alfarabi, *Book of Letters*, ed Muhsin Mahdi (Beirut, 1970), 131.4–134.15. Cited in Lawrence V. Berman, "Maimonides, the Disciple of Alfarabi," *Israel Oriental Studies* 4 (1974): 172–73.

26. Leone Ebreo, *Dialoghi d'amore*, ed. Santino Caramella (Bari, 1929), p. 251.

27. Bruno Nardi, "La Fine dell'averroismo," *Pensée humaniste et tradition chrétienne aux XVe et XVIe siècles* (Paris, 1950), p. 150.

28. Marsilio Ficino, *Opera* I (Basel, 1576), p. 873.

29. Shem Tov ibn Falaquera, *Sefer Reshit Hokhmah*, ed. Moritz David (Berlin, 1902), pp. 72–78. This is taken from a work by Alfarabi, found in the trans. Muhsin

Mahdi, *Alfarabi's Philosophy of Plato and Aristotle,* rev. ed. (Ithaca, N.Y., 1969), pp. 53–67.

30. M. David Geffen, "Faith and Reason in Elijah del Medigo's *Behinat ha-Dat,*" Ph.D. dissertation, Columbia University, 1970, pp. 19–20. The source of the remarks is Paris, Bibliothèque Nationale, MS. hebreu 968, fol 3v.

31. "Themistius said, in *The Heavens and the World* [Aristotle's *De caelo*], that Plato completed almost no investigation, and in most of his investigations he spoke only in a deficient manner, mingled with riddles." Oxford, Bodleian MS. Reggio 23, fol. 141v margin.

32. Oxford, Bodleian MS. Reggio 23, fol 140v, right margin:

Meno, that knowing is remembering
Theatetus, what is knowledge
Timaeus, the nature of the creation of the world
Phaedo, on the soul
The Sophist, on being
Parmenides, on the one and divinity
Symposium, on desire
Philebus, on felicity and the ultimate
The Statesman, prophetic and kingly
Phaedrus, on beauty

This list may not have come from direct knowledge of Ficino's translations, but from mentions of them. In Ficino's letters, IV, 19, he mentions twenty-one works by Plato and comments, "We ourselves have translated all these books of Plato from Greek to Latin":

Meno, on virtue
Theatetus, on knowledge,
Timaeus, on the nature of the universe
Phaedo, on the immortality of the soul
The Sophist, on being
Parmenides, on the single origin of all things and on the ideal forms
The Symposium, on love
Philebus, on the highest good
The Statesman, on government
Phaedrus, on beauty

The letters of Marsilio Ficino III (London, 1975), p. 38.

33. R. W. Hunt, "The Introductions to the 'Artes' in the Twelfth Century," *Collected Papers on the History of Grammar in the Middle Ages.* (Amsterdam, 1980), pp. 117–43; Edwin A. Quain, S.J., "The Medieval Accessus ad Auctores," *Traditio* 3 (1945): 215–64. In 1507, for example, Pietro Pomponazzi opened his commentary on Averroes's *De substantia orbis*: "Before we come to the text, four things ought first to be examined: the intention of the book, its use, order and name. Before them it will suffice to note four others: the proportion, manner of presentation, division and name of the author." Pietro Pomponazzi, *Corsi Inediti dell'Insegnamento Padovano,* vol. 1, ed. Antonio Poppi (Padua, 1966), p. 1.

34. Oxford, Bodleian MS. Reggio 23, fol. 65r, top.

35. Oxford, Bodleian MS. Reggio 23 *Likkutim,* fol 65r.

36. Georg Gelb had demonstrated that the *Dialogues* cite myths from Boccaccio's version in *Genealogy of the Gods*. Riccardo Scrivano, "Platonic and Cabalistic Elements in the Hebrew Culture of Renaissance Italy: Leone Ebreo and his *Dialoghi d'amore*," *Ficino and Renaissance Neoplatonism*, ed. Konrad Eisenbichler and Olga Zorzi Pugliese (Toronto, 1986), p. 138, n. 27.

37. Tasso, *Discourse on the Art of the Dialogue*. pp. 17–41 in *Tasso's Dialogues. A Selection, with the Discourse on the Art of the Dialogue*, trans. with introduction and notes by Carnes Lord and Dain A. Trafton (Berkeley, Los Angeles, London, 1982).

38. Tasso, ibid., pp. 41, 19.

39. Ibid., pp. 19–21.

40. Ibid., p. 25.

41. Yohanan Alemanno, *Likkutim*, in Oxford, Bodleian MS. Reggio 23, fols. 141v–142v.

PART IV

Myth, Midrash, and *Exemplum*
in Medieval Historiography

10

Can Medieval Storytelling Help Understanding Midrash? The Story of Paltiel: A Preliminary Study on History and Midrash

————————————————————————Robert Bonfil

The Story

In *Sefer Hasidim*, the ethical "Volksbuch" of *Hasidei Ashkenaz*, the Jewish Pietists of Medieval Germany (eleventh–thirteenth centuries)[1] paragraph 545,[2] we read the following text:

> I Shabbatai b. Abraham, called Zolgo [= Donnolo] the doctor[—] was exiled from my homeland, the city called Oria, by the Muslim host, on Monday, the 9th of Tammuz, 4085 A.M. in the Eleventh year of the 246th cycle. And then were killed ten just men, rabbis and wise men, of blessed memory—R. Hassadia b. R. Hananel the Great, our relative, relative of my grandfather called R. Joel, and R. Amnon, and R. Uriel, and R. Menahem, and R. Hiyya, and R. Zaddok, and R. Moses, and R. David, and R. Jeremiah and other elders, pious community heads and leaders of the generation and many scholars, and children and women, blessed be the memory of all of them in the world to come, amen. And I was set free through ransom paid on my behalf in the city of Tartan [= Taranto] from the money of my forefathers of blessed memory. I was twenty years old at that time. And my ancestors and relatives were sent in exile to Palorma [= Palermo] and to Ifriqia. And I stayed in the country under the rule of the Romans.
>
> Paltiel was captured and carried away from Oria, in the country of the Lombards, with the same pious men who were captured on the boats. And on that boat was an old man, and he said to Paltiel the lad: "Oh, we were exiled because of you so that you should become a great man. Indeed I dreamed of a tall tree growing from earth to heaven and you were climbing on it.' And when the ships entered the harbour, Paltiel called upon a wise man, an expert

doctor, called Jacob, who was the king's doctor. And that Paltiel had a sharp mind, and he was spicing incense and learned all the medicines. A day came that Jacob the wise man died. And the king fell sick with a headache and sent to call for Jacob and he was told that he had passed away. Then the king enquired whether he had not left a son or a pupil. Paltiel came then before the king. Yet, the king said: I will not take your medicines, because you are still a lad. Paltiel said to him: I shall anoint your feet and you will begin to perspire". Then the king was told: "He is a liar." Paltiel burst out then laughing. The king asked him: "Why do you laugh at me? Don't you know that no laughter is permitted in my presence"? He answered: "This eunuch wanders about, yet how did it come about that while he was injured in the lower part of the body, his beard fell off in the upper part?" And the king was cured and honored him [Paltiel] very much. After some time the king died. And he had two sons, the elder one of whom hated Paltiel. Paltiel then told him: "Rise up and hold the kingship, because all the ministers love you except that certain negro who loves your brother. Let us send to call him and advise him to kill your brother; this will turn his heart towards you." The king followed that advice. After some time Paltiel made something [magic?] and the negro was killed. Paltiel then became a great man, and he asked the king to build the Temple, which was full of debris from the days of Titus, of cursed memory. Yet, the king did not give permission to clear the debris beyond noon time. Paltiel gathered young Jewish men and he himself, together with the young men, cleared the debris. Then they built the Temple and used to pray therein for many years. And Paltiel crowned his son with the king's permission, in Alexandria. And the name of that son was Jacob. After some time he died and he was mourned before the [?]. And when the Muslims realized that a Jew had been crowned as king, they wanted to kill Jacob. And the Great king came and wanted to plough it altogether. After some years, two Jewish leaders wanted to seize power one from the other and that happened in the night of the Day of Atonement, and they beat one another. The king of the Muslims then said: "It was not established by the stars that the Jews pray here." And he ordered to destroy the Temple—until the Spirit of God will descend from Heaven to build it Itself.

Even a superficial reading of this text shows two distinct pieces of biography, which have some elements in common. We are told of two famous doctors, both natives of Oria, both taken prisoner in the course of a Muslim raid on the city. On one of them, Shabbetai Donnolo, we are quite well informed, for he left us a considerable amount of literary production, including a piece of autobiography.[3] On the second one, Paltiel, our knowledge is far less satisfactory. The records concerning his life and activity has reached us in apparently contrasting texts, one of which is precisely the one just recalled. Additional evidence will be cited later, as it will become necessary for developing the main argument of this study. Although there is no necessary relationship between the story of Donnolo's captivity and that of Paltiel, it is not impossible that the two stories in fact stem from the same event, which, as we are told by Donnolo himself, took place in 925.[4] But it is also not unreasonable to think that, although it was not necessarily originally rooted in the same event, for some reason the narrative sequence was so shaped in our text as to convey the impression of a linkage. Be that as it may, there can be little doubt that if this text were examined with the standard tools of the positivistic historical-philological method, our text would be assigned to the genre often called by historians "a mixture of history and legend" or "a legend with a kernel of historical truth."

Such a conclusion would presumably be variously justified. Some would support their argument by drawing attention to the generically fantastic climate of the entire text, apparently a fairy tale; others would prefer to stress the apparent unlikelihood of this or that detail. In any case, effort would be directed toward separating the "truth" from the "legend," using the traditional tools of logic and historical criticism: the search for confirmation in parallel texts; critical internal analysis of the text; and so on. In fact, analyzed in that manner by its first editor, Jehuda Wistinetzki, the first part of our text immediately found some confirmation in the fact that the part of the preceding text concerning Donnolo stems from Donnolo's introductory autobiographical note to his Commentary to *Sefer Yetzirah*, which we are fortunate to have in entirety.[5] However, when confronted with the second part of the story, Wistinetzki could but note: "I have not found this story in its entirety elsewhere, and in fact it is quite difficult to understand many points in it." I must say that I was struck by the prudent circumspection of this note, which after all refrains from declaring the total impossibility of assigning some sense to the apparently fantastic details of the story. Viewed in retrospective, Wistinetzki's scientific caution has proved justified, at least in part. In fact, had he taken into consideration the text of the so called *Scroll of Ahima'az*, brought to publication some decades earlier by Neubauer,[6] but apparently still unknown to him,[7] he would have noted that some of the details of the second part of the document were also confirmed in it. Yet, not only do many details still remain obscure, but the story of Paltiel as we have it in the *Scroll of Ahima'az* is in fact rather different from the story in *Sefer Hasidim*. With considerable omissions, that story reads as follows in Saltzman's translation:[8]

> In those days the Arabians with their armies, with Al Muizz as their commander, overran Italy; they devastated the entire province of Calabria, and reached Oria, on the border of Apulia; they besieged it, defeated all its forces; so that the city was in dire distress; its defenders had no power to resist; it was

taken by storm; the sword smote it to the very soul. They killed most of its inhabitants, and led the survivors into captivity. And the commander inquired about the family of R. Shefatiah. He send for them and had them appear before him. And God let them find grace in his eyes. He bestowed His kindness upon R. Paltiel, His servant, and let him have favor before him. And Al Muizz brought him to his tent, and kept him at his side, to retain him in his service.

One night the commander and R. Paltiel went out to observe the stars. As they were gazing at them, they saw the commander's star consume three stars, not all at one time, but in succession. [Paltiel interprets the sign as announcing Al Muizz future conquests, thereupon gaining the ruler's trust and entering his service as his vizier.] Some time after, Al Muizz went to Ifrikyia [. . .] and R. Paltiel went with him. There he grew in eminence, and added to his fame; he was second in power to the Caliph, his renown spread through all the cities.

At that time, the emperor of Greece sent an embassy with a gift to seek audience with the Caliph of Ifrikyia. [Paltiel humiliated the ambassador, who insolently had said that he would not deal with a Jew for permission to be introduced to the Caliph, first by ostensibly ignoring him for several days until "he came to ask mercy and pardon," then by overwhelming him with a splendid reception and lavish gifts.] Thereupon he dismissed him with honor, to the king of Greece who had sent him.

[. . .]

Upon the death of the ruler of Egypt, the Elders of Egypt [. . .] sent a letter [. . .] to Al Muizz [inviting him to come and promising to be his subjects. Advised by Paltiel, Al Muizz accepted the proposal.] R. Paltiel set out in advance and established the camps; he erected bazaars and places for lodging [. . .] and everything necessary for soldiers coming from distant cities. Then the Caliph and princes and courtiers set out [. . .]. Then R. Paltiel entered Egypt with a division of the forces, detailed them on the walls and towers, so that they might guard the city, the palace and public buildings [. . .] And then the Caliph with all his army marched in [. . .].

Once, on the Day of Atonement, when R. Paltiel was called to read from the Torah, the whole assemblage arose and remained standing in his presence [. . .]. He called to them saying, "Let the old be seated, and the young stand. If you refuse, I will sit down and refuse to read, for this does not seem right to me." When he finished reading, he vowed to the God of his praise 5,000 dinars of genuine and full value; 1,000 for the head of the academy and the sages, 1,000 for the mourners of the sanctuary, 1,000 for the academy of Geonim at Babylon, 1,000 for the poor and needy of the various communities, and 1,000 for the exaltation of the Torah, for the purchase of the necessary oil [. . .].

The growth of his authority which the king, through his bounty, had bestowed upon him over his royal domain, having appointed him over the kingdom of Egypt and of Syria as far as Mesopotamia, and over all the land of

Israel as far as Jerusalem, his eminence and power and wealth with which the king had honored and distinguished him, are recorded in the chronicles of the kingdom of Nof and Anamim.

[When the caliph died, after having placed his son on the throne] the officials appointed to conduct the affairs of Egypt told him lying stories about R. Paltiel [. . .]. The Caliph's fury raged against them; he repeatedly rebuked them. He told R. Paltiel, the prince, all they said. So together they devised a plan of dealing with them [. . .].

One night R. Paltiel and the king were walking in the open and they saw three bright stars disappear [. . .]. And R. Paltiel said, "The stars that have been eclipsed represent three kings who will die this year [. . .]. The first is John the Greek, the second, the king of Bagdad, in the north"; then the king hastening to interrupt him said, "Thou art the third, the king of Teman," but he replied to the king, "No, my Lord, for I am a Jew; the third is the king of Spain." But the king said, Thou art in truth the third, as I said."

And in that year R. Paltiel died [. . .]. In his stead arose his son R. Samuel [. . .]. He brought the remains of his father and mother in caskets to Jerusalem, also the casket containing the bones of R. Hananel, his father's uncle, which had been embalmed [. . .].

A full-fledged analysis of the differences between the two versions would take us too far away from our main issue. Let us limit ourselves to some of the major divergences. In contrast to *Sefer Hasidim,* the text of *Ahima'az* does not contain any critical judgment. *Ahima'az* is squarely hagiographical. Although it mentions the Sultan's courtiers' jealousy of Paltiel, and the pomp displayed on the occasion of his funeral, it does not register any negative consequence. It does not mention any construction and subsequent destruction of the Sanctuary. The Day of Atonement, so negatively charged in *Sefer Hasidim,* is in the *Scroll of Ahima'az* a highly convenient framework for underlining the grandeur of Paltiel. The Muslim raid on Oria is almost factually reported in the *Scroll,* but according to it Paltiel was not transferred to Ifriqia as a prisoner, but as a member of the highly esteemed family of Shefatia; once the Sultan entered Oria, he is said to have inquired about that renowned family and had its members follow him—much as the tradition of German Jews would have Charlemagne take with him the family of Rabbi Kalonymos.[9] Moreover, Paltiel as remembered by Ahima'az was not a doctor, but an astronomer. Consequently, he did not achieve a position of prominence because of medical excellence, but rather because of his talent as administrator, diplomat, and military commander. The figure of Paltiel that emerges from the *Scroll of Ahima'az* is thus, mutatis mutandis, much closer to the traditional portrait of Shemuel Ha-Nagid[10] than to the Paltiel described by *Sefer Hasidim.* No wonder, then, that considerable confusion arises as to the "real" story of this man. Even Paltiel's identity is still to be discovered.

Modern scholars have tried to apply the tools of historical-philological method to the two texts and unravel the knot of historical truth perhaps contained in them.[11] Basing themselves on various Arabic historiographical texts, whose reliability has barely been exposed to critical scrutiny, various identifications have been proposed. All of them are plausible. Yet, they present difficulties and leave important questions unanswered. On the whole, they call for a high degree of readiness to adopt speculative plausibility as effective historical possibility. Unless one is inclined to dismiss the text altogether as fiction, this is definitely too high a price to pay to satisfy critical doubt! Bernard Lewis, for instance, identified this Paltiel with Musa ben El'azar, physician to al-Mu'izz, who accompanied him from North Africa to Egypt, and is the subject of several entries in the two chief Arabic works of medical biography. He was the author of various books, and the father of several sons who followed him in his profession.[12] The reference to al-Mu'izz is perhaps one of the few points on which there can be no doubt: al-Mu'izz is in fact explicitly mentioned in the *Scroll of Ahima'az*.

Yet, Lewis's hypothesis does not provide a full answer to every question. For instance, these Arabic works do not say that Musa held a high political position. Nor has Lewis a plausible explanation as to how Paltiel became Musa or why in these biographical works he is said to have passed away in 963, in the same year as his son 'Aun Allah ben Musa, who converted to Islam, and his other son Isaac ben Musa.[13] And one might add other questions of the same kind. On the other hand, supportive arguments can also be tentatively added to those offered by Lewis. For instance, the fact that 'Aun Allah ben Musa may sound in Hebrew Eli'ezer or El'azar ben Musa, and that Eli'ezer (God helped) would suit the notion of escaping a great danger, like Paltiel (God was my rescue), might support Lewis's suggestion to some extent.[14] Anyhow, Moshe Gil has proposed an alternative. Instead of Musa ben El'azar, Gill would prefer Faisal ben Saliḥ, a Fatimid statesman and military commander. This identification would indeed quite reasonably explain many details that remain obscure in Lewis's hypotheses.[15] Yet, as Gil is well aware, he does find a proper answer to numerous other details. In sum, for the time being no identification has satisfied the historian's curiosity, even if one be prepared to dismiss a priori as absolutely mythical details such as the construction and subsequent destruction of the Third Sanctuary.

I shall not try to offer an alternative explanation. At this stage, it seems that we have really reached the extreme limit of positive knowledge, where history and myth merge indissolubly. Yet, however important the "real" story of Paltiel may be, it seems that the importance of the way it was recorded is still greater for the history of Jewish culture. Among other aspects, I would point out one that is particularly relevant to actual scholarly research. I refer to the fact that from this story the world of Hasidei Ashkenaz appears to be much more closely related to the cultural reality of Southern Italy than is usually assumed or may be inferred from the quite well-documented account of the emigration of Italian Jews to the Rhineland. Indeed, not only do the *Scroll of Ahima'az* and *Sefer Hasidim* both contain a story stemming from the same Islamic area, but the *Sefer Hasidim* linkage of the story of Paltiel with that of Shabbatai Donnolo quite clearly shows that the story reached the Rhineland from Italy. In other words, not only were Hasidei Ashkenaz genealogically related to Italian Jewry, as is already very well known; their cultural tradition, up to now considered as unique and essentially rooted in German soil, included also elements from the heritage of Italian Jews. I shall not insist here on the enormous implications of this conclusion, already stressed elsewhere by me and Ivan Marcus,[16] for the understanding of the sociocultural setting of Hasidei Ashkenaz. In particular, that conclusion, would certainly militate in favor of the recent strong argument put forward by Peter Schäfer against "any attempt to see the ethical code of the German Pietists as deriving solely from contemporary Christian influences."[17]

Rather, for our discussion here, it is important to point out that the radical differences between the two versions of the story of Paltiel leave little doubt that the branches must have forked out of the same trunk long before their being written down in the two separate sources, yet some time after the reign of al-Mu'izz (953–975). In other words the split must have occurred some time between the last decades of the tenth century and the first decades of the eleventh. This conclusion goes very well with all the positive evidence so far collected on the Jewish settlement in the Rhineland.[18]

Preliminary Reflections on the Process of Mythologization

Let us now look at the making of such texts and their possible significance for the history of Jewish culture. Let us focus on the text of *Sefer Hasidim*, and ask, Assuming a priori that the story contains some "fantastic" details, such as the construction and subsequent destruction of the Sanctuary, is it possible to discern in it only one or perhaps more than one level of mythologization?[19] Furthermore, assuming a priori that the emergence of a mythical component is always aimed at helping to place an account at the service of some actual interest, can we determine that we have here one or more than one insertion of that kind?

Here too we have no basic tools of analysis other than those of historical philology. A cautious use of these immediately reveals that there is plenty of room to argue that most of the mythologization of our text was indeed carried out far away from the geographical and chronological area of Hasidei

Ashkenaz. As is well known, according to the traditions concerning the visit paid by 'Umar to the site of the Temple Mount immediately after the conquest of Jerusalem by the Arabs in 638, some Jews started to clean the place from the rubble that covered it. We have different accounts of that story, from Arab as well as from Jewish sources, and the relationship between them is not very clear. The Jewish sources may have drawn on the Arab, just as it is not impossible that the Arab chroniclers were influenced by stories they heard from Jews.[20] In any case, in view of the fact that we know from more than one source that soon after the Arab conquest of Jerusalem, Jewish settlement was in fact reinstated there, we may quite safely assume that the story of Jewish participation in the cleaning of the Temple area first took narrative shape in the chronological setting of the conquest. Broadly speaking, it opposed the Christian tradition, which claimed that among the privileges granted by 'Umar to the Christian population of Jerusalem was that of reinforcing the prohibition on Jewish settlement in the city. If so, apart from the possible nature of other interests that this first distant formulation might have been intended to serve, and about which much room remains for speculation, there can be little doubt that such a formulation in fact came into being soon after the Arab conquest of Jerusalem in 638.

When was the detail of the building of the Sanctuary added? In the present state of our knowledge, I do not see any reason to exclude any moment between 638 and the first formulation of the story of Paltiel; that is, soon after Paltiel's death. It may have been formulated any time before Paltiel, in a context absolutely unknown to us, and subsequently inserted in the story of Paltiel, just as it may have picked up the tradition of the cleaning of the Temple space and adjusted it to illustrate the Paltiel hagiography. If some speculation be allowed, it might be argued that the very working of the text as we have it in *Sefer Hasidim* may support the view that the detail concerning the Sanctuary was originally formulated before Paltiel and subsequently inserted and adjusted to his story. In fact, although the typology of the talmudic stories relating to the destruction of the Second Temple may also have played some role in shaping the *exemplum* of our story, nevertheless, for reasons that will soon be evident, the actual wording of the text does not state very clearly what exactly was the effect of the Caliph's wrath: Was it the destruction of the town, that is, of the Jewish community, where Paltiel's funeral took place? Or was it rather the Sanctuary itself, as the inner logic of the tale would require and as the use of the word *ploughing* would support, alluding to the destruction of the Temple on the Ninth of Av, as recorded by the Mishnah (*Ta'anit* IV. 6: *neḥresha ha-'ir*—the City was ploughed)? In other words, the ambivalent sense of that ploughing may possibly furnish the rhetorical device leading to the linkage of two stories relating two different destructions. In any case, it would seem rather unlikely that this detail was inserted in the story of Paltiel *outside the Islamic area;* that is, in the Christian West. An absolutely independent translation to the Christian West of two different traditions stemming from the Islamic area (the story of the cleaning of the Temple area and the story of Paltiel) to be casually matched in a third, Western, story (that of Paltiel, enriched with the details regarding the Sanctuary) would indeed seem much less probable than the translation of one single tradition. If we are right in this assumption, the story of Paltiel reached the West *after* the "fantastic" detail of the building of the Sanctuary had been incorporated into it. This reasoning should also lead us to exclude the translation to the Christian West of two different versions of the story, one to Southern Italy, that recorded by the *Scroll of Ahima'az,* and one to the Rhineland, that recorded by *Sefer Hasidim.* We may therefore conclude that the story of Paltiel reached the Christian West before the splitting of the two branches of the cultural heritage and that the radical differentiation between the two versions is in fact subsequent to that splitting. In the version recorded by Ahima'az the detail of the building and subsequent destruction of the Sanctuary was suppressed along with many other details, whereas it was preserved in the version recorded by the Hasidei Ashkenaz, who in turn suppressed most of the details recorded by Ahima'az.

In the story as we have it in *Sefer Hasidim,* Paltiel's death brought about some notable disgrace on the Jews. More specifically linked to the great pomp displayed on the occasion of his funeral. According to the story, on that occasion, the royal position of Paltiel was exposed to public attention, thus giving rise to an outburst of hostility and subsequent immediate action on the part of the Muslim ruler. One is tempted to refer here to the unfortunate funeral procession of 1011 that, according to Goitein, may have led the Egyptian Jewish leaders to the decision to erect the Geniza.[21] Of course, I am not proposing to identify that funeral with the funeral referred to in the story of Paltiel as we have it in *Sefer Hasidim,* although such an identification is, in my opinion, not to be ruled out. I am rather stressing the common typological potential of the stories, rooted as it is in medieval mentality, on more than one level; that is, that of the paramount social importance of funeral pomp organically linked to conspicuous lamentation, indeed boisterous threnology and, as such, to its implications for the definition of social excellence for and by Jews living under Gentile rule. All this was of constant concern for Jews in the Middle Ages—a constant of *tres longue durée,* as Fernand Braudel would have it. Whatever the event echoed in our story, it must have matched the idea of achieving the height of *grandeur* with that of disgrace following the improper exhibition of it. It makes no difference to our discussion if the attribution of responsibility for the negative phase of the story to Paltiel's son is in fact a piece of genuine evidence or rather an adjustment dictated by the need to maintain the hagiography intact. For a significant analogy, one may refer to the case of the persecution suffered by the Jews of Granada as a consequence of the improper behavior of Yosef, son of Shemuel Ha-Nagid, as we have it in Ibn Daud's *Book of Tradition*.[22] In any case, the linkage between two antithetic ideas, that of *grandeur* and that of disgrace following the improper exhibition of it in the context of funeral pomp, conferred on the story the character of *exemplum* valid for historical contexts other than the one at its origin.

If so, it would now follow that while the story of the disgrace following Paltiel's funeral was suppressed by Ahima'az together with the story of the construction of the Sanctuary, the responsibility for recording the story more or less as we have it in *Sefer Hasidim* should be assigned to the person who adapted that story to the Northern European historical context. Here it was indeed recorded as exemplary of the disastrous effects of the pride of Jewish leaders and it was stored in the context of moral teachings relating to proper behavior in the synagogue. The matching of the two different moral teachings would seem to follow quite naturally from the content of the story as well as from the needs of the new social reality. The content indeed included the idea of condemnation of pride as well as that of the disgrace of the most significant of all synagogues, the Holy Temple. The new social reality included a great deal of rivalry in the seizing of leadership and power, in the course of restructuring Jewish society after the collapse of the ecumenical Oriental hegemonies. It contained, moreover, the revolution of the demographic configuration of the Jewish people at a time of strong migratory trends and the "colonization" of new worlds, particularly that of the Rhineland. In that framework the necessity of redefining the value of the different components of social prominence—saintly life, knowledge, geneology, familiarity with the Gentile rulers, and so on— was a necessity of primary importance. And, last but not least, one should always bear in mind that precisely in that framework the entire idea of a sacred space proper to the cultural self-definition of the Jews was itself undergoing restructuring. The centrality of the synagogue for that definition was now challenged by the fortune of the *yeshiva*, the "holy *yeshiva*,"[23] as people affiliated with it would characterize it, figuring it in the image and likeness of the ecumenical Oriental *yeshivot*. One need not make a great effort to locate within *Sefer Hasidim* itself a great deal of evidence that all these themes were indeed central in public debate, teaching, and propaganda, within the society reflected by the book. There can be no doubt that social tension of the kind reflected in our story is more characteristic of times of deep change in social structure than of periods of relative stability. In settings of basic social change, tension becomes acute; it manifests itself violently; it may be detected very easily in historical monuments. Such a manifest intensity immediately makes evident the actuality of the story. For the limited purpose of our discussion here, it is not necessary to elaborate further on the precise opinion of the author or the compiler of *Sefer Hasidim* on any of the themes just mentioned. It is enough to stress the actuality of the themes themselves for the society contextual to the book. Yet, *actuality* does not necessarily imply *novelty*. We may axiomatically assume that social tension is one of the immanent components of any social grouping in any time. One cannot then exclude the possibility that the matching of condemnation of leaders' pride with that of indecent behavior within the sacred space of the synagogue, as also of the improper exhibition of grandeur in funeral pomp, stressing the particularly disastrous effects of such an exhibition in diaspora contexts, may actually have preceded its insertion in *Sefer Hasidim*. It may therefore not be impossible that the story reached its final stage of evolution sometime between Paltiel's death and the date of the composition of *Sefer Hasidim*.[24]

To sum up, it seems quite clear that the story of Paltiel as we find it in *Sefer Hasidim* displays more than three consecutive stages of mythologization. On the other hand, it does not seem possible to say exactly how many stages there were, nor to determine exactly when and where they took place. Finally it is quite clear that the process stopped after the story was written down. To be sure, historians may still go on asking who Paltiel "really" was and what was his "true" story. We certainly should not exclude the possibility that new findings will help to define more precisely what happened and when, even if we may wonder about historians' professional capacity to reach the extreme frontier separating reality from myth.

Needless to say, considerations of the same kind may be made regarding the version recorded in the *Scroll of Ahima'az*.[25] For our discussion here, it is sufficient to notice that, whatever the mythological dimension of the *Scroll of Ahima'az*, the focusing of the Ahima'az story on al-Muizz, and the date of composition of the *Scroll* definitely restrict the chronological limits of the last stage of elaboration to the tenth and eleventh centuries. In any case, the evidence we have so far gathered with the assistance of historians certainly enables us to reflect on the nature of the process of mythologization and its significance for the history of medieval Jewish culture.

The Implications of Orality and the Relationship to Midrash

The fact that our story was recorded in the West in two rather different versions, written down in two different places, very distant from each other, no matter how complementary they may appear to the historian's scrutiny, together with the fact that, as fare as we know, the process of mythologization was interrupted after it was written down, leads us to assume a correlation between the phenomenon we are studying observing and the implications of orality and writing in cultural activity. After all that has been said by sociologists, anthropologists, and psychologists, we may here axiomatically assume that in a framework in which cultural activity is characterized by orality, mythologization of the kind we have here observed is not only more frequent than in cases where cultural activity is characterized by writing, but is even an essential and organic component of every actual definition of cultural identity in its adaptation of tradition to changing social contexts. Goody and Watt presented the relevant findings in an article written twenty-five years ago,[26] which has by now become a classic in this field. According to Goody and Watt,

> What the individual remembers [in an oral culture] tends to be what is of critical importance in his experience of the main social relationships. In each generation, therefore, the individual memory will mediate the cultural heritage in such a way that its new constituents will adjust to the old by the process of interpretation that Barlett calls 'rationalizing' or the 'effort after meaning'; and whatever parts of it have ceased to be of contemporary relevance are likely to be eliminated by the process of forgetting.

Goody and Watt called this kind of organization of cultural tradition, characteristic of oral societies, *homeostatic*, that is, analogous to the homeostatic organization of the human body by means of which it attempts to maintain its present condition of life through a continuous process of checks and balances, such as digestion and elimination.[27] To students of midrash, such a definition may perhaps recall Kadushin's idea of organic thinking.[28] Anyhow, in speaking of social bodies one naturally means a process of social digestion and elimination, where *social* of course includes "cultural." Thus, through the mechanism of forgetting or transforming those elements in a cultural heritage that cease to have a contemporary relevance, a certain process of merging myth and history takes place.

To be sure, medieval Jewish society of the eleventh and twelfth centuries was not a preliterate society of the kind posited by Goody and Watt in their study. It should rather be defined *quasi-literate*, in the sense that the written and oral types of transmission of knowledge coexisted already and that most people were dependent on a small, albeit rapidly increasing group of "learned" who fulfilled a mediating function between the written word and the oral word.[29] Moreover, Goody's claim for total homeostasis must probably be somehow qualified.[30] In fact, there is now a considerable amount of literature about the differences and the relationship between oral and written transmissions of knowledge as well as about their social implications.[31] In the light of modern findings, the entire question of Jewish cultural transmission in the Middle Ages should be reconsidered in depth. Yet, such a task clearly encompasses the limits of the present study. For our purpose here, we will assume the following: (1) until it was written down, the story of Paltiel was included in that part of traditional knowledge assigned to oral transmission; (2) oral transmission was governed in the Middle Ages by dynamics similar, even if not identical, to those governing transmission of knowledge in preliterate societies; (3) there exists a close relationship between the way in which knowledge is transmitted and sociocultural context in which messages are actually uttered.

All these assumptions are not self-evident. The first point is the most difficult to assess. A satisfactory demonstration should presuppose the preliminary thorough reconsideration of the question of Jewish cultural transmission in the Middle Ages, which is still a desideratum. Only after having properly defined which kind of knowledge was assigned to written transmission and which to oral, would one be in a position to decide safely to which the text we are dealing with belongs. Our assumption is therefore stated here on an admittedly axiomatic basis. The question ideally will be addressed fully in a full-fledged future study. In the meantime, previous partial conclusions relating to other traditions, transmitted within the very same framework in which the story of Paltiel was transmitted, namely the *Scroll of Ahima'az* and the *Sefer Hasidim*, should be sufficient to argue at least for the plausibility of our assertion.[32] The second point assumes also axiomatically that despite the difference in the contents of cultural transmission, Jews thought and behaved much the same way as non-Jews living in the same historical context. If so, there would be no essential difference between Jews and non-Jews as far as the *outillage mental* underlying and governing mechanisms of cultural transmission is concerned. According to this line of reasoning, even if we knew nothing about European Jews, it should be argued that we could a priori assume that, as far as the general *outillage mental* was concerned, including attitudes toward oral and written communication, their situation was not different from that of their Christian neighbors. On the level of correct scientific method, the burden of proof would rather fall on those who would deny our assumption. Consequently, our second point here relies totally on the findings of scholars who have investigated non-Jewish medieval cultural contexts and have quite satisfactorily shown its general validity in those contexts. As for the third and last point, it follows almost immediately from the second and may in fact be considered a corollary of it.[33]

Thus, assuming that the story of Paltiel was first committed to oral transmission, the general model, first suggested by Goody and Watt, will provide an initial key to understanding the differences between the contents of the two surviving versions. In fact, having already assumed that the evidence of common cultural traditions testifies to common social roots, the comparison between what was recorded in one version and omitted in the other should therefore probably permit the singling out of a first set of elements in which sociocultural development diverged. Let us remark for instance that the elements of major concern in the *Scroll of Ahima'az* seem to be the confrontation with imperial Byzantine grandeur combined with a sense of deep contempt for the Byzantine world. The overall impression conveyed by the text of *Ahima'az* very much recalls that conveyed by Liutprand's memoir of his embassy to the Byzantine emperor.[34] In *Ahima'az* one is struck by Paltiel's close intimacy with the sultan, although this motif is hardly noticeable in *Sefer Hasidim*. The climate of *Sefer Hasidim* is indeed very different from that of the *Scroll of Ahima'az*. A thorough application of such a comparative approach would lead us very far from our main issue here.[35] It is sufficient to note its possible usefulness to the study of changing medieval Jewish mentalities in disparate historical contexts.

Contrary to the situation in totally preliterate "oral societies," in societies where cultural transmission and activity is carried out within a setting implying the diffusion of writing, an opposite trend takes place. To avoid misunderstandings, let me stress here that the key word in the last sentence is *diffusion,* not just *writing.* It is indeed a well-established fact that in the medieval period, written and oral transmission of knowledge and texts coexisted. Yet, for the limited purpose of the argument put forward in this essay, dwelling on the complexities of the interface between the oral and the written seems as unnecessary as was dwelling on possible necessary qualifications of Goody's most general thesis, especially within frameworks of quasi-literate societies, in the sense already specified. [36] Following Goody and Watt, diffusion of writing favors awareness of inconsistency, fosters comparative and critical attitudes, gnoseological and epistemological doubt, even skepticism.

> One aspect of this is a sense of change and of cultural lag; another is the notion that the cultural inheritance as a whole is composed of two very different kinds of material; fiction, error and superstition on the one hand; and, on the other, elements of truth which can provide the basis for some more reliable and coherent explanation of the gods, the human past and the physical world.[37]

It seems almost superfluous to linger extensively on these conclusions, which may now appear as some kind of "Columbus egg." The model in its entirety would thus provide further keys to understanding. It would perhaps explain why after *Sefer Hasidim* the "fantastic" story of Paltiel fell into oblivion, notwithstanding the fact that the teachings and the lore of Hasidei Ashkenaz found their way into the corpus of medieval Jewish culture.

The model we borrowed from anthropologists focuses almost exclusively on *forgetting* or *transforming* the elements of the cultural heritage. We however understand transformation as including sheer invention. The mechanism of transforming an already inherited element of culture into another is in fact essentially identical with the mechanism of producing what subsequent critical analysis, alerted by awareness of inconsistency, may eventually label a novel invention. I would argue that the mechanism is essentially the same as that of hermeneutics, in all the possible connotations of the term, with the stipulation that we are dealing with oral transmission. In oral transmissions of knowledge, I would maintain, hermeneutics tend indeed to be identical with what the Hebrew culture called *midrash*, in all possible definitions of the term.

My suggestion runs as follows. First, I would suggest to adopt that part of the argument that Weiss Halivni advances in stressing the roots of orality in the evolution of the semantics related to the term *midrash*.[38] According to Halivni,

> The standard definition of the root *drash*, "to inquire," "to seek out" and, derivatively, "to exposite" [texts], which is adequate for biblical, sectarian and Tannaitic literatures, is seemingly not adequate for Amoraic literature. There are numerous instances in both Talmuds where the root *drash* introduces fixed laws accompanied by neither biblical exposition nor logical inquire. [. . .] It is generally assumed that the word *darash* preceding a fixed law means that the law was promulgated in public. [. . .] It is quite possible, therefore, that the use of the word *darash* preceding fixed laws in Amoraic literature was justified on the basis of its public posture. In Tannaitic times biblical exposition, Midrash, was taught in public either as part of worship in the Synagogue following the reading of the Torah, or in some other manner. In the course of time the root *drash* became attached not only to biblical exposition but to any teaching done in public, so that later on with the emergence of Mishnah, when fixed laws were also taught in public, the root *drash* was transferred to fixed laws announced in public as well. Thus in Amoraic times the root *drash* was employed both for scriptural exposition and for introducing fixed laws. The latter usage was justified on the grounds that, like Midrash of old, it too was public. Paradoxically, [. . .] The Amoraim did not transfer the use of the root *drash* to the exposition of Tannaitic texts, apparently out of fear that a similar usage would blur the distinction between the two texts.[39]

Given The overwhelming specific weight of the Bible in Jewish traditional culture, it is only natural that most of this culture was rooted in biblical teaching. In the light of the process delineated by Weiss Halivni, it is only natural that Midrash came gradually to widen its semantic field and to include all exposition of traditional knowledge not committed to writing. Defining exactly that field as well as its gradual mutations over time would certainly be out of the range of this essay. In any case, it seems that *Midrash Halakhah* found its way more easily to written records, whereas the writing of *Midrash Aggadah* came much later. As has recently been argued quite convincingly, the prohibition of committing this part of traditional knowledge to writing may very well explain the absence of historiographical written production in Tannaitic and Amoraic times.[40] If so, the application of the term *Midrash* should not be restricted to biblical inquiry and exposition, as appears to be the general trend among contemporary students of Midrash.[41] Indeed, it seems to me that such assumptions do not take into due consideration that part of Midrash which is most properly *aggadah*, namely myth and history. Therefore, I would insist on the cumulative effect of the possible evolution, suggested by Weiss Halivni, and maintain that, although generally linked to biblical verses (in part probably as a mnemonic device, absolutely necessary in oral performances), *Midrash* should be more broadly understood; namely, as oral teaching of traditional knowledge. Then, focusing on that part of midrashic production which contains myth and history, I would propose to read in Urbach's recent suggestion that *midrash* fulfilled in Jewish civilization functions analogous to those of *history* in Greek civilization, much more than a rhetorical device intended to justify the absence of historical literary production among Jews of the talmudic epoch.[42] In other words, following and extending Urbach's idea perhaps beyond its authors contention, I would maintain that as far as some form of discourse on the past was concerned, within the "pastless" view of the past, of the sort that characterizes preliterate societies and that can be assumed to characterize that part of traditional knowledge committed to orality,[43] viewed as intellectual activity, Midrash included history. Thus, in that case, viewed as intellectual production, midrash and history totally overlapped.

I must say that producing a systematic and detailed proof of the entire argument would require not only much more space than may be allowed in a single essay, but also much more evidence than I am at the moment able to produce. Some partial evidence may nonetheless be offered—I hope it will encourage others to proceed along this path and make the task easier in the future. In fact the etymology *midrash* overlaps that of history, for both terms indicate *seeking information, inquiry,* and *exposition.*[44] These meanings taken together include *exegesis* and *exposition of a text,* in all possible ways and by all possible techniques. But with reference to ancient societies, comparable to oral ones, they also include *adjustment of meaning* and even *sheer invention* of new meanings. The only limitation to this kind of activity seems to be logical plausibility, according to the critical awareness of the person who actually performs it. As has been pertinently noted by students of the interface between fact and fiction, Cicero classified *fabula, historia, and argumentum* as a single species of *narratio. Fabula* he defined as that which had neither truth nor verisimilitude; *historia,* the account of things done in the remote past; *argumentum,* a fictional but nevertheless possible action, like that of comedy. Yet, a fourth-century Virgilian commentator already identified *historia* with *argumentum.*[45] The Ancients were perhaps more aware than later historians of the fact that one cannot easily distinguish between *mythopoiesis* and *historia.* Indeed Strabo listed them very incisively together in characterizing the Academy of Athens as the place where one might find *mythopoiias sychnas kai historias.*[46] In fact, although Cicero's distinction in his definitions of *historia* and *argumentum* would later be diligently rehearsed by Isidorus of Seville in his *Book of Etymologies,*[47] were we to read his *History of the Goths* from our modern standpoint, we would no doubt hardly agree with him as to the actual application of the distinction he apparently accepted. Should one be prepared to prescind from the question of textuality, that is, the question of what precisely is the subject of inquiry and exposition, and limit oneself to discourses relating (no matter if among other things) what happened in the past, the identification of *midrash* with *history* would present itself as almost self-evident.

In fact, students of midrash have given definitions much broader than the one tentatively suggested here. According to one definition, recently proposed by A. Shinan and Y. Zakovitch, "Midrash is a mode of approaching a text—derived from a religious world view and motivated by various needs (historical, moral, literary, etc.)—which enables and encourages multiple and even contradictory meanings to be discovered in the text, while the intention of its author(s) is perceived as elusive."[48] Such a definition seems indeed to broaden our field twice over.

First, it does not confine itself to specific texts, the authors are prepared to consider any text, whether "oral or written, as long as it is fixed in form . . . by its having achieved the status of sacred or quasi-sacred text," yet not necessarily because of some divine origin; the authors are in fact prepared to include here every kind of "important" text, importance being defined for instance by "its great antiquity or its immense importance in the culture."

Second, the definition refuses to consider Midrash merely as a literary genre or even as a form of expression; accent is placed rather on *content, approach,* and *intention.* The content of the text must be "important," the approach as well as intention must be "serious." In fact they must be serious responses to contextual challenges— for instance, "historical" ones. It is not quite clear what exactly is meant here by *historical,* the term is used as definitely distinct from "social, literary fashions, etc." In any case, Shinan and

Zakovitch are thus prepared to include within their definition even paintings or sculptures "such as Michelangelo's Moses or the murals of the ancient synagogue of Dura-Europos, which depict biblical episodes." The last specification may be rather misleading. In fact, the authors' professional interest in biblical and Rabbinic themes may encourage further misinterpretation as to the actual field of textuality they are pointing to. Yet, in the light of what has been said, one must then refer to biblical texts as to mere examples of "important texts," not as an indication that only biblical texts are to be considered. In that vein, midrashic activity would come to designate any serious interpretation of reality whatsoever, inasmuch as reality itself is assigned importance for the cultural perception of the Self and is perceived through the mediation of a text (written or oral).[49] One may thus not only be persuaded to identify midrashic activity with history, even with that history of which the narrator was indeed an eyewitness—in that case, *memory* would provide the text. One might rather say that history is more exactly included in Midrash, as part of it. We might even push the argument *ad limitem* and have Midrash cover the entire field of gnoseology. Midrash would thus be equivalent to the search of meaning tout court. In fact, Ithamar Gruenwald's programmatic discussion,[50] which the author generously made available to me before I began to write this essay, would point in that direction.

Yet, to my mind, the conditio sine qua non to be verified before such definitions can legitimately be applied to Midrash, in the sense given by general consensus to that term prior to modern scholarship, is that we are dealing with an intellectual activity strictly committed to orality. This limitation already imposes itself almost naturally through another deeply rooted meaning of the root *darash* in Hebrew, one which is probably also connected with the origin of the term, as Weiss Halivni has argued.[51] If so, any definition of Midrash should not dismiss that original association of the root *darash* with orality.

If we are now prepared to refer to orality not just as to an activity performed orally, but to the sociocultural setting properly pertaining to what anthropologists would call *oral societies*, namely, the commitment of the transmission of cultural heritage to orality, *midrash*, however strictly or broadly defined, would mean the transmission or adjustment of inherited culture within a framework characterized, at least at one stage, by orality. As such, Midrash would include history, inasmuch as history would be conceived as strictly linked to myth, as in fact it is in oral societies. Midrash would embody the mythical heritage of Jewish society, in a variety of formulations, reflecting a variety of adjustments to different sociocultural settings, sometimes impossible to define precisely, but whose presence proper philological inquiry may at times uncover, as in the case of the story of Paltiel. Such a definition of *Midrash* certainly agrees with Heinemann's definition of it as creative historiography.[52] It therefore suggests rather rhetoric than logic, inconsistency more than cogent argumentation, not rarely even puzzling paradoxality, rather Ciceronian *exhornatio rerum* than plain *narratio rerum*, apodictic education more than critical search for knowledge, and more a public characterized by *infantia* than by *senectus*. To some extent, inconsistency is even granted disciplinary legitimacy; *'ein meshivim 'al ha-midrash*, one does not ask questions on Midrash, is indeed an axiomatic methodological rule for a proper understanding of Midrash. Significantly enough that characteristic institution of Jewish civilization, the *beth midrash*, was, at a certain moment translated into Greek by *oikos paideias*. The term *paideia* indeed carries a great deal of the above mentioned meanings. Moreover, structurally linked to these meanings, is the implication of entertainment, of ludicrousness, not rarely of "scandalous" joke, in brief, of ludic activity. It is perhaps not by chance that synagogues and *batei midrash* were chosen as lapidar opposites of theatres and circuses, in opposing the nature of the Jewish civilization to that of the Greek.

Limited to societies committed to orality for the transmission of knowledge, all these characteristics are common to Midrash and to history. Let us stress again that this conclusion should not be overlooked because of the fact that most midrashic activity is confined to biblical and Rabbinical literature, for this fact is an almost natural consequence of the paramount importance of these fields for Jewish culture. As is well known to anyone familiar with what is currently labeled as midrashic literature, they are by no means exhaustive of the entire horizon of Midrash. On the contrary, it will perhaps not be a wild exaggeration to say that for talmudic times most of the historical knowledge stemming from Hebrew sources is embodied in midrashic literature. In any case, to the medieval mind, still shaped by orality, Midrash was then "simply" a most general quest for meaning carried out in the field where myth and history organically merged with the entire cultural heritage of Jewish society. In other words, as long as that mind, educated in the wake of the classical rhetorical conception of historiography, was shaped in a socio-cultural setting characterized by orality, *midrash* would include history as a part of the transmission and adjustment of the entire body of inherited culture.

At this point, it may be useful to add that the semantic overlapping of Midrash and myth-history would not appear alien to the cultural perception of medieval Jews. In fact, it seems quite clear that to a Jew of the time of Ahima'az and of the author or compiler of *Sefer Hasidim*, the story of Paltiel was midrash no less than biblical exegesis and exposition. This is explicitly stated by Ahima'az himself, who, in biblical mood, defined his work as *midrash sefer*.[53] Following this line of reasoning, the discovery of modern scholars that medieval Jewish historiography, such as Ibn Daud's *Book of Tradition*, contains much of midrashic chronology[54] should indeed be read not only as a value judgment but rather as an integral part of a proper definition of medieval Jewish historiography itself.

The affinity between the contents and the mechanisms of medieval *transmission of traditional knowledge committed to orality* and Midrash, as perceived by the medieval mind, may thus propose the former as a more general definition of the latter. Viewed as such, Midrash would then at a first stage include every kind of traditional knowledge transmitted orally.[55] At the origin, it would thus include the entire Oral Law (*Torah she-be-'al peh*), *Midrash Halakhah*, and *Midrash Aggadah* altogether, as well as folk stories, edifying anecdotes, and so forth. As this corpus was gradually committed to writing, beginning with *halakhah*, Midrash came accordingly to be affected by a process of gradually losing its characteristics. It thus came to be gradually dissociated from *halakhah*, then committed to writing. At this stage, Midrash came to signify also books containing knowledge so far transmitted orally and from then onward written down according to the criteria of selection and ordering adopted by the editors, following considerations that will not interest us here, yet are of paramount importance for the understanding of the history of Jewish culture. This phase engendered one of the most significant semantic splitings of the root *DaRaSH*; although the root *DaRaSH* itself, as pointing to intellectual activity, maintained the meanings of the usual practices of oral interpretating and teaching of written texts (including preaching), the output of such activity was carefully separated from Midrash viewed as literary production, which came to signify more specifically the books in which the traditional knowledge was written down, and by synecdoche every single tradition actually included in them or which, by virtue of its contents, might have been included. Finally, the relatively rapid diffusion of writing from the twelfth century onward, had as an almost inevitable consequence the rapid drying of the productive vein of composition of new midrashim even in the sense of books.

Ahima'az' labeling his work as *Midrash Sefer* is perhaps a most telling example of the application of the term to new literary compositions containing knowledge other than the one crowned by the sacrality of religious tradition. Yet it was exceptional. In fact, it still remains unique. It is therefore impossible to decide if we are confronted with an already outmoded terminology or rather with an unsuccessful attempt to create a Hebrew word for "history" within a cultural context in which history was still governed by the classical rhetoric tradition linking it to orality. Further research will ideally throw more light on this point.

Actuality of Midrash?

For what they are worth, some more reflections on the possible implications of what so far has been said will be added. We have already noticed en passant that, from our modern standpoint, it is of course true that where cultural transmission is governed by some degree of orality, historical sensibility as we conceive it will be negatively affected. In the light of what has so far been said, and since no postbiblical Jewish society may be considered totally oral, this statement should be understood in the more general sense that historical sensibility is negatively affected in proportion to the *degree of orality* present in cultural transmission. It is not at all easy to find a way to define what constitutes a *degree of orality*, nor a fortiori for indicating parameters for measuring it. We may probably try first to define the *degree of orality* by the width of the gap between the literati and the laity, the attitude toward the written text as well as the place and the role played by such texts in cultural activity, by factors affecting the diffusion of written texts, such as technology, economic conditions, censorship, and so on. We may then assume that the degree of orality should also be defined by the degree of readiness to refer uncritically to the inherited cultural tradition, and of the sense of organic belonging to it. Finally, in the light of what has been said, historical awareness of change should in any case be a very good parameter for measuring a degree of orality. Generally speaking, some degree of orality would thus be discovered even in our modern society. Yet, the evolutive process suggested previously should dissuade us from adhering to modern tendencies of scholarship adopting the term *midrash* as a synonym or a metaphor of any kind of modern hermeneutic activity.

Midrashic original production was indeed mortally wounded in the same period in which European society underwent its first major shift from an oral to a written tradition. It was indeed in this period that the center of Jewish cultural activity shifted from the synagogue to the *yeshiva*. This means that it shifted from generally religious, almost cultic practice, to academic study; from poetics, implied by the so called *payyetanic* production, to dialectic; from the rhetoric of homiletics, to logic. In that same period, cultural activity concentrated on written texts, to be read, explained, glossed, or harmonistically interpreted when critically confronted with contradictions arising from other written texts. It hardly needs saying that these texts consisted mostly of the various tractates of the Babylonian Talmud. It must then be no mere chance if that same period was the last one in which full-fledged midrashim were composed—think, for example, of *Bereshit Rabbati*, *Sekhel Tov*, or *Bemidbar Rabba*. As the writing-oriented attitude to cultural activity progressed, midrashic activity waned, together with *piyyut*. This is not to say that such activities disappeared. But, by then they were no doubt facing constant challenge. Midrash was sent on its way out of the main road of cultural creativity. Where philosophy spread, even the inherited midrashic literary production was scrutinized and interpreted metaphorically or allegorically—and it is enough to refer to Maimonides and the virulent *querelle* over the figurative interpretation of Midrash which went on for centuries.

The one and major field in which midrashic activity still displayed great vitality in the period subsequent to the shift from oral to written culture was that of kabbalistic literature. This was also certainly not by mere chance. Orality still played a much greater role in the transmission of esoteric traditions than it played in the case of exoteric ones. Yet, even so, one should not forget the fact that the very publication of the *Zohar* was carried out under a pseudepigraphical covering. The next phase of crucial restructuring was that of the printing revolution. It has been noticed that, although for some reason Goody and Watt do not dwell on the implications of printing for understanding the significance of the shift from oral cultures to written ones, there can be little doubt that their general model also applies to the restructuring of culture caused by the diffusion of printing.[56] Now it would perhaps be more fitting to say that printing led mostly to a temporary filling of the gap between popular and elite culture, strengthened the critical approach to reading, increased possibilities of checking information, and so on. All this was one more mortal blow at Midrash. The metaphoric or allegoric meaning of *midrash* thus came to represent the last refuge of religious minds challenged by the critical approach to texts and intolerance of inconsistencies. What made sense in a distant past, no longer made sense in the modern era. And rightly so, because, once fixed in written texts, unless one consciously manipulated it, it was no longer possible to adjust it to changing reality, as had been done in oral settings. Midrash was definitely on its way out of critically oriented cultural activity.

It is for this reason that I would not agree to blur the line of definition between specific midrashic activity and gnoseology or hermeneutics. In our written-oriented attitude to culture, *midrash* came definitely to be coterminous with *poetically fantastic* as opposed to *scientifically true*, with *nonexistence* as opposed to empirically tested *existence*, in short with *imaginaire* as opposed to *real*. Should we wish to restore its pristine vitality, we should be prepared to make our way back and resuscitate those epochs in which poetics were science and the imaginary merged organically with the real. This might perhaps be a fine intellectual exercise, a kind of ideal plunging into purely aesthetic experience.[57] To assign it real significance, one should add the two essential components of "orality" already mentioned: the inner sense of organic belonging to the inherited cultural tradition, and the readiness to relinquish critical sensibility, at least as much as oral societies are ready to do. In a word, one should be ready to get out of history and choose myth as existential reality. I do not deny the possibility that such a choice might eventually signify discovering the deep meaning of human life, for which ultimately nonexistence is certainly more real than existence, the *poetically fantastic* more important than the *scientifically true,* the *imaginaire* more real than the *real.* But, to my mind, it is quite impossible to make such a choice consciously. If orality and midrash may persist in our cultural context, it is only on the unconscious level.

Notes

1. On *Sefer Hasidim* and its sociocultural context among the Jewish communities of the Rhineland, see Ivan G. Marcus, *Piety and Society. The Jewish Pietists of Medieval Germany* (Leiden, 1981), where the relevant bibliography up to 1981 is listed; idem, "Hierarchies, Religious Boundaries and Jewish Spirituality in Medieval Germany," *Jewish History* 1.2 (1986): 7–26; and, most recently, Peter Schäfer, "The Ideal of Piety of the Ashkenazi Hasidim and Its Roots in Jewish Tradition," *Jewish History* 4.2 (1990): 9–23.

2. *Sefer Hasidim* is quoted here from Wistinetzki's edition, 2d ed. Frankfurt am Main, 1924; reprint Jerusalem, 1969).

3. On Donnolo and his literary legacy, see Andrew Sharf, *The Universe of Shabbetai Donnolo* (Warminster, 1976) and Giuseppe Sermoneta, "Il new-platonismo nel pensiero dei nuclei ebraici stanziati nell 'Occidente latino (riflessioni sul Commento al Libro della Creazione di Rabbi Sabetai Donnolo,' in *Settimane di Studio del Centro Italiano di Studi sull 'Alto Medioevo, XXVI: Gli Ebrei nell 'Alto Medioevo* (Spoleto, 1980), pp. 867–925, where the relevant bibliography is listed.

4. As for the Muslim raid on Oria, it is mentioned by Arab as well as by Christian chroniclers. See, for instance, Annales Barenses, *MGH, SS,* V (Hannover 1844, reprint 1963), p. 52: "Hoc anno [925] Orie capta est a gente Saracenorum mense Iulio"; Lupus Protospatarius, ibid., p. 53: "[a. 924] capta est Oria a Saracenis nense Iulii, et interfecerunt cunctos mares, reliquos vero duxerunt in Africam, eos venundantes." Ibn 'Idhari, *Histoire de l'Afrique et de l'Espagne intitulee Al-Bayano' l-Maqrib,* trans. E. Fagnan, Vol. 1 (Algiers, 1901), p. 271: "En 313 (28 mars 925), le chambellan Abou Ah'med Djafar ben 'Obeyd dirigean contre la Sicile une expedition ou il fit de nombreuses conquetes, entre autre la ville de Wa'ri (Oria) ou il massacra six mille combattants et fit dix mille prisonniers." I do not know why Moshe Gil persists in identifying Donnolo's town with Aversa instead of Oria. See Moshe Gil, "The Jews in Sicily Under Muslim Rule, In the Light of the Geniza Documents," *Italia Judaica; Atti del I Convegno Internazionale, Bari 18–22 maggio 1981* (Rome, 1983), p. 87.

5. See Wistinetzki's note in his edition of *Sefer Hasidim.*

6. There is already a huge bibliography on the *Scroll of Ahima'az.* Most of the relevant bibliography is listed by Robert Bonfil, "Tra due mondi. Prospettive di ricerca sulla storia culturale degli Ebrei dell 'Italia meridionale nell 'alto Medioevo', *Italia Judaica. Atti del I Convegno internazionale, Bari 18–22 maggio 1981* (Rome 1983), pp. 135–58, of which an augmented Hebrew version is is to be found in *Shalem. Studies in the History of the Jews in Eretz-Israel* 5 (1987): 1–30; idem, "Mythos, Retorica, Historia? Iyyun bi-Meghillath Ahima'az" [Myth, Rhetoric, History? A Study in the Chronicle of Ahima'az], in *Tarbuth ve-Chevrah be-Toledoth Israel bi-Yemey ha-Beynayim*

[Culture and Society in Medieval Jewry. Studies Dedicated to the Memory of Haim Hillel Ben-Sasson] (Jerusalem, 1989), pp. 99–135. The Hebrew text of the work is available in the nice edition of Benjamin Klar (Jerusalem 1944), reprinted by M. Spitzer (Jerusalem, 1974). An English translation is also available in *The Chronicle of Ahima'az*, trans. with an introduction and notes by Marcus Salzman (New York, 1924; reprint, 1966).

7. Unless we understand the words *in its entirety* as hinting precisely to the *Scroll of Ahima'az*.

8. In Salzman's translation, the entire story of Paltiel is in pp. 88–97.

9. On this particular tradition see Aryeh Grabois, "Demuto ha-haggadit shel Karl Ha-Gadol ba-mekorot ha-'ivriim shel yemei ha-beinayim" [The Legendary Figure of Charlemagne in Medieval Hebrew Sources], *Tarbiz* 36 (1967): 22–58; Joseph Shatzmiller, "Politics and the Myth of Origins: The Case of the Medieval Jews," in Gilbert Dahan, ed., *Les Juifs au regard de l'histoire. Melanges en l'honneur de Bernhard Blumenkranz* (Paris, 1985), pp. 49–61; Ivan Marcus, "History, Story and Collective Memory; Narrativity in Early Ashkenazic Culture," *Prooftexts* 10 (1990): 365–88. And see Avraham Grossmann, *Hakhmei Ashkenaz ha-Rishonim [The Early Sages of Ashkenaz]* (Jerusalem, 1981), pp. 35–44; Simon Schwarzfuchs, "L'opposition Tsarfat-Providence: La formation du Judaisme du Nord de la France," *Hommage à Georges Vajda. Etudes d'histoire et de pensee juive*, ed. Gerard Nahon and Charles Touati (Louvain, 1980), pp. 135–50.

10. See Jefim Schirmann, "Shemuel Ha-Nagid ki-meshorer" [Shemuel Ha-Nagid, the Poet], and "Milhamot Shemuel Ha-Nagid" [The Wars of Shemuel Ha-Nagid], in *Le-Toledoth ha-Shirah ve-ha-Dramma ha-Ivrith* [Studies in the History of Hebrew Poetry and Drama] (Jerusalem, 1979), pp. 149–215.

11. The relevant bibliography is listed by Moshe Gil, *Eretz Israel ba-Tekufah ha-Muslemith ha-Rishonah* [Palestine During the First Muslim Period], 634–1099 (Tel-Aviv, 1983), Part I, pp. 299–302. To this one should add Menahem Ben-Sasson, "Italy and 'Ifriqya from the 9th to the 11th Century," *Les relations intercommunautaires juives en Mediterranee et en Europe occidentale* (Paris, 1984), pp. 34–50; idem, "Rashei ha-Tzibbur bi-Tzefon Africa" [Communal Leaders in North Africa], *Pe'amin; Studies in the Cultural Heritage of Oriental Jewry* 26 (1986): 132–62.

12. Bernard Lewis, "Paltiel. A Note," *BSOAS* 30 (1967): 177–81.

13. See Ibn al-Qifti, *Ta'arikh al-hukama*, ed. Lippert (Leipzig, 1903), p. 320; Ibn Abi Usaybi'a, *Tabaqat al-atibba*, Vol. 2 (Cairo, 1882), p. 86. And see Hasan Husni 'Abd al-Wahhab, *Waraqat 'an al-hadara al-'arabiyya bi-Ifriqiya* (Tunis, 1965), pp. 301–4. I wish to thank Joanna Weinberg for having supplied photocopies of these sources and Haggai Ben-Shammai for having translated them for me.

14. I do not understand Goitein's remark, apparently endorsed by Gil, that the name Eli'ezer should be ruled out, because of its association with the name of a slave, for "who would give his boy such a name in a period so slavery conscious?" See Shlomo Dov Goitein, *A Mediterranean Society*, Vol. 2 (Berkeley, Calif., 1970), p. 575, n. 9. Eli'ezer was also the name of Moses son (Exod. 18:4). To my mind, such a name would fit very well our case.

15. Gil, ibid.

16. See the essays quoted in notes 6 and 9.

17. See Schaefer, "The Ideal of Piety."

18. See Grossman, *Hakhmei Ashkenaz*; Simon Schwartzfuchs, "L'opposition Tsarfat-Provence."

19. Such an a priori assumption is in fact legitimate because as far as our knowledge goes and the possibilities of critically checking evidence allow us to state, at least as far as the story of the building and subsequent destruction of the Sanctuary is concerned, no such events ever took place. As for "myth," it is used here in the common meaning of "traditional tale" in which fantastic elements are variously inserted in the report of what actually happened.

20. The relevant bibliography is listed by Moshe Gil, *Eretz Israel*, Part I, pp. 42–61.

21. S. D. Goiten, "Hayyei Avoteinu le-or kitvey ha-geniza" [The Life of Our Forefathers as Reflected in the Documents of the Cairo Geniza], *Te'uda I: Cairo Geniza Studies*, ed. Mordechai A. Friedman (Tel-Aviv, 1980), pp. 9–10 and p. vii of the English abstract.

22. See Abraham Ibn Daud, *The Book of Tradition (Sefer ha-Qabbalah): A Critical Edition with a Translation and Notes by Gerson D. Cohen* (Philadelphia, 19677), pp. 75–76.

23. See, for instance, Isaac b. Moses of Vienna, *Or Zaru'a*, Rosh Ha-Shanah, #275 [*The Responsa of Rabbenu Gershom Meor Hagolah*], ed., annotated, and prefaced by Shlomoh Eidelberg (New York, 1955), #32, pp. 98–100.

24. The semantic ambiguity conveyed by the use of *ploughing* (the *ploughing of the City* as rhetoric hyperbole for the ploughing, that is, the *destruction of the Sanctuary*) may also have played some role in allowing the understanding that what was destroyed because of the Caliph's wrath was the town, whereas the Sanctuary itself was eventually destroyed at a later date, "After some years," as a consequence of a prima facie not self-evident intervention of the Caliph. And it is not impossible that the wording of the final sentence on the effect of the Caliph's wrath was also adapted to convey the impression that "he wished to plough it," although in fact he did not do so.

25. I hope to elaborate on this point in a forthcoming study.

26. J. Goody and I. Watt, "The Consequences of Literacy," in *Literacy in Traditional Societies*, ed. J. Goody (Cambridge, 1968), pp. 27–68.

27. Ibid., pp. 30–31.

28. Max Kadushin, *The Rabbinic Mind* (New York, 1952)

29. See F. H. Bauml, "Varieties and Consequences of Medieval Literacy and Illiteracy," *Speculum* 55 (1980): 237–65.

30. See I. Vansina, *Oral Tradition as History* (London and Nairobi, 1985), pp. 120–23.

31. A full bibliographical note would be out of place here, besides being also out of the present writer's competence. To the formation of the view presented here, the following have been particularly useful: Bauml, "Varieties and Consequences"; I. Vansina, *Oral Tradition: A Study in Historical Methodology* (London, 1965); idem, *Oral Tradition as History*; David Henige, *Oral Historiography* (London, 1982); Paul Thompson, *The Voice of the Past; Oral History* (Oxford, 1978); idem, "Oral History and the Historian," *History Today* 33 (1983): 24–28; Walter J. Ong, *Orality and Literacy. The Technologizing of the Word* (London and New York, 1982); Brian Stock, *The Implications of Literacy* (Princeton, N.J., 1983); Paul Zumthor, *La*

Lettre et la voix. De la "litterature" medievale (Paris, 1987). All of them list rich bibliographies up to the dates of their publication.

32. Reference is made to the studies listed in note 6.

33. For the social meanings of messages of oral tradition, a very useful and schematic outline is provided by Vansina, *Oral Tradition*, pp. 94–146.

34. See, for instance, Johannes Koder and Thomas Weber, *Liutprand von Cremona in Konstantinopel. Untersuchungen zum Griechischen Sprachschatz und zu Realienkundlichen Aussagen und Seinem Werken* (Vienna, 1980); Michael Rentschler, *Liutprand von Cremona. Eine Studie zum Ost-Westlichen Kulturgefälle im Mittelalter* (Frankfurt am Main, 1981).

35. I hope to address this in detail in a forthcoming study, already mentioned in note 25.

36. Reference may be made, for instance, to Jack Goody, *The Interface Between the Written and the Oral* (Cambridge, 1987). For the issues dealt with in this essay, one will find most useful Avigdor Shinan, "Sifrut ha-Aggada: Beyn Higgud 'Al Pe U-Massoreth Ketuva" [The Aggadic Literature: Written Tradition and Transmission], *Meḥkerey Yerushalayim be-Folklor Yehudi [Jerusalem Studies in Jewish Folklore]* 1 (1981): 44–60 and the literature listed there in notes 9 and 15.

37. Goody and Watt, "Consequences of Literacy," pp. 48–49.

38. See David Weiss Halivni, *Midrash, Mishnah, and Gemara* (Cambridge, Mass., 1986).

39. Ibid., pp. 73–75.

40. The argument was presented in a lecture by Moshe David Herr and I hope will be expanded in a full-fledged forthcoming study.

41. See James Kugel, "Two Introductions to Midrash," *Prooftexts* 3 (1983): 145: "Midrash is an exegesis of Biblical verses, not of books"; and most recently Daniel Boyarin, *Intertextuality and the Reading of Midrash* (Bloomington and Indianapolis, 1990).

42. See Efraim E. Urbach, "Halakhah and History," *Jews, Greeks and Christians; Essays in Honor of W. D. Davies* (Leiden, 1976), pp. 112–28.

43. See Bauml, "Varieties and Consequences," p. 249.

44. On the etymology of *historia* there is already a huge bibliography. See, for instance, Karl Kauck, "Historia; Geschichte des Wortes und seiner Bedeutungen in der Antike und in den romanischen Sprachen," Dissertation, University of Münster, Emsdetten, 1934). For its reception in the Middle Ages, Laetitia Boem, "Der wissenschaftstheoretische Ort der historia im frühen Mittelalter," *Festschrift Johannes Spörl* (1965), pp. 663–93; Rüdiger Landfester, *Historia Magistra vitae; Untersuchungen zur humanistischen Geschichtstheorie des 14. bis 16. Jahrhunderts*, (Geneva, 1972); Gerald Press, "History and the Development of the Idea of History in Antiquity," *History and Theory* 16 (1977): 280–96; Arno Seifert, *Historia im Mittelalter, Archiv für Begriffsqeschichte* 21 (1977): 226–84; Joachim Knape, *"Historie" in Mittelalter und frürer Neuzeit* (Baden-Baden, 1984); Jack M. Greenstein, "Alberti on *Historia*: A Renaissance View of the Structure of Significance in Narrative Painting," *Viator* 21 (1990): 273–99.

45. William Nelson, *Fact or Fiction. The Dilemma of the Renaissance Storyteller* (Cambridge, Mass., 1973), p. 5. See Landfester, *Historia Magistra vitae*, pp. 47–92.

46. Strabo, IX, 1, 17, p. 396. Quoted by John Glucker, *Antiochus and the Late Academy* (Göttingen, 1978), p. 242.

47. Isidori Hispalensis Episcopi, *Etymologiarum sive Originum libri XX*, recognovit brevique adnotatione critica instruxit W. M. Lindsay (Oxonii, 1911), I, pp. xl–xliv.

48. Avigdor Shinan and Yair Zakovitch, "Midrash on Scripture and Midrash Within Scripture," *Scripta Hierosolymitana, XXXI: Studies in Bible*, ed. Sara Japhet (Jerusalem, 1986), pp. 257–77. Quotation is from p. 258.

49. See Yonah Fraenkel, "Meḥkar Sippur ha-Aggadah. Mabbat Le-'atid La-vo" [Research on Aggadic Tales. A Foreview], *Jewish Studies—Forum of the World Union of Jewish Studies* 30 (1990): 22.

50. See Chapter 1 of this book.

51. David Weiss Halivni, *Midrash, Mishna, and Gemara*.

52. Yitshak Heinemann, *Darkei ha-Aggadah* (Jerusalem, 1954), pp. 4–7 and passim. See now also the preceptive analysis of Heineman's interpretation by Daniel Boyarin, *Intertextuality*, pp. 1–11.

53. In Klar's edition, p. 11, 11.4–5. See Bonfil, "Myth, Rhetoric, History?" p. 131.

54. See, for instance, Gerson D. Cohen's remarks in his edition of Ibn Daud's work, *Book of Tradition*, p. 274.

55. Needless to say, transmission in most cases includes performance.

56. Elisabeth L. Eisenstein, *The Printing Press as an Agent of Change: Communications and Cultural Transformations in Early Modern Europe*, 2 vols. (Cambridge, 1979).

57. To my mind, this is the most valuable contribution of modern attempts aimed at actualizing Midrash; see, for instance, Boyarin's already cited fine book.

11

History, Story and Collective Memory: Narrativity in Early Ashkenazic Culture

Ivan G. Marcus

I

T he problem of narrativity has yet to be addressed by students of medieval Jewish historiography.[1] Those who have studied that group of texts that "look like history"—my term for narratives about the past[2]—tend to fall into one of three categories depending on whether they are looking for "facts," literary genres and motifs, or the historical meaning of cultural symbols. The first group I would call "historical positivists,"[3] the second, "folklorists,"[4] and the third, "anthropological historians."[5] The first hopes that a sequential narrative that purports to tell about a true set of events in known places and specified times is mainly, partially or even slightly factual. The value of such a text to this historian is defined in proportion to its degree of facticity. Hence this historian has a special obligation to demonstrate the reliability of the narrative's descriptive accuracy. Great pains must be taken to reconstruct the best possible state of the text—every letter can be a significant datum about a person, place or date. Similarly, the positivist reader needs to establish with a high degree of probability the relationship of the text to all possible literary models or influences which could undermine the text as factually credible.

The second scholar of history narratives has no such burden. Because he either assumes that facticity is irrelevant or does not care about it, the accuracy of the text is significant but for a different reason. His concern is primarily with the genre or type of narrative that the text represents and with how this specific text is like or unlike others of the same genre. By classifying a narrative that looks like history as a legend—a tale about a specific place or person from another time—the issue of facticity is not only avoided; it is denied.[6] On the other hand, if a narrative is classified as hagiography (sacred lives) or martyrology (sacred deaths), it is then compared on formal grounds with other holy biographies or accounts about traumatic acts of religious suffering and witnessing. The question: Did they actually suffer or die that way? does not arise. The very questions that motivate the interest of the historical positivist are irrelevant to the folklorist. In large measure, the style in the text is what counts, not the representation of events outside the text, let alone events distinct from their representation.

The third approach which I call anthropological history is a departure from both of the others and yet combines features of each in a unique way. The historian assumes that the narrative presents a set of symbolic expressions of experiences or events that can be known only as mediated through the narrative. In this respect, there is considerable overlap with the folklorist: both agree that the symbolic layering of the text is important in and of itself without any "external" referents. But like the positivist, and unlike the folklorist, the anthropological historian assumes that the text as written preserves an expression of an actual historical extratextual reality. That historical reality is not reducible to an event or fact but exists in the mind of those who wrote, edited, copied, owned, read and reread the narrative. Any living relationship to that text is part of historical experience and of the imagined literary world formally constructed in the text itself.

If we review the canonical texts of medieval Jewish historiography, we see at once that they *are* the standard texts because they have been gathered together based on a shared assumption about what medieval historiography is supposed to be. These are the texts that look like history based on the positivist's perspective that facts are embedded in these narratives or form some proportion thereof. They are thought to be narratives that record events that actually happened. The collection and the approach of the positivists is based on the nineteenth-century Rankean epistemology that governs most academic historiography to this day. It posits that the past can be retold *"wie es eigentlich gewesen"*—as it actually happened.[7] But taxonomy is not a "given"; it is a function of prior assumptions about what the historical narrative is supposed to be.

Thus the "historical" texts included in various anthologies by Neubauer, Dinur, Kahana or Meyer are mainly those the editors assume contain facticity about the past.[8] They assume that true representation of past events is what should be sought in a "historical" narrative. Moreover, such monographs as Avraham Grossman's study of the immigration of sages to early Germany or Robert Chazan's study of the 1096 anti-Jewish Rhenish riots and his reflections on medieval Jewish historiography in general[9] focus almost exclusively on the facticity of narratives that are not in reality documentary "sources."[10]

Not that events and "facts" do not exist out there "behind" these texts, but they are not "in" them, and the persistent assumption that they are leads to few positive results and, more significantly, avoids a more appropriate analysis that would make historical sense of what the type of source can tell us.

But it is not at all obvious that the positivist approach and its logically derived anthology of texts are either the only ones or the ones that enable one to reach the very goals its practitioners seek: to discover what Jews— thinkers and more ordinary Jews—thought, felt and wrote down about the past. The second approach, that of the folklorist, leads to a different anthology based on a wider range of literary genres that have in common a narrative representation of the past. The table of contents of Dan's collection of narratives includes such an alternative collection, based, as it is, on literary models that incorporate texts that look like history as part of a broader set of categories.[11] Anthologies of stories, such as Bin Gorion's, reflect this orientation as well.[12] Those texts that represent the past are included because they exemplify a genre of narrative, not because they are presumed to record "what actually happened."

The literary folklorist's goal is to explore the wide range of literary creativity demonstrated by the memorable—i.e., remembered—stories that are preserved in many literary structures. Not past "events" provide the key but the literary creativity of the "Jewish people." To discover this requires first undertaking a comparison between Hebrew or Yiddish or other Jewish versions of international motifs or stories and then asking what makes the Jewish version culturally distinctive. Thus the folklorist is not engaged in a purely formalistic inquiry but rather in a kind of cultural and historical quest for the uniquely Jewish aspect of comparable motifs and narratives. Nevertheless, compared to the positivist historian, the folklorist focuses on the inner world of the texts studied, not on the way the narratives about the past report or represent "what actually happened." Examples of such a formalistic approach to medieval hagiographical texts or *exempla* include studies by Zfatman, Alexander, Werses and Yassif.[13]

The third approach, that of the anthropological historian, also generates its own canon based on a special agenda. Like the folklorist's, this agenda is broad and includes some texts that the folklorist includes because they are "stories" and others that the positivist excludes for the same reason. Like the positivist's, the anthropological historian's anthology contains narratives that purport to represent/record/comment on a remembered past time. This narrows the range compared to the folklorist's, even as the inclusion of stories, not just texts that "look like history," gives it more breadth than that of the positivist.

The goal is not "facts" or "literary creativity" but something I would call "historiographical creativity." At issue is not many literary genres of stories that represent the world but many types of pasts remembered in symbolic forms. This is a critical distinction between the second and third type. The agenda of the anthropological historian is not, as in the case of literary-folkloristic analysis, to study the forms and motifs and filiations of a story. It is to penetrate the history of symbolic representations that claim to express a collective memory of an individual leader, local community, region or global Jewish experience.

In some ways, the importance and power of the experience being represented requires a near mythic vehicle for it to be remembered and transmitted effectively. Not nitty-gritty details—the stuff of the positivist—are the stuff of collective memory. Rather, heroic stories of foundings, conquest, rescue, self-sacrifice are. A collective memory is based on a collective forgetting of everything but one considered theme; the spotlight requires a blacked-out stage. Everything else must be removed = forgotten, so that one person, place or thing will be seen = remembered.

I would like to illustrate the third approach first by remembering an earlier study of a narrative text that "looks like history" from medieval Spain—"the Story of the Four Captives" in Abraham Ibn Daud's *Sefer ha-Qabbalah (Book of Tradition)*.[14] Following a consideration of Gerson D. Cohen's analysis of this narrative about the divinely arranged founding of a new rabbinic academy in Muslim Cordova, I would like to reconsider a functionally parallel but culturally distinctive "foundation story" from Ashkenaz. It portrays Charlemagne, not a Muslim Caliph, as the founder of the Mainz Jewish community in Christian Europe. This will lead, by way of conclusion, to some suggestions about what historical narrativity is and how it "works" especially in early Ashkenazic cultural memory.

II

The pioneering character of Gerson D. Cohen's revisionist study of Ibn Daud's twelfth-century classic has not been sufficiently appreciated. Viewed from the end of the present century, his work can now be seen as a turning point in postmodern Jewish historical scholarship that points towards the new anthropological Jewish history. Cohen analyzed in a detailed and powerful monograph the story of four rabbinical sages who were captured at sea and distributed to new, western centres of rabbinic learning in Alexandria, Egypt; Kairowan, North Africa, and Cordova, Spain (Ibn Daud ignores the fourth).[15] Prior to Cohen's monograph, scholarly discourse on this charming text fell into those two categories which I have called the "positivist" or the "folklorist." He consciously rejected those two approaches and proposed instead an interpretive strategy that I have called the "anthropological historical" approach.

Here is an excerpt of the narrative and my précis of Cohen's analysis in which the possibility of a symbolic historical reading is proposed:

Prior to that, it was brought about by the Lord that the income of the academies which used to come from Spain, the land of the Maghreb, Ifriqiya, Egypt, and the Holy Land was discontinued. The following were the circumstances that brought this about.

The commander of a fleet, whose name was Ibn Rumahis, left Cordova, having been sent by the Muslim king of Spain, Abd ar-Rahman an-Nasr. This commander of a mighty fleet set out to capture the ships of the Christians and the towns that were close to the coast. They sailed as far as the coast of Palestine and swung about to the Greek sea and the islands therein. [Here] they encountered a ship carrying four great scholars, who were traveling from the city of Bari to a city called Sefastin, and who were on their way to a Kallah convention. Ibn Rumahis captured the ship and took the sages prisoner. One of them was R. Hushiel, the father of Rabbenu Hananel; another was R. Moses, the father of R. Hanok, who was taken prisoner with his wife and his son, R. Hanok (who at the time was but as young lad); the third was R. Shemariah b. R. Elhanan. As for the fourth, I do not know his name. . . .

The sages did not tell a soul about themselves or their wisdom. The commander sold R. Shemariah in Alexandria of Egypt; [R. Shemariah] proceeded to Fostat where he became head [of the academy]. Then he sold R. Hushiel on the coast of Ifriqiya. From there the latter proceeded to the city of Qairowan, which at that time was the mightiest of all Muslim cities in the land of the Maghreb, where he became the head [of the academy] and where he begot his son Rabbenu Hananel.

Then the commander arrived at Cordova where he sold R. Moses along with R. Hanok. He was redeemed by the people of Cordova, who were under the impression that he was a man of no education. Now there was in Cordova a synagogue that was called the College Synagogue, where a judge by the name of R. Nathan the Pious, who was a man of distinction, used to preside. . . . Once R. Nathan explained [the law requiring] "immersion [of the finger] for each sprinkling," which is found in tractate Yoma, but he was unable to explain it correctly. Thereupon, R. Moses, who was seated in the corner like an attendant, arose before R. Nathan and said to him: "Rabbi, this would result in an excess of immersions!." . . . On that day, R. Nathan the Judge walked out, and the litigants followed him. However, he said to them: "I am no longer judge. This man, who is garbed in rags and is a stranger, is my master, and I shall be his disciple from this day on. You ought to appoint him judge of the community of Cordova." And that is exactly what they did. . . .[16]

Cohen noted that many scholars had sought to make sense of this account, starting with the early nineteenth-century scholar, Judah Loeb Rapoport (Shir), and including such luminaries as Graetz, Schechter, Poznanski,

Aptowitzer, Marx, Assaf and Mann, among others.[17] He divided them into two camps:

> The one dismisses the story as pious legend, based perhaps on a grain of truth, and contends, therefore, that students need not trouble themselves about squaring internal contradictions. However, in the absence of conclusive evidence that the story is pure fiction, the other and minority group refuses to discredit the story and accepts it as basically correct. Where there are internal contradictions, the statements are emended; where there are patent misstatements of fact, they alone are summarily rejected.[18]

The lengths to which positivist historians would go to square new data with the facticity of a historical narrative are revealed in a report about one of the four scholars in Ibn Daud's account. We recall that one of the scholars captured at sea who founded a new academy was R. Hushiel, the father of Rabbenu Hananel. In 1899 Solomon Schechter published a letter from the Cairo Geniza[19] in which R. Hushiel writes to R. Shemariah b. Elhanan, another of the "captives," that he, R. Hushiel, had come to Kairowan but makes no mention whatsoever of being captured at sea.[20] Undaunted by this new "fact" that blatantly contradicted the version in Ibn Daud's narrative, a scholar as accomplished as Jacob Mann resorted to the pure conjecture that there must have been two contemporary scholars named R. Hushiel, one captured at sea and the other the author of the Geniza letter.

Although Cohen worked within the dominant paradigm of positivist historiography, he acutely sensed the inadequacy of this approach when applied to a narrative that looks like history but that exhibits signs of a literary imagination. The positivist scholars either accepted the narrative as factual and made emendations to "correct" the account or left the discordant details alone but dismissed the narrative as a "pious legend," grist for the mill of others—I would say "folklorists"—not of historians.

Instead of following either of these alternatives, Cohen proposed a third approach which points the way to an "anthropological historiography": "It is the purpose of this paper to demonstrate that, on the one hand, the account is a fiction and was probably not intended by its author to be read as factual history and that, on the other hand, the text and data which have come down to us in *Sefer ha-Qabbalah* are essentially as Ibn Daud wrote them."[21] And after isolating various literary sources from which the author might have constructed his story, Cohen concluded: What we are dealing with "is not a historical account but a homily, a romance with a moral."[22] The point? "The fact that the 'four' scholars came to their new homes by divine fiat provides the rationale for the break of Jewish communities throughout the world with the Babylonian academies."[23] Cohen further showed that the dates in the narrative, which violate known "facts," were purposefully symmetrical and symbolic, pointing to pairs of events that were designed to console the present-day reader: "The significant point about these schematized dates in *Sefer ha-Qabbalah* is that history is always shown to conform to a pattern. It is in this very orderlines [*sic*] of history that Ibn Daud finds a source of consolation, a source of hope that history will yet vindicate the Jewish hope for redemption."[24]

And yet, Cohen also pondered "the historical substratum of the tale,"[25] which involved expressing Spanish-Jewish regional autonomy from the previously dominant Babylonian centers and even signs of local family rivalries discussed in an episode of the narrative not quoted above. In short, real trends and conflicts were refracted in the narrative, but through a symbolic narrative prism that was designed to reassure a Jewish readership that God favored the Jews, in general, and that the Jewish academy of Spain, in particular, was the legitimate heir of the Babylonian Geonim.

Cohen put it this way: "In the tradition of the philosophers of his day, Ibn Daud felt that fables were a means to a higher end—the education of the masses to good conduct. Historical facts as such were probably of little value to him. What mattered most was their effect. However, even in his moralistic tale he left the door open to the initiates of his day to see the fictional character and religious-political significance of a story he attributed to the divine plan."[26]

Cohen transcended the dualistic typology of either/or when it came to narratives that looked like history. He assumed correctly that a text need not be either "fact" or "fiction," but that "fiction" itself could embody another kind of historical reality. Writing before the study of "collective memory" became fashionable, his assessment of this Sefardic text moved in that very direction.

III

Among the texts from Ashkenaz that look like history are brief accounts about the founding of new Jewish communities such as Mainz in the Rhineland. Like the Story of the Four Captives, the accounts from Ashkenaz deal with the medieval European problem of new cultural beginnings and the problem of the relationship of the newer European communities in the West to earlier, classical civilizations in the East.

This Jewish tradition is part of a larger cultural phenomenon during the Middle Ages in Western Europe. At that time, one of the indicators of a community's cultural emancipation from earlier eastern centers was the use of a version of a story that describes a transfer of power or culture from East to West. Even in ancient times, the name "Europe" was connected with this historical shift from East to West, and some even wanted to understand the name "Europe" as being etymologically connected to 'E-R-B/Ma'aRaB (Hebrew: Evening/West), "the land of the setting sun." Even if the etymology is imagined, mythology established that Europa was a Phoenecian goddess with whom Zeus fell in love. He turned himself into a bull to win her heart, and she climbed on his back and swam westward with him until they landed in Crete.[27]

Christians and different Jewish communities used a similar story. Communities that came into existence after ancient Rome were aware of being culturally "belated." They were conscious of being established in the wake of earlier classical cultures. Thus, several foundation stories that play on the idea of transfer from East to West tend to justify the community as legitimate heirs of classical cultures and civilizations. And since the latter often as not were also great political powers in their day, the transfer motif applied to political rule (*translatio imperii*) as well as to cultural activity (*translatio studii*).[28]

Several foundation stories exist among key medieval European Jewish communities. The texts in which they are preserved include *Megillat Aḥimaaz* from southern Italy in the eleventh century;[29] the Story of the Four Captives in Ibn Daud's *Sefer ha-Qabbalah* about Muslim Spain;[30] and cycles of historical lends connected to the Frankish king, Charlemagne. The latter in particular served to consolidate the memory of certain circles as the only legitimate heirs of an earlier culture from the East. In general, the foil for new Western Jewish communities was not Rome, but rather Babylonia, or Palestine, or both.

Among the Jewish communities that made use of the legend of Charlemagne, two stand out: Narbonne, in southern France, and the Jews of the Rhineland, in Germany. Regarding the historical setting of the former, it is likely that the emergence in the twelfth century of a story that Charlemagne founded the Jewish community of Narbonne is part of that community's response to the challenge posed by the contemporary rise to prominence of new Jewish communities in nearby Christian Spain.[31] Similarly, there is reason to ask why R. Eleazar of Worms (d. ca. 1230), author of *Sefer ha-Roqeaḥ* and an important descendant of the Qalonimos clan that had helped found Mainz in the tenth century, wrote down his version of the Charlemagne story in the late twelfth or early thirteenth century. In part, he was responding to another challenge, that of the newly ascendant rabbinic dynasty of Rashi and especially the Tosafist scholars of Champagne in Northern France.

Below is a well-known version of this narrative. The text appears in a commentary to the prayerbook that R. Eleazar wrote down:[32]

> They received the esoteric traditions about the arrangement of the prayers as well as the other esoteric traditions, rabbi from rabbi, all the way back to Abu Aaron, the son of R. Samuel the Prince, who had left Babylonia because of a

certain incident, and he was therefore required to travel all over the world. He came to the land of Lombardy, to a certain city called Lucca. There he found our Rabbi Moses who composed the liturgical poem (which begins) *"eimat nora'otekha,"* and he transmitted to him all of his esoteric traditions. This is R. Moses bar Qalonimos, son of R. Meshullam b. R. Qalonimos b. R. Judah. (Now R. Moses) was the first who emigrated from Lombardy, he and his sons, R. Qalonimos and R. Yequtiel, and his relative R. Itiel, as well as the rest of the people who counted. All of them were taken from Lombardy by King Charles who resettled them in Mainz. There they grew to prodigious numbers until 1096 when the Lord visited His wrath upon the holy communities. Then were we all destroyed, utterly destroyed, except for a few of our relatives who survived including R. Qalonimos the Elder. He transmitted (the esoteric traditions)—as we have written—to R. Eleazar Hazan of Speyer. Eleazar Hazan transmitted them to R. Samuel (the) Pietist and R. Samuel (the) Pietist transmitted them to R. Judah (the Pietist). And from him did I, the insignificant one, receive the esoteric traditions about the prayers as well as other traditions.

Many have written about this narrative that looks like history, especially with the intent of determining the degree to which this story is "true" in the sense of being "factual."[33] As we saw, similar effort was made regarding the Story of the Four Captives,[34] and the same can be said about the Charlemagne account about Narbonne[35] or about Aḥimaaz's rhymed narrative from southern Italy.[36] This approach is understandable, even though it is doubtful that any real progress can be made here because the sources are not documentary in character. Even if one date or another happens to be found in such a narrative, as is the case with one of the parallels to the Mainz account,[37] it is highly doubtful that it is reliable. Apart from errors due to manuscript transmission, we should consider the purposely fabricated symbolic dates found in Ibn Daud's account, as Gerson Cohen demonstrated.[38]

A different approach would not ask, Are there facts here as opposed to legends? but: Why were these and not other legends created and preserved? What is their historical significance in the collective memory of this community? In this way we confront two distinct, related, aspects of the meaning of a narrative that looks like history. On the one hand, we are asking, Does the content of the narrative as constructed and remembered, have historical meaning? And on the other hand, we want to know what can be learned from the narrative and from other evidence about the fact hat this narrative appeared only at a specific point in time, long after the time the narrative itself claims to represent. "Content" and timing are related but distinct historical features of collective memory.

This approach, which I call the "anthropological historical" one, takes the data in the narrative seriously even though it is not considered factual. It views the details as part of the collective memory of a community or of a subgroup in it. It pays attention to the context of the narrative—its selection of protagonists and plot—and it also focuses on why the narrative appeared when it did.

The Mainz Carolingian story suggests true historical recollections embedded in it despite the fact that there was no such event.[39] Among other things, it reminds us that the gradual emergence of northern European Jewish societies was made secure for individual Jewish merchants, in the ninth century, and for German Jewish communities, in the eleventh, by the charters that were first issued by Carolingian monarchs or their imitators. In this sense the story preserves a true "fact," for the Carolingians gave legitimacy, security, and support to the early Ashkenazic merchant communities. Immigration from Italy and France, not a single "event," "founded" the earliest communities; but the story that remembers such an event incorporates the true memory that Charlemagne (d. 814) and his son Louis the Pious (d. 840) played an important part in the early history of Ashkenazic community building.[40]

In another sense, too, the narrative of a transfer from Italy to Germany resonates with a true historical process that took place in the Frankish Empire. Not only does it recall that some of the Jewish immigrants to Mainz were Italian Jewish merchant families, but it parallels the ways that Charlemagne organized his newly constituted and fragile empire around Roman models which he had brought to the Rhineland to his newly conquered lands in the north. Whether it was a Roman version of the Benedictine Rule or of Canon Law codes, he sought Roman models. Consciously or not, the idea of building a northern community on Italian models, found in Eleazar's account, echoes the true historical memory of the Carolingian Renaissance.[41]

But we should also remember that the Mainz foundation narrative, emphasizing Qalonimos' priority in the founding of that community, does not accurately reflect what we know of the power elite in the early Mainz academy. The Qalonimides were not the leaders of the communities "in the beginning" but only in the second half of the eleventh century. Thus, neither the first great rabbinic leader of Mainz, Rabbenu Gershom ben Judah "Light of the Exile" (d. 1028), nor his successor, R. Judah b. Meir ha-Kohen, were of Qalonimos stock. The same was true for the next generation of leaders there and in the newer academy of Worms.[42] It was only in the later eleventh century that the Qalonimos members begin to dominate some of the older communities, and Speyer, a newly founded spin-off community from Mainz in 1084. Thus, while R. Eleazar's account correctly remembers that his ancestors immigrated early, it forgets that they "arrived" late.

And it was this very belatedness that made the sudden fall so annoying. Just as they were gaining control, they lost it in 1096. As R. Eleazar put it,

"They grew to prodigious numbers until 1096 when the Lord visited His wrath upon the holy communities. Then were we all destroyed, utterly destroyed, except for a few of our relatives who survived including R. Qalonimos the Elder."[43]

On top of the devastating losses the German rabbinic elite incurred in the anti-Jewish riots of 1096 came the simultaneous rise of brilliant French outsiders—Rashi and his descendants. Soon even German students were lured to France to study, whereas a generation earlier, Rashi and his future son-in-law, R. Meir, had gone to the Rhineland. The center had shifted from East (the Rhineland) to West (Champagne), and R. Eleazar's writing down his self-serving claims to being the legitimate continuation of Babylonian traditions—as had Ibn Daud—constitutes a rear-guard action in the defense of the Qalonimides of early Ashkenaz against the *nouveau arrivés* Rashiides of Champagne. The use of the *translatio* motif is, in part, a response to the Qalonimides' awareness of a loss of mastery, as the French elite displaced the German clan of founders.

This and other features in the narrative point toward a new understanding of its appearance in the post-1096 world, and more particularly in the late twelfth or early thirteenth century. The Charlemagne legend is part of R. Eleazar's commentary on the prayerbook, and grew out of the German Pietist tendency to write down their traditions starting in the late twelfth century. This conserving activity is a German-Jewish trend that began in the early twelfth century when the descendants of Rabbenu Gershom collected and recorded early Ashkenazic customs. In the twelfth century, we have other collections of early German-Jewish customs, such as R. Eliezer bar Natan's book of law and tradition. It is no accident that he evidently authored a Hebrew narrative about the riots of 1096 and wrote liturgical poems commemorating them. The German Pietists continued this Ashkenazic tendency to conserve early local traditions and write them down.[44]

Parts of the pietist ideal were ancient and consisted of several intersecting features that cannot be reduced to an anti-Tosafist ideology.[45] Nevertheless, the medieval historical stimuli which helped precipitate the pietistic ideal in written form may be related to other anti-French polemical trends we find among the German pietists. The German pietists wrote down their traditions—among them R. Eleazar's narrative about Charlemagne and the founding of Mainz—as a response to the preeminence of the Tosafist movement which surpassed the German scholars stuck in the conservative backwaters of the Rhineland. They clung to their early customs and bragged that they and they alone were the First Families of Ashkenaz. History seemed to be passing them by; they expressed their sense of themselves in a narrative that looks like history.[46]

In another Ashkenazic text that looks like history, we find a trace in collective memory of the competition between the German and French Jewish subcultures in Ashkenazic Europe, and it reinforces our interpretation of the Charlemagne narrative. In a late medieval cycle of Hebrew and Yiddish hagiographical stories about R. Judah the Pietist and his father, R. Samuel, we find a story about R. Samuel. The Yiddish collection is called the *Mayse-bukh*. It includes much older oral and written traditions from the Rhineland and Regensburg. One such story reports a mysterious encounter between R. Samuel the Pietist, of Speyer, and a Rabbi Jacob, apparently, Jacob b. Meir or Rabbenu Tam, the most brilliant of the French Tosafists. My translation of the more original Hebrew version follows:[47]

> A story about Rabbenu Jacob from Rame[rupt][48] who had always wanted to see Rabbenu Samuel. One time R. Samuel exiled himself for seven years— some say for nine years—and came to the very town where R. Jacob lived. He asked which was the Rabbi's house. They showed it to him, and he lodged there. While he stayed there he never spoke a word of Torah.
>
> R. Jacob asked R. Samuel: What is your name? He answered him: Samuel the Parchment Maker—and there was a wild and simple fellow in those days who had that name—and (R. Jacob) showed (R. Samuel) no special respect.
>
> When R. Samuel left the next day,[49] one of R. Jacob's students said to him: Rabbenu Jacob, my master and teacher, yesterday when you asked the guest who lodged with you what his name was he answered you correctly, "Samuel who prepares skins which are called 'parchment'." (That is) because he is thoroughly familiar with their contents. I am convinced that he is R. Samuel the Pietist. (R. Jacob) said to the student: Why was he so quiet? He never said a word to me! The student answered: It was on account of his extreme humility that he did not say anything to you. R. Jacob said: I want to ride after him and bring him back with me so that I can find out for sure. If you are lying I will excommunicate you. The student replied: I know that he is R. Samuel the Pietist.
>
> And R. Jacob and some of his students rode out. When they overtook R. Samuel, R. Jacob said to him: Come back to the house with me. Forgive me for not honoring you appropriately and do not deny that you are R. Samuel the Pietist for it was disclosed (*hugad*) to me clearly (that you are). And now come with me. R. Jacob urged him (to do so), and the Pietist went with him. They spent two weeks there, and after R. Jacob told the law to his students, R. Jacob and R. Samuel went by themselves into the same room and remained there in communion and did what they did. After fourteen days, they left one another.

The Yiddish version in the *Mayse-bukh* elaborates the story in significant ways. Especially important is the way R. Samuel is characterized in the beginning of the story. The text reads as follows:

Once upon a time there lived a great man called R. Jacob, who had heard a great deal about R. Samuel, the Pious, the father of R. Judah, the Pious, and desired very much to see him. One day R. Samuel went abroad to study and came to the very town in which R. Jacob lived. So he went to the house of R. Jacob to take up his lodgings there without making himself known, for he was afraid lest he would derive a special advantage on account of his great learning, and it is not permitted to derive profit from the Torah.

R. Jacob never spoke to him all the time that he was with him, for he thought that he was a simple fellow. Finally, however, R. Jacob said to him: "My dear friend, what is your name?" He replied: "Samuel." Then R. Jacob asked him: "Have you a surname?" He replied: "I am called Samuel the Parchment Maker, after my trade." R. Jacob thought that he was in truth a parchment maker and showed him no more respect than any other guest.

When R. Samuel was leaving, R. Jacob and his pupils accompanied him for a short space, while R. Samuel went some distance ahead with one of R. Jacob's students. When R. Jacob had returned to the town, R. Samuel said to the young man: "Your master asked me yesterday what my name is and I told him that it was Samuel Parchment Maker. I gave myself that name because of my occupation, for I know thoroughly the whole Torah, which is written on parchment.' With these words R. Samuel left the young man and went on his way.

When the student returned home, he told his master what the stranger had told him. Then R. Jacob said: "I am sure that he was R. Samuel the Pious and that he purposely refused to make himself known so that I should not show him any special honor, as in fact I did not." And turning to the young man, he said: "Let us hasten after him, perchance we may overtake him and bring him back with us, but assuredly you are not telling me a falsehood." The young man replied: "God forbid that I should tell you a falsehood." So R. Jacob hurried after Samuel, came up to him and intreated him so long that R. Samuel consented to come back with him. As soon as they had reached R. Jacob's house, they entered a room and stayed there ten days and ten nights and no man knew what they were doing. Then R. Samuel left R. Jacob, having been shown great honor. May the Lord, blessed be He, grant that we benefit by their merits through the ages.

Although in this story R. Samuel's traveling incognito serves as a plot device to create irony (the "great man" R. Jacob is contrasted to R. Samuel whom he thinks is a "simple fellow") and suspense (when will R. Jacob discover who his guest really is?), it also embodies some the competing values of German Hasidism and of French Tosafism and gives priority to German pietism by "remembering" that Rabbenu Tam wanted to meet R. Samuel, not the other way around.

One of the cardinal sins of the Pietist is to enjoy personal honor,[50] and from a Pietist perspective, Tosafists who flaunt their learning and crave personal recognition are sinners. The Hebrew version starts out with R. Samuel as the embodiment of Hasidism—he goes abroad in self-exile and does not talk to R. Jacob because of his extreme humility. R. Jacob is portrayed as being insulted. The stranger did not honor him by talking to him, and R. Jacob in turn dismisses him. The pietist follows pietism; the Tosafist is frustrated in seeking to be honored. In the later Yiddish version, R. Jacob is frustrated in now being able to bestow honor on R. Samuel, even though that is the last thing that a Pietist would want.

In tension with this scheme is the question of R. Samuel's learning and his play with his identity as a Parchment Maker. We readers know that he is not a "simple fellow," but exactly what kind of learning does the story claim for him? In the Yiddish version, there is contamination of Pietism by the Tosafist ideal. Thus, R. Samuel is traveling not as a penitential exile but "to study." Moreover, he is portrayed as being learned, like R. Jacob. This is totally missing in the Hebrew version.

Yet, we cannot tell even from the Yiddish version what kind of learning is being claimed for him. We know from other sources that R. Jacob Tam held the radical view that a Jew should not study the Bible or the Mishnah as subjects in their own right, but should study only the Babylonian Talmud which is filled with quotations from both earlier texts.[51] R. Samuel provides no evidence of his talmudic learning. Indeed, he explains his name to R. Jacob's student by saying enigmatically: "I gave myself that name because of my occupation, for I know thoroughly the whole Torah, which is written on parchment." (The Hebrew version insists that the name is self-deprecatory and not a sign of learning at all.) The answer is ambiguous. Does it mean "the whole Torah" as a Hasid would know it, with hidden associations of each word and letter? Or, does it mean R. Jacob's Torah, i.e., the Babylonian Talmud? We are not told.

The ending of the story, however, resolves the tension in the story by having R. Jacob learn his former guest's identity, thanks to a student's insistence (Hebrew version) or to R. Samuel's revealing himself to one of R. Jacob's students (Yiddish version). In the original story, R. Samuel remains humble; in the Yiddish retelling, R. Samuel turns out not to be so humble after all—for he reveals his knowledge to the student solely in order that R. Tam can guess who he is and subsequently honor him. This penultimate resolution of the plot compromises Hasidism. But the real denouement occurs in a mysterious final encounter between the two when R. Jacob and R. Samuel spend ten days (or two weeks) together in seclusion. Is R. Tam teaching the Hasid new Tosafot? Hardly. That would have occurred in public in the academy. The story suggests that R. Samuel is disclosing some secret revelation in private to R. Jacob. This explains why the story opens with R. Jacob's wanting to meet R. Samuel. Together the opening and the mysterious meeting at the end frame the suspense story that turns on the hidden identity of the visitor.

On balance, then, this Ashkenazic story, reported first in Hebrew and modified significantly away from Pietist values in Yiddish, makes R. Samuel to be more important than R. Jacob. It is R. Jacob "the great man" who "desired very much to see" R. Samuel and who ends up doing so, apparently to his advantage. Even though R. Samuel's Pietist ethos has been contaminated by Tosafist pride and learning, the core of the story gives greater value to R. Samuel and, in the end, suggests that R. Tam learned something other than Babylonian Talmudic dialectics from R. Samuel. In this subtle and fascinating story about R. Samuel we find a reflection of the rivalry between the Hasid and the Tosafist that is also reflected in R. Eleazar of Worms's use of the Carolingian narrative about the founding of Mainz. It is a German-Jewish version of the political-cultural transfer of Jewish life from the East to the West, via Italy. Not "facts" but historical meaning and ultimately historical creativity can be disclosed in such sources.

IV

The Ashkenazic narratives that look like history differ significantly from Sefardic texts such as Ibn Daud's.[52] To begin with, the Muslim-Sefardic narratives are mainly concerned with the rabbinic elites in Jewish society, whereas the Ashkenazic texts generally describe a broader social spectrum. When they are about the elite, it is not necessarily the rabbis or academy that is central.

Thus, Ibn Daud called his book *Sefer ha-Qabbalah* because it consists primarily of lists of rabbinical figures, generation after generation, from Moses to his own time in medieval Spain. Moreover, it seeks to establish one basic truth: "each great sage and righteous man . . . received (true teachings) from a great sage and righteous man."[53]

Ibn Daud did not invent this genre: the same focus on the rabbinic elite and its claim to teach true tradition is also the dominant feature of three earlier works: a lengthy *responsum* by Rav Sherira ben Hanina Gaon (d. 1006) about the rabbinic schools and chains of learned authorities in the Baghdadi academies;[54] an anonymous text from Muslim times called *Seder Tannaim va'Amoraim*;[55] and even of a narrative written in Kairowan by a former observer of the academies and communal conflicts in Baghdad in the early tenth century, the Narrative of R. Nathan the Baghdadi.[56] These texts argue for the legitimacy of rabbinic authority and law in the face of sectarian doubters called Karaites or argue that in a Christian society, where Ibn Daud lived, Judaism is ancient and still authentic because it was reliably transmitted through the ages by the sages.

The Ashkenazic anthology of narratives that look like history is not characterized by chains of rabbinic teachers through the centuries nor does it have the same ideology. The Ashkenazic texts focus on Jewish communities or families. Thus, from early medieval Italy, we have *Sefer Yosippon*, a sophisticated working of the biblical narrative through the Greco-Roman era that ends with the Roman defeat of the Jews at Masada in the first century C.E.[57] Another member of the same community produced *Megillat Aḥimaaz*, a narrative written in rhymed prose in the mid-eleventh century. It includes stories about the author's ancestors who were miracle workers, liturgical poets and communal elders.[58]

Even more clearly concerned with whole communities are the narratives from northern Europe. They include short narratives about persecutions from early Ashkenaz, especially the anti-Jewish riots in the Rhineland in the spring of 1096 or 1147—the so-called Crusade Chronicles[59]—hagiographical *exempla* preserved in Hebrew and Yiddish about rabbinic or medieval sages (*Mayse-bukh*);[60] anonymous *exempla* about pietists (*Sefer Ḥasidim*);[61] elaborate cycles of tales about heroic figures such as Alexander or Arthur recast into Hebrew.[62]

The Italo-Ashkenazic narratives also contain an ideological purpose of their own: they describe the Jewish people as a holy community of *hasidim*—Pietists—and emphasize that the self-image of Ashkenaz is of a community of righteous saints.[63] *Sefer Yosippon* looks like a continuation of the Bible because it too narrates the sacred history of Israel but continues the story down to Masada. Although, like the Bible, it is concerned with political rulers and their struggles, it emphasizes that the Jews of Italy are *hasidim*, charismatics who have a special relationship to the holy.

This theme is reflected in an Ashkenazic tradition that the first major German rabbinic figure, Rabbenu Gershom, copied out the Bible, the Talmud and *Sefer Yosippon*.[64] It makes little sense to connect the latter work with two central canonical Jewish sacred texts if we think of *Yosippon* as a "history book" or paraphrase of Josephus, both modern anachronisms. Regardless of the facticity of the tradition, its being remembered means that Ashkenazic Jews thought that *Yosippon* was about the sacred people of Israel, comparable to the Bible and Talmud. The same presupposition underlies the preservation of the entire genre in Ashkenaz of narratives that look like history.

Like *Yosippon*, the *Narrative of Aḥimaaz* also contains many vignettes of people who are not powerful or remarkably learned but who are described as holy and righteous, descended from the saintly exiles of Jerusalem. In addition, the 1096 German-Jewish narratives, which do include significant reports about the power brokers and their efforts to influence the political leaders of the towns or even the Emperor, away in Italy, stress portraits of holy martyrs including women, males who are not rabbis and even children. The phrase *Kehillah Kedosha* (Holy Community) is central in the Ashkenazic narratives.

The miracle tales in *Aḥimaaz* or the narrative *ma'asim* (*gesta*, deeds) about R. Samuel or R. Judah are matched by the acts of martyrdom represented in the 1096 narratives: they are about holy people and about a holy community. Although influenced by the earlier narratives about ten rabbinic martyrs,[65] the Ashkenazic canvas is society itself, not just rabbinic heroes. The language used to describe these men, women and children is the rhetoric of the Temple,[66] not the learning of the academy. Again, Rabbi Eleazar of Worms' narrative introduction to his rewriting of Proverbs 31 (A Woman of Valor) describes his wife, whom he called a *ḥasidah* (Pietist woman)[67] and his two teenage daughters, not rabbinical colleagues.

The Muslim-Sefardic Jewish narratives that look like history stress continuity with an earlier classical past as the basis for Sefardic legitimacy, similar to the Muslim concept of *isnad.*[68] Uninterrupted tradition is how we know that we understand properly the will of God. And the Story of the Four Captives underscores this feature, showing how God used the Caliph to establish four new centers of Jewish learning to succeed the older institutions of rabbinic authority that had declined in Babylonia.

In R. Eleazar of Worms' Carolingian account of Mainz, on the other hand, a king helps an Italian-Jewish family "found" a whole community. It was the community that grew prodigiously until 1096. The focus is not on rabbinic elites and their continuity, but on the discontinuity in a community brought about by migration and trauma.

The Ashkenazic texts seem to emerge especially at times when communal status is in decline, in comparison with an earlier time. The occasion for writing down a narrative about the past is not idle curiosity or even family pride or community self-respect but a perceived change or loss. Thus, *Yosippon* was written in the ninth or tenth century, when Italian Jews were becoming aware of the Babylonian influences supplanting Palestinian ones; Aḥimaaz wrote in the mid-eleventh century, after the political climate in southern Italy had changed dramatically from the Byzantine world described in the narrative. The 1096 German-Jewish narratives describe reactions to the loss of German-Jewish religious hegemony in northern Europe and the crisis of confidence in the Carolingian peace that they had enjoyed for a century and a half. And the narrative exempla in *Sefer Ḥasidim* are responding, in part, to a post-Tosafist world in which the old Italo-Ashkenazic values of Pietism have been challenged by the upstart French Tosafists.

The emphasis in Ashkenazic narratives on the story of the changing holy community makes the remembered changes in the life of the community comparable to a dense, partially obscure, sacred text that requires interpretation. The Mainz tradition about Rabbenu Gershom significantly juxtaposes his copying out Scripture, the Talmud and *Yosippon*, a story about the Sacred

People. The latter complements the Bible—the Written Torah—and the Talmud—the Oral Torah—because in Ashkenaz the life of the sacred people is the Living Torah. Its glosses we call "historiography."

The idea that the postbiblical story of the people of Israel is a sacred text is reinforced further by a distinctive feature of the Ashkenazic legal tradition. Whereas the Muslim-Sefardic law codifiers, including R. Joseph Karo, the author of the *Shulḥan Arukh,*[69] decided the law based on the weight of earlier Muslim-Sefardic rabbinic authorities, what counted in Ashkenaz, where Jews had to improvise, was *minhag*[70]—the customary religious behavior of the people. These practices were canonized as legitimate precedents, and, even more important, as a valid process. The people's behavior in the earliest days of European Jewish settlement, before they possessed the text of the Babylonian Talmud, remained paradigmatic for all time. It remained canonical even after they got the Talmud. By the twelfth century, when comparisons of authoritative texts were made, and lived practice was seen to contradict explicit talmudic texts, the latter were reread—we would say grossly forced—to conform to the behavior of the sacred community, the living text of Israel.[71] In effect, the lawyers accepted what the sacred people did as normative.

The concept of a righteous or holy people, whose deeds are the subject in Italy and Ashkenaz of narratives that look like history, is the key to understanding these texts' cultural meaning. Just as Jews in Ashkenaz wrote commentaries to the Hebrew Bible, the Talmud, the standard texts and liturgical poetry in the prayerbook, so too they glossed the living text of the sacred people. What the people did was comparable in Ashkenaz to Scripture and the Talmud. As new customs developed, Ashkenazic authorities continued to view them as legitimate *minhag* even if no precedent could be found in earlier written authorities. The people itself was the authority.

These texts also create narrative Hebrew prose that complements the Bible and rabbinic Midrash in a new way. They do not strictly follow biblical syntax or narratives; nor are they "midrashic" in texture because they are not attached to a biblical text as a model or archetype. Unlike the Rabbinic midrashim from late antique Palestine or the biblical commentary literature that develops in Baghdad and Muslim Spain and then in northern Europe, these texts do not subordinate themselves to the Bible. Rather they are their own text and subordinate the Bible to themselves. They quote, paraphrase, and adapt biblical images, allusions and diction for the sake of clarifying and enriching a narrative that is new, but the narrative is independent of any one earlier authoritative text. It is the people's remembered deeds that are being glossed. And so, just as a peculiarity or discontinuity in a sacred written text may elicit a midrashic response, so a discontinuity in the text of the sacred communities provoked a narrative response. Traditional Ashkenazic "historiography," then, is analogous to but distinct from midrashic glosses on the Bible. It is a commentary not on the Written Torah but on the Living Torah, the "holy seed" (Ezra 9:2), the "holy people" (Isa. 62:12)—Ashkenazic Israel. Finally, the historiographic traditions suggest an unsuspected complexity in Sefardic and Ashkenazic cultures. The same Sefardic elites that crossed the religious boundaries of the Muslim or Christian world and participated in the sophisticated courtier culture of Baghdad and Cordova and Toledo, also maintained their Jewish authenticity by chaining themselves to an ancient anchor, the earlier generations of rabbinic sages.

For the Jews of Ashkenaz, on the other hand, clear cultural boundary existed between themselves and Christians whom they viewed as pagans. Protected from outside contamination, the Jews of Ashkenaz thought of themselves as Pietists who were the living heirs of the ancient centers of Palestine and Babylonia. Their ancestors and their own lives embodied legitimate meanings of the Torah as much as the ancient rabbinic texts which they studied.

Notes

1. Scholars of medieval Jewish historiography have rarely questioned rhetorical issues in the texts. See Moritz Steinschneider, *Die Geschichtsliteratur der Juden* (Berlin, 1905), Adolf Neubauer, ed., *Mediaeval Jewish Chronicles*, 2 vols. (London, 1887), Preface; Salo W. Baron, "Histories and Homilies" in his *A Social and Religious History of the Jewish People*, 18 vols. to date (Philadelphia and New York, 1952–91), 6:152–234 and his *History and Jewish Historians* (New York, 1964), chapters 6–9; Moshe Shulvass, "Knowledge of History and Historiography in Medieval Ashkenaz," [Hebrew] *Sefer hayovel lerabbi Hanokh Albeck* [Albeck *Festschrift*] (Jerusalem, 1963), pp. 465–95; Haim Hillel Ben-Sasson, "On the Chronographic Tendencies of Medieval Jewry," [Hebrew] in *Historionim ve'askolot historiot* [Historians and Schools of History] (Jerusalem, 1963), pp. 29–49; reprinted with documentation in *Retsef vehevrah*, ed. Joseph Hacker (Jerusalem, 1988), pp. 379–401, 485–87; Yosef Haim Yerushalmi, "Clio and the Jewish Historians" in *American Academy for Jewish Research Jubilee Volume*, 2 vols. (New York, 1980), pp. 607–38, enlarged in his essay, *Zakhor* (Seattle, 1982). On the latter, see Ivan G. Marcus, "Beyond the Sephardic Mystique," *Orim: A Jewish Journal at Yale* 1:1 (1985): 35–53 and Roberto Bonfil, "Esiste una storiografia ebraica medioevale?" *Atti del congresso tenuto a S. Miniato, 7–10 novembre 1983* (Rome, 1987), pp. 227–47 and "How Golden Was the Age of the Renaissance in Jewish Historiography?" in *Essays in Jewish Historiography (History and Theory*, Beiheft 27), Ada Rapaport-Albert, ed. (Middletown, 1988), pp. 78–102. In addition to the other essays in Rapaport-Albert's collection, see, too '*Iyunim behistoriografia*, ed. Moshe Zimmerman, *et al.* (Jerusalem, 1988).

Compare: Jacques Le Goff, *Time, Work, and Culture in the Middle Ages* (Chicago, 1980); Roger D. Ray, "Medieval Historiography through the Twelfth Century: Problems and Progress of Research," *Viator* 5 (1974); 33–59; Lawrence Stone, "The Revival of Narrative: Reflections of a New Old History," *Past and Present* 85 (1979); 3–24; Pierre Nora, "Between Memory and History: *Les lieux de Mémoire*," *Representa-*

tions 26 (1989): 7–25, the last kindly called to my attention by David Roskies; "The New Philology," a symposium in *Speculum* 65:1 (January, 1990), especially, Gabrielle Spiegel, "History, Historicism, and the Social Logic of the Text in the Middle Ages," pp. 59–86. For a general survey of medieval Latin "historical" narratives, see Beryl Smalley, *Historians in the Middle Ages* (New York, 1974).

2. This circumlocution is used to leave open the issue of the narrative's facticity. A phrase such as "narratives about the past" appears to side with the positivists and assert that what is historical about a text is its factual value. On the fact-fiction issue, see also the penetrating comments of Meir Sternberg, *The Poetics of Biblical Narrative* (Bloomington, 1985), pp. 23–35; Lee Patterson, *Negotiating the Past: The Historical Understanding of Medieval Literature* (Madison, 1987); L. Valensi, in *History and Anthropology* 2 (1985), pp. 283–305; and Natalie Zemon Davis, "Du conte et de l'histoire," *Débat* 54 (1989): 138–43.

3. In medieval Jewish studies, see below, n. 9.

4. See Dov Neuman (Noy), "Motif-Index of Talmudic-Midrashic Literature," 2 vols. (Unpublished Ph. D. dissertation, Indiana University, 1954), pp. 633–54; Dan Ben-Amos, "Narrative Forms in the Haggadah: Structural Analysis," (Unpublished Ph. D. dissertation, Indiana University, 1967); Zvi Malaki, *Sugiyot besifrut ha'ivrit shel yemei habeinayim* [Topics in Medieval Hebrew Literature] (Tel Aviv, 1972), pp. 13–24; Eli Yassif, "On the State of the Field: Folklore Research and Judaica" [Hebrew] *Yedion* 28 (1988): 3–11 and below, n. 13.

5. Cf. Jacques Le Goff, "Préface" to reprint of Marc Bloch, *Les rois thaumaturges* (Paris, 1983), p. ii, who refers to Bloch as "le fondateur de l'anthropologie historique" which means, in effect, of the history of mentalities. I would rather shift the focus to "l'histoire anthropologique," the difference lying in the latter's taking development more seriously than the former with its renowned interest in structures and consistent features over "la longue durée." See Fernand Braudel, "History and the Social Sciences: The *Longue durée*," in Ferdand Braudel, *On History* (Chicago, 1980), pp. 25–54 and his masterpiece, *The Mediterranean and the Mediterranean World in the Age of Philip II*, 2 vols. (New York, 1972–1974). In recent Jewish historiography, the essays of Robert Bonfil are fundamental. See in particular the studies cited above, and "Between the Land of Israel and Babylonia" [Hebrew] *Shalem* 5 (1977): 1–30; "Myth, Rhetoric and History? An Inquiry into *Megillat Aḥimaaz*" [Hebrew] in *Tarbut veḥevrah betoledot Yisrael bimei habeinayim* [H. H. Ben-Sasson Memorial Volume] (Jerusalem, 1989), pp. 99–135; and chapter 10, above. See, too, my studies, "From Politics to Martyrdom: Shifting Paradigms of the Hebrew Narratives of the 1096 Crusade Riots," *Prooftexts* 2 (1982): 40–52. On this, see the reply by Robert Chazan, *European Jewry and the First Crusade* (Berkeley, 1987), pp. 308–9 and my reply in *Speculum* 64 (1989): 685–88. See, too, my study, "Hierarchies, Religious Boundaries and Jewish Spirituality in Medieval Germany," *Jewish History* 1 (1986): 7–26, and my essay, "Toward an Anthropological History of the Jews," in *The State of Jewish Studies*, Shaye Cohen and Ed Greenstein, eds., (Detroit, 1990), pp. 113–27.

6. See the distinctions in Dan Ben-Amos, Introduction to *The German Legends of the Brothers Grimm*, Donald Ward, ed. and trans., 2 vols. (Philadelphia, 1981): 1:x.

7. See Leopold von Ranke, "Preface" to his *Histories of the Latin and Germanic Nations from 1494–1514*, excerpted in Fritz Stern, ed., *The Varieties of History* (New York, 1956), p. 57.

8. See Neubauer, *Chronicles;* Ben Zion Dinur, *Yisrael bagolah* [The Jews of the Diaspora] (Tel Aviv, 1858–1972); Avraham Kahana, *Sifrut hahistoria hayisraelit* [Jewish Historiographical Literature] (1922–1923; rpt. 2 vols.; Jerusalem, 1969); Michael A. Meyer, *Ideas of Jewish History* (New York, 1974).

9. See Avraham Grossman, *Ḥakhmei Ashkenaz harishonim* [The Early Sages of Ashkenaz] (rev. ed., Jerusalem, 1989) and Chazan, *European Jewry* and in *History and Theory.*

10. See Dominick DaCapra, "Rhetoric and History," in his collection, *History and Criticism* (Ithaca, 1985), pp. 19–20: " 'documents' are themselves texts that 'process' or rework 'reality' and require a critical reading that goes beyond traditional philological forms of *Quellenkritik.*"

11. Joseph Dan, *Hasippur ha'ivri bimei habeinayim* [The Hebrew Story in the Middle Ages] (Jerusalem, 1974), esp. chaps. 5–6, 9–14, 17–19.

12. Micha Joseph Bin Gorion, *Mimeqor Yisrael: Classical Jewish Folktales,* 3 vols. (Bloomington, 1976).

13. See Sara Zfatman, "*Maaseh Book:* An Outline of a Genre of Early Yiddish Literature," [Hebrew] *Hasifrut* 28 (1979): 126–52; Tamar Alexander, "Folktales in *Sefer Ḥasidim,*" *Prooftexts* 5 (1985): 19–31; Shmuel Werses, "On the Formal and Genre Characteristics of the Stories in *Sefer Ḥasidim,*" [Hebrew] *Meḥqarim beqabbalah, befilosofia yehudit, uvesifrut hamusar vehahagut* [Isaiah Tishby *Festschrift*], eds., Joseph Dan and Joseph Hacker (Jerusalem, 1986), pp. 349–68; and Eli Yassif, "Folktales in *Megillat Aḥimaaz,*" *Yad le-Heiman* [A. M. Haberman Memorial Volume], ed. Zvi Malakhi (Jerusalem, 1984), idem, "*Exempla* in *Sefer Ḥasidim,*" *Tarbiz* 57 (1988): 217–55.

14. R. Abraham Ibn Daud, *Sefer ha-Qabbalah (The Book of Tradition),* ed. and trans. Gerson D. Cohen (Philadelphia, 1967).

15. Gerson D. Cohen, "The Story of the Four Captives," *Proceedings of the American Academy for Jewish Research* 29 (1960–1961): 55–131. On a related source, cf. Robert Cohen, "*Memoria para os siglos futuros:* Myth and Memory on the Beginnings of the Amsterdam Sephardi Community," *Jewish History* 2 (1987): 67–72.

16. Cohen, *Sefer ha-Qabbalah,* pp. 63–66.

17. Cohen, "Story," p. 70.

18. Ibid., p. 71.

19. On the Geniza, see S. D. Goitein, *A Mediterranean Society,* 5 vols. (Berkeley, 1967–1988): 1:1–28.

20. Solomon Schechter, "Geniza Specimens. A Letter of Chushiel," *Jewish Quarterly Review* 11 (1899): 643–50.

21. Cohen, "Story," p. 71.

22. Ibid., p. 95.

23. Ibid., p. 23.

24. Ibid., p. 105.

25. Ibid., p. 114.

26. Ibid., p. 123.

27. Denys Hay, *Europe: The Emergence of an Idea* (New York, 1957), p. 1.

28. Ernst Robert Curtius, *European Literature and the Latin Middle Ages* (Princeton, 1953), pp. 28–30. For examples from Amsterdam and Poland, see,

respectively, Cohen, *"Memoria para os siglos futuros,"* and Bernard Weinryb, *The Jews of Poland* (Philadelphia, 1972), pp. 17–19.

29. Benjamin Klar, ed., *Megillat Aḥimaaz* (Jerusalem, 1945); English translation, Marcus Salzman (New York, 1924).

30. Cohen, *Sefer ha-Qabbalah.*

31. Jeremy Cohen, "The Nasi of Narbonne: A Problem in Medieval Historiography," *ASJ Review* 2 (1978): 45–76.

32. R. Eleazar b. Judah of Worms, *Peirush hatefillot* (Commentary on the Prayerbook), Paris, Bibliothèque nationale Heb. MS 772, f. 60r.

33. See Grossman, *Ḥakhmei Ashkenaz*, pp. 27–44 and Bonfil, "Between the Land of Israel," p. 23, n. 81, which applies *mutatis mutandis* to all positivist studies of all these foundation accounts.

34. Cohen, "Story," pp. 70–74.

35. Arthur J. Zuckerman, *A Jewish Princedom in Feudal France, 768–900* (New York, 1982) and cf. J. Cohen, "Nasi of Narbonne," *passim.*

36. Klar, Afterword, *Megillat Aḥimaaz*, pp. 111–24.

37. Grossman, *Ḥakhmei Ashkenaz*, pp. 31–33. To Grossman's two manuscripts of the short, third tradition (p. 33), add Parma, Biblioteca Palatina, Heb. MS 540, p. 18.

38. Cohen, *Sefer ha-Qabbalah*, pp. 189–222.

39. Bonfil, "Between the Land of Israel," *passim.*

40. A. Graboïs, "Le souvenir et la légende de Charlemagne dans les textes hébraïques médiévaux," *Le moyen âge* 72 (1966): 5–41.

41. See Judith Herrin, *The Foundation of Christendom* (Princeton, 1987), pp. 390–44; Pierre Riché, *Daily Life in the World of Charlemagne* (Philadelphia, 1973), p. 231.

42. Grossman, *Ḥakhmei Ashkenaz, passim.*

43. See above, pp. 372–73.

44. See Grossman, *Ḥakhmei Ashkenaz*, Chapter 9; Ephraim E. Urbach, *Ba'alei hatosafot* [The Tosafists] 4th ed. (Jerusalem, 1980), pp. 173–84. By "conserve," I do not mean "write down facts." The medievals selected and reshaped what they remembered. See the bibliography cited above in notes 1 and 2.

45. See Ivan G. Marcus, *Piety and Society: The Jewish Pietists of Medieval Germany* (Leiden, 1981). The antiquity of the Pietists' vision and peculiar practices is becoming ever more obvious. I accidently noted the similarity between the sins for which the German Pietists wrote penitentials and a Heikhalot text. Cf. *Hekhalot Rabbati* pars. 198–99 in *Synopse zur Hekhalot-Literatur,* Peter Schäfer, ed. (Tübingen, 1985) (= *Heikhalot Rabbati*, chap. 13, *Beit hamidrash,* ed. Jellinek, reprinted 6 vols. in 2 [Jerusalem, 1967], 3:93). Peter Schafer has found many such parallels and will publish his results shortly in an article in *Jewish History.* Supporting a pre-German origin for much of German-Jewish Pietism are the studies of Robert Bonfil who has pointed to Pietist roots in the Christian culture of early medieval southern Italy. See his "Between the Land of Israel," p. 22, where he calls for students of German-Jewish pietism to consider this thesis. I agree, and would add that we should also look eastward, to Palestine, Syrian Christianity and Babylonia.

46. Haym Soloveitchik, "Three Themes in the *Sefer Ḥasidim,*" *AJS Review* 1 (1976): 339–57, insisted that the Tosafist movement was also responsible for the

ideology of German-Jewish Pietism: radical modesty was a response to Tosafist arrogance. However, in view of Schäfer's and Bonfil's work and the negative conclusions I reached about Soloveitchik's thesis (*Piety and Society*, p. 168, n. 80), this is not persuasive. On the other hand, a German Pietist response to the French Tosafist movement is likely to be responsible for the timing and animus of the Ḥasidim's written campaign. It does not account for the contents of their ideal which was ancient. Cf. Moshe Idel, *Kabbalah: New Perspectives* (New Haven, 1988), pp. 250–53 who argues, *mutatis mutandis,* for a similar relationship existed between Maimonides and the writing down of early kabbalistic traditions. Both phenomena, as well as Maimonides' own relationship to the ancient Mishnah of Rabbi Judah the Prince and the Tosafist's own revival of the pre-Geonic dialectical texture of the Babylonian Talmud—four contemporaneous parallel Jewish developments—are all part of what I have called "the renaissance of Jewish spirituality in the twelfth century," on which I am preparing a separate study.

There are other signs of a German anti-French polemic that bear on the argument that the Mainz Charlemagne narrative should be seen in this light. For example, R. Judah the Pietist, R. Eleazar of Worms's teacher in pietism, vigorously attacked "the people of France and England" for changing the wording of the liturgy, thereby subverting the numerological-cosmic meanings he associated with the words and letters of the correct—i.e., German-Pietist—text. See Ephraim E. Urbach, Introduction to Abraham b. Azriel, *Sefer 'arugat habosem* 4 vols. (Jerusalem, 1939–1963): 4:73–111; Joseph Dan, "On the Historical Character of R. Judah the Pietist," [Hebrew] in *Tarbut veḥevra,* pp. 389–98. In addition, the German-Jewish Charlemagne legend is political propaganda and should be seen in a wider context. In the late twelfth century, the German Emperor, Frederick I Barbarossa, and a strong French monarch, Philip Augustus, used the legend of Charlemagne to bolster their own claims to legitimacy. See Peter Munz, *Frederick Barbarossa: A Study in Medieval Politics* (Ithaca, 1969), pp. 242–44.

47. The Hebrew text is found in Jerusalem, Heb. MS 8° 3182, f. 131r–131v which was published by N. Brüll in "Beiträge zur jüdischen Sagen- und Spruchkunde im Mittelalter," *Jahrbücher für jüdische Geschichte und Litteratur,* 9 (1889): 26–27. Another MS of the Hebrew version is Frankfurt am Main, Stadt- und Universitätsbibliothek, Heb. MS Oct. 35 in which the story appears on fols. 94a–94b. The Yiddish version is in the *Mayse-bukh* (Basle, 1602) and is translated in Moses Gaster, *Maaseh Book* (Philadelphia, 1934), pp. 317–19. On the differences between the two versions and the dependence of the Yiddish on the Hebrew, see Zfatman, "*Maaseh Book,*" p. 132. Our analysis below confirms Zfatman's relative dating, at least as far as this story is concerned.

48. So MS Frankfurt. On the identification, see Urbach, *Ba'alei hatosafot,* p. 192, where n. 58 is missing, and pp. 66–67 for other references to Rabbenu Tam as "Rabbenu Yaakov."

49. MS Jerusalem clearly reads: "lemoḥorat" (the next day) (f. 131v, line one); in Brüll it is garbled as "le'aḥeret"? and paraphrastically translated, "Als" (when). MS Frankfurt reads: "lemaḥar."

50. See Marcus, *Piety and Society,* chap. 2.

51. See Tosafot to *b. Avoda Zara* 19b s.v. yeshalesh; *b. Qiddushin* 30a s.v. lo.

52. The issue of historiography is not discussed in H. J. Zimmels, *Ashkenazim and Sephardim* (London, 1954).

53. Cohen, *Sefer ha-Qabbalah,* p. 3.

54. *Iggeret Rab Shrira Gaon,* ed., Benjamin Lewin (1921; rpt. Jerusalem, 1972).

55. *Seder Tannaim va'Amoraim,* ed., K. Kahan (Frankfurt am Main, 1935). See Shraga Abramson, "On the Textual History of *Seder Tannaim va'Amoraim,*" Y. Gilat, et al., eds., '*Iyyunim besifrut HaZaL* [Studies in Rabbinic Literature] (Ramat Gan, 1982), pp. 215–47.

56. Neubauer, *Mediaeval Jewish Chronicles,* 2:77–88; Kahana, *Sifrut,* 1:59–70. Two later works that follow this pattern are Abraham Zacuto, *Sefer yuhasin hashalem,* ed., H. Filipowski (1857; rpt. Frankfurt am Main, 1924), and Gedalia Ibn Yahya, *Shalshelet haqabbalah* (Venice, 1587).

57. *Sefer Yosippon,* ed., David Flusser 2 vols. (Jerusalem, 1978–1980).

58. Klar, *Megillat Ahimaaz, passim.*

59. A. Neubauer and M. Stern, eds., *Hebräische Berichte über die Judenverfolgungen während der Kreuzzüge* (Berlin, 1892); A. M. Haberman, *Sefer gezeirot Ashkenaz veTsarfat* (Jerusalem, 1945); Shlomo Eidelberg, ed. and trans., *The Jews and the Crusaders* (Madison, 1977).

60. See above, n. 47.

61. See *Sefer Hasidim,* ed., Jehuda Wistinetzki with an introduction by Jacob Friemann (Frankfurt am Main, 1924), based on MS Parma, Biblioteca Palatina H 3280, edited in facsimile by Ivan G. Marcus (Jerusalem, 1985). On the exempla, see the references cited above, n. 13, and Ivan G. Marcus, "Narrative Fantasies in *Sefer Hasidim,*" in *Rabbinic Fantasies: Imaginative Narratives from Classical Hebrew Literature,* ed. David Stern and Mark Jay Mirsky (Phila., 1990).

62. See *The Book of the Gests Alexander of Macedon,* ed., Israel J. Kazis (Cambridge, Mass., 1962); *King Artus,* ed. and trans., Curt Leviant (New York, 1969).

63. See Bonfil, "Between the Land of Israel," pp. 21–22 and Haym Soloveitchik, "Religious Law and Change: The Medieval Ashkenazic Example," *AJS Review* 12 (1987): 205–21. *Sefer Yosippon* is a narrative about the people of Israel, as a whole, and especially about the family of the Hasmoneans. It includes special asides about families of Pietists, such as the mother Hanna and her seven sons. These features of the text make it a transition between biblical narratives about the people of Israel and Ashkenazic narratives about special groups of communities and personalities of great piety.

64. Alexander Marx, "Rabbenu Gershom, Light of the Exile," in his *Essays in Jewish Biography* (Philadelphia, 1947) and Grossman, *Hakhmei Ashkenaz,* p. 160.

65. For the texts, see Gottfried Reeg, ed., *Die Geschichte von den Zehn Martyrern* (Tubingen, 1985) and Esther Jo Adler, "Justice, Justice . . . or Love? A Structural-Thematic Analysis of *Midrash Eleh Ezkerah:* the Ten Martyrs" (Unpublished Ordination Thesis, H.U.C.–J.I.R., 1987).

66. Marcus, "From Politics to Martyrdom," p. 43.

67. Haberman, *Sefer gezeirot,* p. 165; Ivan G. Marcus, "Mothers, Martyrs, and Moneymakers: Some Jewish Women in Medieval Europe," *Conservative Judaism* 38 (1986): 34–45.

68. Fazlur Rahman, "Islam: An Overview," *Encyclopedia of Religion,* ed., Mircea Eliade (New York, 1987), Vol. 7:309. For the conservative bent in Muslim-Sefardi Jewish culture, consider this quotation by a student of a student of Rav Yehudai

Gaon, an ideologue of the gaonic movement in eighth-century Sura, of Rav Yehudai's own basis of authority: "Whenever you asked me (the law), I made a decision only when there was proof for it from the (Babylonian) Talmud and when I heard the decision from my teacher and my teacher from his teacher." See "Pirqoi ben Baboi," in Louis Ginzberg, ed., *Ginzei Schechter,* 3 vols. (1928–1929), 2:558–59. Cf. R. Abraham Ibn Ezra, Commentary to the Torah on Exodus 3:22: "One is not to rely on any book not written by the prophets or sages based on tradition."

69. Isadore Twersky, "The Shulhan Aruk: Enduring Code of Jewish Law," *The Jewish Expression,* ed., Judah Goldin (New York, 1970), pp. 322–43.

70. Israel Ta-Shema, " 'The Law Follows the Later Authorities'," [Hebrew] *Shenaton hamishpat ha'ivri,* 6–7 (1979–1980): 405–23; "*Halakha, Minhag* and Tradition in Ashkenazic Judaism in the Eleventh and Twelfth Centuries," [Hebrew] *Sidra* 3 (1987): 85–161.

71. Jacob Katz, *Exclusiveness and Tolerance* (New York, 1961), pp. 24–36 and Soloveitchik, "Religious Law," *passim.* Cf. Jean-Claude Schmitt, *La raison des gestes dans l'occident médiéval* (Paris, 1990), pp. 132–33 and 382, n. 98: "Dès son apparition, l'ancien français 'geste' désigne simultanément une histoire et une 'race', un lignage" (p. 132).

12

Sefer Yosippon: History and Midrash

Steven Bowman

This chapter will argue two theses derived from its title: first, that the *Book of Yosippon* is a history in any definition of the term. Whether it is totally reliable for reconstructing the ancient history of Israel is another matter. The anonymous author of *Yosippon* produced an historical narrative that served the purpose of interpreting the past for his and subsequent generations. He used the methods of the historian's craft and was faithful to the sources at his disposal. If modern scholars differ with some of his interpretive results, it is the fate of all of us to be revised on the basis of better source materials and other points of view. The second will argue for an expanded definition of the term *midrash* based upon the biblical origins of the term, which allows for a dual usage of *midrash* in the Middle Ages. One usage is an historical narrative that expands the biblical narrative, a form of narrative commentary that illuminates or rather interprets the text for the pleasure of the reader. The second usage is a technical method for interpreting and developing the text for the intellectual training of the reader as well as the halakhic process of creating a socioreligious reality for the Jewish community. Thus *midrash* should be understood on both levels: as narrative history-exegesis, and as a method, a question implicit for various categories of mediaeval Hebrew literature.

The *Book of Yosippon* is the major literary creation of medieval southern Italian Jewry to have survived in Hebrew, and its influence is still to be found on various aspects of the contemporary Jewish experience. It is not without controversy however. Whereas *Yosippon* is structured as an historical narrative of ancient Israel and her fateful encounter with Rome, modern scholarship is somewhat divided over the question of the date of composition and even more so the genre of literature to which it belongs. Two opposing interpretations are summarized in the following: "Sefer Yosippon is a narrative about the people of Israel, as a whole, and especially about the family of the Hasmoneans. . . . Sefer Yosippon looks like a continuation of the Bible. . . . It makes little sense to . . . think of Yosippon as a 'history book' or as a paraphrase of Josephus, both modern anachronisms."[1] On the other hand is the standard view: "Josippon, historical narrative in Hebrew, of anonymous authorship, describing the period of the Second Temple, written in southern Italy in the tenth century. . . . Considering the period in which he lived, the author was a gifted historian, aware of his responsibilities and endowed with excellent historical insight."[2]

This was not the case in the Middle Ages. Already in the tenth century there are hints that *Yosippon* was recognized as a major contribution to Jewish knowledge. Rabbenu Gershom, *me'or hagolah*, made his own copy of *Yosippon* as well as the Bible and Talmud.[3] These three texts came to be considered as the sacred and secular history of the Jews that illuminated and were illuminated by the encyclopedia of rabbinic scholarship contained within its oral tradition. By the eleventh century, it was cited as authoritative for the history of the Second Commonwealth period in Rashi's commentaries. Already by the latter's time, *Yosippon* had become attributed to Josephus Flavius and indeed was considered as the Hebrew original that Josephus alludes to in his works. In subsequent generations, the corpus of material called *Yosippon* grew by accretions as various scribes and editors added, subtracted, inserted whole treatises, and otherwise treated *Yosippon* as a traditional post-biblical text. The eclectic edition of *Yosippon* produced by Judah ibn Moskoni in the fourteenth century reflects the most important stage in the ongoing uncritical development of the *Yosippon* corpus.[4]

Hence the first questions that the scholar must resolve in the study of *Yosippon* are those of time and place. Then the serious task of establishing a text becomes crucial before attempts to analyze and categorize *Yosippon* are possible.[5] The efforts of Judah ibn Moskoni were a welcome contribution that indeed saved the corpus of *Yosippon* from oblivion. As he related, he came across fragments and excerpts in the libraries of Aegean Jews whole he was on his self-appointed task to write a supercommentary on Ibn Ezra.[6] Eventually he collected a sufficient number and patched them together into a consecutive narrative. Subsequently this *Yosippon* formed the uncritical text from which the hundreds of printed editions from the sixteenth and the twentieth centuries derived.[7]

In 1953 David Flusser announced his intention to edit the original *Yosippon*, which he claimed antedated the Moskoni edition by nearly 400 years.[8] His M.A. thesis at the Hebrew University was a critical edition of the Res Gestae Alexander, which he identified as an eleventh-century insertion into the text of *Yosippon*.[9] In 1978 appeared his critical edition of *Yosippon* with extensive annotations, followed by a volume of notes, excursuses and variant reading in 1980.[10] Flusser's edition, like Moskoni's is eclectic, as a single manuscript of the original *Yosippon* is not extant. Still, our ability to work with the text has been increased greatly through his scholarly efforts, and any study must perforce begin with his analysis and comments on the text.

Flusser has praised the *Yosippon* he presented as the work of a consummate historian whose methodology is comparable to our contemporary scholarly standards and whose literary skills are enviable. He dates his edition to 953 and places the author perhaps in Naples, where he had access to the excellent library of Duke Johannes III (928–968), which the latter had renewed in memory of his wife. The anonymous author was fluent in Latin, perhaps reflecting his training as a physician, with an excellent command of biblical Hebrew. Moreover, he has a highly developed historical imagination tempered by a keen historical sense.[11]

Flusser's dating of this *Yosippon* is based on an internal date that the author supplies following a scribal injunction.[12] Based on several of the data the text relates that date to the beginning of the tenth century, critics have challenged the accuracy of Flusser's identification.[13] Elsewhere, however, Flusser has averred that *Yosippon* should be dated, regardless of the date supplied in one manuscript, between ca. 900 and 965. The latter reflect the termini *ab quo* and *ad quem* of two historical situations described in his first chapter, a Table of Nations depicting his contemporary world.[14]

Moskoni provides further information on the question of the date of *Yosippon* in his citation of a Latin manuscript from the end of the sixth century.[15] Hence a Hebrew translation of the Latin Josephus could not have been extant before that date.[16] Further we may argue that a Hebrew history of the Second Commonwealth could not have been composed in southern Italy before the flowering of the Hebrew renaissance there in the ninth and tenth centuries. We may summarize the current situation as follows: *Yosippon* was written sometime before the middle of the tenth century possible as early as the late ninth century. One text of *Yosippon* that forms the core of Flusser's edition is dated to 953 and may reflect the time of a later edition rather than the original Hebrew author. Pending the discovery of another manuscript, the question of an original Hebrew *Yosippon* prior to Flusser's edition must remain mute.

The second question that has been raised by critics is that of genre. Is *Yosippon* a history as defined by nineteenth-century standards or is it a fictive narrative as defined by twentieth-century literary criticism?[17] To what extent has the analysis of eleventh- and twelfth-century Hebrew sources such as the *Megillat Ahima'az* (south Italy) and the *Sepher Ha-Kabbalah* of Abraham ibn Daud (Spain) necessitated a rereading of *Yosippon* as literature rather than as history? A more important question, to be examined later, is the relationship of the discipline of history to the discipline of midrash in its biblical and Rabbinic senses. In what sense can we say that *Yosippon* is a historical midrash, and how does this type of midrash differ from the midrashic techniques of the legal, ethical, or narrative commentary of its predecessors? Is there a case to be made for the prior existence of historical midrash in Jewish tradition? And, if the methodology employed by the author compares with the methodology of midrash, how does it compare to the methodology of the historian in pursuit of that craft?

From a different perspective, this last question was illuminated in the seminal analysis of the "Story of the Four Captives" by Gershom Cohen in his edition of RABaD's *Sepher Ha-Kabbalah*. There Cohen elicited both the polemical aspect of the latter's work and the fictive nature of his account of the spread of talmudic scholarship to new centers in Spain and North Africa.[18] The contributions of Robert Bonfil to the study of *Megillat Ahima'az* are presented more fully elsewhere in this volume. His studies legitimately challenge the efficacy of that poetic hagiography as an historical source read uncritically.[19] The point to emphasize here is that *Yosippon*, unlike *Sepher Ha-Kabbalah*, is neither a contemporary polemic nor a contemporary apology. It was therefore not necessary for the author of *Yosippon* to generate a fictive account of recent history to telescope a more complicated political process. One of the contemporary by-products of RABaD's reality was the spread of local Jewish centers of learning throughout the fragmented Islamic world. We might note here that the rise of talmudic academies of major import in Jerusalem in the tenth and eleventh centuries is not germane to RABaD's argument and hence this historical phenomenon is completely ignored by him.[20]

To return to our former question, the relationship of the discipline of history to the discipline of midrash may shed some light on an understanding of *Yosippon*. History and midrash have numerous parallels—some obvious, others obscure—especially insofar as ancient historiography is involved.[21] Although a full discussion of their relationship is beyond the parameters of this chapter, two points may be explored here: purpose and method.

The purpose of history to the Greeks was to recall the truth—*aletheia* in Greek, with the meaning "that which should not be forgotten." Hence "history" was the narrative format by which exemplary deeds were recorded for posterity. Both Herodotus' ethnographic forays that complemented his analysis of the Persian wars and Thucydides' political analysis of the Peloponnesian War were written as narratives and came to be considered by posterity as "historiography." For our purposes, it is sufficient here to emphasize the ethical didactic nature of Greek history writing.[22]

The purpose of midrash, as it appears in the Bible, is not that much different. As a term, it occurs only twice in the Book of Chronicles; that is, contemporary to the classical Greek historians. The word is derived from the root *DaRaSh*, which has the meaning of "seeking," usually in conjunction with requesting oracular guidance. In other words, it is a technical term used by a class of religious (priest, prophet, and the king as priest) functionaries whether in the service of the state or more directly as representatives of God to the people. As a noun it has the meaning in its two appearances as the prophet's reported result of such an investigation.[23] The Hellenistic translation of Chronicles renders *midrash* (2 Chron. 24:27) as *"biblios"* (book) and *sepher midrash* (2 Chron. 13:22) as *"graphe"* (writing); that is, a simple correlation based on the translator's contemporary understanding of Greek literature. Both history and midrash in this ancient sense were, then, reports of things to be remembered for the future edification of the people.

For that purpose, Thucydides cross-examined witnesses to elicit the best account of battles and policies, thereby setting the standard for future Greek scholarship. Later Greek and other followers of the discipline would use his work as a model for presenting the past to their contemporary generation. As a respected source Thucydides also became the literary standard for the portrayal of that history. Not only would his phraseology be alluded to, but also events would be cast according to the formulas he used, Hence, for example, depictions of the plague in the reign of Justinian and in the fourteenth century would follow his model description of the plague in fifth-century Athens.[24]

The Bible, too, in particular Kings and Chronicles, provided the model for Rabbinic midrashic representations of Israel's history and folklore. These Rabbinic midrashim, essentially commentaries on various stories and themes in the Bible, were loosely read as histories by medieval Jews. The question is whether *Yosippon* falls into this category of midrash or into the category of fictive narrative as defined by modern terminology.

A second meaning of the term *midrash* as used by the Rabbis is what we might call "method." There the rabbis would expand on the biblical meaning of the stem *DaRaSh*—to seek not only the meaning but, more important, the lesson to be derived from the text. By this methodology they would expand on the rhetorical tools they inherited from the Bible and those they adopted from the Greeks to read the Bible as an "open text"; that is, as a text into which they could pour their developing concepts and formulations of Judaism. Although it is clear that Josephus used both meanings of *midrash* in the compilation of this "histories," it is not clear whether *Yosippon*'s methods were derived directly from the Rabbinic oral tradition or whether he followed the patterns set by Josephus and his biblical sources, which the author knew intimately. Any analysis of the book and its value as historical source must perforce begin with a systematic evaluation of these various possibilities.

Flusser has shown that the author of *Yosippon* used the following sources: some extant and some no longer extant chronicles of Roman, Italian, and barbarian Vandal history; the Vulgate Old Testament and Apocrypha, which he rendered into a Hebrew drawn from the *Tanakh;* Latin versions of the Pseudepigrapha; the Christianized Latin epitome of Josephus made from the Greek in the latter half of the fourth century and known as Hegesippus; and explanatory additions drawn from his contemporary reality.[25] Where Flusser was able to check the Hebrew text against the Latin sources (including the variant manuscripts available to the author), he found that the author followed them carefully (save where he misunderstood the garbled Latin) and supplied the necessary corrections and summaries in conformity with modern scholarly demands. Occasionally the author did err in his interpretation; however, few modern scholars escape similar criticism. Hence, although *Yosippon* does not read like a modern history (and neither does Josephus we should emphasize) nonetheless the author's methodology does meet modern standards. Not only is he an effective guide to the period, but his conclusions even anticipate modern scholarly interpretations based on the recently discovered Dead Sea scrolls.

Whereas the term *midrash* can be read on two levels, either biblical or Rabbinic, my argument is that the author of *Yosippon* uses the methods of both uses of the term, though without acknowledging either through any specific reference to the term *midrash.* [26] On the first level, his narrative is the result of his scholarly investigation and critique of what he considered to be authoritative sources for the story he would arrange and tell. In the main these are the Bible as he had it and Joephus as he had it. On the second level, the language that he used to communicate his story was drawn from biblical and Rabbinic (i. e., mishnaic) Hebrew. Therefore he had to intermix two Hebrew styles as did his contemporary colleagues in different Judaic disciplines (e. g., poetry, philosophy, law) with his vernacular tongues. Moreover, as a *maskil,* that is, a scholar of his sources, he played with *ekphrasis,* already a biblical rhetorical device (cf. Gen. 19:5 and Jud. 19:22) known in the middle ages as *shibbutz.* Thus he spiced his narrative style with phrases drawn from his sources sometimes for literary style, other times as illusions to an expanded meaning of his text, and sometimes for the pleasure of word play.

The author of *Yosippon* has given us then a midrash in form, style, and method. But his midrash is also a history (much like Josephus), as defined by both his critical approach to the sources and by the narrative form in which the results of his investigations are presented to the reader. A comparison of *Yosippon* to *Sepher Ha-Yashar* may point up the differences between these two types of midrash. The latter is a narrative summary of the Pentateuch and Joshua recently argued to have been written in the late sixteenth century.[27] It follows the biblical text with additions from a number of medieval midrashim, including stories lifted verbatim from *Yosippon.* The author of *Sepher Ha-Yashar* does not use non Hebrew sources, and the Hebrew material he does include is used uncritically. Being a literary retelling of the biblical story and apparently without polemical or apologetic intent, it reads much more like a novel than the scholarly historical study of *Yosippon*.

The thesis of *Yosippon* is the relationship between Jerusalem and Rome, which he may have derived directly form Josephus, if not from Hegesippus. At the same time he functioned within a Jewish historiography that he had inherited from the Bible. The Bible contains the story of humanity with specific emphasis on one branch of it, the Jews, their relationship to the creator of the heavens and earth, to the land that was promised them, and to the city that they appropriated as their national and religious capitol for all time. Josephus, or rather the Bellum Iudaicum that was available to the author, represents the tragic (inevitable, as in the Greek sense) relationship between Rome and Jerusalem, respectively, the imperial and religio-spiritual capitols of the Mediterranean. Insofar as Josephus' apology was stated, the Jews fought well and thus deserved Roman respect both from the government and Roman society. Behind this apology there was a concern that the hatred against Jews and the antagonism toward Judaism prevalent in the Greek-speaking east Mediterranean world would, attending the Roman victory, find a welcome in the Latin-speaking western Mediterranean. His *contra apionem* was written to refute these attitudes as expressed in Greek tracts and ideally to avert that possibility.

From the Bible then the author of *Yosippon* could have derived his cosmopolitan and nationalist perspectives and from Josephus his national pride in Jerusalem. A combination of these themes will introduce us to the author's weltanschauung. His first chapter is a tenth-century commentary on Genesis 10, the family of humankind. Although of immense importance to modern scholarship, the author's purpose follows the biblical precedent; that is, to structure the world and Israel's place in it through the framework of a family of nations divided among the three sons of Noah who, having scattered throughout the world, represent the intermixed peoples located in Europe, Asia, and Africa. Just as Genesis introduced this human kinship as a religious concept—ethnography in the form of a family history with the important new idea of human integrity and ultimate unity—it was followed as a model by the authors of Chronicles, Josephus, *Yosippon*, and Joseph ha-Kohen in the sixteenth century.[28] Thus our author continues the pattern of Jewish historiography, which is based on a world-view particular to the Jews.

To illustrate his main thesis, which we believe to be the relationship between Rome and Jerusalem as one of the grand themes of history, we shall look now at three specific chapters (of the eighty-nine in Flusser's edition). Although the author may have legitimately derived this theme from Josephus or more likely Hegesippus, the situation of the Jews in the mid-tenth century was secure enough (the Western Christian massacres and oppression of the Jews was a century in the future and the Byzantine persecutions had ended a decade before) for this independent and proud Jewish intellectual to challenge Rome and its heirs in his history.

The author records Rome's growth from an outlaw lair to a metropolis with a physical empire that stretched to the limits of the known world and mistress of huge resources. The first of our three chapters (chapter #2) relates the legendary history of Rome, the story of Romulus, the rape of the Sabine women, the chronicle of her kings and their accomplishments, Rome's first encounter with Africa (which shows perhaps some of the author's medical background), and the early history of Carthage. Into this material, which derives perhaps from some lost epitome of Livy, the author weaves his Jewish and Near Eastern material that would not be inappropriate for contemporary students of Rome to follow. From a modern perspective, his Roman material appears legendary, albeit based on lost sources. Both this material and its Jewish ramifications are commingled here for the first time in Hebrew literature.

Most interesting, he introduces an apocryphal Zepho ben Eliphaz, a scion of Esau (mentioned in Gen. 36:11) who was exiled to Egypt by Joseph after the latter's capture of Zepho when he harassed Joseph's attempt to bury his father Jacob in Hebron, Zepho later escaped to North Africa, where he offered his military services first to the Carthaginians against the Vandals (whom the author calls Guandali following the Italian) and then later to Rome. Eventually Zepho became king of Rome and received the names of Janus (due to the wonderful act of killing a cattle-devouring dragon) and Saturnus. He ruled Rome for fifty years. The story of Zepho has no antecedents in Jewish medieval literature or, rather, we should say the author's source has not survived. The possibility exists that the story is a creation of the author of *Yosippon*. In fact the careers of both Zepho and Aeneas, at least insofar as the author has structured them, may have been modeled on that of David. Although this technique is commonly identified with Midrash (even Bible), it should be noted that it is not at all rare among ancient historians and other classical literature.

What is of particular interest to us here is the impression gained from the story of Zepho and the later reference to Romulus, which may be a harbinger of the author's grand theme in his history. First, Zepho is a descendent of Esau, which allows for an explanation of the Jewish identification of Rome with Edom. (Edom is the traditional enemy of the Jews in medieval Hebrew literature and usually applied to Rome or Byzantium.)[29] Just as Jacob supplanted Esau in the land of Israel, henceforth named after the former, so Joseph exiled Zepho. Ultimately their respective descendents, the Jewish tribes in Israel and the mixture of peoples called Romans, engaged in an internecine war that led to the destruction of Jerusalem. This destruction was not necessarily wished for by Rome (surely different from Rome's attitude toward Carthage). Zepho, after all, had carved out a new career for himself; in the process, he was deified in the Roman pantheon as Janus, god of war and peace.[30] Romulus was afraid of David's reputation as a conqueror all his days, and even enclosed the seven hills with a wall out of this fear. And, finally, both Vespasian and Titus attempted to reconcile the rebels in Jerusalem up to the moment of the destruction of the Temple.[31] The author's respect for Roman power is balanced by his national pride in Jewish history, which he felt was as important as that of Rome. Therefore, he viewed (or at least portrayed) Roman and Jewish history not only as interwoven but also as genealogically interrelated from its very beginning.

The author's second major excursus on Rome serves a similar purpose. The chapter introduces Rome as a potential ally of Judah the Maccabbee and its structure shows a national pride that raises the Jews to a level of geopolitical strength equal to that of Rome. After juxtaposing Rome and Judah, the author epitomizes the Roman war with Hannibal, the portentious clash between Rome and Carthage that stained Italy and North Africa with the blood of myraids. The author apparently made use of a Latin epitome of Livy that is no longer extant. This lost chronicle was full of fanciful and legendary material and outright errors that resulted partly from a telescoping of that eventful period the author could not control. The critical care with which the author of *Yosippon* managed the sources that we can check elsewhere in his text indicates that he faithfully followed that error-filled history of Rome that he used as his source. His book may therefore be of some use to classicists and students of medieval Roman literature in reconstructing this unknown source whose influence may yet be discovered among other authors. Despite its historical inaccuracies it is a tribute to the author's literary skill that this chapter reads so well, with its drama and pathos.

The author of *Yosippon* is determined to present the Punic War as a life and death struggle of historical importance, as indeed it was. The author's purpose in doing so was not to magnify the story of Rome, however, for his real intent is borne out by the conclusion of the chapter. There Judah receives a letter from the Roman Senate offering an alliance between Rome and Judah, about whose bravery and victories the Senate had heard so much. Rome, now the mistress of the western Mediterranean, approaches Judah as an equal who is the potential power broker in the eastern Mediterranean. In this chapter the author successfully raises Judah's guerrilla victories against the Seleucids to the same level of historical importance as Rome's life and death struggle with Carthage. (An interpretation that might not seem as arbitrary as it would at first glance, if we remember that eventually pagan Rome succumbed to a spirit coming out of Jerusalem.)

His third chapter follows this theme, although here it is presented as a warning to the Jews. When the war against Rome was about to break out, the support and assistance of Agrippa the Ethnarch was sought by the fighters. In a magnificent speech Agrippa pointed out the folly of war with Rome, which had attained a position of world power. How foolish it would be for Jerusalem with her limited resources to take on the might of Rome. His description of the Roman Empire is among the best that has reached us and draws on material that the author of *Yosippon* had already introduced in his introductory chapter, his invaluable table of nations, and would allude to in other speeches by Josephus later during the war.

The author structures his argument based on his source in Hegesippus. He lists the mighty people whom Rome has subjugated and emphasized those who had conquered the Jews in the past. All now served Rome and many supplied auxiliaries to fight against Jerusalem alongside her legions. If each people, Agrippa argues, were a match for the Jews in the past, what would be the possibility of Jerusalem overcoming their combined strength and the ineluctable march of Rome toward world hegemony according to God's plan. The author's view of the rise of Rome, than, is inextricably linked to Jewish history as evidenced in our summary of these chapters. His thesis developed through his narrative is as much a history as that of Hegessipus and that of Josephus. His critical use of sources is part of the tradition of history writing already well developed in the ancient world by both Thucydides and Josephus. The author of *Yosippon* is unique however among classical and medieval historians in the sense that he is writing about the ancient past and does not, as Flusser has pointed out, bring his story up to his contemporary present.

Yosippon has shown us, inter alia, that Midrash can be used on two levels: a narrative macro-level, much like the literary storyteller who reuses some past either as background or framework for his story, and a linguistic micro-level of word play or phrase allusion (*ekphrasis*). It shows us too that Midrash can be an historical narrative whether written by a prophet in the biblical period or by a medieval Jewish scholar. It also demonstrates that a scholarly historical study can use midrashic techniques just as it uses the literary narrative commentary. Hence, although history can be termed a form of midrash, it is insufficient to refer to a work of *Yosippon*'s scholarship as midrash without a qualifying definition of the term.

Several examples of *Yosippon*'s method illuminate the author's varied skills as scholar and stylist as well as his methodological use of *choice*, an important tool the historian uses to structure a cause and effect narrative to illustrate his thesis. The first is the author's chapter on Mordechai and Esther, which he drew from the Vulgate Esther and apocryphal additions. Whereas, the biblical text mentions only that Esther fasted and prayed before approaching the king, the author felt a dramatic need to fill in that lacuna. This expansion of a biblical text is central to midrash and represents the continuation of biblical commentary already existing in ancient times—as evidenced in the Aramaic and Greek translations of the Bible (the former surviving in Qumran manuscripts and the latter in the Septuagint). In this latter literature the text survives intact, yet becomes alive for later generations by its expansion via contemporary notes drawn from some oral tradition or adduced de novo. (The addition of speeches created by the author is a regular feature of ancient historiography as well.) In the elliptical scene of Esther's preparations, the author sought for some way to enhance and embellish the scene. He found it in *Asenath and Joseph,* a pseudepigraphal work from Hellenistic Egypt available to him in Latin translation. There he found in a prayer uttered by Asenath reflecting her feelings as a convert to Judaism. The author adjusted his translation accordingly and put this prayer into the mouth of Esther—a brilliant touch that integrates a piece of ancient Jewish literature into his reworking of biblical narrative that was preserved in the expanded Christian version of the Bible.[32]

The second example is the author's satire on the vicissitudes of the Roman papacy. Here the author shows this mastery of sardonic wit. Josephus (*Antiq.* 18, 66–77) relates the story of the high-born Roman lady Paulina, a devotee of Isis, who was seduced by Decius Mundus, of equestrian rank, through the clever ruse of bribing a priest of Isis to influence Paulina to sleep with the god Anubis. The fait accompli, Mundus later visited her in his true identity and asked for a return engagement. The lady was mortified and begged her husband to seek redress from the emperor. Tiberius, in turn, destroyed the Temple of Isis, crucified the priests, tossed the statue of Isis into the Tiber but merely exiled Mundus on the grounds that he was a victim of his own passion.[33]

This story recalls the wonderful tale of the seduction of Alexander's mother Olympia by Nectabenus, the Egyptian pharaoh and magician, as recounted by Pseudo-Callisthenes, a story that was extremely popular in the Middle Ages in the many languages that rendered the Res Gestae Alexander.[34] What our author did however was to put new wine in old bottles. By ingeniously quoting from the Vulgate Gospels, he has lifted a salacious tale of religious hypocracy from Josephus to the level of religious satire. In several key places in the tale Paulina is wrapped in the words that so clearly cloak Mary: "Blessed art thou, O Paulina, above all women, etc.," so that any Hebrew reader is clearly aware of the allusion to the mother of Jesus who was impregnated by the god of the Jews. When we recall the state of Rome's virtue in the tenth century, which was as tarnished as the city's surviving monuments, then we can appreciate the author's mordant allusion to the current chastity of the leaders of Christianity. Our author in a brilliant literary play has transformed Josephus' story into a guarded attack on the church.[35] The reworking of older stories and motifs to make a contemporary point has been pointed out by biblicists and folklorists alike.[36] As in the case of "modelling" noted earlier, this method, also central to Midrash, is a device not uncommon among historians especially of an earlier age when literary and rhetorical techniques carried equal weight with uncritically transmitted source material.

The third example is a skillful and ultimately a Rabbinical reading of a biblical verse. That is, by changing one word in the phrase he gives the biblical allusion a meaning that is opposite to its use in Chronicles. It is worth perhaps citing the verse and its two contexts to illustrate this last point. Chapter 25 of *Yosippon* relates the death of Judah the Maccabbee. There Judah's main force flees, leaving him with only his veteran core consisting of "his brothers and 800 youth with him from the youth of Israel who did not turn tail nor retreat." The last phrase is worded differently in Chapter 17, where the author cleverly puns on the verbal roots *sov* and *shuv* (*asher lo yassobu peneihem ve-lo yashuvu mipnei kol*—also applying to his veteran core). Here, in Chapter 25, however, he uses the phraseology of 2 Chronicles 29:6 in an innovate way.

The context of Chronicles is Hezekiah's repair of the Temple and his order to cleanse the sanctuary of Assyrian abominations, which the priests had installed there in recognition of his father Ahaz's submission to Assyrian hegemony. The text castigates the Levites thus: *va-yassebu peneihem mi-mishkan YHWH va-yittnu 'oref* ("and they turned their faces from the temple of YHWH and presented the back of the neck," i.e., fled). What the author does is add a negative to this castigation thus making it into a positive phrase to honor the courage of Judah's veterans. By doing so, he redeems the cowardice and profanation of the Levites of the seventh century B.C.E. that Hezekiah failed to do, because he stopped only the foreign sacrifice without cleansing the Temple. Judah's veterans, on the other hand, are praised for having fulfilled the command of the great biblical king in contrast to the failure of the Levites. This *ekphrasis* with its clever word play produces a new version of kingship and priesthood: not Hezekiah son of David and the profaned priests of his day, who did not fight, but rather Judah son of Aaron and his *non*priestly veterans who did fight for Israel and the Second Temple of YHWH. Thus the author has used a biblical allusion to condone the non-Davidic kingship of the Hasmoneans.[37]

These midrashic techniques parallel the rhetorical and literary techniques of ancient historians and scholars in other disciplines as well. Yet the use of both midrash and rhetoric by the author do not detract from his identity as an historian. Rather, as Flusser has shown, his critical treatment of his sources and his historical insight, which make his narrative a trustworthy reconstruction of Israel's ancient past, qualify him as an historian of superior quality for his time.[38] True, from the perspective of Jewish literature, one may loosely call his work a midrash; however, it is our contention that such a designation must be qualified, at the minimum, by the adjective historical.

Notes

1. Ivan G. Marcus, "History, Story and Collective Memory: Narrativity in Early Ashkenazic Culture," *Prooftexts* 10 (1990): 380 and note (above, ch. 11; p. 270, n. 64). To be sure, Marcus is offering only an opinion rather than a critical study of *Yosippon*, yet he misreads *Yosippon* through the prism of this enlightened reading of early Ashkenazi narratives. He does not distinguish in this article between history and historiography in their modern usage nor between the Italian and German phases of early Ashkenazi narratives.

2. David Flusser in *Enclyclopedia Judaica*, vol. 10, pp. 296 f.

3. Cf. David Flusser, "The Author of the Book of Josiphon: His Personality and His Age" [Hebrew] *Zion* 18 (1953):109–26; and his Hebrew essay, "The Author of *Sefer Josippon* as a Historian," *Mekomam shel toldoth 'am Yisrael be-misgereth toldoth he'amim* (Jerusalem, 1973), pp. 203–26. In addition to the encyclopedia article cited in the previous note, see also his "Josippon, a Medieval Hebrew Version of Josephus," in *Josephus, Judaism, and Christianity*, ed. Louis H. Feldman and Gohei Hata (Detroit, 1987), pp. 386–97.

4. See this author's *The Jews of Byzantium 1204–1453* (Birmingham, Ala., 1985), pp. 134 ff and notes.

5. On the craft of the historian, see G. J. Renier, *History, Its Purpose and Method* (London, 1950; reprinted Macon, Ga., 1982), passim.

6. His preface is translated in ibid., document #87, pp. 283 ff.

7. An extensive list is available in H. Hominer, *Sepher Josippon,* 4th ed. (Jerusalem, 1978).

8. See note 3.

9. "An "Alexander Geste" in a Parma MS," *Tarbiz* 26 (1956–57):165–84.

10. *The Josippon (Josephus Gorionides)*, published by the Bialik Institute in Jerusalem.

11. See studies cited in notes 2 and 3.

12. The rabbinic injunction is introduced by the phrase *'tze ve-ḥashov';* see *Seder Olam* (ed. Neubauer, *Mediaeval Jewish Chronicles* II (Oxford, 1895) Chapter 30 middle (p. 66); *Tractate Avodah Zarah (MS. J. T. S.)*, ed. S. Abramson (New York, 1957), fol 9a; and *Yalkut Shimoni* on Daniel 8. I should like to thank Benzion Wacholder for these references. The texts and interpretation are discussed in my

forthcoming annotated translation of *Yosippon.*

13. See R. Bonfil in the Israeli Hebrew newspaper *Davar* (September 28, 1981), pp. 13–14, and his "Tra due mondi: Prospettive di ricerca sulla storia culturale degli Ebrei nell'Italia meridionale nell'Alto Medioevo," *Italia Judaica. Atti del I Convegno internazionale Bari 18–22 maggio 1981* (Rome, 1983), pp. 156 f.

14. As pointed out by Flusser in his encylcopedia entry. Although it should be admitted that Flusser leans rather heavily upon the date of 953 as the date of composition.

15. See his introduction printed in H. Hominer's edition of *Yosippon* (Jerusalem, 1978), p. 39.

16. Indeed Judah ibn Moskoni ascribes the translation of Josephus's Hebrew original into Latin by Pope Gregory I himself!

17. See note 1 and the quote in the text cited there.

18. *Sefer Ha-Qabbalah. The Book of Tradition by Abraham ibn Daud* (Philadelphia, 1967); and his "The Story of the Four Captives," *PAAJR* 29 (1960–61): 55–131, especially pp. 71 and 114.

19. See above, ch. 10; and Bonfil's earlier study, cited there, p. 250, n. 6 (Ed.). An analysis of *Megillat Ahima'az* against the background of contemporary Byzantine hagiography was proffered by Stephen Benin, "The Chronicle of Ahimaaz and its Place in Byzantine Literature" [Hebrew], *Jerusalem Studies in Jewish Thought* 4 (1985–86):237–50. Especially interesting is his discussion of the *Toldoth Yeshu* in this context.

20. The marriage of Bustanai to the daughter of Yezdegerd as reported in RABaD's chronicle should also be subjected to the same methodological analysis both for the seventh-century reality as well as the tenth-century polemics within the political structure of Babylonian Jewry. The results of such an investigation may well be as illuminating as Cohen's analysis of the "Story of the Four Captives." Indeed, Cohen defines RABaD's story of the four captives as a "historical romance" (ibid., p. 114). "Within the artistic motifs there have been woven subtle Jewish midrashic ideas and chronological devices—such as historical symmetry and *gematriot.* Ibn Daud, we submit, should be read for what he was: not a historian, but an artist, a preacher and a moralist, whose aim was to demonstrate that the Eternal of Israel will not fail or forsake his people." One should be careful of applying Cohen's useful methodology indiscriminately to other medieval sources.

21. The relationship of midrash to ancient historiography has not been subject to scholarly investigation. Currently midrash is being studied by students of literature and literary criticism without recourse to its *Sitz im Leben* as a facet of ancient rhetoric. On the writing of ancient history in the ancient world, see Albert A. Bell, Jr. "Josephus ad Pseudo-Hegesippus," in *Josephus, Judaism, and Christianity,* (Detroit 1987), pp. 349–61; and the observations of David J. Ladouceur, "Josephus and Masada," ibid., pp. 95–113.

22. See Arnaldo Momigliano, *Studies in Historiography* (New York, 1966), pp. 127–42; and M. I. Finley, *Aspects of Antiquity. Discoveries and Controversies* (New York, 1968), pp. 44–57.

23. See Michael Fishbane, *Biblical Interpretation in Ancient Israel* (Oxford, 1988), p. 245 and passim; also see *midrash* in *Encyclopedia Judaica,* vol. 11

24. See Momigliano, *Studies in Historiography,* pp. 211–20. For the influence of Thucydides in Josephus, see H. St. John Thackeray, *Josephus, the Man and the Historian* (New York, 1929).

25. See note 3 and Flusser's review of Franz Blatt, *The Latin Josephus* . . . (Aarhus, 1958), in *Kiryat Sefer* 34 (1959):458–63.

26. See Fishbane, *Biblical Interpretation,* pp. 418 ff, for an extended discussion of this process in early Rabbinic midrash.

27. Joseph Dan, *Sefer Ha-Yashar* (Jerusalem, 1985).

28. Just as *Yosippon* was the model for the latter's book, so, too, he took his nom de plume from the author as he understood. Hence Josephus becomes *Yosippon* due to the mistake of later readers, whereas Joseph ha-Kohen took his name directly from *Yosippon* as his contemporaries understood the name of the author.

29. This identification resulted from a kind of love-hate relationship between Jerusalem and Rome on a parallel to the topos Jacob (later called Israel)-Esau (from Edom).

30. I am in doubt at this point if there is any intent on the part of the author to allude to a later similar career.

31. There are chronological difficulties in making Zepho contemporaneous with Carthage and David with Romulus. Although the author tried to structure a chronology in Chapter 2 from the legendary and garbled material he had at his disposal, his results do not conform to modern scholarly reconstructions.

32. David Flusser, "Joseph and Asenath, A Hellenistic-Jewish Novel" [Hebrew], *Dappim le-mehkar ba-siphrut* 2 (1985): 73–82.

33. A translation with commentary of this chapter will appear in my 1988 essay "Italiah shel Yavan in the Tenth Century" to be published by the Oxford Centre for Hebrew and Postgraduate Studies in its *Proceedings of the Spring Symposium at Yarnton Manor.*

34. The Parma manuscript of the Res Gestae Alexander omits this story; however, it was translated into Hebrew by the fourteenth-century French scholar Immanuel ben Jacob Bonfils; see Israel J. Kazis, ed. and trans., *The Book of the Gests of Alexander of Macedon* (Cambridge, Mass., 1962), pp. 59–63.

35. To add a touch that seems to anticipate Hollywood, the author mistakenly translated the rank of Mundus—equestrian—as racetrack driver! In this general context it is interesting to recall Benin's discussion of *Toldoth Yeshu* in connection with *Megillat Ahima'az;* see note 19.

36. See Fishbane, *Biblical Interpretation,* passim; and Susan Niditch, *Underdogs and Tricksters: A Prelude to Biblical Folklore* (San Francisco, 1987).

37. Perhaps this midrash hints at the author's familiarity with the tradition that the messiah would come from the House of Aaron.

38. Flusser's edition is annotated in rigorous scholarly fashion including the identification of the author's sources and an analysis of how he used them. He also points out where the author erred in his interpretation or relied on a poor source. In other words, *Yosippon* has been enveloped in a modern critical commentary so that the original text has become useful for student, researcher, and general reader. The Hebrew reader can test this thesis at present; the English reader will be able to use my forthcoming annotated translation.

Index